Democratizing the Corporation

The Real Utopias Project

Series Editors: Erik Olin Wright and Tom Malleson

The Real Utopias Project embraces a tension between dreams and practice. It is founded on the belief that what is pragmatically possible is not fixed independently of our imaginations but is instead shaped by our visions. The fulfillment of such a belief involves "real utopias"— utopian ideals grounded in the real potentials for redesigning social institutions.

In its attempt at sustaining and deepening serious discussion of radical alternatives to existing social practices, the Real Utopias Project examines various basic institutions—property rights and the market, secondary associations, the family, and the welfare state, among others—and focuses on specific proposals for their fundamental redesign. The books in the series are the result of workshop conferences, at which groups of scholars respond to provocative manuscripts.

Democratizing the Corporation: The Bicameral Firm and Beyond

Edited by Isabelle Ferreras,
Tom Malleson, and Joel Rogers

VERSO

London • New York

First published by Verso 2024
Collection © Verso 2024
Contributions © Contributors 2024

1 3 5 7 9 10 8 6 4 2

Verso
UK: 6 Meard Street, London W1F 0EG
US: 388 Atlantic Avenue, Brooklyn, NY 11217
versobooks.com

Verso is the imprint of New Left Books

ISBN-13: 978-1-80429-453-6
ISBN-13: 978-1-80429-454-3 (UK EBK)
ISBN-13: 978-1-80429-455-0 (US EBK)

British Library Cataloguing in Publication Data
A catalogue record for this book is available from the British Library

Library of Congress Cataloging-in-Publication Data

Names: Ferreras, Isabelle, editor. | Malleson, Tom, editor. | Rogers, Joel,
  1952- editor.
Title: Democratizing the corporation : the bicameral firm and beyond /
  edited by Isabelle Ferreras, Tom Malleson, and Joel Rogers.
Description: London ; Brooklyn, NY : Verso, 2024. | Series: The real
  utopias project | Includes bibliographical references.
Identifiers: LCCN 2023041740 (print) | LCCN 2023041741 (ebook) | ISBN
  9781804294536 (trade paperback) | ISBN 9781804294550 (ebook)
Subjects: LCSH: Management—Employee
participation. | Employee empowerment.
  | Corporate governance. | Democracy—Economic aspects.
Classification: LCC HD5650 .D448 2024 (print)
| LCC HD5650 (ebook) | DDC
  658.3/152—dc23/eng/20231020
LC record available at https://lccn.loc.gov/2023041740
LC ebook record available at https://lccn.loc.gov/2023041741

Typeset in Minion by Biblichor Ltd, Scotland
Printed and bound by CPI Group (UK) Ltd, Croydon CR0 4YY

Contents

Preface

This volume was written in a time of crisis. A health crisis in the form of a global pandemic whereby workers were lauded as "essential" yet simultaneously denied protective gear or sick days. A crisis of war and occupation from Palestine to Yemen to Ukraine. A crisis of systemic racism epitomized by the police murder of George Floyd and the discovery of Indigenous children's bones beneath their old school grounds. A crisis of inequality, where a handful of grotesquely rich men possess the wealth of half the entire planet. And underlining all of these, the cold specter of environmental collapse.

Times of crisis are often times of despair. Which is why it is more vital than ever to elaborate alternatives that can provide hope via a glimpse of a better world. Antonio Gramsci once counseled radicals to counterbalance the pessimism of the intellect with the optimism of the will. The purpose of the Real Utopias Project is to foster both: to nurture the optimism of the will by expanding the force of intelligent and sensitive engagement with the world.

The project began in the early 1990s, galvanized by its leading force, Erik Olin Wright (and named by Joel Rogers during one of their weekly Sunday walks), in order to carefully explore institutional alternatives to the reigning capitalist order. As Erik once described it:

> These alternatives (1) embody our deepest aspirations for a just and humane world—thus "utopia," and (2) can to a greater or lesser extent be built in the world as it is, prefiguring the world as it could be, and

moving us in that direction, thus "real." The objective is to formulate visions for radical alternatives embodying the emancipatory values of democracy, equality, and solidarity that also specify realistic steps for solving existing problems.

This volume, the ninth in the series, began in 2017 when Erik heard Isabelle speak on economic bicameralism and invited her to write the anchor essay. In the spring of 2018, Isabelle visited Erik at the University of Wisconsin–Madison where, with the help of his students, many happy hours were spent discussing, critiquing, and revising the proposal; he also arranged for the project's accompanying conference to take place at the Institute for Future Studies in Sweden (though the COVID-19 pandemic would move it online). Alas, he would never attend this conference. Shortly thereafter, he was diagnosed with acute myeloid leukemia and passed away in January 2019, at the age of seventy-one. His passing left a hole in the lives of all who knew him: his family and friends, colleagues and generations of adoring students, and the international socialist movement of which he was a giant. His passing tore a hole in the sail of our vessel. We patch it up as best we can, but it can never be made whole.

Before he passed, he asked me to take over as coordinator of the Real Utopias Project, a truly profound honor, though truthfully one that I, as with all who loved him, would have much preferred to be unnecessary for many more years to come. This volume and those that will come later continue this project, as was his wish. All of us who help to carry it forward do so with his memory lightening our steps and fueling our conviction that in the deep fullness of time his vision of real utopias, which we glimpse now ever so partially across the horizon, will yet coalesce into that new and brighter reality that he helped us to see and to forge.

Tom Malleson

Acknowledgments

This volume would not have been possible without the support of many friends and colleagues.

Isabelle Ferreras wishes to particularly express her deep gratitude to Erik Olin Wright and Tom Malleson. Erik commissioned her anchor essay and engaged with incredible energy in every aspect of it until his untimely passing. It was a tremendous pleasure and honor to learn from him. The anchor chapter also improved immensely from the lively participation of his sociology graduate students at the University of Wisconsin–Madison during spring of 2018. Although all limitations remain Isabelle's, her essay benefited from the generous feedback of Joshua Cohen, Tom Malleson, and Benjamin Sachs. Miranda Richmond Mouillot was an outstanding editing partner throughout the writing and revision of the essay. Upon Erik's request, Tom took over from Erik's coordination role with incredible energy and vision. Erik was profoundly right to believe that Tom would be well suited to follow in his footsteps. Tom is as talented and generous as Erik, and it has been a true pleasure to collaborate with both them and Joel Rogers.

We extend the most heartfelt appreciation to the wonderful scholars from many countries and across multiple time zones who took part in the conference, wrote chapters for this volume, and patiently went along with our incessant editing. We are grateful, too, for the Institute of Future Studies in Stockholm, particularly its director, Gustaf Arrhenius, and the administrative and logistical support provided by Helen de Canésie, Ludvig Beckman, Niels Selling, and Vuko Andrić and financial support provided by the Riksbankens Jubileumsfond (Swedish Foundation for Humanities and Social Sciences). Thanks especially to the Havens Wright Center for Social Justice at UW–Madison for their ongoing support with the Real Utopias Project, especially Joel Rogers and Patrick Barrett. We are also extremely appreciative of Fred Block and the *Politics and Society* board for their continued support and solidarity. Thanks also to Asher Dupuy-Spencer, Sam Smith, and the Verso team. We are truly grateful to you all.

Most of all we thank Erik Olin Wright for building this project and for carrying us on his shoulders still.

Tom Malleson, Isabelle Ferreras, Joel Rogers

Introduction

Tom Malleson and Joel Rogers

This volume of the Real Utopias series goes to the epicenter of everyday domination in our society: the private, profit-seeking corporation. In the lead essay, Isabelle Ferreras proposes to cure the abuses of its "private government" by giving the employees and owners equivalent powers and mutual veto rights in corporate decision-making in a bicameral governance structure.[1] Taking a "voice" approach to equalizing power within the corporation, as opposed to a shared-ownership model, she invites us to consider firms as political entities. Ferreras draws from the history of political democracy's extension of the suffrage and, most notably in the United Kingdom, the addition of a "Commons" chamber to the old aristocratic "House of Lords," which was for so long the sole source of government. Her suggestion of a "bicameral firm"—with workers and capital investors possessing equal numbers of board representatives—would extend and deepen the practices of codetermination that exist today in many German firms.

As conceived by its founding editor and moving force, Erik Olin Wright, Real Utopias are well-worked-out suggestions for reform in policy or practice that make plausible assumptions about human behavior, are not so far from present social organization and power realities to be fanciful, and whose execution could (on these same assumptions) grow and stably reproduce. Given the amount of attention the desire for greater worker voice in firms is getting these days, Ferreras's "bicameral firm" is not obviously fanciful. Whether it can plausibly find accumulating agency and work well enough to survive and flourish, much less support further movement toward what Ferreras says is her real ideal for the firm—worker cooperatives collectively owned and governed by the workers themselves—is for the reader to judge.

There can be no question that capital has grossly abused the power granted it in the present corporate form, or of the dominance of that power over our lives. And the idea of beginning to correct that abuse by equalizing the power of workers and of capital within the firm has undeniable appeal. The central objection—that doing so would be catastrophic for productivity—has by this point been laid to rest.[2] And while the idea of extending some semblance of democracy to the management of private firms today seems difficult to imagine, its analogy to the initially gradual but then very rapid expansion of political democracy is potentially instructive.

Recall that as recently as two hundred years ago, the very idea of a fully representative democracy—that all adults should have an equal right to govern their country, typically instituted through an electoral mechanism of "one person, one vote"—would have struck the average person on the street of New York or Paris or Mumbai or Mexico City as extremely far-fetched and unlikely. At that time there was not a single democratic state in the entire world. The more radical idea of democracy—that *wherever* there is significant power being exercised by some human beings over others, whether in the state or town or farm or factory or plantation or church or university or marriage, that power should be accountable to, and ultimately governed by, the people affected by it—would have seemed not just far-fetched but also fantastical. And yet, over the years, the democratic ideal slowly and gradually became more and more powerful, galvanizing social movements and political parties, inspiring rebellions and even the occasional revolution. If political democracy is defined simply as a government chosen through universal suffrage among the people it governed, there was not a single democratic country in the whole world in 1900; yet by 2000 there were 120 (out of 192 countries).[3] Today democracy is the norm for the majority of the world's people.

But of course—and this is the focus of this collection—the same basic rights of voice have not spread into the firm. Democracy in the political sphere has been rigidly cordoned off from democracy in the economic sphere. Massive undemocratic organizations in the form of multinational corporations have come to dominate our economies. Of the world's one hundred largest economies—measured by revenue or value of product—only twenty-nine are countries; seventy-one are corporations. Walmart is bigger than Spain; Exxon is bigger than New Zealand; Apple is bigger than India.[4] The dominance of these gigantic firms employing millions of people, with their top-down governance structure, is arguably a central cause of some of the deepest problems facing society today.

One such problem is the widespread sense that actually existing democracy is failing as a form of government to get citizens the results they might reasonably expect. Worldwide, the democratic advance has slowed and partially reversed, and democratic norms and institutions are weakening.[5] Scholars have documented a number of ways in which corporations threaten political democracy. These include extensive lobbying of government, spending huge amounts of money on media and public relations to bend people's minds to their priorities, threatening to go on investment strike—that is, cutting investment, leading to reduced revenues and laid off workers—or even leaving the country altogether if their demands are not met.[6] Because of these overwhelming powers, many people increasingly see corporations as akin to Dr. Frankenstein's monsters: legally created by states but now running wild, no longer controllable by their original creators.[7] As more and more of the most important decisions that impact people's lives are made by far-off CEOs or bankers or money-managers—frequently making decisions on the other side of the globe from where one lives—it is easy to feel disempowered and disillusioned; there is an increasingly pervasive sense that corporations are pulling the strings, while the governments, and we the citizens, are merely puppets being yanked this way and that. It is both significant and foreboding that many large democracies, including the US, Brazil, Mexico, the UK, and Australia, are experiencing their highest-ever recorded levels of democratic dissatisfaction. In the US, such levels have risen by over a third in just one generation, resulting in a situation where more than half of the entire populace say that they are dissatisfied with democracy.[8] What follows from that dissatisfaction varies. It can inspire pro-democracy reforms and progressive social movements. More commonly, however, it inspires reactionary movements or nihilism.[9] It is an ominous sign of global trends that in 2020 the heads of the most powerful countries in the world—Trump in the US, Putin in Russia, Modi in India, Xi in

China, Bolsonaro in Brazil—were largely united in their contempt for democracy.

Not only do corporations threaten our political democracy, but, in a more visceral and tangible sense, they also rule our daily lives. Most people spend most of their waking hours at work, and much of that work revolves around taking orders and following commands. Since most employment contracts cannot cover every possible kind of task that might be required, what employment contracts really establish—and this is particularly true for lower-skilled workers with less bargaining power and fewer alternative options—is the parameters of their obedience and subservience. In our working lives, most of us are essentially servants. Indeed, it was not too long ago when the standard language used in legal discourse reflected this fact more honestly than it does today, by referring not to "employers" and "employees," but to "masters" and "servants."[10] The language used today has changed, but the fundamentals of the underlying situation have often not.[11] The relative lack of freedom, equality, and self-determination at work, from the constant feeling of being bossed around, the frequent dismissal of one's ideas, the exclusion from decision-making, the fear of the boss, and the daily, subtle reminders that one is subordinate—all of this accumulates in a stew of alienation, resentment, anger, and poor health.[12] Across the world, a staggering 85 percent of people dislike their job (only 15 percent feel "engaged").[13] Fifty percent of American employees report quitting a job at some point in their career in order to get away from a boss, and one in five British workers admits to hating their boss.[14]

In addition to democratic deficits, a second major problem flowing from the top-down governance structure of large firms is that of inequality. In the US, CEO-to-worker compensation ratios have gone from roughly 20:1 in the 1960s to 351:1 today, as median incomes have stagnated while CEO salaries skyrocket.[15] In addition to income inequality within firms, large corporations exacerbate economic inequality throughout society in other ways, too, such as by pressuring governments to lower corporate tax rates, and avoiding payment of their taxes (through loopholes and tax havens), both of which sabotage the state's capacity to improve equality by public investments or redistributive cash transfers.[16] Over the past forty years, for example, statutory corporate tax rates among member states of the Organisation for

Economic Co-operation and Development (OECD) fell by nearly half, from 42 percent to 23 percent, and use of tax havens has exploded—together removing tens of trillions of dollars from public budgets.[17] Today, we have levels of inequality unseen since the beginning of the past century: the top 10 percent of the population claims 52 percent of world annual income and 76 percent of world wealth, compared to the bottom 50 percent's 8.5 percent and 2 percent, respectively.[18]

Issues of declining democracy and globally worsening inequality have many determinants and are complex, with many positive and negative feedback loops over varying durations. But clearly one major and ongoing source of these problems is the asymmetry of power at the heart of the economy: the divergent interests between the owners of the shares of the corporation—shareholders who are generally richer, white, male, and mobile—and its employees, who are typically much poorer, racially and gender diverse, and geographically bound. The fact that corporate governance gives shareholders so much power and workers so little creates multiple problems that ripple across society.[19] Clearly shareholders have little reason to desire either workplace democracy inside the firm or an empowered democracy in society at large, since both threaten their control over the firm and thus their ability to maximize profits. Likewise, shareholders have strong motivation for the corporation to avoid taxes via tax havens, and CEOs have obvious incentives to try to inflate their own salaries—all of which drive up inequality. It is very doubtful that the workers in these firms would make the same decisions, since in many cases their interests are quite different if not diametrically opposed; the problem is that the asymmetry of the rules of firm governance means that workers are banned from steering the firm.

The idea of workplace democracy is an old one. In the West, it was defended first by various anarchists and syndicalists who saw it as part and parcel of a broader set of revolutionary changes that they hoped would replace every top-down and "authoritarian" institution in society with bottom-up, self-governing ones.[20] The idea was also picked up and defended in the late nineteenth and early twentieth centuries by a variety of iconoclastic radical democrats, including dissident Marxists, democratic socialists, anti-racists, as well as the occasional liberal.[21] For instance, John Stuart Mill, perhaps the most influential liberal theorist of all time, argued in 1848 that the form of association, however, which if mankind continue to improve, must be expected in the end to predominate, is not that which can exist between a capitalist as chief, and work-people without a voice in the management, but the association of the labourers themselves on terms of equality, collectively owning the capital with which they carry on their operations, and working under managers elected and removable by themselves.[22]

Over the roughly two centuries since demands for workplace democracy first surfaced in collective action, there have been many diverse attempts to put it into practice.[23] Among them are

- *Trade unions*: In most countries, the most important institution for promoting worker voice and power is the union.[24] Although unions are not typically intended to give workers any direct control over the firm's actions, they do provide protections and bargaining power.[25] As economist G. D. H. Cole once put it, unions provide workers with a "brake" but not the "steering wheel."[26]
- *Employee stock ownership plans (ESOPs)*: In the US, ESOPs enjoy broad bipartisan support as a mechanism for increasing worker ownership.[27] The basic idea is that ESOP legislation provides companies with tax breaks to incentivize the sale of ownership shares to internal workers (which often occurs when the initial founders wish to retire and prefer not to abandon the firm to a competitor).Today there are over 10,000 ESOPs, roughly 3,000 of which are majority held or 100 percent owned by employees.[28]
- *Codetermination* (or *Mitbestimmung* in German) is the practice of giving workers the ability to elect a certain portion of the governing boards of large firms (usually one-third, though up to half in large German enterprises). This practice is most widely associated with Germany, where it has been firmly established since 1976, though it also exists in a number of other European countries such as Austria, the Netherlands, and the Scandinavian countries.[29] Although codetermination has never existed in the Anglo-American countries, it has gained more attention in recent years than perhaps ever before. Jeremy

Corbyn in the UK, as well as Elizabeth Warren and Bernie Sanders in the US, all developed prominent codetermination legislation as central parts of their economic policy platforms in their respective bids for prime minister and president.[30]

The chief strength of these three models is that they are eminently feasible: they have existed for many years in many places and are widespread and stable (ESOPs exist only in the US but are widely spread there). We have extensive evidence showing that they work reasonably well, and we have quite a lot of understanding of how to further scale them up.[31] Their major limitation is that they are not fundamentally transformative: they do not solve the heart of the problem because even within these models workers remain largely subservient to shareholders (though the degree of subservience may be somewhat softened).

On the more radical side of the spectrum, the most prominent model is that of worker cooperatives.

- *Worker cooperatives* are firms that are collectively owned by the workers themselves and governed on the basis of "one worker, one vote."[32] In small co-ops, workers might make collective decisions in a participatory fashion, whereas in large ones, they necessarily elect their management or members of the governing board. The best-known example is that of the Mondragon Corporation in the Basque region of Spain, a conglomerate that included (in 2017) ninety-eight worker co-ops (as well as many noncooperative firms) with over 80,000 employees and total resources of about €25 billion (in 2014).[33]

The major advantage of worker co-ops, with both ownership and control residing with the workers, is that they are truly democratic. This makes this form of firm organization central to most visions of a genuinely democratic society.[34] Their major weakness is that they are so rare and marginal—in most countries, worker co-ops represent less than 1 percent of firms (in the US, there are only 465 co-ops out of 6.1 million employing firms, that is, 0.0076 percent of enterprises).[35] This means they are currently unable to offer a real alternative for the vast majority of working people; nor could the expansion of the worker co-op sector in itself do anything to challenge the power of the Amazons and

Walmarts of the world. Moreover, any significant expansion in their number and size would require a vast shift of power and resources away from wealthy and powerful shareholders (with their wealthy and power-ful political allies) toward relatively impoverished and weak workers (with their relatively weak political allies). Achieving this at the scale needed for an economy to be actually dominated by worker co-ops is not a short-term possibility. At best, it will take time.

We find ourselves, therefore, in a familiar bind. At some point, all progressive projects face this fork in the road: do we aim for more immediate, realistic, and feasible change, which risks remaining super-ficial, or do we strive for radical, transformative change, which risks remaining infeasible and utopian?

A major virtue of Isabelle Ferreras's proposal is to inspire, without indulging in delusion, by recommitting to democracy itself. Intention-ally aiming for that narrow window between superficiality and utopianism, it is a practical, realistic model yet simultaneously bold and radical enough to offer profound differences to people's lives

She finds the history of the UK and other predemocratic states instructive. Instead of jumping from undemocratic institutions straight to democratic ones (a transition that, due to the balance of political forces, in many cases was simply impossible), they supplemented older feudal institutions with more democratic ones, assigning them both power in their new government. In the UK case, that meant adding the House of Commons to the old aristocratic House of Lords. Analogously for the firm, workers would get their own chamber, along with one reserved for capital. The radicalism of this suggestion is underscored by its modesty. Bicameralism does not directly disturb capital and certainly does not expropriate it, but it does check its abuse of power. It seeks to "build a bridge for firms so that they can move away from capital despotism and transition toward democracy" (this volume, page 29).

Of the models discussed above, the bicameral firm is most similar to codetermination. It, too, would be imposed through legal fiat; it would apply only to large firms; and it would seek to democratize the work-place by altering the governance structure of the firm (i.e., reforming the composition of the board), not through the extension of ownership rights. Neither regular workers nor the worker representatives on the board would "own" the corporation—shareholders would continue to do that—but workers would acquire increasing say over its actions—indeed a collective veto power. The major difference is that whereas codetermination leaves shareholders with the majority decision-making power, bicameralism wouldn't. In most German firms (and all non-German examples), codetermination provides workers with a fraction of board seats, between one-third and a half. Even in German firms larger than 2,000 workers, codetermination grants only "quasi-parity": workers get half the seats, but in case of a tie, the deciding vote is cast by shareholders, which enables them to retain their dominance.[36] In bicameralism, by contrast, the two chambers would be completely equal in authority, each having veto power over the other. Hence another way to view Ferreras's "economic bicameralism" is to see it as a model of "true parity codetermination."

The appeal of bicameralism is obvious. If the crux of the problem is that CEOs (and other senior executives) run large corporations in order to maximize profit for themselves and international shareholders, with little concern for inequality, democracy, or environmental protection in their home country, then such problems may well be significantly improved by shifting some executive control to workers. Since workers occupy a different social location, it stands to reason that they would make different decisions. Since they are typically far poorer than CEOs and upper management, they will have more desire to compress wages at the top and raise them at the bottom (hence reducing inequality). It also seems likely that they will have more desire than shareholders to see their firm actually pay its fair share of taxes (not evade them through tax havens) since poorer workers will typically benefit more from the public services such taxes provide than do richer shareholders (again reducing inequality).[37] Additionally, since workers are more deeply rooted in their home community than scattered shareholders, they are likely to have different priorities in terms of caring for their environment, having a robust democratic political system (that corporations do not undermine), as well as having much less desire to threaten to move the firm to a different country in search of cheaper labor and fewer social regulations (since this would mean sacrificing their own jobs).[38] In sum, given that workers are typically poorer, more rooted in community, and possess more heterogeneous interests than simple profit-maximization, it stands to reason that their empowerment would help to bring the behavior of the corporation closer in line with the broader public interest. Bicameralism would not solve all conflicts of interest, but it might well soften them by aligning corporate behavior somewhat closer to the common good.

Naturally, this proposal raises many questions, explored in the detailed essays responding to it, such as:

- Foundationally, what about private firms make them public enough to warrant this intervention?
- Who are the appropriate "constituents" that need their interests represented in the firm?
- How should bicameral firms be financed?
- What should be the role of unions within bicameralism?
- Is it better to pursue the bicameral strategy of expanding workplace democracy on the basis of legal guarantees to voice, or on the basis of expanding worker ownership?
- Do proposals for workplace democracy complement or conflict with other progressive goals (such as reducing inequality, protecting the environment, and combating racism)? And where exactly are the points of synergy and mutual support?

Each of the contributors wrestle with these vital questions and more. And though there is much disagreement, every reader who makes their way through the volume will find that such disagreement nevertheless sparks considerable illumination.

The responses to Ferreras's proposal are divided into four broad sections:

Democracy at Work

- Carly Knight argues that the best way to justify the bicameral firm today is to learn the lessons of earlier twentieth-century Progressive Era thought, which conceptualized the corporation as a "public" rather than a "private" entity, due to a capacious understanding of what constitutes the public interest.
- Marc Fleurbaey develops a stakeholder approach to the firm, which he uses to gain insights into the strengths as well as the limitations of workplace democracy.

The Corporation and the Law

- David Ellerman analyzes the nature of the corporation and argues that the key issue facing society is not the ownership of the corporation per se but rather the employer–employee relationship. The best avenue for transforming this relationship, he suggests, is a novel co-op-ESOP model.
- Robert Freeland examines the prospects for democratizing the corporation in the context of US corporate law, arguing that current law offers greater prospects for democratizing the corporation than are typically realized, though he also warns of significant barriers.
- Lenore Palladino analyzes how codetermination or bicameralism could practically work within the current institutional context and legal framework of the United States. She highlights a number of difficult procedural and substantive issues that would need to be addressed, offering a range of plausible solutions.

Nuts and Bolts of Economic Bicameralism

- Max Krahé argues that in order for bicameral firms to survive, they need to be situated within a supportive ecosystem, including, in particular, a supportive financial system. He outlines the dangers and constraints placed on democratic workplaces by the current undemocratic financial system.
- Thomas Ferretti and Axel Gosseries question whether bicameralism is the best model for workplace democracy (compared to worker cooperatives and codetermined firms), pointing to issues of potential domination by investors as well as efficiency concerns in terms of the ability to attract capital investment.
- Simon Pek analyzes the research on best practices of governance of worker cooperatives, multi-stakeholder co-ops, and union co-ops, in order to identify areas of concrete improvements to the proposal for bicameralism.

Economic Democracy: The Big Picture

- Bo Rothstein examines the prospects for workplace democracy by considering the important example of Sweden. By recalling the famous experiment of the Meidner wage earner funds, and analyzing the resistance to economic democracy of the world's strongest union movement, Rothstein highlights some major obstacles to the bicameral project.
- Christopher Mackin discusses the proposal for the bicameral firm in terms of some of the broader debates concerning workplace democracy. He does this by analyzing key issues concerning the contemporary context, normative justifications, and competing visions of how transition to workplace democracy might occur.
- Ewan McGaughey connects the proposal of the bicameral firm to the broader field of economic democracy. He outlines five essential principles of economic democracy and develops a sympathetic critique of the bicameral proposal.
- Sanjay Pinto argues that any project for economic democracy must reckon with the context of racial capitalism. Drawing inspiration from W. E. B Du Bois and Fannie Lou Hamer, the chapter considers how efforts to expand worker power must contend with the racial hierarchy that marks the socioeconomic division of labor and the related use of racial distinctions to thwart labor solidarity.

Finally, in a reply to the many comments on her paper, Isabelle Ferreras discusses the main contours of her proposal. She sharpens the discussion not only by clarifying disagreements with the commentators but also by identifying her agreement with at least some who incorrectly thought they disagreed with her. But, as you will see, she does not back down from or significantly change any part of her original suggestion.

I.

The Proposal

1

Democratizing the Corporation: The Proposal of the Bicameral Firm

Isabelle Ferreras

> *With enterprises as with the state, democratization requires favorable conditions, conditions that do not arise spontaneously, inevitably, or "naturally." Favorable conditions must be created.*
> —Robert Dahl, *Democracy and Its Critics*

The Challenge

So far in Western history we have limited the scope of democratic government to a relatively narrow sliver of life that society views as "political."[1] For most, business is an entirely separate piece of the pie. Indeed, the idea that the political and the economic are and ought to be separate has been taken for granted for so long that it can seem impossible, or at the very least implausible, to challenge. In "capitalist democracies," the equality and voice of citizens is a guiding principle of government when it comes to affairs of the state.[2] In most firms, however, these same citizens have little of either: capital owners, by virtue of their investment of money in the firm, are granted nearly exclusive political rights. But the inequality baked into firms, markets, and the broader economy has always spilled back into the political arena and endangered political equality, and today it threatens the viability of political democracy itself. The contradiction between democracy and capitalism is rapidly reaching a point of crisis, washing away the credibility of democratic governments, drowning all faith that "the system"—that is, political democracy in its current form—can actually address the grave problems citizens face today, in particular a life with access to such vital resources as good education, health, transportation, safe food, clean air, and water—in short, a livable environment. This essay will offer a new strategy for an old and very simple proposal: that people ought to be recognized as equal citizens in the workplace, too. The idea that workers have a legitimate right to participate in the government of their work life, where they invest the vast majority of their time and effort, is receiving renewed attention.[3] As the need to inject new life into our political democracies in the global age becomes ever more urgent—the project to strengthen, "deepen and extend democracy"—democratizing corporations is becoming a more and more legitimate and desirable goal.[4] How to get there remains a momentous challenge, and tackling it is the task of the present essay.

The Problem

The Nonprivate Logic of the Work Experience

"All human beings are born free and equal in dignity and rights," announces article 1 of the Universal Declaration on Human Rights, signed in 1948 by fifty nations as the world confronted the atrocities of World War II. As many thinkers have articulated over the years, from Mill to Pateman, from Dahl to Ellerman, the fact that this fundamental principle is not upheld in the workplace significantly damages the credibility of the democratic project.

Every day, working citizens of democracies experience a huge contradiction.[5] The political regime governing their everyday lives outside the workplace has evolved much faster than the political regime governing their lives inside the workplace. In the workplace, work is still carried out under a very particular regime known as *employment*. Because we frame this regime as an "economic" one, firmly established within a "free" market, we lose sight of the fact that, if we dare to describe it empirically, it is essentially a political regime of government and one that establishes the *subordination* of workers, who sign most of their freedom over to their employers for the duration of their employment. This is clear in the very word "economy," which comes from the Greek *oikos-nomos*, meaning "household management," and indeed the master-slave relationship was central to the ancient Greek *oikos*. The remains of the master-slave relationship, which Aristotle calls despotism,[6] and which defined this primitive form of employment, carried over in employment arrangements as the world industrialized and contractualized labor became the norm: essentially, what happened over time was that people gained the right to sign *themselves* into slavery for limited times, rather than someone else signing them over.[7] But farm, factory, shop, and workshop have all continued to be governed as closed *oikoi* privately managed by a "master" (or their delegates). This subordination rings out from time to time in the language of work; until recently, workers were often known as "hands," and their employers as "masters." In her recent account, Elizabeth Anderson describes workplaces as enclaves in which "private governments" rule the lives of otherwise-free citizens.[8] However, Paddy Ireland reminds us that earlier in the history of industrial capitalism, legal realists in corporate law had already noted that the rights exercised by employers were "most accurately seen as delegations by the state . . . of a discretionary power over the rights and duties of others," which is not subject to direct democratic control. These rights are a form of what Robert Hale called "private government," delegations of public authority to "unofficial minorities."[9]

But of course, the world has changed. These enclaves are not so private; in the twenty-first century they exist at the center of our democratic societies, and in addition to being our workplaces, they are often sites of knowledge-sharing and sociability, of consumption and entertainment, all at the same time. The Habermasian tradition identifies the public sphere as the social fabric of interactions that nurture the possibility of a free and democratic society, and contemporary workplaces are part and parcel of what people who work experience as the public sphere. This has always been so, but our current service-based production regime, with its intensive focus on consumption, is more firmly a part of the public sphere than ever before: think about an Apple store, and all the functions it serves beyond being a mere workplace. The shift of the workplace into the public sphere was accelerated in the twentieth century with the creation of labor law as a separate body of law, as well as with the growth of collective labor rights, unionization, and the invention of collective bargaining. The 1980s accelerated the shift even more, as Western economies moved from an industrial to a service-based production regime, which is now entirely demand driven—meaning customer oriented. This is a sociological observation: as the economies of most Western democratic countries have become largely service based, in the eyes of workers, the workplace, even when constituted remotely, cannot be differentiated from the public sphere. While many may still be busy in the production line of a factory, well away from customers, in the "fissured" workplace of the twenty-first century, employees often maintain some contact, direct or indirect, with those they serve.[10] This may include engineers from a buyer company coming through a plant; users to whose needs they immediately cater; trainees; patients; or customers they interact with online, over the telephone, or face-to-face. Furthermore, as citizens all over the world have more purchasing power (and more things to consume), they are more often in others' workplaces. The fissured experience of the workplace today—be it at a Foxconn plant or a store along the Champs-Elysées, a hospital in rural Texas or an attorney's office in Buenos Aires—is more centered than it once was around persons who are not coworkers. A curious thing has happened during this shift toward a service economy, which has brought with it a weakening of labor rights and unionization; a blurring of the well-ordered positions of principal and agent, master and subordinate workers; and less and less state attention "from the outside." Very *visibly*, because workplaces are so much more public, the building blocks of labor contracts (minimum wage, maximum hours of work, health and safety issues, etc.) that ensure a basic framework of decency for workers are eroding away, and workers have less and less access to institutional structures through which they can express solidarity or gain better conditions or compensation. The situation of Uber drivers compared to that of drivers employed by a cab cooperative is a good example of this shift. The old imposed frames are not working anymore, and the presence of customers and other outside parties has in some ways become emblematic of the fissured workplace. The delivery person bringing the mail, the truck driver dropping off production parcels, the legal advisor and reputation specialist working with the in-house PR team—all of these citizens observe each other and are observed. Such a work environment cannot possibly be experienced as private by workers. Instead, it is experienced as a continuation of the public realm, in which private rules are enforced with ever-increasing severity.

This has created an entirely new level of tension and contradiction in the lives of workers. Outside the workplace, they are expected to behave as responsible citizens, as voters capable of taking a stance on major political and social issues. Both in and outside of the workplace, they are expected to behave with courtesy toward others—to treat them with respect, as equals in dignity and rights. Then, at their jobs—in places, circumstances, and settings they know best, in which they are arguably the most qualified to assess situations and make decisions—workers become subordinates. They cease to be equals. Instead they become "subordinates" thanks to the labor contract—tools, resources, "human capital"—a phrase that acquires an eerie ring when one realizes that firm government is run unilaterally by those whose rights depend entirely on capital *ownership*.

This contradiction is tied to the dominant tradition of economic liberalism in the West, according to which anything economic is emphatically not public.[11] The notion of "public," as used here, does not mean state-run or state-owned but rather refers to the sociological notion of a specific "interaction regime."[12] To consider the work experience as nonpublic (private, in other words) means suspending the norms of equality in dignity and rights that underpin the democratic public sphere. In the dominant tradition of economic liberalism, an employee, when she steps into her workplace, steps into the *oikos*, the (supposed) "boss's place," where the boss's rules apply. That tradition assumes that there is an *owner* of the firm, which from a legal standpoint is nonsensical, as we shall see later on.[13] Neoclassical economics as a field, and particularly the economic theory of the firm, has nevertheless continued to endorse this wrongheaded notion, and models of work organization and customer service relationships prevalent today take for granted the subordination of the employee to the employer and the customer.[14] Whether labor is viewed as the "labor input" in the capitalist firm's production equation or the material manifestation of the dystopian ideal Marx described as driving capitalism, a relationship of domestic subordination governs work. To a Marxist, this leads to a specific form of alienation. To a neoclassical economist, it is merely efficient. To use Marx's critical term, the worker is a *commodity*, one tool of production among many, all of which are there to serve a project decided upon by a corporation's capital investors. In this view of the firm, the instrumentality goes both ways: by choice or by necessity, workers are employed so that a firm's capital investors can make money; at the same time, workers submit to employment by the firm in order to make money for themselves.

The Critical Intuition of Democratic Justice at Work

Moving away from this theoretical description, let us examine the reality on the ground. In more traditional industrial production regimes, divisions of labor inspired by Taylorism and scientific management were considered fundamental to the organization of production, to the point that firms only included top management and key engineers in charge of overseeing the work process in their governance and the design of work organization. Today, in a strongly service-based economy powered by knowledge, the link between the success of firms and the motivation of their employees is much more direct. As Charles Sabel pointed out over two decades ago, problem-solving in the contemporary firm more often than not requires that conception and execution divided in the Taylorist approach be reunited.[15] For firms focused to any degree on service performance and innovation, employees are the driving force, not one production factor among many. In a high-skill service context, it is obvious that employees cannot properly understand the issues they must resolve without putting themselves in the place of their customers— in other words, without employing all dimensions of their human selves. Indeed, these human selves and perspectives become central to their experience of work. This is true for low-skill workers, too. A survey of the growing literature in talent management shows that their performance depends on their feeling involved with the tasks they must perform.[16] Although the critique of contemporary, renewed forms of Taylorization has focused on a vision of workers as mere cogs in well-designed wheels, it has been amply demonstrated (and is clear to anyone who has carried it out) that work can never be totally reduced to such an alienating experience.[17] The more employers try, the more they increase turnover, sick days, work-related injuries and mental illness, and worker burnout, all of which lessens performance and poses a serious threat to workflow and service delivery.

Sophisticated firms are increasingly aware of this and expect high levels of commitment, motivation, and loyalty from many of their workers. But these are intertwined with workers' own attitudes to their work, and because both the liberal tradition and critical social theory have largely failed to expand the scope of the public sphere to include the firm, the implications of this beyond mere issues of worker motivation has been largely ignored.[18] Extensive research in the sociology, psychology, and anthropology of work has shown that people's attitudes toward work go well beyond the instrumental (work is carried out for a wage), meaning that not only do workers experience being treated as instruments as unjust; they also do not feel that their own relationship to their work is instrumental.[19] Certainly, they define it as "earning money to be able to meet your needs outside of work." But at the same time, individuals *also* perceive their relationship to their work in expressive terms of *meaning*: it provides social inclusion, a sense of usefulness, a sense of independence, a sense of service provided, or a sense of mastery—that is satisfaction with tasks performed combined with some form of autonomy.[20] For people engaged in labor that we are accustomed to defining as meaningful, such as doctors, teachers, or scientists, this may seem obvious. But sociological research has shown that it holds true even for workers in low-skill jobs that are repetitive and draining, with no opportunity for career advancement or access to a job ladder. As I highlight in my own research, a fundamental dimension of what lies at the heart of the work experience is people's own conceptions of justice.[21] As the workforce becomes more educated, and involved with conceptualizing the service to be performed, questions of what is just, right, or fair become part of work in many more visible ways, beyond the more classic industrial mobilization around compensation, work rhythm, and safety: while these remain as valid and necessary as ever, especially in the gig economy, the questions employees feel empowered to address are evolving in scope.[22] In 2018 alone, internal discussions surfaced from within several major firms in which employees voiced opposition on expressive grounds to their own top management. In May, thousands of Google employees wrote to their CEO, Sundar Pichai, and asked him to drop the "Maven Project," which provided artificial intelligence to a Pentagon drone program.[23] Dozens of employees resigned in protest. In June, Microsoft employees protested a contract with US Immigration and Customs Enforcement because of its inhumane policy of separating children from their parents.[24] In August, US employees of Twitter objected to opaque processes surrounding decisions to shut down accounts for inappropriate content.[25] In November, Google employees organized the first transnational walkout in the company's history, voicing their condemnation of the top management's handling of the sexual harassment, systemic racism, and gender inequality that have plagued the life of the organization, and asking for "real change." Thousands of employees met outside Google offices in San

Francisco, New York City, Dublin, London, Zurich, Haifa, Tokyo, and Singapore.[26] These movements speak to the centrality of conceptions of justice in workers' work experience.[27] Amid both the hype and the fear, it seems unlikely that human knowledge will become less important to our knowledge economy. The workplace is automating rapidly, and workers may be weighing in on fewer and fewer "technical" decisions. But if anything, as robots become more and more common, human knowledge and judgment will become more precious and all the more central a feature at work. Firm efficiency will depend more than ever on the quality, the expertise, and the motivation of what one might refer to, far more appropriately, as its labor investors.

To grasp the specific logic through which workers experience their labor, I use the notion of the *critical intuition of democratic justice*. I use this term in the tradition of the critical social sciences, the Frankfurt school in particular.[28] From complaints about unfair compensation to burnout or full-fledged participation in a demonstration, I use this term to describe the notion that working people want to be treated according to the simple standard of the first article of the Universal Declaration of Human Rights: as "equals in dignity and rights." As "equals in dignity," they are equal "in rights," too: I argue that this critical intuition extends to the inclusion of voice, that they ought to be heard and represented, as well. While they have no guarantee that this standard will be applied in the workplace, it is nevertheless part and parcel of the citizenship they share with all those who give life to the firm—principal, manager, worker. When serving others within the context of a commercial economic transaction that is regulated by a contract, workers, even if they have lost all hope of respect and fair treatment as they discharge the obligations agreed upon in that contract, are highly aware of the injustice of their conditions. For workers in low-skill service jobs, donning a cashier's smock does not mean shedding their desire for equal dignity. But equal dignity is often not a part of their work experience, and workers confront unfairness with a deep sense that their voices are not heard. However resigned they may be to the *reality* of the work contract in our liberal economies, the *democratic ideal* of our liberal societies hints at an unsettling question—an unvoiced expectation of voice:[29] Why should such interactions not be governed according to the ideal of equality of dignity and rights with which the public space in democratic societies is governed?

This question, arising from the contemporary work experience, flags an urgent problem. When this critical intuition of democratic justice goes unrecognized in the workplace, a great tension emerges, at times unstated, certainly underestimated but clearly felt. My understanding of this tension is anchored in the study of "capitalist democracies."[30] To live in a "capitalist democracy" must mean, in particular, to live out this great tension between our critical intuition of democratic justice and the power structures of capitalism.[31] This tension between democracy and capitalism has great destructive power—not to destroy capitalism in the short turn but to destroy democracy instead. Democracies promise their citizens equality. But, even in political democracies, that promise has been shut out of the workplace. Workers are citizens, not instruments, and their civic lives are built around a promise of equal voice on which their work lives fail to deliver. Citizens aspire to and expect a voice in their lives and futures—in and outside the workplace—and the power structures of the contemporary corporate firm mute, deny, and even strangle that voice by granting exclusive *political rights* only to certain citizens, those with capital investments.[32] While democracy is built on the idea that all citizens deserve equal say in the government of their present and future, capitalism removes that equal say from the government of firms, giving rise to an experience of constant contradiction. In everyday work life, this contradiction glimmers through in words of anger or of resignation, in ordinary indignation, in gestures of discouragement or exasperation. It may also be observed lurking behind phenomena affecting workplace efficiency, such as absenteeism, lack of motivation, or lagging innovation. More intensely and more personally, it may take the form of workplace suffering, which runs the gamut from nagging physical and psychological problems to burnout and work-related suicides.[33]

The Capitalist Firm as a Political Entity Governed by the Corporation

The above considerations lead us to critically examine what a firm is. There is no question that a firm has economic dimensions. However, these should not obstruct the sociological reality of what a firm is: a form of *political entity*, which is owned by no one.[34] It is an entity whose existence depends on ongoing decisions about the goals of the coordinated actions pursued within it, which are bound up in issues of efficiency and justice and depends on two major forms of investment, capital and labor. Their investments are mutually dependent: without one or the other, the capitalist firm would cease to function. It is an entity that affects the lives of many, including consumers and community members whose physical proximity means they are touched by its activities. Capital investors are stakeholders, too. Labor investors, however, are the only constituency formally governed by the rules and decisions of the firm.

Yet, the current legal reality of the firm speaks to another understanding entirely. Firms are, in fact, governed by investors, who organize their capital through the corporation; no equivalent right has yet been granted to workers. This is not to say that workers do not have access to other forms of organization: it is legal in many places for them to organize in unions, for example. My point here, though, is that they possess no institutional mechanism *within* the firm and *equivalent* to the corporation through which they are able to have an equal say in the government of their firms. To expand democracy into the economic realm, it would be both just and expedient to recognize the right of workers to organize along the same lines as capital investors—in other words, through an institutional mechanism that would grant them the right to participate in governing the political entity in which they are at least as intensely involved.

The terms "corporation" and "firm" are often conflated, so let me underline that a *corporation* is, in legal terms, merely a vehicle for organizing capital investors.[35] It is part but not all of the broader entity that is the *firm*. Strangely enough, firms have no real existence under the law; instead, the corporation stands as a kind of proxy for the firm. It has been anointed as the vessel that holds the legal personality that makes it possible for a business endeavor to operate in our social and legal systems. It is crucial, then, to recall that this is nothing more than a historically contingent convention, albeit one with tremendous impact, created by states in order to delegate a portion of their power and activity.[36] Through corporations, states grant business endeavors rights and responsibilities, shield their individual investors, and treat them as a legal party in court. Legal personality shields shareholders from personal liability for wrongdoing and separates their personal assets from their business holdings. Shareholders, even majority shareholders who are deeply involved in the day-to-day operations of corporations, are shielded and protected from accountability for the wrongdoings of those corporations.[37] Corporations' rights include entering into private contracts for both labor and trade, but they often go far beyond that. In the United States, for example, they have come to include free speech—and, by extension, participation in the political life of the nation.[38]

Shares may be bought and sold, listed and delisted. It is possible to know precisely who owns them. The same is not true of the corporation itself: legally, and contrary to what most people think, no one is the owner of a corporation; rather, people own shares in it. The corporation itself is, legally speaking, its own legal entity, owned by no one.[39] If the concept of ownership at the level of the entity cannot be applied to the corporation, it is even less applicable to the firm. It may be useful, at this juncture, to point out another entity no one owns, which is the state.[40] Similar to states, corporations have special tribunals, courts, and arbitrage systems through which their problems are adjudicated and in which their voices are legitimate and heard. Corporations are distinct, "real entities" granted legal personality.[41] This is where the distinction between a corporation and a firm becomes particularly necessary to underline, as the corporate structure comprises only shareholders—in other words, *not the entirety of the firm*. A *corporation*, in sociological terms, forms part but not all of the broader entity that is the *firm*. What about the firm, then? What of the people who work there? The communities affected by its operations? The customers who buy the goods it produces? Who has a right to have a voice in the life of a firm? Once we have noted this crucial distinction between the legal reality of the corporation and the sociological and economic reality that it fails to encompass, it becomes clear that a corporation, while an important element in the firm, cannot describe the larger and very real entity of the firm. Because, as Jean-Philippe Robé aptly puts it, a firm is "built around" one or many corporations.[42]

Identifying a Path away from Corporate Despotism

I call attention to this misconception here because defining firms as political entities offers a new way to raise critical questions about firm government and accountability. It also opens the door to a rich vein of inquiry into the history of political entities and, in so doing, points out a possible path to transition. Our goal here is not to belittle or delegitimize the institutional design already in place for capital investors in firms. It is highly developed, and recognized by corporate law; we wish to take it seriously. But I am suggesting that it is high time we abandon the shortsighted notion that the corporation *is* the firm. Acknowledgment that the firm is broader in scope and that it is a fundamentally political entity allows us the perspective to see that a firm's government must represent its constituents—not only those legally organized and represented via the corporation but also its other constituency: its labor investors. Any government requires proper institutions, with appropriate sets of rights and responsibilities for its constituencies—in the case of firms, for all who invest in them, whether their investment takes the form of capital or of labor. Currently, as figure 1.1 makes clear, only those who invest in the corporation's capital (the constituency of the corporation) have the right to representation in the government ruling a firm.

Let us now return to the context of contradiction between democracy and capitalism. There is indeed a serious tension between the idea of granting the political right to govern a firm to the owners of its corporation's capital, and the idea that all human beings ought to be recognized as equal. This tension is caused by the contradiction between the standard underpinning capitalism, which is that the economy should be

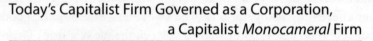

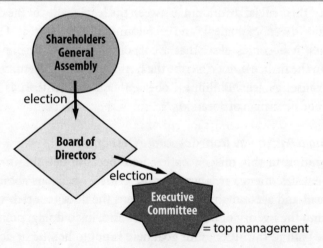

Figure 1.1. Today's capitalist firm governed as a corporation

run by those who own and invest the capital in it, and the ideal under-pinning democracy, which is that all human beings are equal and have a right to a voice in decisions regarding their lives and futures. There are two ways out of this contradiction. The first is to give more, if not all, of the power to capitalists. This is the route we are currently taking. Around the world, citizens are electing officials who promise to run our governments "like a great American company," trading transparency for expediency, public goods for private profits.[43] As described in the first section of this essay, firms are internally built around the political regime of domestic servitude. If the exclusive right to govern is held by capital investors and all those who invest their labor in the firm are subordinate to these capital investors, with little to no voice in the firm's direction or its future, then this way out of the contradiction is in fact a road to capitalist despotism. Consider Donald J. Trump, the 46th president of the United States, as an instructive example. Trump's "America First" platform granted more rights to capital investors and industry heads. Trump himself has long been proud of being the despot of "his own" firm—the Trump Organization—an attitude clearly reflected in his choice of business name.[44] Shares in the Trump Organization, further-more, are not publicly traded, meaning that none of its activities are subject to even the minimum accountability standards that the Securi-ties and Exchange Commission requires of publicly traded companies. The Trump Organization, managed by master Trump and his children, really is the perfect embodiment of the *despotes*'s dream, overseeing its own *oikos-nomos*.

We will not tread any further down this path into the contradictions between democracy and capitalism: descriptions of the disastrous track it is cutting through our lives fill the pages of our newspapers every day. Instead, let us examine the second way out of the contradiction, which is to give more power to democracy, specifically by *extending* and *deepening* it into the economic realm.[45] This is, in fact, a way out of the contradiction that is broad enough to include the capitalist economy within it—which cannot be said of the other way out, which would simply give all signifi-cant voice and power to capital. For democracy, as the political philosopher John Dewey so eloquently wrote, is an experiment, an ideal, a project; it is always in the process of becoming. This fluid and flexible way forward has the potential to inject new life not only into the democratic project but also into the economy itself. Ultimately, I believe, it has the potential to move

us beyond capitalist despotism entirely and into a renewed and democratized form of market economy.[46]

The reference to struggles for emancipation is useful for framing my
transition to the third and last part of this essay: the proposal. What
does it mean to emancipate? The term "emancipate" comes from the
Latin *emancipare*: "to free a slave," derived from *e-manu-capare*: to cease
to hold by the hand. In the Roman Forum, slave owners signaled
their intent to purchase a slave by taking him by the hand. "Emancipation" thus implies a release from slavery, guardianship, domination,
alienation—from constraint in general, be it physical, moral, emotional,
or intellectual. In concrete terms, it is used to describe a situation in
which a given category of the population is granted the same rights that
others have already secured. Progressive actors in history have fought to
emancipate colonies, slaves, ethnic groups, or women. Now it is time to
emancipate workers. For anyone concerned with nurturing the democratic project, the state of disenfranchisement faced by workers the
moment they enter the workplace is cause for alarm—and for serious
thought. If democratic politics is losing credibility among today's ever
more disaffected citizens, the power and reach of global corporate firms
are major culprits.[47] But, although the workplace is the locus of public
life in which democracy is most lacking today, firms have managed to
stay off our political radar. The centuries-long struggle for human
emancipation must now set its sights on the corporate firm. In a world
increasingly dominated by global finance capitalism, which threatens to
crush the long struggle for democratic rights, the firm is the new
frontier.

Proposal: The Bicameral Firm

We have seen that while the corporation is often taken for the whole of
the firm, it is only a part of that much-larger entity. Because the former
has been taken for the latter, capital investors have until now had exclusive right to the institutional channel of representation provided by the
corporation, and thus exclusive (or near-exclusive, if meaningful labor
rights exist, depending on national contexts) say in the government of
the firm. There is no equivalent institutional channel of representation
for the firm's other main constituents, its labor investors. As discussed

above, for this and other reasons, from the perspective of labor investors, the nature of firm government is despotic.[48] There is nothing new in the idea of granting voice to workers: labor law in many countries grants voice to employees, most broadly by guaranteeing at least minimal rights to organize through unions. Works councils guarantee European workers the right to be consulted on certain key issues, for example. In Germany, the *Mitbestimmung* ("codetermination") system grants representatives elected by workers an equal number of seats on the supervisory boards of larger corporations.[49] And yet, throughout the world, and even in the case of German codetermination (as shall be explored below), the government of firms has remained monocameral; that is, it features a single-chamber legislature. As specific systems of industrial relations have developed in different capitalist democracies, it is meaningful to recognize these institutional settings and the collective rights gained by the labor movement as evidence of a general intuition that labor investors ought to have a voice in the government of the entity to which they make such a vital contribution. But nowhere do any of these representative bodies have the weight of corporations in deciding the fate of firms—except, of course, in worker-owned and -governed firms.

Hence, it should be pointed out that the reverse of the despotic corporate firm—that is, a monocameral firm governed by labor investors—does actually exist in the world as we know it, in the form of worker-owned and -governed firms.[50] While such firms live up to the ideal of democracy as applied to economic organizations, they are a marginal presence in the economy.[51] The issue this essay seeks to address is how to deepen democracy in the broader economy *as we know it*, in order to build a bridge for firms so that they can move away from capital despotism and transition toward democracy. Looking at the example of the monocameral worker-owned firm, one obvious strategy is to facilitate worker buybacks of the capital invested in their firm. Employee stock ownership plan (ESOP) legislation in the United States has helped many firms transition to being fully "worker-owned and -managed." Although that is a commendable ideal, a path to extending and deepening democracy in economic life must include and address the case of firms where capital investors are present and wish to remain so. Firms governed by capital investors who are not also its labor investors currently lack a strategy for democratization.

Learning from Political History: Bicameralism as a Primer

So how do we do it? If we recall the parallel previously pointed out, between firms and states as political entities that are not owned by anyone, it is logical to examine the history of how political entities became democratic for clues as to how democratic transitions may be brought about in firms. This history, and in particular the history of democratic revolutions, reveals that shifts from despotism to democracy have been managed through what I call a bicameral moment. By this I mean the moment when those in power realize that they must share that power equally or risk losing it altogether. The continued prosperity of Western societies has been made possible through these moments of emancipation, in which a dominated—and often more numerous—group in a given society secured the same rights as the despotic minority and began to participate in government. The first bicameral moment may be traced back to Roman antiquity (497 BCE), when tribunes of the plebs were granted veto rights over all decisions made by the patricians; perhaps the best known is the creation of the House of Commons alongside the House of Lords in modern Great Britain. In each instance, a single institutional innovation was put in place—that of bicameral politics—engineered to generate productive compromise between two constituencies with distinct and usually divergent sets of interests.

Today, it seems ridiculous to imagine England governed by its landowners, to think of the House of Lords ruling alone. If we apply the same logic to the contemporary capitalist firm, it begins to seem far less reasonable—and far less inevitable—that it be governed by a board representing its shareowners alone. Today our societies are in the midst of economic and democratic crisis. Firms are restructuring, offshoring, outsourcing, shrinking or closing, actively fissuring in order the meet the never-ending demands of their corporations for return on investment.[52] Some politicians are exploiting these realities to stoke popular anger; workers and citizens are losing motivation in the workplace and trust "in the system"; and authoritarian politicians are wooing voters with regressive, demagogic political agendas. Firms' problems cannot be solved from the outside alone; both history and the global reach of firms make nationalization both unrealistic and undesirable. And while a full-fledged transition from capital to labor-governed firms that preserves their monocameral institutional structure may be realistic in the case of firms with capitalization small enough to be fully acquired by their workers and properly managed by worker representatives who already possess the requisite skill sets, the government of larger entities will require appropriate training and skilled upscaling to build govern-ments worthy of that name that meet the three basic conditions for just rule: being *legitimate, reasonable,* and *intelligent.*[53] Our challenge today is to help firms—and the societies in which they function—evolve toward this goal, and to create an economic fabric that actually meets the requirements of a democratic and sustainable society.[54]

Before we move on to the question of whether the bicameral govern-ment of firms meets the three conditions of just rule in philosophy of law, the next section will examine an important distinction between the two main levels at which a firm must be governed within a democratic society.[55] The first is external: firms are, and should be, subject to regu-lation by the societies in which they function. The second is internal: firms, as political entities in and of themselves, are the site of rule and government. This essay addresses this second level of government only. However, some words are necessary about the ways in which these two levels are interconnected.

Two Constituencies Necessary to the Capitalist Firm: Capital and Labor Investors

The project of the bicameral firm will be described in detail further on, but for now let us say that it relies on an investor model, not on a stakeholder model. It views the capitalist firm as comprising two constit-uencies, made up of incommensurable classes of investor—capital investors and labor investors—and assigns a chamber of representatives to each one. Inside these two classes, depending on the specifics of the firm and industry, more specific distinctions may be necessary, as well. For now, let us proceed with the observation that a firm's operations depend on the joint investment of labor and capital; without either of them, the firm ceases to exist.

Obviously, the legal system and support (infrastructure, education, health, etc.) provided by the state in which a firm operates are of crucial importance. Given the series of investments made on behalf of society by the state, the state also has a legitimate claim to governing rights over the firm. Yet, from the perspective of a democratic society, *deepened* and *extended*, per our goal here, the role of the state would not lie in direct control over firms, as was the case in communism, which featured state-owned and -run economic entities. Here, its role would be to set the proper internal requirements (appropriate sets of rights to be applied in the government of firms) and external requirements (public ownership, competition, market design, antitrust regulations, consumer protection code, etc.) for the firm's activity. Particularly with regard to these internal requirements, the state would promote and protect, via proper legal equipment and fiscal incentives, forms of legal structuring for firms that fit the state's own commitment to a democratic society. My essay thus focuses on the internal dimension only.

The emergence of the platform economy highlights the usefulness of the distinction between two classes of investors in any firm. Capital investors invest in Uber on the understanding that some labor investors will be willing to drive their cars for Uber's customers. Until Uber has an automated car fleet, it will have no value at all to its capital investors without these labor investors. By signing commercial contracts rather than labor contracts with its drivers, Uber is fully embracing the fallacy of *reductio ad corporationem*, essentially behaving as a corporation seeking to withdraw entirely from the firm.[56] This strategy should not fool us, however: Uber not only has responsibilities as an employer; it would actually have no value without labor investment.[57] It would be more descriptively accurate to view firms like Uber as having interdependent classes of investors that include all those upon which the possibility of existence of Uber as a *firm*, not as a mere *corporation*, depends. Drawing our attention to this situation, which has not yet been addressed, is one of the goals of this proposal.[58]

Who Are the Labor Investors?

Assuming a functional democratic society is in place, then, all conditions being equal, capital investors are a necessary but not a sufficient condition for the success of a firm. A firm requires labor investors, as well. Although exceptions may exist, under the current conditions of global financial capitalism, there are no grounds for considering that capital investors have—by nature or culture—any greater loyalty to a firm than its employees, or desire its continued existence or prosperity more strongly.[59] In fact, capital investors are far more mobile and less committed than the people working in the firm. Not only are labor investors generally more dependent on and attached to their firms;

they are also vital to its proper functioning. In the context of publicly traded companies, because a labor investment is far less "liquid" than that of shareholders, the risk borne by labor investors is greater than that of capital investors. After all, when a firm is in trouble, a capital investor might choose to sell her shares. All that will be lost to her—the maximum risk she has taken, in other words, thanks to the clause of limited liability—is the value of the share, which, at worst, drops to zero. The same is not true of labor investors, for whom the risk is far greater: a labor investor cannot change jobs nearly so easily, and in cases where they are required to move homes or retrain to obtain new work, they may end up in debt—with less than zero, in other words.[60] The sociology of work has identified various forms of investment made by those who work; these include educational investments through which employees develop skills that, though potentially attractive to other firms, are not necessarily transferable, or even valued in other parts of the labor market.

So who counts as a labor investor? At a theoretical level, anyone who invests their labor in a firm is eligible to be considered as one of its labor investors. This obviously includes, but is not limited to, employees directly and contractually linked to the corporation's representatives. Subcontracted workers, outsourced workers, and independent contractors are often just as vital to a firm's operations and, in these cases, have their rightful place in the constituency of labor investors. This does not necessarily extend to all subcontracted workers: a firm employee catering to a significant number of client firms does not necessarily have a right to voice in each of them; rather, that worker would have a right to voice in their own "home company." However, a worker in a firm that manufactures products exclusively for a single company (parent or not) should most certainly be counted as part of the labor constituency of that larger firm, as the future of their labor investment is directly dependent on the decisions made by the firm (parent or not). In the platform economy, the category of labor investors is crucial if we hope to successfully outgrow the problem of the circumventing of the labor contract by corporations—which treat their drivers, riders, etc. as mere trade providers, thus escaping their responsibility as employer. Indeed, those who contribute labor to certain endeavors in the platform economy might do so through significant investments of time that do not fit the category of wage work or imply any sort of (labor) contract; they are, nevertheless, crucial investors of labor, without which the risks undertaken by the capital investors would make no sense. In addition, they might be clearly governed by the algorithms designing the service provided. Here it is helpful to return to the example of Uber drivers, whose lives are governed by the algorithms powering the app, and whose labor investment is as crucial to the platform's success as capital investment.[61] In specific markets, such as social media, users are content providers: the value of Facebook, for example, depends entirely on the content investments of its users. In such cases, there are good reasons to consider users as labor investors. This proposal hopes to draw attention to these open and pressing questions and to offer a path to rebuilding solidarities across legal categories with the concept of labor investors.

This raises the question of the role of stakeholders—the broader community affected by the operations of the firm, including local residents and customers. Here, we recall the two layers of democratic regulation identified earlier. It is important to keep in mind that firm parliaments would be subject to *external* (public and state) regulation, which are just as vital to the project of extending and deepening democracy into the economy. In the context of the democratic state, stakeholder groups are already granted an indirect say through the choice of representatives in state government, whose role is to set the proper framework and regulate the activity of firms (through consumer protection, environmental regulation, etc.).[62] I believe it is most appropriate for a wider array of stakeholders to be empowered to democratically influence the context and environment within which firms operate, and to limit or orient their development—but that these should be categorized in the first instance as *external*. This is particularly clear when it comes to ecological considerations, which should not depend on any given firm's willingness to make decisions that respect the concerns of some or all of its stakeholders. The matter of the environment is hugely consequential and should be central to public power's control over firms via proper regulatory framework and systems of sanctions. The same logic applies to the concerns of key stakeholder groups, such as customers and other affected community members. Pragmatically, it is reasonable to assume that the interests of those groups would be better known to labor investors, and therefore better represented by them, since, through their work, they are most likely to be in direct and regular contact with those stakeholders. Labor investors are also more likely to live in the communities in which they work, meaning that a two-house firm parliament would be more likely to channel the views and concerns of a wider array of stakeholders. In the context of the democratic state, stakeholder groups are already granted an indirect say through the choice of representatives in state government, whose role is to set the proper framework and regulate the activity of firms (through consumer protection, environmental regulation, etc.). However, firms wishing to extend the voice of stakeholders could decide to set up consultative bodies in order to better inform their own decisions. This is, after all, what corporate firms in social democratic states currently do with their own workers, through works councils.

It is also to be hoped that this would strengthen firms' ecological commitments, since community members have a vested interest in preserving the places where they live. It is logical to assume that placing power in the hands of labor investors who live in the places where they work means placing more power in the hands of communities with a vested interest in remaining part of a viable ecosystem. And while, as mentioned above, it is also to be fervently hoped that environmental-protection policies will also be developed and applied externally to the firm, the community, and even the state, the proposal for economic bicameralism is, in the meantime, intended to foster the reconstruction of political functions and entities that have been destroyed by legal engineering in order to avoid taxes and regulation or locate key rents in specific parts of the value chain. The intent of this *real utopia* is to offer a tool that will help us to transcend the current legal limitations that bind firms to earnings-driven corporations (perceived as networks or as *nexuses of contracts*), in order to reconstruct the political entities that they are, with a view to better inserting them in the overall (open-ended) political global architecture of a society committed to the ideal of democracy and the respect of the planetary boundaries. The vital threat to our planet we now face makes it all the more urgent that we nurture the ideal of democracy at the global level and a renewal of public power.

The Bicameral Representative Government

Economic bicameralism describes an institutional design of firm government that takes seriously the legal and sociological difference between the corporation and the firm. It does not conflate them by attempting to bring labor investors into the government of the *corporation*, as do approaches such as corporate social responsibility (CSR), false-parity codetermination, B Corp, limited employee-shareholding plans, and so on. Such attempts uphold the supremacy of the corporation by continuing to enroll labor investors in the projects of *corporate* government. Democratizing the firm ends the corporation's despotic power over the firm by giving labor investors true voice in the government of this joint endeavor. The perspective offered here recognizes the fact that the corporation legally structures and organizes capital investors, while the firm still lacks its own legal structure and adequate institutional design. These remain to be established, which can be done through the parallel organization of labor investors into a second representative chamber. That, in a nutshell, is *economic bicameralism*. It consists of two chambers, a "capital investors' chamber of representatives" (what is currently known as the board of directors) and a "labor investors' chamber of representatives." These two chambers would form an elected representative government that would work together to govern the firm. The government's executive branch—its top management—would be appointed by the two chambers together. To set the rules governing the existence of the firm, executive management would have to receive a majority vote in both houses. This is why I refer to a two-chamber parliament, in which a majority (50 percent plus one) of representatives in each chamber would be required for the firm's parliament to pass any legislation. In a bicameral firm, the executive branch, or top management, would serve to help forge joint understanding and constructive compromises, and to build shared visions for the firm's future. Both chambers would, as a general rule, meet together in order to maximize deliberative capacity and collective learning, and to ensure transparency with the executive branch, and their shared goal would provide ample common ground and positive basis for dialogue: it is in both chambers' interests to keep the firm functional and prosperous. Figure 1.2 illustrates this institutional design.

The practice of bicameralism in history allows for a number of ways to determine the role assigned to any given firm parliament. Depending on how bicameralism is applied, the executive branch may have more or less power or may even find itself in competition with the legislature. We have to reimagine what this classic structure would look like in the context of the firm: applied to a bicameral firm, the top management, or executive committee, would serve as the executive branch of government. Members of the executive branch would be appointed by and held

Real Utopia: The *Bicameral* Firm with a Two-Chamber Parliament

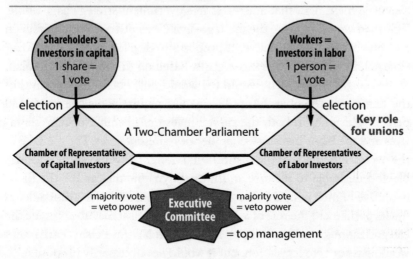

Figure 1.2. Proposal: The *bicameral* firm

accountable to the firm's two chambers, whose members would hold seats won through legislative elections. The executive branch's members would have to be approved by a majority in both chambers; that is, 50 percent plus one vote in each. This would require top management to secure and maintain the trust of a majority in both chambers. A vote of no confidence could thus oblige the top management to submit a new management plan or to resign and place itself in the running against others to win the approval of both chambers for a new executive to be formed. Of course, more sophisticated governmental arrangements also exist, in which legislatures are composed through uncoordinated election cycles that yield different (asymmetric) majorities in the two chambers, with executive branch members appointed at other points in the election cycle. This is the case in the United States, where the framers of the Constitution intentionally sought to secure powerful checks and balances using the divided and competing influences of the legislative, the executive, and the judicial branches of government. The structure put forward in this proposal, in which the executive is appointed by the legislature, is much simpler. It is a balanced, more classic version of bicameralism that does not reflect the internal divisions present in the American version.[63]

Once the firm's executive government has been appointed by the two chambers, its first act would be to issue a policy statement in the form of a management plan that addresses its government strategy as a whole. This plan would indicate the main goals the executive seeks to pursue in a given year and the initiatives it proposes to develop, both internal and external, in order to reach those goals. Based on this management plan, the executive government would (or would not) obtain the approval of the firm's two chambers. Approval would require a majority vote (50 percent plus one) in both the capital investors' chamber of representatives and the labor investors' chamber of representatives. For the sake of the overall efficiency of the institutional design, it would seem reasonable and desirable to nurture an internal dynamic that grants the firm's executive branch considerable control over the legislative agenda, leaving its parliament the role of a "policy-influencing arena," to combine the categorizations used by Philippe Norton and Nelson Polsby. Parliament would pass or veto legislation, but it would not necessarily propose it.[64]

The central change economic bicameralism seeks to effect is to allow both classes of investors in the firm, through the representatives they elect to the capital and labor investors' chambers, to participate in decisions relating to all key aspects of the life and ends of the firm, without exception. In a bicameral government structure, all of a firm's decisions would be subject to approval by its two constituencies' representatives. In concrete terms, this means that what is currently known as the supervisory board or board of directors, which represents shareholders, would be obliged to recognize the firm's other constituency. Like the board of a classic corporation, a bicameral legislature, meeting monthly, would remain a representative system of government, not a form of direct participatory democracy. The existence of such a two-chamber firm parliament would completely alter the incentive structure of a firm's top management. The executive would remain in the driver's seat, but its role would be as a kind of chauffeur to a group that agrees (or is working to reach such agreement) on where it is going, so to speak. Its core function would be to present and foster productive debate over potential routes and destinations along the way—the ends and the means to reach an overarching goal shared by all parties, in theory at least, which is to remain invested in a prosperous operation.

Obviously, the very existence of a labor investors' chamber of representatives would provide a channel of representation that would foster more internal deliberation and participation among labor investors, in view of changing the nature of decisions with regard to both ends and means. Bicameral legislature is, strictly speaking, an innovation in the domain of representative systems of government, but, more important, it can be leveraged to generate significant effects on levels of participation inside the firm. Economic bicameralism is a proposal that, to use Erik Olin Wright's terms, seeks to "extend" the principle of democracy beyond its traditional field, while also "deepening" its application, giving it much more force and meaning.[65] It would meaningfully involve labor investors in deliberation and decision-making in their firm. The very existence of a labor investors' chamber of representatives would change the entire internal culture of the firm, giving workers a channel through which they would have an effective voice in their work lives. It would help to ensure that their conceptions of justice and their own expressive rationalities are respected.

Bicameralism and the Three Classic Conditions for a Just Government
Studying the theory and history of bicameralism in the existing literature on the subject, we see that it has, time and again, been tested against three classic conditions for just rule: it lays a framework for legitimate, reasonable, and intelligent government. As we shall see, this holds true for the government of firms.

Broadly speaking, every state's transition to more democratic government has at least passed through a bicameral phase. Bicameralism remains highly relevant in political democracy: currently more than half of the world's nations, including all federal countries, are governed by bicameral assemblies.[66] This is because the exercise of legislative power by equal chambers that complement, confront, and balance one another is one of democratic political history's most important inventions, instrumental in shifting power from the hands of a single person (tyranny or monarchy) or a small number of people (oligarchy) to a broader majority (democracy). Studying the practice of bicameralism over the centuries, we note that the establishment of a second legislative chamber representing the other constituency of the political entity and granting it a *veto* right is considered the condition for a (more) legitimate, reasonable, and intelligent government. This does not mean that those conditions are fully realized at all times but rather that the practice of bicameralism is a necessary condition to advancing these conditions. Legislative

representation through bicameral politics provides *legitimate* government in that it channels the voices of the constituencies of the political
entity. It is *reasonable* in that each branch of government is limited by
being balanced by the others. Finally, it is *intelligent* in that it provides
rational representation for both sets of interests. The latter two justifications complement each other and are also desirable in and of themselves:
we all wish to be governed reasonably and intelligently, through legitimate, viable compromises among heterogeneous (or even antagonistic
claims) voiced by a society's two constituent bodies. This threefold
motivation drives bicameral innovation.[67]

For the condition of *legitimacy*, we may look to the example of
William of Orange, who, at the turn of the eighteenth century and in the
wake of the English Revolution, placed legislative power in the hands of
Parliament, while retaining executive powers for the throne. At the same
time, he upheld England's recognition of a fundamental distinction
between the House of Commons, which represented the people, and the
House of Lords, which "represented property":[68] *both together* were
considered to be the legitimate source of legislative power, and *both
together* were considered necessary to balance and legitimate the power
of the executive, thus ensuring the proper functioning of British society.
England resolved the social conflict of its revolution by recognizing that
the country was composed of two classes with conflicting constituencies. Only by engineering a way for them to work together could the
Crown hope to retain and effectively exercise executive power. Rather
than trying to suppress or efface this conflict, it set up a government
whose legitimacy depended on the ability of the two classes to cooperate
with each other. A bicameral firm with a house of representatives for
both labor investors and capital investors would bring about such a
balance of powers within the firm.

The theory of the separation and balance of power is fundamental to
the second condition of just government—that it be *reasonable*.[69] This is
what attracted America's founding fathers to bicameral politics.
However, they did not at first justify bicameralism in those terms; it was
initially adopted as a means of balancing power among states. Congress
was created to federate individual states into a union, with a bicameral
representative body whose Senate recognized states as individual entities with equal rights and powers, and whose House of Representatives
federated the population as a whole, across those states.[70]

In a sense, one might say that a "reasonable" government provides a productive response to situations in which parties with opposing interests fear the other party's ascendancy. In the case of the United States of America, as Gordon Wood points out, the separation and balance of powers was a response to criticism from anti-federalists, who were opposed to the idea of a House of Representatives on the grounds that it gave too much power to "the people"—that is, to people who were not members of the elite.[71] As Elaine Swift explains, the Senate was designed as an "American House of Lords" whose members, limited to two per state, could boast not a nobility title but "high social and economic status, substantial political autonomy, and sweeping legislative and executive power."[72] In other words, as Giancarlo Doria points out, the Senate would be "a bulwark against the excesses of democracy, and particularly of popular transient impressions—as part of that system of check and balances which they were beginning to consider the true essence of the new, republican government."[73]

Reasonable government exercises a pacifying function through the balance of two sets of powers, acting as a bridge, a buffer, or a facilitator between them, as well as between the two sets of powers taken together and the executive.[74] In the case of the fledgling United States, its architects considered that it helped strike a balance—deemed reasonable at the time—between the interests of individual states and the nation as a whole (of course, the interests of original tribes were not considered in this debate), but also acknowledged the need for a balance of powers between the "common people" and "the elite," each of whom feared that rule by one would disempower the other—although in a supposedly classless society this acknowledgment was largely a tacit one.[75] The same fear and mistrust exist in capitalist firms today: although different countries acknowledge it more or less openly, the "labor/capital" divide is very real and keenly felt. Granting them equal representation in a bicameral government is a reasonable response to the concerns of both interest groups in a way that monocameral firm government, because it vastly overrepresents the interests of capital, cannot be.

Among the three conditions for just rule, commentaries by legal philosophers and political theorists most often cite *intelligent* government as the ultimate justification for bicameralism. Two chambers representing two sets of interests but united under the common goal of governing a single entity will, through cooperation, debate, and due process, exercise power more wisely and make more intelligent decisions than they would working alone. In John Stuart Mill's words, bicameral politics counters "the evil effect produced upon the mind of any holder of power, whether an individual or an assembly, by the consciousness of having only themselves to consult."[76] A second chamber ensures there is a place for mature and reasoned argument in the legislative process; as Donald Shell puts it, it "allow[s] for second thoughts."[77] Democratic government, in other words, is epistemologically superior.[78]

If bicameral rule is to meet the conditions discussed above in the context of the firm, full parity is necessary. If both groups do not have veto power over each other's decisions, there can be no equity in the representation of the two constituencies—and therefore no *legitimate*, *reasonable*, and *intelligent* government.

Originality Compared with German Codetermination

The German *Mitbestimmung* (codetermination) system of representation, known as the most advanced form of workplace democracy in the capitalist context—not including full-fledged worker-owned and -governed cooperative firms—features parity between employer and employee management on the board of large firms. So what differentiates the bicameral firm from German codetermination, making it a distinct and original proposal? The answer is simple: in contrast to economic bicameralism, *Mitbestimmung* upholds the monocameral system of firm government and does not actually provide truly equal representation. As the graphic on the next page shows, the single chamber in the *Mitbestimmung* system—the board of overseers or supervisory board—is composed of an equal number of employee and shareholder representatives, *but* it is chaired by a president appointed by the *shareholder* representatives only, not the employee representatives. Not only does this president run the board; they cast the deciding vote in case of deadlock. In the crisp words of German legal scholar Franz Gamillscheg, German codetermination is a form of "false parity."[79] In reality, shareholders enjoy a one-vote majority at all times, as the president they appoint is always able to cast the deciding vote. Economic bicameralism, in sharp contrast, is not weighted in either direction: it requires 50 percent of the vote plus one within *both* the labor investors' and the capital investors chambers of representatives to appoint the executive committee and approve any decision. Each chamber thus has equal veto power, requiring a majority in *each* of them.

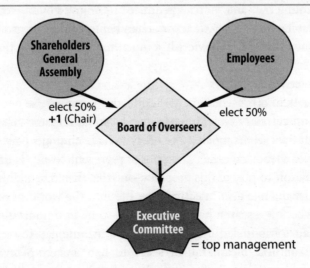

Figure 1.3. Today's codetermination German firm

Mitbestimmung, as figure 1.3 makes clear, requires a simple majority *within a single board*, in which, as we have seen, shareholders have a perpetual edge, since they (and not the labor investors) appoint its president, who has the right to cast a deciding vote over the numerically equal members from both sides.

The major difference between economic bicameralism and "false parity" *Mitbestimmung* is therefore that economic bicameralism is not merely a technique for managing—or even co-managing—firms. Although its ends include the management of production, work organization, and hierarchy, its scope is much broader than that, encompassing all decisions affecting the direction, activity, return on investments, and future of the firm. It is thus a form of *government*: it establishes ends, not just means, and capital and labor investors are represented equally and have equal voice in all strategic decisions.[80] In a bicameral firm, decisions must be approved by a majority (50 percent plus one vote) in *both* chambers—that is, worker representatives enjoy a collective veto right on any decision to be taken at board level. In a bicameral firm, unlike in a *Mitbestimmung* board, you cannot claim you have a legitimate majority to set the course of a firm by merely convincing one worker representative to vote with the capital investors. To approve a decision, a majority of the voters within *each* chamber is required. In sum, granting the same veto right as the one enjoyed by the representatives of capital investors in their own chamber to workers' representatives in *their* own chamber is obviously a much more demanding threshold.

Key Role for Trade Unions

The process of representation and collective compromise between the houses will certainly be an intense one: a capital investors' chamber of representatives seems much more likely to have homogeneous interests than would a labor investors' chamber of representatives.[81] Here, unions have a key role to play in this process—one that would be highly beneficial to firms, while also injecting new life into the world of organized labor. As recent research has shown, the decline in unionization in the past decades has fueled the growth of the income gap in our economies.[82] Economic bicameralism seeks to halt and help reverse this decline and in this way, hopefully, will contribute to a significant reduction of that income gap since unions, if they embrace the idea, should play a central role in the establishment of bicameral governments in firms—and thus see their membership rise again.

The goal of economic bicameralism is to change the way power is held over and in firms. Current institutional settings of industrial relations and collective labor rights (bargaining rights, union rights, etc.) were designed with an understanding of the economy and the firm that placed firms within the regime of domestic subordination and viewed the work experience as mainly instrumental, labor at best as the "junior partner" to capital, and workers and management in adversarial terms. Their intent was to provide an institutional channel for labor outside of the actual workings of the firm in order to ensure that workers would not be (too) exploited as they were used as instruments to pursue the firm's ends. Their goal was never to work within the actual governments of firms to involve their forgotten investors in the determination of the ends they were pursuing with capital investors, pursuing the conditions of their emancipation. By contrast, this is a central, explicit goal of economic bicameralism. Given their long history of providing voice for workers, it seems only fitting for unions to redeploy as a vehicle for labor investors' collective representation in the firm.[83] They are well positioned to help prepare employees to run for election to the labor

investors' chamber of representatives and to train them to serve effectively if elected.[84] Indeed, given their history and their contemporary
role, one ventures to imagine that they would develop into the equivalent of political parties. In a sense, they already are, in that they are
vehicles for workers' representation—the only problem being their
diminishing influence everywhere on the planet. Since economic bicameralism strengthens worker representation, it is to be hoped that it will
counter this problem, if unions choose to align themselves with it. With
any representation of a broad range of people comes interest divisions
based on skill, sector, location, cultural sensibility, and so on. Unions are
uniquely prepared to help shape and overcome such divisions with their
experience in nurturing deliberation inside dialogical institutional
settings. In their seminal paper on the differences between the logics of
collective action among capital and labor, Claus Offe and Helmut
Wiesenthal point out that workers need dialogical institutional settings
to help reveal and form their preferences, contrary to capital, who
behave much more easily as an "interest group" unified behind a clear
interest.[85]

It might be objected that unions do not have a history of prioritizing
the advancement of firm interests. Yet, this is only logical given the
history of capitalism to date. So far labor organizations have, at best,
been co-opted into comanaging firms (in other words, managing
means and not ends within a fixed, corporate-imposed, nonnegotiable
framework). Never have they helped to govern them (in other words, to
decide on ends and goals). If unions have from time to time acted
irresponsibly under current systems of comanagement, one might
actually argue that such behavior was provoked by the fact that their
cooperation is something of a sham: at the end of the day, all parties
know that in a corporation-ruled firm, the capital investors have all the
real power. With the exception of true-parity Montan *Mitbestimmung*
and cooperatives, unions have never been asked to take on any meaningful power and to participate in the actual government of firms, and
never been placed in a position of direct and practical responsibility
over firms' futures. If labor investors were placed on equal footing with
capital investors and could participate in decisions regarding the firm's
future, then it is to be expected that they would not only be strengthened but also behave responsibly toward their fellow worker-citizens
and hold themselves accountable for decisions affecting the life of the

firm given the mechanisms of accountable representation enabling bicameralism.

Finally, it should be noted that economic bicameralism is not intended to provoke economic conflict or intensify firm competition by enlisting workers to uphold a new brand of corporate patriotism. In this sense, the historical role of unions is crucial: they are and should be the traditional vehicle for solidarity among labor investors, across trades and industries, and already possess an arsenal of tools to help devise strategies to strengthen that solidarity within and among firms across trades and industries.[86] The transformation of unions into transnational political parties of labor investors would help to achieve one of the overarching goals of this proposal: to bring about the democratization of firm government at the transnational and even the global level, in order to help democratize globalization in the absence of public authorities capable of exercising much meaningful control over these transnational political entities.[87]

Governing at the Transnational Level? Such Labor Investors' Chambers Already Exist!

The institutional design of the works council emerged at the local level in many industrialized countries (including fledgling attempts during the twentieth century in the United States), spread to the national level in most Western European countries after World War II, and then, at the close of the twentieth century, took shape at the European level.[88] This evolution attests to an intuition running through the history of industrial relations: that workers should bear collectively on the government of the firm. So far, such councils have been consultative bodies, although in some countries and on certain issues they may make binding decisions—for instance, with respect to issues related to health and safety conditions. With a little imagination, it is easy to see how such councils, composed of elected worker representatives from various sites and countries, might evolve into full-fledged chambers of representatives with powers equal to the boards of corporations. It is not such a huge leap: in the words of the Auroux law on the establishment of works councils, which was passed by the French Parliament on October 28, 1982, "they are citizens in the *polis*; workers must be citizens in their firms as well" (see fig. 1.4). The scaling up of worker representation is also only logical given the evolution of the economy: starting in the early twentieth century, firms began scaling up from the local to the national to the transnational. If workers are to be citizens in any meaningful way in today's firms, their citizenship, too, must be scaled up to today's global economy.

The proposal of the bicameral firm should be seen as a way to take the concept behind works councils seriously, making them as important as a corporation's board of directors. Moreover, noting that a second chamber has *already emerged* at the firm level is a crucial observation. A bicameral firm scales up the rights exercised by works councils as they currently exist; I argue that they should be as expansive as the rights exercised by a board of directors. The context of the United States does not offer this obvious bridging institution, and the goal of this essay is to point out that the philosophical principle of economic bicameralism, whether or not bodies like works councils already exist, offers a path forward. It should be noted that, as McGaughey recently described, movement toward democracy at firm level is also part of a long but neglected tradition in the United States.[89] In fact, a law was passed in 1919 by the State of Massachusetts to enable companies to give their employees the opportunity to elect their own representatives to the board of directors. This represents the world's oldest codetermination law continuously in force, and with that history in mind, Julie Battilana and I have proposed translating the philosophical principle of bicameralism into a "dual majority board," where top management appointments and decisions require two majorities of voters in what is currently considered to be a college of voters inside a single board, whatever the colleges' respective sizes.[90]

As a parallel to the corporate board of directors, the labor investors' chamber of representatives should be established at the same level. Consider the imaginary case of the PEER Group, a transnational firm with around 360,000 employees worldwide. Around the globe, labor investors would vote for representatives in a "one labor investor, one vote" system. Thus, workers at a PEER site in California would vote in elections for the chamber of representatives for the entire PEER Group, not just a chamber of representatives for the site in California. If we imagine that there are around 35,000 PEER employees based in sites in the US, then, through a system of proportional representation, each site would send representatives to the PEER Group labor investors' chamber

Transition Path: Toward Economic **Citizenshi**

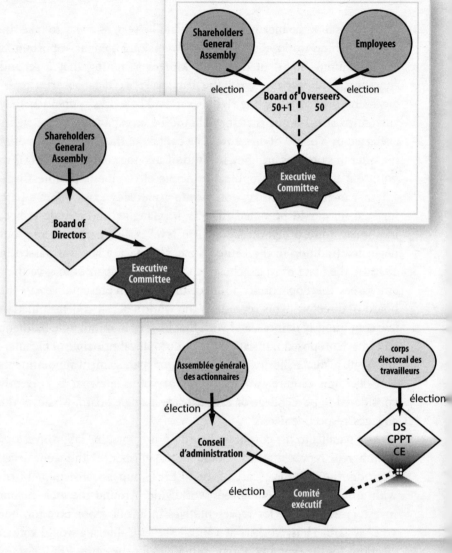

Monocameral Corporate .. Social democratic .. Mitb

Figure 1.4. Transition toward economic citizenship = the intuition at the heart of
the institutional relations in the firm

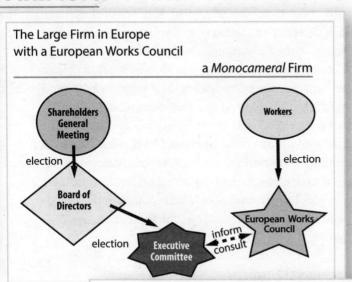

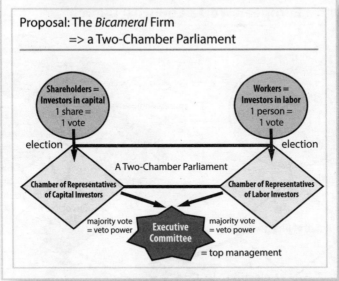

of representatives. In the PEER Group, about 10 percent of its labor investors' chamber of representatives would be elected from the US.[91]

Implementation is complex and requires constructive imagination. It is not, however, the first time something of this scope has been attempted: in 1994, a directive of the European Union established that all corporations present in the EU countries with more than a thousand workers in a single country, or with more than 150 employees in at least two countries, must organize elections among their employees to send representatives from each country to sit in a European works council.

Today, more than a thousand of these EWCs exist, meeting at least once a year with management from the European level, which informs them of the corporation's economic situation.[92] Through them, union delegates are able to collect important information and coordinate potential strategies across borders and sites. This requires, at the practical level, that firms fund travel and translators for these meetings. The

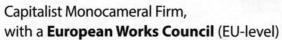

Capitalist Monocameral Firm,
with a **European Works Council** (EU-level)

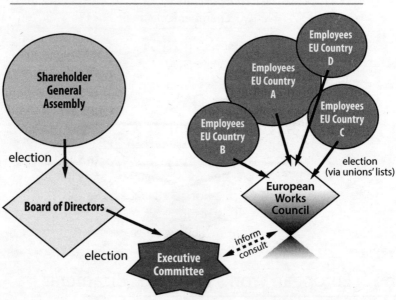

Figure 1.5. Capitalist monocameral government of the firm with a European works council

very existence of these EWCs shows that gathering representatives from various countries is a feasible operation and that positive collective learning is taking place. However, EWCs are consultative bodies; their purpose is not for labor investors to take part in the government of their firms. Nevertheless, it should be noted that a few firms have scaled these works councils up to the global level, with the help of union federations.[93] These world works councils function as consultative arenas for transnational firms, representing all employees at the global level and fostering the exchange of knowledge among workers and across union organizations. In this completely voluntary initiative, we may begin to see the outlines of a true labor investors' chamber of representatives at the global level. The present proposal would grant these representative councils veto power over all decisions currently made by the corporation's board (see fig. 1.5).

From Here to There

Bicameral legislature is easily replicable because it harnesses a dualistic social dynamic present in capitalist democracies and transforms into progress the structural conflict this dynamic produces. Economic bicameralism constitutes a "real utopia" as it offers a constructive response to what Ernest Mandel called a "transitional demand." Such transitional demands, he argued, can help society advance toward what is "bound to become a struggle which shakes the very foundations of capitalism."[94] Economic bicameralism offers an institutional, "transitional" structure that makes it possible for firms to transition from unicameral capital ownership and control in the form of the corporate firm to unicameral worker ownership and control—that is, "cooperative" firms in which labor and capital investors are the same. It can, in other words, help firms to become self-governed and truly democratic. To achieve full ownership and control (what is usually referred to with the misleading term "self-management"), labor investors could buy out a corporation's shares from its capital investors. As mentioned earlier, this already exists as a legal possibility in the highly capitalist United States through federal legislation passed in 1974, which allows labor investors to constitute a trust in the context of an ESOP, via which they can take control of the capital of the firm in

which they work. The trust is empowered to borrow the funds necessary to buy out the former shareholders in the corporation. If this were
in fact their goal, a bicameral phase of firm government would allow
labor investors to hone their government and management skills
before they transitioned to governing without capital investors in a
monocameral, worker-controlled firm.

Framing Private Property

I agree with Ralf Dahrendorf that Marx, in considering ownership of the
means of production as defining the coordinates of the class struggle,
was generalizing from a specific historical situation.[95] According to
Dahrendorf, what divides one class from another is power. If we are to
make sense of the despotism of capital investors in our economic situation, we must understand private property as generating power, which
is only possible when it comes bundled with (political) rights. As M. R.
Cohen pointed out nearly a century ago,

> history is full of examples of valuable property privileges abolished
> without any compensation, e.g. the immunity of nobles from taxat-
> ion, their rights to hunt over other people's lands, etc. It would be
> absurd to claim that such legislation was unjust.[96]

We should bear Cohen's point in mind when considering a way out of
the contradiction between capitalism and democracy: private property
is a relative, historically situated concept, and we can only fully understand it in the context of the social relationships it fosters and depends
upon. Economic bicameralism respects the private property of capital
owners. Yet, it reorganizes the rights associated with that property.
Rather than depriving shareholders of their rights, it extends the same
rights to the firm's other constituency, its labor investors.

Positive Benefits

Given the colossal returns capital investors have managed to extract
from unjust economic structures, one can only conclude that they have
taken the power gained from the bundling of political rights together
with property and abused it.[97] Here, reapplied to the behavior of corporate boards of especially major transnational corporations,[98] let us quote
again Mill's words, which are as crisp and clear as they were nearly two

centuries ago when he wrote, against monocameral legislature, of "the evil effect produced upon the mind of any holder of power, whether an individual or an assembly, by the consciousness of having only themselves to consult."[99] Our democratic societies can do better—indeed they must do better—because they know better. Economic bicameralism would advance the democratic project of equality in the economy and give workers the capability to transform the realities of their work lives and to engage in self-government. Economic bicameralism does not seek to layer one more institutional scheme on top of an already-bureaucratic corporate firm. It is designed to affect the firm as a whole and its output—to change not only the distribution of the wealth generated by the firm and to occupy itself with the returns on *both* capital and labor investments (and in this way to address the need, or not, to grow endlessly, the nature of the end products and services offered by firms), but also to positively affect the overall design of the work experience and of work life in general, as experienced by workers, by ensuring that labor investors have effective access to self-government, hence to valuing their own expressive relationship to work, and can contribute to the design of the goals of their activities and the best ways to organize them effectively.[100]

Economic bicameralism should be envisioned as a key tool for reordering the general architecture of the economic field in order to embed it, to echo Polanyi, in the overall architecture of the democratic society.[101] It is not intended to replace or destroy other tools: it remains vital to strengthen currently existing collective bargaining practices at all levels, as well as any other practices that help to expand workers' and unions' voice in governing the market conditions that affect their lives. And of course, existing regulations (fundamental rights such as the right to strike, labor market regulations, financial market regulations, etc.) should be upheld. Economic bicameralism, by establishing a better balance of power between labor and capital at the firm level, seeks to strengthen these tools, not weaken them. To cite another "real utopia," the need to *deepen* democracy at the state level is not lessened if life in cities is made highly deliberative and participative.[102] Democratizing the corporate firm is just one dimension, albeit a crucial one, of the complex architecture of a democratized economy that actually lives up to the ideals and norms of our democratic societies.

Adverse Conditions

One thing this model of government does not promise—at least not from day one—is to enhance the efficiency of the firm in the narrow, market-oriented sense of that word. There are administrative costs to organizing an effective transnational bicameral legislative structure, and all the more so if its two chambers are not rubber-stamp bodies. If the labor investors' chamber of representatives chooses complex forms of internal negotiation and conflict resolution, it seems unlikely to enhance firm efficiency from the point of view of pure market competition. There is a well-established literature on how the efficiencies of worker cooperatives arising from such assets as loyalty and commitment may be attenuated by the increased transaction costs of democratic govern-ance, particularly in the case of highly heterogeneous groups of worker-owners. At the same time, motivation, commitment, and inno-vation capabilities should be higher among labor investors in such an institutional context, and these should translate into positive market results. At best, we can say that the implications for market efficiency are neither simple nor immediate. Yet, if states considered such structures to better echo their own commitment to freedom and equality, then state authorities might provide significant support to firms choosing to undertake such transitions by granting them tax incentives and advan-tages, which would translate into a direct competitive advantage.

The classic Marxist view of capital's power centers on its mobility—investments can be allocated, bought and sold, divested, and so on. The right of capital owners to choose to invest is not affected directly by economic bicameralism, nor is the power that comes with making basic investment decisions. This, too, might undermine the efficiency and power of labor investors' chambers. Indeed, under the current regime of capital mobility across borders, state legislatures must worry about the "business climate" and often sacrifice various values to the interests of capital as a result. A labor investors' chamber of representatives would in some ways be in this position. It seems essential, then, for the state to establish certain incentive mechanisms and particularly to encourage responsible financial actors able to support and underwrite bicameral firms, at least during the initial stage. Once made, an investment in a bicameral firm would obviously be constrained differently from a classic investment in a corporate firm. This is one of the desired outcomes of economic bicameralism: to change the system of constraints on capital in order to address short-termism, which is one of the gravest ills of global financial capitalism. From this perspective, the history of German codetermination attests to the possibility of anchoring capital in its investments. While German business federations tend to criticize code-termination as being "anti-business," Germany has nevertheless remained the envy of Europe for its ability to maintain strong industry in the highly competitive global era.

Incentive Mechanisms

Clearly, a bicameral transition would require a significant mobilization of both capital and labor investors of the firm. The radically progressive step forward would be for states to make access to the benefits enjoyed today by corporations, that is, legal personality and limited liability, conditional on a firm's government structure, granting it only to firm governments with bicameral structures, or governments that have otherwise been deemed reasonable, legitimate, intelligent, and fitting with the democratic values of that state—the fully democratic firm, that is, the labor investors' governed firm, aka the worker cooperative. Certainly, a more gradual shift beyond current monocameral corporate firms to the bicameral form would be easier politically. In the short term, fiscal incentive mechanisms might be implemented by democratic states interested in encouraging businesses to meet their overall commit-ment to nurturing a democratic society. In practical terms, this would mean lowering the corporate tax rate for firms that commit to a bicam-eral transition. In the past, states have lowered corporate tax rates for reason less glorious than this. After a period of transition, it is to be assumed that bicameral government will generate a more productive form of work organization in firms, as one of its central goals is to bolster two key drivers of commitment in the workplace by supporting labor investors in their search for mastery and autonomy in their own lives, and responding to their own *critical intuition of democratic justice* at work. Today, absenteeism generates enormous losses for firms.[103] The bicameral government of firms might become a competitive advantage, which, combined with a lower corporate tax rate, would ultimately help them to outcompete corporate firms. It seems only fitting for a demo-cratic society to discourage capital investors from investing in despotically governed organizations that run counter to the basic values of democracy.

To help firms make the transition from bicameral government to labor-investor government (see fig. 1.6), public authorities might consider adopting ESOP legislation similar to what exists in the United States.[104] In addition to this legislation, which enables labor investors to form a trust and buy back the shares of their firms, public authorities should seek ways to make capital available to these trusts at favorable interest rates, perhaps through public and community banks.[105] If this funding is properly channeled and monitored, then one of the most intractable barriers to the development of a thriving cooperative sector will finally be lifted. Up until now, the major stumbling block to the spread of cooperatively run firms has been access to (supportive) finance. With proper state support, the risk previously associated with lending to "worker cooperatives" would be greatly mitigated by a transitional bicameral phase, which would help workers prepare for full government of their own firms. In this way, bicameralism for the firm makes the real utopia of a fully democratic firm a much more concrete

Regulative Ideal: The **Democratic Firm,**
Labor-Governed and -Owned

A Labor Monocameral Firm

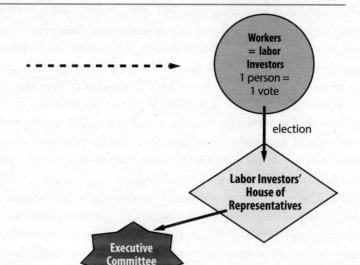

Figure 1.6. Regulative ideal: the democratic firm

prospect. Equally, the billions owned by employees though pension funds could also be mobilized in a consistent strategy—that is, to support firms that commit to fully respecting and including their labor investors in their own government.

To Conclude: About the Limits of Corporate Social Responsibility and the Sustainable Development Index

Using a critical and reconstructive perspective, I have anchored this essay in what I have named the "critical intuition of democratic justice" (at work) as a way to explore the idea that people (who invest their labor in work) consider that their own conceptions of justice ought to matter in the decisions that concern them (including in the realm of their work life, from the work experience to the arrangements of the firm).[106] We have seen that the most innovative businesses have already figured this out. Capitalism, as always, has taken note of the *political critique* of the restraints on worker's autonomy—and productivity—generated by the despotism of capital investors, and is recycling it.[107] As Herbert Marcuse pointed out, its ability to undermine it by this co-option should not be underestimated: business school courses in participatory management and methods for "liberating the firm" abound without addressing the core problem of extractive, unicameral firm government.[108] We cannot hope for our economy (let alone our democratic societies as a whole) to advance in any lasting, sustainable, constructive way if the firms that drive it are governed in a capitalist, despotic fashion. The institutional model of bicameral politics offers a tested and reliable solution. It should be expanded to include firms. Indeed, addressing the government of the firm will make a major contribution to many of the most pressing challenges of our times.

It will help reduce inequality by ensuring that bargaining between capital and labor takes place at its core.[109] It will help us to meet the challenge of globalization by offering an actionable, internally legitimate response to the failure of states to provide a normative and binding framework for transnational corporations and their value chain.[110] Firms that adopt bicameral government structures will become less unilaterally oriented toward capital gains. It is likely that they will assign greater value to functioning public authorities and services and the goods that states have the potential to deliver (education, health, environmental protection, etc.). And as firms cease to fight against the very existence of state capacities, the potential will be even greater for states to cooperate on a proper framework in order to regulate transnational firms.

Economic bicameralism offers a response to the challenge of innovation and motivation, fostering the working conditions firms require by providing new ways to combine and reconstitute the moments of conception and execution of work.[111] It could help to further enrich deliberation over the future of technological changes, including AI and robotization; after all, since they are so significant to the future of workers, it is only fair that decisions regarding such changes, which directly impact labor investment in the firm, be deliberated over with workers. It will help counter the rise of extreme right-wing and populist movements by aligning the experience of citizenship in the *polis* and at work. It will help to fight the corruption of political democracy by injecting new hope into a demoralized demos and empowering labor and civil society actors, not only corporations;[112] in particular, it will help to renew the trade union movement by building a stronger and more constructive role for it at the economic and political level. Democratizing firms is a constructive contribution to all these pressing challenges.

Meeting the challenge of environmental sustainability means, at the minimum, a full transition to a post-carbon model of development by 2050, according to an assessment by the Intergovernmental Panel on Climate Change.[113] Transnational firms (TNFs) have a great deal of responsibility for making this transition, and it is time to see them for what they are: the engine that powers our carbon-producing economic model. As such, it is crucial that they be regulated and reorganized in ways that will allow us to enter the kind of post-carbon economic model of development the planet needs to survive. A single figure is enough to capture the primacy of TNFs to the future of our planet: one hundred TNFs are responsible for 71 percent of global carbon emissions.[114] By enabling higher levels of return on labor investment, economic bicameralism can help to shake off our obsession with endless growth and in so doing aid our economies in achieving greater sustainability by building shared prosperity.[115] Labor investors are not buffered from the effects of environmental devastation by wealth and mobility to the extent that capital investors are, so including their voices in the government of firms would add positive pressure from the inside to encourage firms to concern themselves with limits of our planet and the ways we access and share its resources.[116]

Democratizing the corporation offers a powerful response to the pressing need to transition our economy into a post-carbon model. Indeed, the capitalist despotism that has been the model for governing corporate firms has been instrumental in generating the terrible state in which our planet finds itself: the corporation is the extractive institution par excellence as it treats *by design* everything, environmental and human resources alike, as mere instruments in its quest for more capital returns. It is thus unlikely that more of the same despotism will lead us out of the impasse in which we find ourselves today. If we want that transition to happen, and if we want to reach decisions that will actually lead us to a nonextractivist economy, then leaving the government of firms to capital investors is certainly unreasonable, illegitimate, and highly unintelligent. Labor investors must be brought to the table and seriously weigh on firms' strategies, which will include all the qualitative decisions that firms must make for that transition to happen.

The first two decades of the twenty-first century offer stinging proof that *corporate social responsibility* is a failed strategy. As labor practices around the world make clear, asking capital investors to respect labor's right to organize is futile—and the consequences are dire. In an era of global finance capitalism, the corporation is, more than ever, an institutional vehicle crafted to respond to the interests of capital investors. Where capital investors hold all real power, organized labor is left with only crumbs. The CSR experiment was certainly worth trying, and it has produced a series of interesting soft-law, self-administered developments (new forms of codes of conduct or corporate forms such as B Corp, Social Benefit Company, etc.). It is now evident, however, that institutional design and legal rights matter. It is urgent that efforts be focused at that level, as well. In the absence of a global state, *deepening* democracy depends on *extending* it to areas that have so far been kept segregated from it. The economy and the corporation thus require our full attention.

The time has come to recognize that firms, especially transnational firms, which have such power over our lives and our futures, are political entities and, as such, must be democratized from the inside to fit the commitment of our societies to a democratic and sustainable future. To do so, we must move beyond our limited view of the corporation *as* the firm and institutionalize the firm as a whole. Capital has access to representation through the corporate board that, for the time being, is governing the whole of the firm. Labor does not—not yet! Truly organizing labor would mean obtaining for it the same sets of rights that capital holds through the corporation. It is urgent that we reaffirm for workers the principle of equality "in dignity and rights" stated by the Universal Declaration of Human Rights. This means creating equivalent institutional channels for them, within the structure of a bicameral firm. The capitalist corporate firm as we know it should become as obsolete and preposterous as a monarch ruling with no parliament. If unions and social movements truly wish to further workers' interests and dignity on this earth, they must move toward a fuller understanding of democratic citizenship—one that is broad enough to embrace the economic, as well. The future of organized labor depends on it—as do the future of our democratic societies and our ability to move beyond the current extractive capitalist regime. Firms are the new frontier in the democratic experiment. It is time for citizens at work—whether they bear the title of partner, collaborator, manager, leader, employee, or simply worker—to truly become *equals in dignity and rights* within the firm.

II.

Democracy at Work

2

The Progressive Era's Public Firm

Carly R. Knight

On the morning of September 13, 1899, an assemblage of politicians, labor organizers, scholars, businessmen, and farmers filed into Chicago's Central Music Hall to discuss the future of the American economy. The assembly included such notable figures as William Jennings Bryan, Samuel Gompers, and William Bourke Cockran, all gathered to discuss the singular issue that had transfixed the American public over the previous years. The past decade had witnessed the "trustification" of American business, as new mammoth and seemingly indomitable national manufacturing corporations had begun to monopolize state and local marketplaces. More than an abstract threat, these corporations were feared to have increased prices, watered stock, undercut local business, and fomented political corruption.[1] More threatening still, the fact that states competed for corporate charters meant that states were caught in a "race to the bottom" to accommodate these new corporate giants, rendering state regulations impotent against consolidation. This trend, which would only gain steam over the subsequent years of the "great merger movement," sparked a national conversation about what, precisely, "trusts" were and how to address them.[2] So, on this Chicago morning, under the gaze of a captivated American public, these thinkers gathered to consider the future organization of the American corporation.

The participants of the Chicago Conference on Trusts came to the question of how to reconcile growing corporate power with democracy with a very different set of background assumptions than those that animate public conversation today. The American public had not yet accepted that corporations existed primarily to realize shareholders' interests. As Dudley Wooten, a member of the Texas state legislature, opined to much applause: corporations "were only meant for enterprise of a quasi-public character" in service of the public good.[3] On the question of trade-offs between corporate power and democracy, Wooten pronounced, "There are some things more valuable, more to be desired, and more worthy to be contended for by a free people than mere industrial activity."[4]

While the participants of the Chicago Conference differed in their oppositional or accommodationist stances toward the trusts, a unifying solution that developed from the debate was one that has reemerged today as a salve to imperious corporate power. To reorganize a corporate form that was amicable to a democratic vision of America, the conference coalesced around the idea of moving corporate chartering out of the domain of the states and into that of the federal government. As Attorney General R. S. Taylor argued, "The interests of investors in the shares of [trusts] is a small consideration beside the interest of the general mass of people whose food, clothing, and transportation are controlled by them."[5]

Proponents of federal chartering believed that the federal government could better secure the public interest than the states—but not because state legislators were insufficiently public oriented or were captive to some incipient notion of shareholder value. On the contrary, by this time, many states had already adopted laws against concentration.[6] Rather, the participants of the Chicago Conference understood that state-level chartering in an increasingly integrated national economy created overpowering incentives to capitulate to corporate demands. And as long as at least one state accommodated corporate concentration—as New Jersey had done in 1893 by allowing corporations to own shares in other companies—state-level regulators were effectively powerless.[7] As Bryan, the perennial presidential candidate, orated,

> [it is] impossible for the people in one state to depend for protection upon the people in another state . . . I believe that no complete remedy will be found for the trust until the federal government . . . lays its hands upon these trusts.[8]

If a systemic solution was needed, that was not what Americans got. Over the next fifteen years, the movement for federal chartering would fail, riven by differences among American Progressives about the purposes and extent of federal regulation.[9] The "race to the bottom" among the states would eventually descend even further—as encapsulated by the 2017 offer by Stonecrest, Georgia, to change its name to "Amazon" should it be selected as the winner to house Amazon's second headquarters. The failure of the federal chartering movement is worth keeping in mind today, as progressives again debate proposals for corporate reform. Because at the end of the nineteenth century, Progressives understood that the problem was not the ideological primacy of shareholders' property rights—an idea that remained incipient among the capitalist class. The problem was structural.

Isabelle Ferreras offers an incisive and radical proposal for a more democratic economy: the "bicameral" firm. In what follows, I will argue that twentieth-century Progressive thought may offer important insights as scholars today build upon this proposal and others in reimagining a more democratic economy. First, I will discuss Ferreras's theoretical argument on the "public" nature of the modern firm. Throughout the late nineteenth and early twentieth centuries, legal scholars grounded claims about the public nature of the corporation in legal theory— building on either the *history* of the corporate form or on an *intrinsic* analysis of where corporate privileges originate. This tendency has at times been taken up by modern-day progressives when, for instance, they argue that corporations' public obligations are grounded in the privileges they receive from charters.[10] By contrast, Ferreras grounds the "public" nature of the modern firm not in corporate history or in legal theory but in the actual *practices* of contemporary firms. Specifically, she argues that contemporary customer-oriented firms operate as modern-day "public spheres." This pragmatist orientation, I argue, better approximates historical understandings of the corporation's public nature and offers a more solid foundation for justifying their regulation. However, I suggest we should go further in resuscitating Progressive Era notions of the public firm, which were based in a capacious notion of the public interest.

Second, I suggest that if we take seriously the issues raised at the Chicago Committee on Trusts, then Ferreras's bicameral firm must be seen as only a partial solution to the problem she identifies—that of antidemocratic corporate power. This is not to take away from the strengths of Ferreras's proposal; all real-world policy proposals are necessarily partial. However, there are inherent limitations to policy solutions aimed at a level below the structural source of the problem. In this case, it is inadequate to rely on firm-level solutions to deeply structural market-level inequalities. In discussing features of twenty-first-century capitalism that render firm-level solutions of limited efficacy, I argue that a new progressivism must not lose sight of the goal to ultimately make firms matter *less* for the well-being of citizens.

The Public Nature of the Firm

Across political theory, law, and the social sciences, there is an interest in reinvigorating an investigation into the political nature of the corporation.[11] As political theorist Abraham Singer summarizes, the idea is that "firms should be understood as political in the empirical and conceptual sense such that we see them as being similar to states . . . or the direct result of government action."[12] Contemporary theorists have made three primary arguments that private corporations are, in fact, political entities. The first relies on a *genealogical* approach, where scholars point to the fact that corporations have historically been understood as semipublic entities vested with political power. Second, some scholars have adopted an *intrinsic* approach, arguing that, irrespective of the corporation's history, the *current* set of privileges and rights that corporations enjoy exist only by virtue of government-granted political power. Finally, some theorists have argued that corporations are public, not because of where they came from or how they were made but because of what they *do*. Ferreras's proposal is built upon this later, pragmatic approach, and I will argue below that this approach offers the most persuasive basis for reconceptualizing the firm for our modern economy.

Genealogical, Intrinsic, and Pragmatist Approaches to Corporate Theory
Corporate history is often used by scholars to argue that corporations should be considered political, or quasi-public, entities.[13] Pointing to the historical novelty of the shareholder theory of value, these scholars denaturalize, and thereby unsettle, the corporation as a wholly private vehicle for capital accumulation. For instance, American scholars cite

the fact that the colonies were originally corporations and that early American corporations were associated with public works projects like canals, bridges, and turnpikes.[14] As Oscar and Mary Flug Handlin demonstrate, in antebellum Massachusetts the early corporate form was limited to organizing groups of persons into *governmental* entities, such as towns and parishes. When faced with inadequate state budgets that limited their capacity to meet citizens' demands for infrastructure, Massachusetts state legislators built upon this experience to use corporations for the novel end of organizing *capital*, setting "to unfamiliar service a versatile and trusty form."[15] The corporation as a mode of organizing persons into governmental entities goes back even further, to medieval times. In *The Asymmetric Society*, James Coleman makes explicit the link between history and our contemporary evaluation of corporate rights: "To learn more about the [corporate] form necessitates learning more about the structure of rights under which a given form arises. And a useful place to begin is back in the 13th century."[16] By demonstrating how recently we turned toward a private conception of the corporation, such scholars denaturalize the purely private view, opening space for reconceptualization.

If genealogical approaches unsettle our assumption that corporations are necessarily private entities, *intrinsic* approaches argue that today's corporations retain some of their historical governmental features by virtue of their legal structure.[17] In his groundbreaking article, David Ciepley argues that corporations are "not constituted through private contract, but are government fostered."[18] Specifically, Ciepley points out that the capacity of a corporation to contract as an individual entity depends on a set of legal privileges that separate corporate assets and liabilities from those of its shareholders; these are the privileges of limited liability, entity shielding, and asset lock-in. Crucially, Ciepley argues that there is no way for contractual arrangements among shareholders to re-create these government privileges. For instance, for a corporation's assets to be shielded from investors' liabilities, every shareholder would have to contract with every creditor to prevent them from claiming firm assets in instances of bankruptcy. Because "corporations rely on government to override the normal market rules of property and liability," corporations are thereby governmental entities.[19]

Both genealogical and intrinsic approaches also appear in early twentieth-century debates about the corporate form. It was not uncommon to see those advocating for the grant view of the corporation, for example, to cite corporate history.[20] In a particularly notable instance, Robert Ludlow Fowler cites corporate history in arguing for state regulation:

> Corporations are not novel social phenomena but as old as high civilization . . . By a natural extension from these first examples of an artificial legal personality have come the modern commercial and trading corporations . . . The recognition by the State of an aggregation of persons as a single pluralistic person . . . has been always, under all systems, the distinctive feature of corporate bodies.[21]

Similarly, much of the legal history debate about the nature of the corporation was centered around theories about, fundamentally, what corporations *were*: a political entity, a legal abstraction, or a natural form of human organization.[22] The intrinsic analyses offered at the time often lacked the analytic heft of those being put forward today, relying as often on analogy as on legal argumentation.[23]

However, an important conceptual corrective to emerge from the Progressive Era was that the proper way to think about corporate theory was not to focus on intrinsic analyses of corporate logic—a move that tended toward endless, esoteric debates.[24] Rather, as philosopher John Dewey urged, quoting Charles S. Peirce, corporate legal theorists should follow the "pragmatic rule" in developing conceptions of legal entities: "Consider what effects, which might conceivably have practical bearings, we conceive the object of our conception to have. Then, our conception of these effects is the whole of our conception of the object."[25]

In other words, Dewey encouraged a pragmatist view of the corporation, one that comprehends its character not by where it came from or how its organized but by what it *does*. While the genealogical approach may denaturalize the corporation, it does not offer reasons why we should consider firms *today* to be public. And while it is important to demonstrate that publicly traded corporations depend on government-originated privileges, these arguments are less relevant for the new way firms are increasingly owned and organized in today's American economy.[26] Thus, it is this pragmatic approach, and how it can be used to justify a public view of the corporation, to which I now turn.

To Be Affected with the Public Interest

Recently, scholars have employed versions of this pragmatist approach in arguing that firms should be considered "political" or "public" in some way. In her proposal, for example, Ferreras relies upon the notion of the public sphere to justify the "nonprivate logic of the work experience" (this volume, p. 16). Specifically, Ferreras argues that because our "current service-based production regime" is customer oriented and largely service based, "the workplace cannot be differentiated from the public sphere" (p. 18).[27] Ferreras argues that it is the contact between workers, customers, and the larger public—"the delivery person bringing the mail, the truck driver dropping off production parcels" (p. 18)—that has eroded any semblance of workplaces as private entities. Because, Ferreras argues, workplaces (more so than ever before) act as a primary location wherein people experience the public sphere, it is particularly crucial that firms be democratized.

However, while Ferreras powerfully illustrates the contradictions inherent in workers' lives—of public workplaces subordinated to private rules— it is not clear that this public-sphere argument offers the strongest foundation for corporate democracy. First, by defining firms' public nature by their degree of customer or public orientation, this seems to imply that workers in service firms would have more of a claim to democratic workplace relationships than, for example, those in manufacturing firms. Second, this view mistakes a consequence of unequal employment relations for its cause. The fact that workplaces are more public today than in the past draws attention to hierarchical workplace relations, but it does not account for what gives rise to them. Finally, this view limits the claims for democratic firm governance to those who are employed by the firm. Yet it is clear that the power that modern-day firms wield over individuals extends more broadly than just over the workforce they employ. Competitors, customers, the environment, and individuals generally considered to be firm "stakeholders" are all affected by firms' decision-making powers.

Thus, while a public-sphere approach does justify regulating corporate governance, alternative theoretical traditions grounded in a pragmatic approach may go further in recasting corporations as political entities. First, as Ferreras herself discusses, the idea that corporations are political because they *act* like governments has been foundational to a long line of socialist thinking.[28] For instance, in *A Preface to Economic Democracy*,

Robert Dahl grounds the right to workplace democracy on features of economic associations that are analogous to those of states—specifically that workers, like citizens, are operating within an organization that makes "binding" *collective* decisions that affect their lives.[29] For Dahl (at least in his later work), it is this parallel between governments and business enterprises that justifies workplace democracy: "*If* democracy is justified in governing the state, then it must *also* be justified in governing economic enterprises."[30] More recently, Elizabeth Anderson, in *Private Governments*, draws on Weber's discussion of the state as a "compulsory organization" to argue that governments exist "wherever some have the authority to issue orders to others, backed by sanctions."[31] Here, because companies are governmental in their effects—crucially, by acting in a way that exerts dominion over workers' lives, issuing orders and enforcing sanctions—workers have a right to a democratic voice. One particularly beneficial aspect to this argument is that it justifies corporate democracy in the fissured workplace that Ferreras describes. What matters here is ultimately that managers issue orders and enforce sanctions; the contingency of workers having a formal employment relation, interacting with customers, or operating in a public workplace is secondary.

At the same time, taking on board a pragmatist definition of corporations as political in their effects opens the door to a more capacious understanding of who has a claim over corporate governance. For instance, some early twentieth-century Progressives argued that the power to regulate corporations was based in their status as public entities—not on whether citizens were linked to the corporation through their status as employees or as consumers. For example, William Novak chronicles a central idea underpinning the expansion of corporate regulation during the Progressive Era—the "public service corporation."[32] During this period, the category of public service corporations grew to be broader than the public utilities or common carriers—for instance, electric companies, railroads, telegraphs, turnpikes, and bridges—from which the concept originated. Rather, this category was expanded to include all businesses "affected with a public interest"—businesses whose size or importance caused them to affect the public at large. As legal scholar Frank Goodnow explains:

> The regulation which in the case of public utilities was justified on the
> theory that the enterprise was based upon a privilege has since been

extended to enterprises which in no sense owe their existence to the possession of such privileges. The justification for the regulation is found in the mere fact that the public interest is involved.[33]

The notion of "public" here was not that corporations were government owned, nor even government originated. Rather, "public" meant that their operation *in practice* affected the public, and thereby such corporations should not be regulated as though they were wholly private entities. It is this pragmatic notion of a public—that of a collectivity bound together by common experience and a common set of problems—that animated Dewey's pragmatist philosophy of the period.[34]

A powerful feature of this view is that it does not limit those who have a claim to a voice in firm governance to employees alone but instead expands the purview of legitimate government regulation. In order to regulate firms affected with the public interest, the government must regulate markets. That is, firms in industries on which the citizens particularly depend are social, and their markets should be regulated as such. As Rexford Tugwell writes, "When the market is viewed as a social mechanism rather than a private one . . . the problems of price and service control attain a new importance."[35] The Progressive conception of public interest, therefore, offers a broader justification for the regulation of market-wide outcomes, one rooted in the social nature of the market.

It is important to note that there is nothing necessarily at odds about these two approaches to defining firms as public entities in their effects. The effect of companies on the public serves to justify government regulation and undercut the notion of companies as purely private entities. At the same time, companies have very *particular* effects on their employees—decision-making power and the ability to sanction—that likewise give workers a particular claim to a democratic voice. Here, the democratization of firms and government regulation of markets go hand in hand in developing a new progressive worldview of a more democratic economy.[36] A benefit of the twentieth-century Progressive conception of the public interest is that it sensitizes us to the social nature of the market more generally—rather than limited to that which obtains in the worker–firm relationship.

"The Market as a Social Mechanism"

One exciting feature of modern-day progressivism is that there is no shortage of new ideas of how to democratize the economy (as evidenced by the Real Utopias project). Ferreras's proposal thus joins a slate of bold reimaginings of what a more just and egalitarian economy might look like. At the same time, firm-level proposals *must* be paired with market-wide regulations—those that empower governments to design markets for better outcomes and to ultimately make markets matter less for the well-being of individuals.

If structural, federal-level corporate regulation was the necessary corrective that twentieth-century Progressives failed to achieve, it is worth considering whether firm-level proposals may now be of particularly limited efficacy. As Paul Adler has warned, we must avoid seeking a "twentieth century solution to a twenty-first century problem."[37] While there's been much written on this topic, here I mention only two features of our twenty-first-century problems that demand more than firm-level remedies: the between-firm structure of wage inequality, and economic precarity.

First, over the past decades, wage stagnation has increasingly been defined by variation *between* firms. Since 1979, wage growth for American workers has stagnated, becoming divorced from productivity gains.[38] Until recently, scholarship on wage stagnation had focused on *within-firm* explanations. The rise of the theory of shareholder value, competition among CEOs, and the decline of collective bargaining all play a role in firms' capacity to direct profits toward shareholders, rather than reinvesting those gains back into the firm or raising employees' pay.[39] However, this focus on within-firm explanations obscures an important feature of contemporary wage stagnation: since 2000, most of the growth of wage inequality has been *between firms*.[40] As Nathan Wilmers summarizes,

> The growing gap between median and high earners is between high- and median-paying firms, rather than among coworkers at the same firm ... and the declining labor share is due to reallocation toward very profitable firms, rather than redistribution from workers to owners in the same firm over time.[41]

This between-firm model of wage inequality illustrates the "winner-take-all" logic of economic inequality.[42] Superstar firms appear across industries, and the industries most characterized by this model are those where workers' wages have stagnated the most.[43] Superstar firms exacerbate inequality by exercising monopsony power—that is, power of a small number of companies that dominate their markets. Companies that dominate their labor markets are thought to dictate and suppress wages.[44] Through a different mechanism, firms that dominate their *buyer* markets, and are thereby able to set prices, can suppress wages among their suppliers.[45] In addition to stagnating wages, monopsony limits entrepreneurship, lowers job mobility, and narrows the job ladder for workers.[46] If a principal mechanism for wage inequality is *between* firm, then democratizing an Apple or an Alphabet or a Facebook can only do so much to alleviate inequality, particularly for workers in smaller firms within concentrated industries. That is, any proposal for democratizing the market must remain cognizant of the inegalitarian structure *between firms*.

Second, social scientists have drawn attention to the global increase in economic precarity.[47] Precarity in employment reflects the decline in union protections, the growth of alternative work arrangements, the erosion of "good jobs," and the rising sense of insecurity among workers.[48] Yet "precarity" also refers to an increased general exposure of individuals to market forces, an increase propelled in part by growing financialization in the economy and the individuation of social welfare institutions. Between 1980 and 2008, the percentage of workers whose companies offered defined benefit pension plans fell from 38 to 20 percent.[49] Meanwhile, between 1989 and 2001, the percentage of American households whose savings were tied to stock investments increased from 32 to over 52 percent.[50] With Americans' wealth, retirement savings, and income all increasingly tied to unpredictable market cycles, a primary source of dissatisfaction with the economy has been a sense of economic insecurity.[51]

Forming a labor investors' chamber of representatives and treating workers as "investors" has the potential to mitigate some of this precarity. For instance, strengthening the bargaining power of American labor could lead to better health coverage. However, it is unlikely that American employers will ever return to offering the social safety nets they did in the mid-century. The disappearance of such programs is at least partially due to economic trends that cannot be reversed: rising global competition, a shift toward a service economy. Furthermore, in a contemporary labor market characterized by frequent job changes and an economy where firms' long-term stability is far from guaranteed, we need policies that separate workers' economic survival from that of their employers.[52]

What all this suggests is that proposals such as Ferreras's must be paired with novel mechanisms to *insulate* individuals from markets. Luckily, there are no shortage of such plans, many of which draw inspiration from twentieth-century reformers. For instance, inspired by the Fair Labor Standards Act of 1938, Kate Andrias and Brishen Rogers sketch a plan for setting broad-based floors on minimum wages at the sectoral level through the creation of industry-specific wage boards.[53] Jacob Hacker has suggested creating a universal insurance program to provide relief to needy Americans experiencing particularly severe economic shocks.[54] Other plans may include the expansion of the realm of what is decommodified beyond labor, protecting firms themselves from market bubbles.[55] For others still, the solution may require revisiting the Progressive Era notion of the public, expanding the space of what is considered to be a "public" good to domains that are contemporarily seen as private.[56] My own preferred plans are those that call for an unconditional universal basic income, which Erik Olin Wright long advocated as a powerful tool of a broad socialist challenge to capitalism.[57] Beyond their particulars, what unites all of these proposals is an attempt to strengthen the bargaining power of workers by making work matter less—in the words of Karl Polanyi, to limit the extent to which the "market mechanism [is] the sole director of the fate of human beings and their natural environment."[58]

What Ought to Be

In her essay, Ferreras offers a creative, radical, and potentially transformative idea for addressing the deep inequity that characterizes contemporary capitalism. The bicameral firm, Ferreras argues, "will make a major contribution to many of the most pressing challenges of our time"—reducing inequality and short-termism in investing, fighting corruption, and even countering the rise of the extreme right wing.[59]

Altering the governance of the firm—and truly giving workers a voice in the decisions that structure their lives—would indeed represent a transformation in the management of contemporary capitalist enterprise.

At the same time, the structure of the contemporary American economy demands that corporate governance changes must be paired with solutions that free individuals from such heavy dependence on employment. As long as firms—even worker-owned firms—operate within a winner-take-all market whose zero-sum logic is structured by profit-seeking, both capital and labor will be beholden to incentives that too often put them at odds with not only their buyers and suppliers but also their communities and the environment.

The amelioration of capitalism's harms will require a pastiche of solutions, including those like Ferreras's aimed at expanding workplace democracy. The challenge is to remain as ecumenical as possible in our search for remedies, while not losing sight of the complex nature of the problem. As Williams Jenning Bryan once argued, "In a civilized society, the question is not what is, but what ought to be."[60]

3

Workplace Democracy, the Bicameral Firm, and Stakeholder Theory

Marc Fleurbaey

The bicameral firm proposal put forth by Ferreras brings some heralded institutions of representative democracy into the capitalist firm. Critics of such schemes for democratizing the workplace have many objections, but I would like to highlight two of them. First, bringing too many conflicting interests to the table will produce governing gridlock and raise transaction costs.[1] This issue seems particularly relevant to the bicameral firm, which inevitably evokes memories of a Democratic House of Representatives being obstructed by a Republican Senate. A democratic firm with only as much goodwill as exists between strongly opposed politicians in a polarized political theater cannot function very well.

The second criticism is that democratizing the firm blurs the objective of the corporation. Whereas the standard capitalist firm has a clear objective that ends up being measured objectively in the bottom line and the stock price (although the two may diverge systematically sometimes, as one is tied to profit whereas the other is tied to expected dividends and appreciation), a democratic firm with diverse constituencies will have no clear agenda, and this situation is likely to be exploited by the CEO. Ultimately, much will depend on having a charismatic CEO with some vision, and the democratic base will be at best a rubber stamp, at worst a haphazard check or a sheer nuisance.

This second criticism is commonplace among critics of the stakeholder approach to corporate governance. For instance, Joseph Heath disparages the stakeholder approach for failing to define what objective the firm should pursue or, when it is defined (total surplus for all stake-holders, as in J. S. Harrison et al.), for failing to give a practical way to measure it and make it operational.[2]

In this chapter, building on the formal analysis developed in my coau-thored article with Gregory Ponthière, "The Stakeholder Corporation and Social Welfare," I will argue that these criticisms can be addressed.[3] Along the way, one gets an idea of what the firm should do and how it can measure and check what it does. This provides some guidance for how the democratic decision-making bodies of the firm should work and what they should focus on. Workplace democracy is not a panacea. It must not only enfranchise the relevant constituencies, especially workers who are the flesh and blood of the organization; it must also serve the purpose of a direction of management that truly pursues the common good. With an operational depiction of what pursuing the common good means for a firm, a decisional gridlock and a loss of direction is less likely to occur. At least, that is the hope I would like to convey here.

The penultimate section of this chapter delivers a cautionary note. Even if all firms were to behave democratically and "responsibly," as described below, there would remain deep societal issues that these firms are unlikely to spontaneously address and more generally that the market economy is not equipped to deal with. It is important to keep this in mind, not just to put things in perspective but also because these societal issues are not independent of how firms are managed and because they provide some additional ideas about good management.

Stakeholder Theory Revisited

What is a firm? It is a collective venture in which many parties join forces to gather resources from suppliers of equipment and other phys-ical capital, financial backup, labor and ideas, and intermediate goods and services, in order to transform them to serve the needs of custom-ers. All the parties involved stand to benefit from this venture. The suppliers obtain income that they can spend on their own needs, while the customers obtain the goods and services fashioned by the firm.

Let us take the total surplus of the firm to all its stakeholders (includ-ing workers, investors, customers, suppliers, and so on) as the measure of its contribution to society. This is the measure recommended by the literature in stakeholder theory—that is, when it bothers to suggest a measure.[4] As a preliminary step, let us bracket issues of externalities affecting outsiders, and other such complications.

Critics such as Heath and Tirole argue that this notion of total surplus is not practical, because unlike financial profit, which is measured more or less objectively (expected profit is actually a subjective notion, but at least the realized profit is ascertained by accountants), the surplus is a wholly subjective variable that cannot be accurately measured and therefore cannot be used for sound management.[5]

This issue turns out to be solvable, as Ponthière and I argue, because what matters for management, as economic students painstakingly learn in their first year, is marginal calculus.[6] For instance, to know if you maximize profit, you do not need to measure the realized profit; you only need to know how profit varies with any small variation of your production plan. If you hire one more worker, how will that affect the revenue and the cost? Marginal profit is equal to marginal revenue minus marginal cost, and everything boils down to comparing these two terms, expanding the plan when marginal revenue is greater than marginal cost and scaling down in the opposite case. When they finally end up being equal, that is when profit is maximized.

How does that help with the problem of maximizing total surplus instead of profit? Just as profit is equal to revenue minus cost, the total surplus of the firm is equal to the willingness of customers to pay minus the willingness of suppliers (including workers) to accept. First, a few definitions. The customers' willingness to pay (WTP) is the maximum amount they would be willing to pay to obtain the product they buy. If they pay less than that, the difference is their surplus. The suppliers' willingness to accept (WTA) is the minimum amount they must be paid for them to accept to deliver their goods and services to the firm. If they are paid more than that, that is their surplus. Now, let us do a simple accounting exercise, calling "revenue" what the customers pay to the firm and "cost" what the firm pays to the suppliers:

$$\text{total surplus} = \text{customers' surplus} + \text{suppliers' surplus} + \text{profit}$$
$$= (\text{WTP} - \text{revenue}) + (\text{cost} - \text{WTA}) + \text{profit}$$
Since *profit = revenue − cost*, after simplifying the formula one
obtains the promised expression:
$$\text{total surplus} = \text{WTP} - \text{WTA}$$

Since WTP and WTA are highly subjective notions, the critics seem justified in declaring that this notion is, unlike profit, not operational. But let us bring back the idea that it is marginal calculus that matters for management. As it turns out, if the customers and the suppliers do not have market power and behave as "price-takers" in their respective markets, then the marginal WTP of the customers—that is, the maximum amount they are willing to pay for one more unit of the product—is the market price. Likewise, the marginal WTA of the suppliers—that is, the minimum amount they must be paid to deliver one more unit of their contribution—is again its market price. What is more objective than market price?

Therefore, it is not difficult to derive from this observation the management rules that a firm that maximizes total surplus should follow. They are not less operational than the standard rules for a profit-maximizing firm. In fact, they actually coincide with the rules followed by a competitive, that is, price-taking, firm! One way of stating this result is to say that a firm maximizes its surplus if and only if it maximizes its profit while taking all prices as parametric (instead of using its market power by manipulating them).

Let us now bring externalities into the picture. A firm's activities clearly involve many impacts that are not captured in the market WTP and WTA of the parties. In particular, local communities where the firm operates may not be in a direct exchange relationship with the firm, and therefore not have a WTP or WTA featured in the above formula, but nevertheless are substantially affected by the firm. And there are of course large externalities affecting broader populations, including future generations and other species. This adds one more term to the above formula, representing the social value to society of the firm's externalities. Again, marginal calculus will need the marginal social value of the externalities, and this is a standard notion in economic policy. For instance, the social cost of carbon is the marginal social (dis)value of emitting one more ton of carbon (or CO_2). Therefore, a firm that takes account of its externalities will have to incorporate this extra term to its marginal cost. Interestingly, as Ponthière and I have shown, theoretically the firm can maximize the total surplus, including externalities, by maximizing its profit under the same price-taking constraint as above, by computing its profit by subtracting the marginal social value of the negative externalities multiplied by the physical quantity of externalities (e.g., the social cost of carbon applied to the total emissions of the firm),

and symmetrically adding the marginal social value of positive externalities.[7] Not only does it make the firm maximize the total surplus, but
also if this corrected profit is taken as the entry condition in a free-entry
market (i.e., enter if this profit is positive, leave if it is negative), then the
optimal number of firms enter the market and full efficiency is achieved.
This is noteworthy because ordinary profit-maximizing firms generally
fail to enter in the optimal number in a free-entry market (an excessive
number enter because they do not internalize the fact that they steal the
others' business, not to mention externalities).

To sum up: not only is total surplus maximization practical, it also
relies on simple and familiar management rules that mimic the behavior
of a profit-maximizing firm in perfect competition and under suitable
taxes for externalities, and produces efficiency results not only for the
firm but also for the whole market. A general equilibrium analysis further
extends this from one market to the whole economy.[8] Pareto efficiency
can be achieved thanks to responsible firms that maximize total surplus,
meaning that they refrain from using their market power and incorporate an externality tax in their profit accounts. A responsible firm, in
other words, is one that actively measures the quantity of all relevant
externalities, applies a price to them, and then acts so as to maximize
total surplus. It is noteworthy, and quite ironic, that the "market failure"
approach to business ethics that is proposed by Heath, in replacement of
the allegedly impractical stakeholder approach, is essentially implying
the same management rules that have been obtained here on the basis of
total surplus maximization.[9]

There are still two more complications to reckon with. One is that the
firm's production process involves noncontractible variables that are not
handled by the market transactions between the firm managers, the
customers, and the suppliers. Quality of product and maintenance
service, working conditions, effort and dedication at work—many variables are important while being difficult to monitor, or needing
adjustments to unforeseen events, so that constant ex post bargaining is
required between the parties to adjust for that. This can be done by
setting up collective management arrangements where direct negotiations can take place. This is, by the way, a key argument in Ferreras's plea
for giving voice and power to the workers, because they are the prime
party subject to, and responsible for, the vagaries of noncontractible
parameters in the workplace.[10]

Another complication is that total surplus is a definition of the common good that is oblivious to inequalities, as is Pareto efficiency in general equilibrium analysis. If, instead, the common good is defined by a social welfare objective that incorporates a priority for the worse off, then the firm's contribution to the common good has to be recomputed as a weighted sum of each of the individual stakeholders' surpluses, and the nice simplification of the formula that was obtained above no long applies. There are two ways to deal with this issue. The easy one is to let the firm largely off the hook and assign general redistributive issues to the state, hoping that the state will discharge its obligations in a satisfactory way. In practice, this is unlikely to occur. Even if the state does the best it can to address general inequalities, there is specific knowledge of individual circumstances that is available in the firm and will never be mobilized by the state. Therefore, it would be better for the firm to keep an eye on its contribution to inequalities. Regarding economic inequalities, the main topic here is the pay scale, although price differentiation on customer markets may also be a relevant consideration. In terms of the pay scale, workplace democracy is again a natural way to obtain good results, since it is generally observed that more democratic firms tend to avoid the excesses of high CEO pay and miserable wages at the bottom. As far as relational inequalities are concerned, it is even more obviously the responsibility of the firm to protect the dignity of all its stakeholders, and workplace democracy is the only approach offering the promise of full dignity to all involved.

Lessons for Workplace Democracy and the Bicameral Firm

The stakeholder approach described in the previous section involves rather simple management rules that have already been proposed by business ethics authors: maximize profit responsibly by taking prices as parametric, adjusting for the value of externalities, and democratizing the organization to handle noncontractible variables and promote equality and dignity. However practical, these rules may not find sufficient support to be embraced by real-world managers. Internal and external incentive issues need to be addressed.

Externally, the pressure of competition is playing against the responsible firm that maximizes total surplus instead of mere profit. Since maximization of total surplus boils down to maximization of profit under special constraints, as explained earlier, the responsible firm is in fact entering the competition with its wings cut. Shrewd profit-maximizers will tend to uproot responsible behavior, and they have several mechanisms playing to their advantage: they will enter and steal business in markets where responsible firms inevitably leave profit opportunities on the table; they will be more resilient to shocks, thanks to their greater profit; they will take over responsible firms to reform their management and make a profit; and they will be seen favorably by financiers to whom they promise higher returns. All in all, responsible management is as likely to win the market competition as a clean cyclist is to win the Tour de France. Responsible firms have advantages when their management makes stakeholders more accommodating to market fluctuations, because, indeed, these stakeholders are typically more dedicated to the survival of their firm. But it is a general fact of life that competition is a double-edged sword: it selects both the "best" (the fittest) and the "worst" (the cheaters). In the end, market competition does indeed favor the most productive firms; but among them, it ends up selecting the least scrupulous profit-maximizers and the most egregious cost-externalizers. Therefore, responsible management can realistically dominate and thrive in the economy only under strict regulation, stringent transparency rules, and pressure from ethical agents (consumers, investors, workers) who shun the bad firms.

Public regulation should include the imposition of governance norms such as those discussed here and could include more specific monitoring of firms' management and strategies. All aspects of such regulation can be associated with more or less stringent mandated as well as targeted incentive mechanisms, for instance through a modulation of corporate taxes and subsidies. The regulation of corporate governance is, in particular, meant to foster internal monitoring of good management practices.

Internally, the good management rules that maximize total surplus—taking account of externalities, noncontractible variables, and inequalities—need strong monitoring to incentivize the managers. The best-known way to protect the interests of stakeholders, in any setting, is to give them voice and power, and judicial recourse where they can lodge complaints. In the case of management in the firm, judicial remedy is hard to mobilize because of the nonverifiable information that underlies most of the firms' operations. Therefore, participatory mechanisms, by which the stakeholders can intervene and check the management, appear necessary. This is especially the case for workers who stand to benefit or suffer a lot from the quality of management. Reciprocally, giving them direct participation in their workplace is an excellent way to motivate them to act with goodwill in their daily efforts at work and make an investment in skills that are specific to the firm. The case of investors is also particularly relevant. Unlike workers, they cannot really jeopardize the firm by their daily behavior, but they stand to lose from bad management, and their dedication to the firm can protect the firm against market fluctuations and takeover threats. The other stakeholders—ordinary customers and suppliers of intermediate goods and services, as well as local communities—can be less intimately involved in the firm; nevertheless, their involvement can be highly beneficial, as well. Participation by workers and communities is especially valuable with respect to externalities. While financiers tend to focus on financial interests, even if they also care about externalities (as suggested by Oliver Hart and Luigi Zingales), workers and communities are likely to make externalities a higher priority and to bring their direct knowledge of some impacts of the firm's activities. This should buttress the internal incentives to adopt responsible behavior in this respect.[11]

These observations suggest a few insights about workplace democracy, and the bicameral firm in particular, which shall be enumerated in the remainder of this section.

First, one should not hope to see workplace democracy emerge spontaneously as the dominant form in a market economy. While this is not impossible and does indeed occur in certain industries and under certain circumstances, serious legal and regulatory support is absolutely crucial. Ordinary profit-maximizing behavior should no longer be seen as good for the economy but rather as harmful, inefficient, and immoral. Responsible profit-maximization is the only decent option and should be seen as such.

Second, participatory and inclusive governance is needed not only to enfranchise and give dignity to workers—which is good in itself, and extremely important for social justice—but also to provide the right incentives for responsible management of the firm. Just as political democracy is meant to put a check on, and provide adequate motivation to, policymakers, workplace democracy has to do with much more than human rights or well-being. It serves a management purpose.

Third, a democratic firm should not do whatever it likes. The rules of responsible management should serve as essential guidelines. The parties to the government of the firm should not use their voice and power to simply push their own interests and seek to extract as much of the surplus as possible at the expense of the others. This destructive escalation can be prevented by taking the rules of responsible management as the compass. A party can complain that the rules are not followed and is more likely to do so when its interests suffer as a result, but its influence on daily management should stop here. This point should address the worry that democracy in the workplace would be messy—that every party would push and pull in a different direction and the steady compass of profit would be replaced by a permanent war among conflicting interests. With responsible management rules, egregious demands can be silenced. Of course, this does not mean that workplace democracy should only consist in checking the rules and voicing complaints when violations are observed. Another key function of management is to build a strategic vision for the long term—deciding to develop certain activities and scale back others—and the responsible management rules are silent on these issues, except regarding the financial viability condition, which must consist in profit correction for externalities, as already explained. The firm can also decide to engage in a mix of for-profit and nonprofit activities, and so on. Having the relevant stakeholders involved is important and valuable for that, too.

Fourth, this recommendation about how to use the rules of responsible management as a compass can help to address the worry of gridlock in the bicameral firm. If the parties are prevented from pushing their interests without limit, this can avoid conflict triggered by what the other party views as excessive demands. Since conflict in any cooperative venture like a firm is generally about how to share the surplus, it is encouraging to see that the responsible management rules are addressing precisely this type of issue. One could still worry that, in absence of legal recourse, the parties may still ignore the responsible management rules, push their interests shamelessly, and endanger the responsible management and the survival of the firm. This is where the next point may be relevant.

Fifth, it is clear that workers deserve a special place in the governing structure of the firm because of their special human dedication to the firm's operations. This is confirmed by the stakeholder approach delineated here, in which the parties that are more dependent on noncontractible variables have greater stakes and need direct access to renegotiation mechanisms. But this approach also clearly rejects the view that the ultimate democratic ideal would only have workers at the helm (as suggested by Ferreras).[12] All stakeholders should have their interests taken care of through the responsible management rules, and the best way to build internal incentives to that effect is to grant them voice and power. Total exclusion of investors would potentially harm their interests, and exclusion of customers, other suppliers, and local communities is equally imprudent. A three-party governing structure, involving investors, workers, and the remainder, which could be set up with three chambers, or a three-part board, appears an interesting idea to explore. The alternative idea of having non-investor stakeholders represented by external, independent members of the board is frequently aired in discussions of corporate social responsibility, but it seems much less promising as it is strongly dependent on the goodwill of, and provision of appropriate information to, the independent members. In this light, the bicameral firm is a key step forward because it elevates the party (workers) that deserves the highest priority in the current capitalist economy, but it should not be presented as a step toward exclusive labor management. While labor management is much preferable to the current situation, it would not provide the right incentives to take account of all relevant stakeholders, and it would fail to deliver the positive outcomes that responsible management can deliver.

An Alternative Governance Model?

An inclusive governance structure in which all the stakeholders are represented, with no single block holding the majority, may be the best guarantee against shameless demands that would breach responsible management and seek to grab an excessive part of the surplus. If one bloc were to do so, the others would react and object. One would need a coalition of two blocs to make a majority in order to stage a holdup. For instance, investors and workers could collude to discount externality concerns that affect local communities; investors and customers could collude to lower wage costs and obtain lower prices and greater profits; workers and customers could push for retaining earnings and expanding scale at the expense of investors. This could occur, but the dynamics of governance is unlikely to entrench such coalitions because any block can be lured by another to undermine the third one. Moreover, if a holdup operation occurred, beyond certain proportions the violations would become conspicuous, and some form of legal remedy should be possible. These considerations reinforce the idea that one should avoid the domination by one bloc (the current situation in capitalist firms), or the blunt opposition between two blocs (the bicameral firm), and prefer a situation in which every bloc's attempts at a power grab can be curbed by the others. In order to avoid excessive violations of reasonable norms of conduct, Ferreras proposes the introduction of veto rights or super-majority requirements. This may work to some extent, but such clauses reinforce the risk of gridlock between the two parties.

At the end of the day, experimentation may tell what structure of governance is most conducive to promoting responsible management. Once one accepts that workers, equity holders, lenders, customers, suppliers, and local communities all have a claim to participate in democratic firm management, it is still necessary to work out the details of the governance architecture, which may have to be adapted to the context. Capitalist firms are themselves organized in different ways, with some cultural traditions appearing in various countries. The CEO / board / general assembly model is popular in many countries, but in some, such as Germany, a collegial board of directors (*Vorstand*) is monitored by a larger council (*Aufsichtsrat*) in which workers are well represented.

The rather specific management rules that Ponthière and I propose as a compass replacing unbridled profit maximization appear to fit rather well with the German dual structure.[13] The monitoring council could feature a large participation of several blocs, and three blocs could be composed as follows: one with workers and perhaps, as is common in Germany, a few external members representing unions (their role would be to protect the general interests of workers, keeping in mind what happens in the economy at large); one with equity holders and other creditors, whose interests in the profitability and viability of the firm may be sufficiently similar to warrant associating them in the same bloc;

and one comprising stakeholders whose relation with the firm is more distant: customers, suppliers, and local communities, which may have sufficient overlap in many cases to justify being grouped together. The case of contractors working in the firm may have to be sorted out, depending on whether their situation is closer to that of workers or that of other suppliers. If any pair of blocs can control the majority of the vote, while no single bloc can impose its will on the others, the risk of gridlock and the risk of holdup may be minimized.

There does not seem to be a need for separate chambers, in which each bloc would work separately. On the contrary, constant communication and bargaining between the different parties would be made much easier by their common participation in the same assembly. The selection of council members would have to rely on elections, and invitations to declare candidacy would have to be sent by the firm to the relevant stakeholders (a label could be affixed on the product to reach customers whose identity is unknown to the firm).

The collegial board of directors could have three members, each chosen by one bloc of the monitoring council, in order to preserve the inclusive perspective in day-to-day management. However, one of the advantages of the dual structure is that the board of directors would be more independent of the monitoring council than a typical CEO is from their board, and this would facilitate limiting the role of the council to checking that the responsible rules of management are followed by the directors, as far as daily management is concerned. Nevertheless, of course, more general strategic decisions about the long-term orientation of the firm would fall within the remit of the council.

These are mere suggestions and, again, experimentation with various democratic forms is needed to ascertain what works best in each relevant context.

Beyond Workplace Democracy

Workplace democracy is an essential pillar of social justice, first for promoting equality and dignity by itself, and second for providing internal incentives for responsible management. But it is important not to oversell the good contributions that workplace democracy would make to improving society.

Two of the limitations have already been mentioned. First, externalities require that a price be put on behavior that is harmful to the rest of the world, and for some externalities even the most inclusive participatory management will exclude some of the victims. Climate change, for instance, will affect many people who are not yet born and will live all over the world, and it will also harm many species in the ecosystem. Even the most goodwilled firms may fail to accurately measure the social value of their externalities. Ponthière and I have shown that if different firms rely on different social objectives (different degrees of priority for different populations, for instance), then their responsible management, based on the shadow prices they compute independently, will fail to produce an efficient allocation.[14] In other words, coordination is needed for the computation of the social value of externalities, and such coordination has to involve consensus on distributive issues— a highly political domain. This may be a trivial observation, but a fully just society cannot occur without a consensus on what full justice means. Moreover, the incentives to act on this consensus may be lacking at the level of the individual firm. Therefore, public authorities must play a central role in dealing with externalities. We cannot expect responsible firms to spontaneously coordinate and faithfully adopt adequate pricing parameters in their accounting. Taxes and regulations need to buttress private goodwill regarding externalities, just as public intervention must also make sure that competition by irresponsible firms does not undermine responsible management.

As it turns out, there is one market externality that even responsible firms are ill equipped to address. While their entry and exit decisions will be optimal for the economy, their efforts to differentiate themselves from competitors, in order to obtain a greater market share and expand their total surplus, will generally be excessive, as they will fail to see the business stealing that occurs through this channel. Some public intervention may be needed to address this problem, too.

The other limitation that has already been mentioned regards inequalities. Workplace democracy spontaneously contributes to the reduction of inequalities by compressing the pay scale in the organization and by raising the lowest wages. But it cannot resolve large and structural inequalities, including inequalities of wealth, racial and gender discrimination, educational disparities, and so on. Public policy in general and specific regulation for some issues are indispensable, as is generally recognized.

Now, I would like to introduce another sort of limitation of workplace democracy. It is commonplace among advocates of workplace democracy to emphasize that this offers an interesting avenue for keeping the market economy, with all its advantages in terms of productivity and efficient coordination of economic activities, while getting rid of the indignities of capitalism. This is quite true, and it is important to go against the naive doctrine that only overturning the market and dramatically enlarging the role of the state, or some other form of nonmarket regulation (or anarchy), can save us from the evil nature of the current society. But one must go beyond the black-and-white opposition between the complacent appraisal of market efficiency and the sweeping rejection of anything having to do with the market. This essay is not the place to develop a detailed analysis of the pros and cons of various forms of social coordination. Nevertheless, what follows is a brief depiction of what I think is a promising way of thinking about it.

Human interaction is almost all there is to life, given how mutually interdependent we are. There is a natural moral hierarchy among these interactions. Let us put aside the destructive interactions, which are generally viewed negatively, and rightly so (although deviant moralities abound that praise violence and domination). Among the positive and beneficial interactions, the highest form involves selfless, personalized attention to the wants and needs of the other. The lowest form involves selfish, immediate reciprocity, with disregard to the particulars of the partner in trade. There are two dimensions that play a role in this ranking. First, how selfish or selfless is the partner's motivation? Second, how personalized is the attention? The more selfish the motivation, and the less personalized the attention, the lower in the ranking. Most market transactions belong to the lower tier. They do vary in the degree of personalization, and it is more pleasant to have personalized attention than impersonal interaction, as a customer, worker, or in any other economic role. They also vary in the degree of selfishness because of the noncontractible aspects of the interaction. A good partner will not just do their contracted part but will also make sure that the noncontractible part is done well. Some do it for building a good reputation, but many do it simply because it is the right thing to do. However, overall, the world of market transactions is rather bleak, in human terms. Economists often brag about their theorems proving how market transactions are efficient and mutually beneficial, but most models do not have the components that describe this moral hierarchy, so that the low level of mutual benefit is not on the economists' radar.

High-level interactions are desirable and put limits on what the market can achieve. The market is unable to deliver such benefits, not only because it relies on immediate reciprocity and is not conducive to selflessness, but also because many of the high-level interactions involve positive feelings (love, friendship, esteem) that cannot be contracted because they involve personal beliefs and feelings. One cannot pay someone to adopt new beliefs or feel in a certain way. One can bribe someone to pretend with regard to some beliefs or feelings, but this is of little use. This radical noncontractibility shields such interactions from market transactions.

Nevertheless, this shielding is not total, and this is where the question of workplace democracy in the market economy returns. Human interactions distribute social status, an attribute that is a very high priority for most people, and which gives them strong incentives to behave in a way that ingratiates them with others (or subdues them). In our society, economic success is a key element of social success, and this is a strong engine of economic effort, innovation, consumption, and the like (as well as environmental destruction). One cannot pay others to like them, but one can invest in the economic game to gain the esteem of others, and indeed often their friendship or more.

The expansion of the scope of market transactions is dangerous because, while it may bring some price coordination and related efficiency, it also undermines the higher-level interactions that could take place beforehand. In a little valley of the Alps, one of the joys of life once consisted in walking down to the local town in groups, carrying the load together, or following a horse-led carriage. When the automobile arrived, that joy disappeared; everyone was free to go independently, and that pleasant shared experience was not replaced by anything similar. This type of phenomenon has occurred repeatedly, and anyone could write a long list of activities and objects that have been commodified during one's lifetime. Each time, some material efficiency may be gained (not always) but at the cost of desocialization and demoralization.

This does not imply that the market should be severely curtailed and that we should go back to walking shoes and horse carriages. But careful attention should be paid to the quality of social interaction, and sufficient space must be preserved for social bonding, solidarity, and genuine selflessness. Workplace democracy can play a role here. The labor "market" is an awful concept, reminiscent of the slave market and the day-labor markets where, each morning, employers grabbed some men at the corner to perform their labour. Treatment of workers not as external contractors who must submit to orders day in, day out, but as partners in the venture, brings back some potential for higher-level interactions at work. In fact, such interactions do happen, even in the current economy, because coworkers spend time together and make many mutually beneficial gestures without doing so through a market transaction; even between employer and employee, one sees this same mechanism of mutual gift-giving outside of the contract. Further, such interactions make the economy function, and without them, if people reverted to pure transactional behavior, a major drop in productivity and trust would follow. But workplace democracy arguably does a great deal to foster the higher-level interactions, and this benefit should not be underestimated.

However, workplace democracy can only do so much to promote higher-level interactions, and one should not expect the generalization of workplace democracy to spontaneously induce the right degree of market transactions in our lives. A collective deliberation, in society at large, is needed to examine this issue and design regulations that help some interactions and foster the free-share initiatives, while curbing the share-for-sale initiatives that turn various forms of mutual help into a racket.

One last remark: in the current context, it is natural, as I have just done here, to highlight the invasive nature of market transactions and sound the alarm about their deleterious effects on social relations. But one should not forget that market transactions can also be liberating because they can displace abusive nonmarket relations that fall on the negative end of the ranking depicted earlier. Commodification of the work done in childcare and eldercare, on the whole, has freed many women from the presumption that they should devote their lives to their children and their parents and abandon any other personal interest. To sum up, the goal should not be to constrain the market because it is the market. The goal should be to fight destructive and abusive interactions as much as possible, to promote positive ones, and, among them (including the market), seek to preserve and foster the higher-level forms.

Workplace democracy can play a positive role in this respect but a limited one, and we should keep this in mind when discussing the virtues of the democratized market economy.

Conclusion

In brief, this chapter has connected the discussion of workplace democracy and the bicameral firm with stakeholder theory. I have discussed how the democratic firm should be managed (it should not simply do whatever the democratic boards and chambers decide but should stick to responsible management rules); how it can thus avoid losing its compass (in capitalist firms, profit maximization is the compass, and it may remain so in democratic firms, but with some specific constraints); which set of stakeholders should be involved (workers are at the top of the list, but the list is long, and the bicameral firm is too restrictive, while the pure labor-managed firm is even worse); how to avoid gridlock (having more stakeholders at the table can help guard against the risk of one bloc obstructing the other); and what benefits to expect in terms of improved social relations in a market economy (substantial benefits but with important limitations).

Within the firm, workplace democracy is of central importance and can truly change people's lives. Proposals such as Ferreras's bicameral firm keep the flame burning and rekindle a public debate about an ideal that already has a long history and, hopefully, will not be perpetually suppressed. From the perspective of society as a whole, this is also essential because the social structure, and the general degree of democracy, will be substantially affected by the transformation of corporations. But even when this dream is achieved, there still remain three important issues that deserve careful collective deliberation at the highest level: inequalities, externalities, and the quality of social interactions. Workplace democracy does make a useful contribution to addressing each of them, but it is unlikely to suffice.

III.

The Corporation and the Law

4

Fallacies about Corporations: Comments on "Democratizing the Corporation"

David Ellerman

I fully support Isabelle Ferreras's program of finding intermediate joint-governance models—for instance, true-parity versions of codetermination or democratic employee stock ownership plans (ESOPs)—between the current human-rental firm and the "regulative ideal" of the democratic firm.[1]

My comments on Ferreras's "Democratizing the Corporation" will focus on a conceptual framing I believe contains a number of problems that are quite common on the left and are thus doubly deserving of commentary and explanation. Her conclusions do not depend on this framing, but it is so common and conventional that it needs to be discussed anyway.

What Is the Fundamental Defining Institution in So-Called Capitalism?

The problematic assumption is that the legal basis for the conventional firm is the rights attached to the ownership of land, buildings, machines, and other capital assets. This is a version of the very widespread idea, on both the left and right, that the legal basis for the current system is the "private ownership of the means of production," which is interpreted to mean that the ownership of capital assets includes:

- · the rights to the product produced using that capital and
- the rights to the managerial control over the people carrying out the production process.

Yet this is descriptively *incorrect* in the so-called capitalist system.

The "Ownership of the Means of Production"

Karl Marx popularized the capital-based phraseology of "capitalist" and "capitalism." To understand Marx's concept of the "rights of capital" embodied in the "ownership of the means of production," one must go back to the medieval notion of dominion based on the ownership of land. What today we might call the "landlord" was then the *lord of the land*, exercising both political/juridical control over the people living on the land and the rights to the fruits of their labor. As the legal historian Frederic Maitland put it, "Ownership blends with lordship, rulership, sovereignty in the vague medieval *dominium*."[2] Or, as the German legal scholar Otto von Gierke put it simply: "Rulership and Ownership were blent."[3]

By substituting "capital" for "land," Marx carried over this medieval notion of dominion, associated with the ownership of land, to the ownership of capital in his conception of "capitalism."

> It is not because he is a leader of industry that a man is a capitalist; on the contrary, he is a leader of industry because he is a capitalist. The leadership of industry is an attribute of capital, just as in feudal times the functions of general and judge were attributes of landed property.[4]

Marx's blunder has been a staple of socialist thought ever since, as was pointed out by Bo Rothstein:

> It is astonishing that a hundred years of socialist thought have not confronted the basic capitalist idea—that owners of capital have the right of command in the relations of production. The idea behind nationalization, wage earner funds, and the like is in fact fundamentally the same idea as that on which capitalism is based, namely, that

ownership of capital should give owners the right to command in the production process (be they democratically elected politicians, state bureaucrats/planners, workers' representatives, or union officials). Indeed, this is a nice example of what Antonio Gramsci called bourgeois ideological hegemony.[5]

The defenders of "capitalism" were more than happy to accept the view that management rights and the rights to the product are all "an attribute of capital," of the "ownership of the means of production," or of the ownership of "productive property." Hence any change in the management or product rights would be a violation of their supposed property rights. But the usual notion of the "rights to the private ownership of productive property" involves a misconception of property rights that I will call the *fundamental myth*.

The Fundamental Myth

The fundamental myth is that management rights over the people using the capital assets and the rights to the product produced using the capital assets are part and parcel of ownership of those assets. If the management rights are referred to "political rights," then those rights are not in fact attached to the ownership of the capital assets. This hegemonic belief is asserted by thinkers left, right, and center, as seen in the following quote from an English Liberal:

> The owner of capital resources, or the agent who acts on behalf of the owner or a number of associated owners, controls and determines, *in virtue of such ownership*, the process of production and *the action of the workers* who are engaged in the process. In its unqualified form, capitalistic organization is a form of autocracy or absolutism.[6]

John Maynard Keynes also saw the rights to the net returns from using a capital asset in a going concern as being attached to the ownership of a capital asset—as if the asset could not be rented out:

> When a man buys an investment or capital-asset, he purchases the right to the series of prospective returns, which he expects to obtain

from selling its output, after deducting the running expenses of obtaining that output, during the life of the asset.[7]

But this is factually incorrect; Keynes is talking about the "prospective returns" from using the capital asset in a going concern based on the contractual fact-pattern of buying in the complementary set of inputs ("the running expenses of obtaining that output') and selling the produced outputs. Such a set of contracts is not bought when one buys a capital asset.[8] In spite of Marx's imprimatur and the constant ideological assertion of the "rights of capital," it takes nothing more than an understanding of the *renting out of capital* to see the fallacy.

Suppose capital assets are rented out to another legal party, such as Frank Knight's "entrepreneur," who buys, hires, or already owns the other inputs and who undertakes a productive process. Then that entrepreneur, by virtue of being the hiring party (not the owner of the capital assets), exercises the discretionary management rights within the limits of the input contracts (i.e., the management rights) over the people working in that process and has ownership of whatever product is produced. In addition to banks and other financial firms in the business of loaning out financial capital, real estate companies, equipment rental companies, and computer hardware companies are also in the business of hiring, renting, or leasing out physical capital assets.

Let us consider some simple examples. When an individual owns, say, a widget-making machine, then it is easily understandable that the machine could be rented out. But if the individual forms a corporation and puts in the machine and other capital as initial capital, then many people think that the individual's ownership of the corporation somehow makes a fundamental difference in the logic of rentability as if the machine can no longer be rented out. But the machine, of course, may still be rented out, in which case the owner of the corporation does not have the management or product rights in the going concern operation (aka "the firm") using that machine. The process of incorporation does not miraculously transubstantiate the ownership of a capital asset into the ownership of the net results produced using the capital asset in a going concern.

The ownership of capital gives the owner the *negative* or *indirect control rights* over the use of the capital by other parties, as in: "No, you may not use this machine, building, or land." This right is sufficient to make those who nevertheless use the machine, building, or land into trespassers—but it does not automatically make them into employees:

> Central to ownership is the right to exclude others from contact with an item. Ownership thus gives the owner of an item the right to control the uses to which others put it in the sense that he may veto any use of it proposed by someone else. But it does not give him any right to tell anyone to put that property to the use that he wants. *It is not a right to command labor.*[9]

What actually occurs in capitalist societies is that the *positive* or *direct discretionary control* or management rights over employees come from the employer–employee contract, not the ownership of the capital the employees are using. This is a conceptual point about the structure of property rights in the current system. The conceptual point is not about the bargaining power (obviously almost always in the hands of capital owners) or transaction costs involved in renting capital out of a corporation.

The Conner Avenue Plant Example

Does the "ownership of the firm" determine who owns the product? If by "firm" one means a corporation, then there is currently the ownership of a corporation (more on this below), but it is the pattern of contracts (who hires what or whom) that actually determines who owns the product produced using some of the corporation's assets (ownership is not necessary because the assets could always be leased out).

In addition to the fundamental myth's involvement in a common misunderstanding of the "ownership of a corporation," it is also expressed in the usual notion of "owning a factory." But the simple logic of the rentability of capital does not stop at the ownership of a whole factory. In the early 1950s, an automobile manufacturer, the Studebaker-Packard Corporation, had the Packard auto bodies produced in the Conner Avenue plant of the Briggs Manufacturing Company. After the Briggs founder died, all twelve of the US Briggs plants were sold to the Chrysler Corporation in 1953. "The Conner Ave. plant that had been building all of Packard's bodies was leased to Packard to avoid any conflict of interest."[10]

This real-world example illustrates the vacuity of the usual idea that "being the firm" or firmhood is determined by "the ownership of the firm." Where was the "ownership of the firm" that included the ownership of the auto bodies coming off the assembly line or the management rights over the production process? Of course, the shareholders in Studebaker-Packard owned that company, and similarly for the shareholders in Chrysler, but that did not answer the question of "who is the firm" in that going-concern operation. That was determined by pattern of the new market contracts—by who hires, rents, or leases what or whom. If Studebaker-Packard leased the factory from Chrysler, then Chrysler would not hold the discretionary management rights and product rights for the operation of the factory owned by the Chrysler Corporation.

The Misnomer of "Capitalism"

In the Middle Ages, there was no developed market for renting out land, so those governance and product rights were rolled into the medieval notion of ownership as dominion. But capital assets, including land for that matter, are today *routinely* rented out in our so-called capitalist system. Given the central role of the Marxist notion of the "ownership of the means of production," it may be understandable why Marxists cling to the fundamental myth as a matter of quasi-religious dogma. Many defenders of the "capitalist" system seem equally dogmatic in failing to think through the consequences of capital being rentable in a private-property market economy. Yet the whole capital-based narrative emanating from the left, right, and center is mistaken.

Since the management and product rights are not part of the ownership of capital or the means of production in the first place, the whole "great debate" between "capitalism" and socialism or communism (as to whether there should be private or public ownership of the means of production) has been ill formed from the very beginning. It is wrong in the same sense that two centuries ago it would have been wrong to frame the basic social question as to whether slave plantations should be privately owned, government owned, or socially owned.

Even the most prominent liberal philosopher, John Rawls, could not get beyond the framing in terms of the ownership of the means of production or of productive assets (as opposed to personal assets):

- "Under socialism the means of production are owned by society."
- "The first principle of justice includes a right to private personal property, but this is different from the right of private property in productive assets."
- "Welfare-state capitalism permits a small class to have a near monopoly of the means of production."
- "Property-owning democracy avoids this . . . by ensuring the widespread ownership of productive assets."[11]

There is, however, one economist who stands out as the most philosophically and economically sophisticated defender of the so-called capitalist system—and he didn't call it by that name because he was able to trace out the consequences of capital's rentability and understood that the product/management rights were thus not part of capital ownership. He is Frank H. Knight, one of the founders of the Chicago School of Economics. Knight was perfectly clear on "capitalism" being a misnomer and on Marx's role in propagating that myth about capital ownership:

> Karl Marx, who in so many respects is more classical than the classicals themselves, had abundant historical justification for calling, i.e., miscalling—the modern economic order "capitalism." Ricardo and his followers certainly thought of the system as centering around the employment and control of labor by the capitalist. In theory, this is of course diametrically wrong. The entrepreneur employs and directs both labor and capital (the latter including land), and laborer and capitalist play the same passive role, over against the active one of the entrepreneur . . . The superficial observer is typically confused by the ambiguity of the concept of ownership.[12]

If an established economic, political, or legal theorist is such a "superficial observer" as to not think through the consequences of capital being rentable, then there is little hope to get beyond erroneous tropes and libertarian talking points—or Marxist/postmodernist slogans ("It's all about congealed power relations").

In fact, the current system is not characterized by capital being unrentable but rather by *both* persons and capital goods being legally rentable. As the leading neoclassical economist Paul A. Samuelson put it:

"Since slavery was abolished, human earning power is forbidden by law
to be capitalized. A man is not even free to sell himself: he must *rent*
himself at a wage."[13] Similar remarks are made by other economists:

> The commodity that is traded in the labor market is labor services, or
> hours of labor. The corresponding price is the wage per hour. We can
> think of the wage per hour as the price at which the firm rents the
> services of a worker, or the rental rate for labor. We do not have asset
> prices in the labor market because workers cannot be bought or sold
> in modern societies; they can only be rented. (In a society with
> slavery, the asset price would be the price of a slave.[14]

Knight makes a similar point:

> In a free society the larger part of the productive capacity employed
> (as matters stand today in a typical Western nation) consists of the
> services of human beings themselves, who are not bought and sold
> but only, as it were, leased.[15]

Given the power enjoyed by capital owners (including entrepreneurs
with ample access to capital) and the transaction costs involved in
currently reversing the contract between capital and labor, it is almost a
truism that, statistically speaking, it is much more likely that people will
be rented by the owners of capital, not capital being rented by people.
Yet this routine fact should not obscure the *actual* structure of property
rights in the so-called capitalist system.

It is unfortunate that so many economists and conventional classical
liberals think that because they and Marxists all agree on the "rights of
capital" that it must be a valid characterization of the misnamed
"capitalist" system.

Do the Shareholders "Own" a Corporation?

In an apparent attempt to weaken the claim of shareholder primacy, a
number of legal and political thinkers—among them Lynn Stout, David
Ciepley, and Jean-Philippe Robé—have recently emphasized that the
shareholders only own their shares, not the corporate assets, as their

private property.[16] The fact that the shareholders do not own the corporate assets as their personal property is only the other side of the balance sheet from the fact that the shareholders do not owe the corporate liabilities as their personal liabilities.

Stout, Ciepley, and Robé try to argue that since the shareholders do not own the corporate assets as their personal assets, therefore the shareholders (contrary to existing conventional corporate law) do not "own" the corporation. But the ownership of property would usually include the right to buy and sell the property, and the shareholders indeed have the right to buy and sell a corporation by buying and selling a majority of the shares. And the shareholders have the right to throw out the board of directors and the management. Since the shareholders' ownership of the shares gives them these rights over the corporation, their argument can at best be interpreted as the quixotic linguistic suggestion that we avoid saying the shareholders "own" the corporation—in spite of conventional corporate law all being written in those terms and corporations being routinely bought and sold by their shareholders or their agents.

It is also asserted that the particular legal aspects of a corporation (e.g., limited liability and separate juridical personality) are enabled or chartered by the government, and thus that a corporation should have a "social" function (e.g., stakeholder primacy) sanctioned by the government.[17] It is certainly true that the legal aspects of a corporation are created by the government, but that is true of all legal rights (e.g., the private property rights to houses and cars) and all legal institutions; they do not exist as part of the natural world. That is hardly an argument that all private property must bend to some governmental purpose.[18]

On Personal Rights and Property Rights

Perhaps a few words are necessary about the terms "membership" and "ownership." People have many membership rights that are personal rights, while other rights are property rights. For instance, one's voting rights in a city (or municipal corporation) are based on having the functional role of residing in the city, but those rights may not be bought or sold, so they are personal rights, not property rights. Ferreras makes the point that states are not "owned," and that is because the rights of the members/citizens are personal rights, not property rights.[19]

In a cooperative corporation, membership rights are based on the functional role of "patronage" in the cooperative (e.g., working in a worker cooperative or shopping in a consumer cooperative). When membership rights are supposed to be based on having a certain functional or patronage role, then it makes no sense to treat them as alienable property rights. A "buyer" may not have the functional role, and if the person did have the functional role, there would be no need to "buy" the rights.

It is easy to distinguish personal from property rights in terms of inheritability (or "bequeathability"). When a person dies, personal rights (like one's vote in municipal elections) are extinguished, while property rights (like the votes of one's corporate shares) are passed on to one's estate and heirs. When membership rights, as in a conventional corporation, may be inherited or, in general, may be bought and sold, then they are property rights, so then the members are referred to as "owners." Whether the shareholders' ownership of the membership rights is to be called the "ownership of the corporation" is a question of only rhetorical interest.

We should properly regard the conventional corporation as being like a cooperative corporation where the patronage requirement has been reduced to zero, meaning the membership rights become free-floating property rights—that is, inheritable ownership rights.[20]

The Distinction between the Corporation and the Firm

Forty-five years ago, I distinguished between the corporation, which is owned by the shareholders (in the sense of owning the corporate membership rights), and the "firm," which is the corporation as a going-concern making a set of contracts, say, to undertake production by hiring in workers and other inputs in order to produce and sell a set of outputs.[21] The firm-as-a-going-concern is based on a certain pattern of market contracts, and contractual fact-patterns are not owned by the corporation or its owners. The suppliers and customers may choose to make different contracts in future time periods, and the corporation has no "ownership" rights over the behavior of its contractual counterparties.

Jean-Philippe Robé has independently made a similar distinction between "the corporation" and "the firm—the organization built via contracts transferring control over resources to the corporations used to legally structure the firm."[22] He correctly observes that the contractual fact-pattern characterizing the firm is not something that can be owned.

Further Comments on "the Corporation"

My purpose here has been to analyze a miscellany of fallacies blaming the corporate form for a litany of problems. But the corporate form itself, at least in its original conception, is not the problem. Blaming "corporations" for the ills of the current system of renting human beings is like blaming glass bottles for alcoholism—or the legal form of ante-bellum cotton farms for the institution of slavery.

After all, a worker cooperative is also a corporation with the attribute of so-called limited liability (actually, members have zero personal liability for corporate debts, just like they have zero personal ownership of corporate assets). Do left-wing critics of "the corporation" really think worker cooperatives should be reorganized as unincorporated partnerships with each member potentially having full personal liability for the cooperative's debts?

What is important to preserve is the original and ancient idea of a corporation per se as a group of natural persons engaged in certain joint activities "that possesse[s] a juridical personality distinct from that of its particular members."[23] This original conception of the corporation is well described in the legal literature,[24] particularly by Abram Chayes:

> We can here perhaps note a final irony, at least. The concept of the corporation began for us with groups of men related to each other by the place they lived in and the things they did. The monastery, the town, the gild, the university . . . were only peripherally concerned with what its members owned in common as members. The sub-sequent history of the corporate concept can be seen as a process by which it became progressively more formal and abstract. In particular the associative elements were refined out of it. In law it became a rubric for expressing a complicated network of relations of people to things rather than among persons. The aggregated material

resources rather than the grouping of persons became the feature of
the corporation.[25]

The point that is little, if at all, mentioned in the corporate law literature is
that the original joint activity of the members could only be squeezed out
because it was replaced by the joint activity of the employees (including
managers) of the corporation. In conceptual terms, the *absentee-owned*
corporation is a "wholly owned subsidiary" of the human rental relation, the employment contract. The characteristic feature of the current
system misnamed "capitalism" is not the imagined rights of capital
(fundamental myth) but the institution for the renting, hiring, employing, or leasing of persons.

That system-defining legal institution has completely corrupted and
undermined that original conception of the corporation. The *employment relation*—the whole idea of the members of the corporation as
carrying out some joint human activity—was undermined by the legal
institution of the hiring, employing, leasing, or renting people to carry
out those actual human activities undertaken by the corporation.

Then, with the active members replaced by employees, membership
could be debased into the limiting case of "ownership." The corruption
of the notion of membership in the corporation was carried to its logical
conclusion in the modern corporation of the joint stock or limited
liability variety. The partaking in the human activities of the corporation
(e.g., "patronage" in a cooperative) was reduced to zero, thus turning the
membership rights into untethered, free-floating (i.e., no personal functional role requirement for the members) property rights that could be
arbitrarily bought and sold on the market like any other piece of property. And this reduction of the members' personal functional roles to
zero was enabled by the above-mentioned human rental institution
where the "employees" carry out the corporation's human activities.

Thus, the original conception of the corporate embodiment for
people associated together in a joint human activity was turned into a
piece of property, like a piece of real estate or "a large, composite
machine" to be bought and sold in the marketplace.[26] When a recent
occupant of the White House suggested "buying Greenland," the leading
thinkers in political science, economics, and the law as well as various
pundits and thought leaders ridiculed the suggestion. They rightly did
not accept "it's just a real estate deal" as a justification. Yet, the same

thinkers find no problem in the purchase and sale of corporations (whose workforce is many times the population of Greenland); after all, it is supposedly just the purchase and sale of a bundle of assets, since the "aggregated material resources rather than the grouping of persons became the feature of the corporation."[27]

An interesting aspect of the whole corporate governance debate is how so many legal, political, and economic thinkers have conveniently lost sight of the concept of democracy in the organizations where people spend most of their waking hours. There is no doubt about who the people are who constitute an organization (hint: it is not the corporate shareholders). Hence the application of the notion of democratic self-governance to an organization gives a clear answer to the question of who should be the members of the organization. And the human right of self-governance is not a right that applies only in one sphere of life; it is based on human nature that applies everywhere. As John Dewey put it:

> [Democracy] is but a name for the fact that human nature is developed only when its elements take part in directing things which are common, things for the sake of which man and women form groups— families, industrial companies, governments, churches, scientific associations and so on. The principle holds as much of one form of association, say in industry and commerce, as it does in government.[28]

Yet, the human rental relation and the debasement of membership into ownership seems to have eclipsed the democratic ideal in so many learned thinkers today who would otherwise pledge their undying allegiance to democratic self-governance in the political sphere. They seem unable to address the questions (1) Who should legitimately control corporate management, and (2) Who can do so effectively?

The answer to the first question is not even in theory "shareholders' democracy" as Abram Chayes notes:

> The analogy between state and corporation has been congenial to American lawmakers, legislative and judicial. The shareholders were the electorate, the directors the legislature, enacting general policies and committing them to the officers for execution. . . . Shareholder democracy, so-called, is misconceived because the shareholders are not the governed of the corporation whose consent must be sought.[29]

The concept of "shareholder democracy" is analogous to the people of
Russia going through the motions of running multiparty "democratic"
elections of the government of Poland. The democratic self-governance
answer to the first question is: "the people who are governed by the
corporate management."

The answer to the second question about effective governance is:
"The only cohesive, workable, and effective constituency within view is
the corporation's work force."[30] In spite of Robert Dahl's earlier use of the
affected-interests principle, which points toward stakeholders' governance (whatever that might be), when it came to later specifying the
"alternative," he made *no* use of that principle or the stakeholders
theory.[31] He advocated instead "a system of economic enterprises collectively owned and democratically governed by all the people who work
in them."[32]

It is only because of the professionally prudent forgetting of democratic ideals in the workplace that the whole question of corporate
governance and purpose is up for grabs in the first place.

The Property Argument for the Democratic Firm

Isabelle Ferreras is in the distinguished company of political theorists
such as Robert Dahl and Carole Pateman in applying democratic
principles to the workplace.[33] But her argument is one-sided and thus
leads to such one-sided hybrids such as codetermination (true-parity
or not) where the workers have democratic rights but no net income
rights. They are not the residual claimants to the retained net income
that builds up the net asset value of the company. The true members
of a democratic firm, for instance a Mondragon-type worker cooperative, have both the governance rights and the net income and asset
rights in the firm—regardless of whether the net income is paid out
in cash or retained and thus added to the members' internal capital
accounts representing the net asset rights. As only a governance
model, the bicameral firm may be able to affect the income paid out
as labor bonuses (i.e., which are not *net* income), but it is silent on the
claim to retained net income and asset rights—as if the only problem
in the human rental firm was the lack of governance rights. The case
for the bicameral firm as a stepping stone toward the democratic

firm needs to use both sides of the full argument: on the one side, there is the democratic self-governance argument (which Ferreras makes), but on the other side, there is the important fruits-of-the-labor argument, which states that workers, not shareholders, morally deserve the fruits of corporate labor (this argument Ferreras fails to make).

Over a period of time, the production operations (not exchange operations) of the firm create a set of assets (the products or outputs produced by the firm) and a set of liabilities (the liabilities for the inputs used up by the firm). The firm directly (and the members of the firm indirectly) legally *own* those new assets (the products typically sold) and *owe* those new liabilities (typically paid for prior to or at the end of the production time period in question). The normative question of who should be the members of the firm is not *only* the question of who should have the governance rights (a question answered by democratic self-governing principles) but who should be the people who (in their corporate body) jointly own those output-assets and jointly owe those input-liabilities. That normative property question is answered by the old *labor* or *natural-rights theory of property*—people's rights to the (positive and negative) fruits of their own labor.[34]

That is the property-theoretic answer to the question of who ought to be the members of the firm, not the question of the "ownership of the means of production," which does not decide the question since capital goods—indeed, whole factories (as in the Conner Avenue example)—may be rented.

The answer to that question is the people (legally employees or employers) who work in the firm; they are the ones who use up the inputs in the process of producing the outputs—not the absentee shareholders who do neither. In a statement of remarkable clarity in 1944, the Tory scholar, member of Parliament, and public servant Lord Eustace Percy made precisely this point:

Here is the most urgent challenge to political invention ever offered to the jurist and the statesman. The human association which in fact produces and distributes wealth, the association of workmen, managers, technicians and directors, is not an association recognised by the law. The association which the law does recognise—the association of shareholders, creditors and directors—is incapable of production and is not expected by the law to perform these functions. We have to give law to the real association, and to withdraw meaningless privilege from the imaginary one.[35]

When that is done, then the "human association which in fact produces and distributes wealth" will become the firm, and the suppliers of capital inputs and other nonhuman inputs will become the parties to whom the input-liabilities are paid.[36]

The Bicameral Firm

Perhaps the most general point is that the institutional question is misframed as being only about corporate or firm governance (and ignoring property rights to produced outputs and liabilities for used-up inputs discussed in the last section). It is like framing the main institutional question in antebellum America about the legal form or governance of cotton or tobacco farms. The key institution then was the master-slave relation, and the key institution now is the master-servant relation or, in Newspeak, the employer-employee relationship. As Justice Brandeis put it:

> The civilized world today believes that in the industrial world self-government is impossible; that we must adhere to the system which we have known as the monarchical system, the system of master and servant, or, as now more politely called, employer and employee.[37]

The point, presumably, is to suggest transitional forms from the conventional human rental firm to the regulative ideal of a democratic firm. How would "the bicameral firm" transition to a democratic firm? A democratic firm such as the existing examples of democratic firms (e.g., the Mondragon worker cooperatives) is monocameral.

An Alternative "Bicameral" Transitional Firm: The Co-op-ESOP Model

As mentioned by Ferreras, we do have existing models of firms designed to transition to a democratic firm.[38] One important such model is based on the idea of the US ESOP but reformed in order to democratize it. I call this the co-op-ESOP model.[39] In this model, the ESOP trust is replaced by a democratic worker cooperative whose members are all the employees in the underlying corporation. The co-op-ESOP model increases its share of the ownership over a period of years, and when it reaches 100 percent, then the company can be consolidated and collapsed into the cooperative, which would then function as a Mondragon-style worker cooperative.

This model is "somewhat bicameral" since there are, in effect, two boards of directors. The board in the worker cooperative is pure labor representation, but it only accounts for a certain x percentage of the underlying conventional corporation. The other board is the conventional shareholder-representing board—where one of the shareholders is the worker cooperative. The board of the corporation is jointly determined by the other shareholders and the co-op-ESOP (see fig. 4.1).

The co-op-ESOP model is designed to correct for two artifacts of the way the American ESOP was implemented. Firstly, the worker-ownership vehicle is a worker cooperative (with democratic "one member, one vote" governance of its board) rather than a trust with the trustee usually a member of some bank's trust department selected by

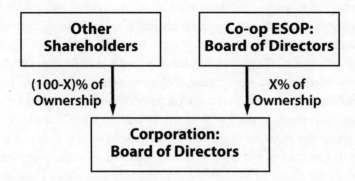

Figure 4.1. Two "boards" in the co-op-ESOP model

management. Secondly, the co-op-ESOP is an ownership acquisition vehicle rather than a special type of retirement plan, so there is no need for workers to retire or otherwise exit to receive some cash payouts.

Moreover, the underlying agreement or "social contract" between the other shareholders (e.g., a retiring founder), the underlying company, and the co-op-ESOP means that the ownership may over a period of years transition to 100 percent in the co-op-ESOP, at which point it could be consolidated into one democratic worker cooperative firm.

The co-op-ESOP model is a generic model designed to work in any country with conventional company law and worker cooperative law. Examples could be established without any special legislation but also without any special tax breaks. Later legislation could then standardize the model, apply some suitable tax incentives, and help spread the model around the economy.

A Brief Description of the Co-op-ESOP Model

The US Employee Stock Ownership Plan (US ESOP) was introduced in the late 1970s, and now there are about 7,000 ESOPs in the US, covering 10 percent of the private workforce. My purpose is to describe a generic model of an ESOP for any country that captures the unique features of the US ESOP and makes some improvements over aspects that were only artifacts of how ESOPs were legislated in the US.

The co-op-ESOP would be a separate legal entity associated with a company (hereafter "Company"). That separate legal entity could be a new type of employee ownership cooperative where each Company employee has a membership and individual account holding their share of Company ownership.

The co-op-ESOP is a vehicle for the employees in the associated Company to acquire, over a period of time, some percent (up to 100 percent) of the ownership of the Company. The shares owned by each employee are kept in the ESOP in an individual share account so the employees will enjoy the rights to the income and capital appreciation rights of the shares, but they may not individually sell, mortgage, or bequeath the shares. The shares will eventually be bought back by the ESOP and redistributed to the current employees.

The US ESOP is *not* based on employees individually making shares purchases out of salary or other income. The Company makes periodic ESOP contributions, much like a form of tax-favored profit-sharing, in cash to the ESOP, which then passes the money through to buy out the shares of an exiting owner (and eventually to buy back employee shares). In other words, part of the Company's income is repeatedly contributed to the ESOP to purchase shares from the owner in order to slowly transition ownership and control from the owner to the workers.

Most of the US ESOPs arose out of the succession of family firms or small- and medium-sized enterprises (SMEs) where the founders wanted to retire or exit to pursue other opportunities. The problem with selling to a competitor is that it usually means the slow death of the enterprise because the competitor typically moves the customer list, some key employees, and eventually all the business to their other facilities. Since family firms can be benefactors to the local community by providing jobs, income, and taxes to support the community, selling out to a competitor may be seen as a betrayal of the community and the local

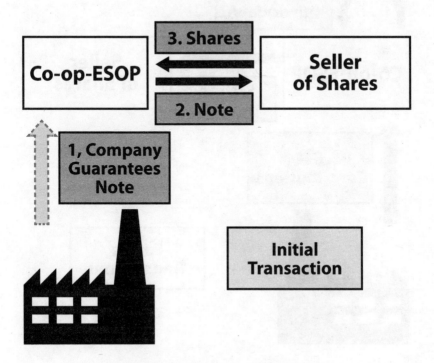

Figure 4.2. Creating a co-op-ESOP, steps 1–3

employees who, for the most part, will lose their jobs. Hence, an ESOP provides an alternative of rewarding the employees who helped build up the company and keeping the jobs, incomes, and taxes in the local community.

One way to understand the co-op-ESOP structure is to follow the steps in all the transactions (see figs. 4.2, 4.3, and 4.4).

Initial Transaction

Step 1: The seller of shares (i.e., the exiting or retiring owner) gets a guarantee from the company that contributions will be made to the ESOP to eventually pay off the note in return for a certain percentage of the shares going to the ESOP.

Step 2: The ESOP issues the company-guaranteed debt note to the seller.

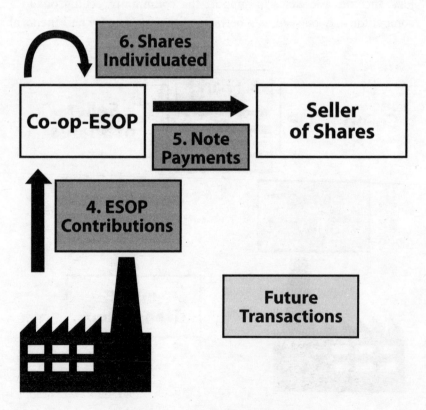

Figure 4.3. Creating a co-op-ESOP, steps 4–6

Step 3: The shares pass to the ESOP. The shares are not individuated to the employees at this stage but are held in an unindividuated "suspense" account.

Future Transactions with Seller

Step 4: The company makes regular (e.g., monthly) cash contributions to the ESOP out of its regular profit.

Step 5: The cash contributions are passed through the ESOP to pay down the note from the seller.

Step 6: Shares equal in value to the principal portion of each note payment are taken out of the suspense account and divided between the individual employee share accounts, usually according to salary.

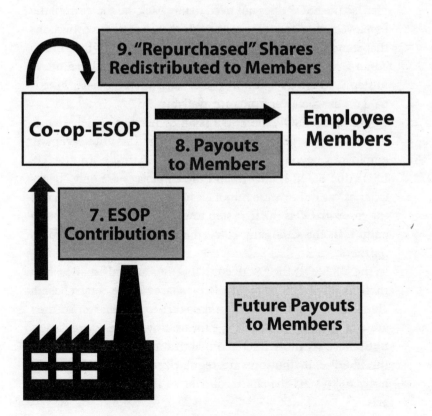

Figure 4.4. Creating a co-op-ESOP, steps 7–9

Future Transactions with Members and Ex-members

Step 7: The ESOP contributions continue on a regular basis.

Step 8: After the seller note is paid off or when the ESOP has funds in excess of the note payments, then the ESOP starts to repurchase the oldest ESOP shares from the employees on a first-in-first-out basis.

Step 9: As the longest-held shares are repurchased from the member (whether still an employee or not), those shares are redistributed to the current employee accounts on the usual basis.

This co-op-ESOP model is an improvement over the US ESOP in several respects:

- The US ESOP was implemented as a special type of retirement plan, so the ESOP does not need to buy back the shares until the employee exits or retires, although there are some provisions that some shares can be repurchased after age fifty-five. In the co-op-ESOP model, the employees "see some ownership money" in step 8, where that "rollover" can start when the seller note is paid off or whenever funds are available.
- In the co-op-ESOP, the ESOP is an ownership vehicle that is democratically governed by its members (i.e., the company employees beyond some probationary period). In the US ESOP, the ESOP is a trust, and the employees are only "beneficiaries," as if they were minors. The democratic governance of the co-op-ESOP is the first step toward building an ownership culture in the Company since the employees are treated as partners.
- In the US ESOP, the ESOP contributions are only made when there is a loan to be paid off or shares to be repurchased. Hence new employees only *then* start to get shares, so they are not owners and do not capture any share appreciation until there are more ESOP contributions. In the co-op-ESOP, the ESOP contributions are regularized to repay the loans/notes or to start the share rollover so this problem does not arise.

One final point is that the co-op-ESOP model builds labor-based membership in the co-op (since all and only the people working in the underlying corporation qualify as members) on top of a company where the membership rights are still property rights—so it is building something structurally new within the shell of the old.

5

Prospects for Democratizing the Corporation in US Law

Robert F. Freeland

Efforts to democratize the corporation have made considerable headway in Europe.[1] A majority of EU member countries have passed legislation requiring some form of worker representation on boards of directors or corporate governance committees. Though labor often remains a distinct minority in these schemes, there is at least a growing recognition that such representation is needed. The situation is different in Anglo-American countries, especially in the United States. The US is the center of the shareholder value movement—an approach that explicitly places the interest and power of shareholders above those of other constituencies. The idea of democratization and worker representation has gained little traction here and is subject to resistance in political, legal, and academic circles. Indeed, proponents of the US model contend that "there is no longer any serious competitor to the view that corporate law should principally strive to increase long-term shareholder value," confidently declaring that the shareholder-value model marks "the end of history in corporate law."[2] The consequences of such Anglo-American exceptionalism extend well beyond borders. Because US corporate law looms large in global markets, both the US model and the zeal of its ideological proponents impact economic relations around the world.

In this essay, I examine the prospects for democratizing the corporation in the context of US corporate law.[3] In the spirit of my late colleague Erik Olin Wright, I seek to understand the "obstacles, possibilities, and dilemmas" facing those who would attempt to transform existing capitalist institutions—in this case corporate law and the structure of corporate boards—in ways that make them more equitable and that promote human emancipation and flourishing.[4] In doing so, I engage in a dialogue with the work of Isabelle Ferreras, which frames many of the more specific themes of this volume.[5] I argue that efforts to democratize the corporation reveal a set of deep tensions within US corporate law. On one side US law is "enabling"—it provides enormous latitude for participants in the corporation to design and alter the rules of governance in almost any way they see fit.[6] Here US law offers greater prospects for democratization than is typically recognized. At the same time, however, the values and assumptions underlying US corporate law are often biased toward shareholder primacy. This creates ongoing ideological and material barriers in both corporate law and supporting institutions that serve as strong obstacles to democratization. Identifying these obstacles is a first step in transforming them.

The Legal Nature of the Corporation

Before discussing democratization, it is helpful to outline some key characteristics of the corporation and to dispel a few common misunderstandings. The corporation is a specific type of legally recognized actor. In legal parlance, it is a juridical personality or legal "person" before the law—one that possesses an unlimited lifespan. It is the corporation itself—the corporate person—that is a rights-bearing entity that owns assets, enters into contracts, serves as an employer, issues shares, and carries out economic activity. And it is the board of directors that is most closely identified in law with "the corporation itself." The board is the most powerful actor in the corporation, possessing full legal rights and responsibilities for making decisions and approving policies. For this reason, efforts to democratize the corporation typically focus on board membership and structure.

While the centrality of the board is well known, the relationship between the board and shareholders is often misunderstood. Economic accounts typically conceptualize corporate shareholders as "principals" and the board of directors (as well as officers and executives) as "agents" of shareholders who are subject to their control. This is incorrect.

Legally, corporate officers and managers are agents of the corporation itself (the juridical personality), while "neither officers nor directors are agents of the stockholders."[7] Crucial here is the fact that shareholders— both individually and collectively—lack the power of control over directors that is characteristic of a principal-agent relationship.[8] To put it a bit too simply, shareholders cannot issue affirmative orders to the board. Indeed, shareholders' formal powers are quite limited in US law. In large, publicly traded corporations, shareholders typically have the sole power to elect board members (usually via annual elections), they can nominate board members if they are willing to pay the proxy costs, and they are required to formally vote on certain fundamental corporate changes (e.g., sale or dissolution of the corporation; amendments to bylaws), "but only if the board has formally voted to approve the change and to put it before . . . [shareholders] for approval."[9] Absent board action, even a unanimous decision of shareholders cannot force such fundamental changes. It is thus the board, not shareholders, that has the power and legal responsibility to run the corporation, though share- holders retain veto power over certain important decisions. And while the board is elected by shareholders, board members need not be shareholders.

There is one way in which shareholders do occupy a special status, however. Board members are constrained by fiduciary duties that obli- gate them to act in the best interests of the corporation and its shareholders. As I discuss below, the board's fiduciary duties are a main source of the "shareholder primacy" orientation that permeates US law. But, surprisingly, the rationale for fiduciary obligations also reveals an opening for democratization. The board's fiduciary obligations are rooted in shareholders' position as investors in the corporation. In exchange for investing in the corporation by purchasing shares, stock- holders gain an ongoing right to a portion of future earnings. But their claims to future income, it is said, are always "last in line"—they are paid only after the corporation's other contracts have been honored. Share- holders' power to appoint board members, their veto over important decisions, and the board's fiduciary obligations all serve as mechanisms that protect their position as investors and subordinated creditors. Yet, as many critics have pointed out, various constituencies—most notably employees—also make investments in the corporation.[10] Moreover, their investments are often firm-specific and difficult to redeploy without substantial loss. The upshot is that employees, too, can be conceptualized as residual claimants worthy of board representation.[11]

Most proposals for democratizing the corporation focus on board selection, composition, and structure. Recognizing that the board is the main governing body in the corporation, that the board is not an agent of shareholders, that board members need not be shareholders, and that employees can be investors and residual claimants, they argue that a key step in democratizing corporate governance is to ensure that employees have real and substantial representation on the board. Specific proposals vary, but most implicitly operate via some notion of *quod omnes tangit ab omnibus approbetur*, or the idea that those most directly affected by corporate governance decisions should have a voice in approving such decisions. In what follows I consider the implications of US corporate law for such proposals. What challenges does US corporate law pose to such proposals for democratization, and how likely are such changes to achieve their stated aims if implemented?

Board Structure and Membership: Monocameral versus Bicameral Boards

Most proposals for democratizing US corporations focus on adding employees to a single board of directors. While Ferreras argues for a bicameral form of organization with two separate governing committees—one composed of and representing shareholders; the other, workers—she acknowledges that the single-board approach may be more workable in some contexts. The real issue is to create worker representation on corporate boards so that workers can validate or veto board decisions. In this section, I focus primarily on democratizing a single board of directors, though I comment briefly on the prospect for bicameral boards.

Existing US corporate law assumes a single board of directors and, at least in principle, is amenable to democratization of this board. Corporate laws in all fifty states provide "that a corporation shall be managed by or under the direction of its board of directors," which is "the universal norm in American corporate law."[12] By default, shareholders usually have a monopoly on selecting board members. But because US corporate law is "enabling," in most states this shareholder monopoly of election can be changed by modifying corporate bylaws or articles of incorporation. Even when selected exclusively by shareholders, however, board members need not be shareholders. Thus, even in current US corporate law, there is nothing that prevents the appointment of employees to the board, save the cost of putting them on the ballot.

To say that it is possible for employees to serve as directors is not to say it is likely. Default rules typically give shareholders monopoly power to elect directors. Any changes to this default, or to corporate bylaws, must be approved by shareholders. For this reason, most plans to democratize the corporation call for statutory change to corporate laws that would require employee participation in board selection and/or employee representation on boards. Assuming that such changes at the state level would simply lead corporations to move to a more shareholder-friendly state, most follow Clyde Summers's admonition that such legislation should occur at the federal level.[13] For example, Senator Elizabeth Warren's Accountable Capitalism Act would require large corporations (over $1 billion in revenue) to be chartered at the federal level, and it would further require that at least 40 percent of the directors of such corporations be elected by employees.[14] Other proposals call for more aggressive measures, recommending that: (a) a certain percentage of director seats be filled by employee-directors; (b) such seats be filled by monopoly vote of employees; and (c) voting thresholds be adjusted such that the board could not pass resolutions without employee support (e.g., if 40 percent of the directors are employee representatives, board votes would require support from over 60 percent of the directors to pass).[15]

To summarize thus far: (1) Employee representation on boards is already achievable via existing corporate law, in the sense that directors need not be shareholders. (2) The default arrangement is that such employee representatives would have to be elected by shareholders, who have monopoly power to elect directors absent modifications to articles of incorporation or corporate bylaws, or absent statutory change. (3) Most states allow shareholders to modify bylaws in ways that would reserve seats for employees and/or allow employees to vote for employee directors. (4) Provisions that change voting thresholds are, in principle, also obtainable via bylaw modifications. (5) But substantial changes to either the proportion of employee representation on boards or to voting thresholds and procedures would probably require statutory intervention at the federal level.

When it comes to bicameral boards, the waters are considerably murkier. Corporate statutes in all fifty states currently require a single board of directors. This is a mandatory feature of the law that actors within the corporation cannot change.[16] In principle, at least, statutory law at the state or federal level could override this, allowing for bicameral boards. But the outcome of such a reform might well be uncertain if it were challenged in the courts. US law seemingly has no experience with bicameral boards. Moreover, US corporate law relies on common law traditions, which are deeply rooted in history and precedent. It is thus possible that courts would be hostile to bicameral boards even if they were mandated by statute.[17] Prospects for implementing a bicameral board in the US seem uncertain at best. On purely practical grounds, democratization would thus be easier to achieve with a monocameral model.

Fiduciary Duties of Corporate Directors

Reformers who seek to democratize the corporation "have only two options . . . changing the decisionmaker or changing the decision rule."[18] Proposals to alter board membership and structure aim primarily at changing the decision-makers. As we have seen, both the enabling nature of US law and the possibility of statutory reform make such changes feasible. But if new decision-makers are bound by rules that require them to prioritize shareholder interests, democratizing the corporation will also require that we change decision rules. In this section I briefly outline the most important decision rules in the US corporate model, and I examine to what extent they are consistent with calls for democratization. The core standards of decision-making that I focus on are the duties of care and loyalty, jointly known as fiduciary duties. Although both directors and corporate officers are bound by these duties, I focus only on directors.

Before proceeding, a word of caution. Fiduciary duties are typically defined through case law and precedent rather than via statute. As a result, even though they have been discussed extensively, there are sometimes still differences in how these duties are interpreted by the courts. Crucial here is the fact that directors owe fiduciary duties to both the corporation and to shareholders. It is here that the tensions in US law come to the fore. Speaking generally, US courts are loathe to acknowledge that the interests of shareholders and the corporation diverge, and they give directors wide latitude to determine what constitutes the best interests of the corporation. But when they are forced to choose—typically when a corporation is being sold, dissolved, or taken over—courts often revert to a position that privileges shareholder interests. As the former chief justice of the Delaware Supreme Court put it, "in Delaware, the directors' duties to stockholders must trump their concerns for other constituencies."[19] The shareholder-primacy view is deeply entrenched in the values and assumptions underlying even the courts' interpretation of fiduciary duty.

Directors' Duty of Care

When board members make decisions in their roles as corporate directors, they are obligated to exercise a duty of care. The duty of care constrains directors to act "(1) in good faith, and (2) in a manner the director reasonably believes to be in the best interests of the corporation."[20] The good-faith provision is generally interpreted to mean that directors must act in an informed fashion and must "exercise the degree of skill, diligence, and care that a reasonably prudent person would exercise in similar circumstances."[21] The duty of care seeks to create sanctions for director negligence and/or corruption in decision-making.

The proviso that directors must act "in the best interests of the corporation" raises differences of interpretation. Some observers contend that this requires directors to act in the corporation's interests and "not shareholders."[22] Most, however, translate it to mean that directors owe a duty of care to both the corporation and to shareholders, and they further assume that the two sets of interests are aligned. As D. Gordon Smith puts it, "'The best interests of the corporation' are generally understood to coincide with the best long-term interests of shareholders," and it is usually shareholders who would charge violation of the duty by bringing a derivative suit.[23] In principle this creates a potential issue for democratizing the corporation. If directors pursue a policy that puts non-shareholder interests ahead of shareholders, "the director technically violates the fiduciary duty of care."[24]

This apparent obstacle to democratization is rendered moot in practice by the business judgment rule, which "is a presumption that in making a business decision the directors of a corporation acted on an informed basis, in good faith and in the honest belief that the action taken was in the best interests of the company."[25] The business judgment rule is a presumption on the court's part that directors have not violated a duty of care unless certain specific conditions are met (e.g., gross negligence). It puts the burden of proof on shareholders or others who would challenge directors' actions to rebut this supposition with evidence. Practically, it means that US courts are loathe to second-guess the board's decisions, even when those decisions turn out to be "clear mistakes."[26] Indeed, cases successfully charging breach of the duty of care are exceedingly rare in Delaware.

The business judgment rule has clear implications for democratizing the corporation. Because it gives directors enormous discretion in making business decisions and creates a presumption that they have acted in good faith, it allows them to consider the interests of non-shareholder constituencies when determining the best interests of the corporation. As Margaret Blair and Lynn Stout observe, "Case law interpreting the business judgment rule often explicitly authorizes directors to sacrifice shareholders' interests to protect other constituencies."[27] And at least in principle, courts acknowledge that such constituencies may sometimes include "employees, and perhaps even the community generally."[28] US law thus gives boards clear latitude to consider the interests of employees when determining the best interests of the corporation, though it by no means requires them to do so. Adding worker representatives to the board would, of course, make it more likely that these interests would be taken into account when determining the best interests of the corporation.

Yet caution is warranted, as the discretion of directors in this regard is not unlimited. Courts sometimes point to the limitations of director discretion in their decisions, and they do so in a way that suggests consideration of other constituencies may be subordinated to shareholder interests. This is clearest when corporations are sold or taken over. In *Revlon v. MacAndrews and Forbes*, for instance, the Delaware Supreme Court was careful to state that the board "may have regard for various constituencies in discharging its responsibilities, *provided that there are rationally related benefits accruing to the stockholders.*"[29] Indeed, the court explicitly ruled that when a corporation is sold or dissolved, the directors' duty of care shifts "from the preservation of [the corporation] . . . as a corporate entity to the maximization of the company's value at a sale for the stockholders' benefit." At this point, the board's discretion in determining the best interests of the corporation is subordinated to considerations of shareholder value; other constituencies take a back seat. There is thus a tension between the discretion typically allowed to board members under the business judgment rule and shareholder primacy as an ideology, even within the courts.

Directors' Duty of Loyalty

Directors and officers also have a fiduciary duty of loyalty toward both the corporation and other shareholders.[30] The meaning of loyalty can be notoriously difficult to pin down. At its core it requires corporate directors and officers to refrain from conduct that injures the corporation and, when there is a conflict between their personal economic interest and that of the corporation, to put the corporation's economic interests ahead of their own.[31] The "duty of loyalty . . . imposes an affirmative obligation to protect and advance the interests of the corporation and mandates that [directors and officers] absolutely refrain from any conduct that would harm the corporation."[32] The duty of loyalty also prevents directors from acting in "bad faith" by, for instance, knowingly violating extant law and thereby discrediting the corporation.

The duty of loyalty is concerned primarily with personal self-dealing on the part of directors and officers.[33] Disloyal behavior typically requires that a director personally profit from a specific transaction. Absent evidence of such specific gain, the courts will generally not find that a director has been disloyal. As long as we stick to this narrower definition, the imposition of a duty of loyalty on employee directors would create little challenge to democratization; it would simply require all directors to refrain from plundering corporate or shareholder assets for personal gain. Yet loyalty is sometimes construed to involve clashes between different constituencies. The issues here involve policies that benefit one group of actors, including the directors involved. Corporate officers who sit on the board are typically required to recuse themselves from decisions involving executive compensation, for example. Such decisions must be made by a committee of outside directors who do not have executive positions within the corporation and thus will not personally benefit from such salary increases. Similarly, corporate auditing committees that monitor accounting records often must be composed of outside directors to ensure greater impartiality.

Issues of loyalty concerning conflict between group interests raise more difficult questions for efforts to incorporate employees and other constituencies into board decision-making. Would employee directors have to recuse themselves from decisions involving employee salaries? What about strategic decisions that would potentially entail certain classes of workers to be laid off or cut back? It is difficult to discern ex ante how broadly US courts would interpret the need for such recusals. It is here that the conflicting interests of shareholders and workers come to the fore. Perhaps for this reason, proponents of democratization sometimes advocate the extension of directors' duty of loyalty to employees or other constituencies. If we focus on narrower issues of personal self-dealing, the creation of a director duty of loyalty toward employees is quite realizable, though it would not change much. Doing so would simply prevent directors from plundering employee assets (e.g., pension funds) for gain. At the broader level, though, the extension of a duty of loyalty to multiple constituencies is potentially more problematic. Fiduciary loyalty involves placing another's interests ahead of one's own when there is a conflict. When there are multiple constituencies with distinct and conflicting interests, the standard becomes difficult to adjudicate. There is currently "no guidance [in US law] as to how boards with dual responsibilities to shareholders and other constituencies should balance those sometimes-competing interests in practice."[34] Because existing fiduciary law has developed in the context of a shareholder-primacy model, it has addressed the problem of adjudicating interests by simply prioritizing one group of interests (shareholders) above all others and treating those interests as identical to the interests of the corporation. In a world where multiple interests are represented on the board, this will not do.

What Is to Be Done?

Attempts to alter decision rules present perhaps the biggest challenge to the democratization of the US corporation. Although US law gives boards wide latitude to determine the best interests of the corporation and to consider the interests of workers and non-shareholder constituencies when doing so, it typically privileges shareholder interests above those of other groups when there is a clear conflict. Such conflicts are most apparent when a corporation is subject to dissolution, sale, merger, or acquisition, though those are by no means the only time they arise. In this section, I briefly assess ways in which decision rules might be changed in order to facilitate democratization.

The most sweeping approach would be to create a new legal organizational form that allows for the contractual modification of board fiduciary duties. The law in most US states (including Delaware) already allows for this possibility.[35] Thus, LLC (limited liability company) statutes allow LLC bylaws and articles of incorporation to modify or eliminate director fiduciary duties. What might these modifications look like in the "corporate" context? Consistent with existing law, directors would have a duty of care to act in the best interests of the corporation, and consistent with the business judgment rule, democratized boards would then have wide latitude to determine those interests. The duty of care toward shareholders could be handled in one of two ways. One alternative is simply to eliminate it, such that directors have no duty of care beyond the duty to the best interests of the corporation. A second is to amend it such that the duty of care runs to both shareholders and employees. In either case, what is crucial is that both shareholders and employees be empowered to bring derivative suits charging a violation of the duty of care, for it is primarily through the threat of such suits that the duties are enforced.

Duties of loyalty should follow a similar path, with directors having a duty of loyalty toward the corporation as well as to shareholders and employees. All directors should be (and currently are) precluded from self-dealing behavior that allows them to personally profit at the expense of the corporation. More difficult questions arise when there are clear conflicts between constituencies, such as are manifest in mergers and dissolutions, where a gain for one group might mean a loss for another or for the corporation as a whole. The general rule here should be one of equity: any gains or losses generated by a specific decision in which conflict is manifest (e.g., sale of the corporation) should be borne in roughly equitable measure by the constituencies. It is again crucial that both shareholders and employees have the power to sue for violation of these duties. The general rule of equitable distribution could be overridden in specific cases by a supermajority vote (say, 75 percent) of the board. This would allow the board more flexibility in extraordinary circumstances.

The creation of such changes would by no means be easy. Many states, for instance, have allowed for corporate forms that adopt "constituency clauses" that require the board to "balance" the interests of shareholders and other constituencies, especially in the context of mergers and acquisitions. But such provisions typically lack teeth—they do not allow non-shareholder constituencies to sue for breach of these provisions, meaning that they will effectively go unenforced. And Delaware has been especially resistant to adopting even these more tepid moves toward democratization. One possibility here, as evidenced by Warren's Accountable Capitalism Act, is to create a federal level of incorporation that allows for these more ambitious changes. Such legislation would have to be accompanied by incentives (e.g., tax breaks) that encouraged corporate actors to adopt the new form. But such a move would require a sustained and formidable political program. For now, we can at least outline what the elements of new decision rules should entail.

Will Changing Corporate Law Help?

A final question is whether changing corporate law will actually change outcomes. It seems self-evident that if workers sit on the board, and if directors are not required to prioritize shareholder interests but are allowed or obligated to consider the interests of employees and other constituencies, outcomes will be more favorable to non-shareholder constituencies. Yet US corporate boards already have substantial latitude to consider the interests of other constituencies, though they are hardly required to do so. More broadly, it is widely accepted that boards are in no simple sense obligated to maximize shareholder value.[36] Even the US Supreme Court recently acknowledged that, "while it is certainly true that a central objective of for-profit corporations is to make money, modern corporate law does not require for-profit corporations to pursue profit at the expense of everything else."[37] Yet, as Smith notes, "even though courts do not enforce the shareholder primacy norm, businesses seem quite focused on maximizing profits."[38]

The pursuit of profit and shareholder interests by boards and officers is overdetermined. Dylan Riley notes that eroding capitalism from within faces severe constraints "for the simple reason that capitalist

economies ... are backed by ... institutions that are specifically
designed to eliminate such [alternatives] ... as soon as they begin to
threaten the system."[39] It is not corporate law alone that privileges shareholder interests, but a plethora of institutional constraints. Some of
these are more material in nature, while others are more ideological. But
together they operate to reinforce something like a shareholder primacy
model and to make alternatives to that model appear to be unrealistic.
They thus limit the extent to which change can be imposed on the
system without attacking multiple points.

Capital markets are one well-known source of constraint on board
discretion. To the extent that financial institutions make current and
future share value a central consideration when making capital available, we would expect corporations that fail to maximize share value to
pay more for capital costs. But capital market pressure goes beyond
simple consideration of actual share value. Corporations that adopt
deviant or less recognizable forms of governance may suffer a "legitimacy discount" that makes capital costs higher, even when they perform
well.[40] In the US context, it is not hard to imagine that alteration of
decision-makers and decision rules would be viewed as suspect by
financial institutions and thus face higher capital costs. Shareholder
value is also strongly institutionalized in "markets for corporate control."
The standard argument is that the market for corporate control also
imposes capital costs. If shareholders can freely exit by selling their
shares, they will do so when managers fail to deliver, thereby lowering
stock prices and the cost of raising capital.

Yet one need not believe in a rosy image of a perfectly competitive
market for this outcome to occur. Something like 60 percent of publicly
traded equity in the US is controlled by institutional investors such as
retirement funds and state pension funds.[41] When evaluating investment decisions or exercising their power to vote shares, such investors
typically follow institutionalized guidelines, although they are not
necessarily legally obligated to do so. Private pension funds, for instance,
are required to follow ERISA (Employee Retirement Income Security
Act) guidelines, which obligate the fund to make decisions "solely in the
interest of the participants and beneficiaries."[42] This is generally understood in financial terms: pension funds seek to maximize the value of
holdings. State pension funds and similar holdings are not required
to follow ERISA guidelines, but they generally do so as a matter of

course—a move that confers legal protection if and when questions arise about best practice or duties of care. Similarly, nonprofits and charitable organizations generally manage such investments in accordance with guidelines set out in the Uniform Prudent Management of Institutional Funds Act. While UPMIFA allows for somewhat more discretion in managing investor funds, it too encourages an approximation of maximizing portfolio value. And of course hedge funds and other "activist shareholders" seek to take over corporations in order to maximize returns to hedge fund shareholders—an outcome that is often accomplished by dismembering the corporation that has been taken over. In each case, it is the financial return to shareholders that takes center stage, putting pressure on corporations to pay attention to this metric. Institutional investors will sell shares or put pressure on management when share prices fall, even if those prices do not accurately reflect performance and underlying value. Such behavior is taken to be rational, even if its rationality cannot be demonstrated.[43]

Institutional pressures exist within the corporation, as well. Executive pay for top officers and managers has been increasingly tied to corporate performance as measured by share value. Since the 1980s and 1990s, an increasing proportion of executive pay has been tied to stock holdings, stock options, and bonuses granted on the basis of share performance.[44] With enormous personal remuneration at stake, it is hardly surprising that top executives act to raise share value. To be sure, this trend has certainly been driven in part by corporate boards acting on shareholder-value ideology to approve such measures. But tying executive compensation to share performance has now become an institutionalized expectation among external parties who assess corporate performance. In addition, and paradoxically, this shift has been accompanied by a strengthening of top management power that has "enhanced managers' ability to capture rents."[45]

Finally, and more broadly, I have implicitly argued that the view that the corporation should be run in the interests of shareholders is deeply institutionalized in the US at a moral and cognitive level.[46] The values and assumptions underlying US corporate law lead to a strong sense that such a model is "rational" in the sense of returning highest net value and morally desirable in terms of "how things should be." It would be a mistake to dismiss such sentiments as "mere" ideology, if by that we mean shallow sentiments that are easily changed via evidence or theory.

Although such beliefs are certainly a form of ideology, they also serve as "gap-filling" measures in the courts, and they thereby have very practical consequences.

Changing corporate law is a necessary but arguably not sufficient condition for achieving more equitable outcomes. Changes in corporate law must be accompanied by a multipronged political agenda that seeks to transform supporting institutions. Of vital importance here is altering institutional rules that evaluate corporate and managerial performance solely on the criterion of share value.

Conclusion

There is considerable room within existing US corporate law to democratize the corporation. Although the prioritization of shareholders is built into the default laws governing corporations, the "enabling" nature of US corporate law allows for substantial discretion to move away from those preexisting defaults. Under existing law, there is already substantial room to allow for the representation of employees or other constituencies on the board. As a practical matter, achieving large numbers of employee representatives will probably require statutory intervention, rewriting laws at state or federal levels. The key structural challenge facing Ferreras's proposal is the very notion of a bicameral board.[47] Because there is no precedent for bicameralism in US corporate law, it is hard to know how it might fare. The key "operational" concerns center on the behavioral rules that guide decision-makers. As I have outlined, duties of care and loyalty do allow for boards to consider the interests of non-shareholder constituencies. But true democratization requires rethinking these rules. Perhaps the bigger constraint here is not so much "law on the books" as the ideologies that undergird and reinforce court deliberations and decisions. It is unclear to what extent efforts to "educate the educator" will overcome these constraints, which tend to serve as gap-filling measures when courts interpret the law. None of these are reasons not to pursue a project of democratization. They instead point to the need to anticipate the problems that may arise and the need to devise possible solutions.

6

Economic Democracy at Work: Why (and How) Workers Should Be Represented on US Corporate Boards

Lenore Palladino

For the past four decades, US corporate governance has followed a "shareholder primacy" model.[1] The "law and economics" theory of shareholder primacy claims that the shareholder is the sole corporate stakeholder who makes a risky investment; therefore, the maximization of shareholder value is defended as the sole goal of corporations, and management "agents" owe allegiance only to the shareholder "principals."[2] Under US corporate and labor law, workers have no voice in major corporate decisions, including who to hire and how to compensate a CEO, whether to merge or acquire another firm, what kind of shareholder payments to authorize, whether to outsource production, or whether to engage in aggressive tax-avoidance behavior. Prominent challenges to shareholder primacy have recently appeared from across the political spectrum, and a number of scholars, such as those writing in this volume, have developed a more coherent theory of the corporation. Ferreras argues for reframing workers as *labor investors*, and for transforming corporate boards into a bicameral body composed of both shareholders and workers.[3]

Although worker representation on boards, or "codetermination," is common and largely successful in Germany and other Western European countries, it cannot simply be imported. It is critical to consider how stakeholder governance could work in the contemporary American context.[4] The contemporary US has a labor market with extremely low levels of unionization, high and growing wealth inequality, a service-based and consumption-focused economy with high levels of fissured workforces, and a system of federal labor and securities law but state corporate law. This means that models based on a twentieth-century manufacturing-focused economy are insufficient, as are models based wholly on European institutions. The US does not have centralized union bargaining over the terms and conditions of employment or a tradition of "works councils" at the enterprise level.[5] Labor unions have at times resisted the idea of worker representation on boards as a poor substitute for strengthened bargaining power, while at other times bargaining directly for a seat at the board table.[6]

In this chapter I attempt to improve the proposal for the bicameral firm via two main avenues. First, I briefly point to a supplementary justification for workplace democracy on the basis of the *theory of the innovative enterprise*; such a theory usefully strengthens the normative case for the bicameral firm. Second, I consider a number of specific policy-design questions with which it is necessary to grapple in order for the bicameral firm to ever become a real possibility in the US context.

To begin, I ground the discussion in the theory of the innovative enterprise (TIE), which offers a theoretical framework for the corporation based on how it can transform inputs into higher-quality outputs.[7] The importance of TIE is that it offers a clear normative basis for the argument that workers should have representation on US corporate boards of directors.

In contrast to the neoliberal market-based vision of the corporation in which the most productive firms are seen as the ideal, TIE shows that the innovation process necessarily involves collective and cumulative learning by the workforce, along with long-term financial capabilities that enable management to take risks that can lead to innovation. In the theory of shareholder primacy, shareholders are construed as the primary provider of necessary firm assets because of the mistaken assumption that they provide necessary financial resources. In today's publicly traded corporations, shareholders and asset managers trade stocks among themselves, which does not result in increasing available firm resources. What is actually required for corporations to be productive are the three "social conditions of innovative enterprise—strategic control, organizational integration, and financial commitment—that

support the innovation process."[8] Collective learning cannot be successful without worker participation, as it is a risky and uncertain process
that involves the tacit knowledge that the workforce collectively
constructs along with management. Not only does this framework
clarify the economic benefits of worker participation in corporate
governance, it also provides a clear normative basis for workplace
democracy, since workers—often unlike shareholders—actually have a
substantive view of the production process that they can bring to the
table.

The argument made here is that worker participation on corporate
boards, if established in conjunction with worker organizations and
strengthened collective bargaining, can have similar positive effects in
the United States as codetermination does in Europe, contributing to
increased economic value-creation and rightfully recognizing the
centrality of workers' effort and voice in corporate governance. Assuming that worker representatives have an appropriate mechanism for
sharing information with the workforce, worker representation on
boards will increase the flow of information between employers and
employees, in turn building workers' organizations.

Ultimately, in the long term, I believe that shareholders should function largely like creditors: they should have a claim to the gains (or
losses) of the financial assets that they hold but no managerial power.[9]
However, given the heavy weight of historical precedent of shareholder
involvement with the board, the proposal here focuses on the more
modest idea of integration of labor onto the board, rather than whole-
sale displacement, as the appropriate short-term policy goal in the
United States. I do offer one reframing of the role of shareholders that is
distinct from the Ferreras framework. In today's US economy, for corporations with publicly traded shares, shareholders largely do not
contribute financial resources but instead are better understood as *trad-
ers*.[10] The conventional argument that shareholder primacy is necessary
to induce capital investment, and thus that it contributes to social
welfare, falls apart when confronted with the fact that shareholder
financial assets go to the previous holder of the stock, rather than the
company itself.[11] The trading of financial assets is not investment, as it
contributes nothing to the company's productivity or ability to innovate.
Therefore, shareholders should not be thought of as "capital investors"
in established publicly traded firms, though they may be truly investors

in privately held firms (and in non-US contexts). However, the complex chain of financial intermediation through the asset manager industry means that even in privately held companies where shares are not largely held by one owner or one family, the holder of economic title to shares (a person contributing to their employer pension fund or retirement account) is distinct from the holder of legal title, the asset manager, who is themselves not a "capital investor."

The most compelling justifications for instituting workers as directors include both normative claims that workers should have voice and instrumental claims that voice will improve corporate productivity. Workers serving on corporate boards can participate in business decision-making and create greater visibility and consideration for the effects of those decisions on workers.[12] Employees' firm-specific investments should be seen as a key driver of improved firm productivity over time. As workers become experts in their roles, they produce more efficiently and contribute to shared best practices. Because firms require specific knowledge and experience, employees have highly undiversified risk in the corporation where they work and face significant hardship if their employer shuts down or leaves the country.[13] As Clyde Summers puts it,

> The employees may have made a much greater investment in the enterprise by their years of service, may have much less ability to withdraw, and may have a greater stake in the future of the enterprise than many of the stockholders.[14]

It is much harder to go on unemployment, relocate, or go back to school for new skills if employment ends than for a shareholder to sell shares out of a diversified portfolio. Most employees still hold only one job. As health care and retirement benefits in the United States are typically structured as employment benefits, employees' dependence on the success of the firm runs even deeper than income compensation.

The early history of US industrialization included experiments with various forms of worker representation and employee participation.[15] During World War I, the federal government promoted employee-representation committees, which unions later saw as a postwar organizing vehicle. The growth of works councils in the 1920s was stopped when they were outlawed in the National Labor Relations Act (NLRA) as impermissibly dominated by management, as its drafters saw that it would be challenging to distinguish between workers' organizations where workers could freely participate versus those that served as de facto anti-union vehicles.[16] In the last several decades, even as shareholder primacy became entrenched in the boardroom, worker representatives have served on boards of directors of large business entities in two contexts: as union-nominated directors and as labor-appointed trustees on pension funds. It is time to draw on this history and reinstate workers on corporate boards in the United States.

Policy Design for Worker Representation on US Corporate Boards

Important considerations for how to restructure American worker voice inside corporations include: how workers should elect worker-directors; who may be considered a worker for those elections and who is eligible to serve on the board; what kind of organizational mechanism is necessary for worker-directors to adequately represent workers (including how worker organizations would interact with US labor law and its general prohibition on joint management-labor committees); and what rules should govern the board participation of worker-directors. Moreover, it's important to realize that bringing workers onto corporate boards would be insufficient on its own to substantially shift bargaining power within large US corporations. A constellation of other policy changes is also required, such as sectoral union bargaining, making clear that the fiduciary duties of directors include the interests of a wider range of stakeholders, ending extractive practices such as stock buybacks and excessive executive compensation, and public provision of public goods.[17] Discussions of German codetermination—where worker representation on the board is mandatory for large corporations—consistently note that codetermination is successful precisely because it is paired with sectoral bargaining at the regional or industry level and works councils at the enterprise level.[18] Here I assume that, were the politics in the United States to allow the policy of workers electing board members to move forward, other policy reforms to industrial relations would also be on the table.

In order to understand the policy options available when reforming corporate law, it is necessary to delineate the relationship between US labor and corporate law. US labor law is governed by the NLRA. Issues that are not related to terms and conditions of employment—anything termed a business decision or within the core of entrepreneurial control—is outside the scope of labor law. Under section 8(d) of the NLRA, employers must bargain with the union in good faith only "with respect to wages, hours and other terms and conditions of employment." NLRA section 8(a)(2) protects workers against "company unions" by prohibiting employers from engaging with employees collectively about workplace issues. More specifically, it is an unfair labor practice for an employer to "dominate or interfere with the formation or administration of any labor organization or contribute financial or other support to it." Though this section benefits employees, protecting their right to elect their own representatives, it can also prohibit employee engagement in the production process.[19]

Corporate governance law is state law: the procedures for elections of directors, to whom the board owes fiduciary duty, and how they serve are governed by state statute. Delaware corporate governance law is the de facto corporate governance law of the United States for large publicly traded corporations, as corporations choose their state of incorporation, and have overwhelmingly chosen Delaware as a business-friendly jurisdiction.[20] However, labor law is federal, and in order to both disallow avoidance of state mandates by jurisdiction shopping and ensure the correct interplay between corporate and labor law, federal chartering of large corporations would create the right structure for mandating worker representation on boards of directors.

The following section considers some of the additional specific policy questions that arise once a policy for worker representation on corporate boards is adopted. The key differences from the Ferreras proposal are as follows. First, prosaically, this proposal is just for the United States, with our unique constitutional constraints, precedent, and market structure (though leaving aside government paralysis). Substantively, my proposal unifies workers and shareholder representatives, along with management, in one unicameral body, recognizing the importance of negotiation with the idea that all major decisions require a supermajority. The proposal presented here also intends to enable further development of worker organizations, without which workers cannot elect or be represented by a worker-director, rather than presupposing the existence of strong labor unions and collective bargaining rights. Further detail on each element of the proposal is provided below.

How Many Directors Should Be Workers? Who Can Represent Workers?
Without sufficient representation on the board, worker-directors will
not have the power to affect decisions. A range of proportions may be
appropriate as long as worker-directors have representation sufficient to
exert real power in decision-making. The presence of worker-directors
and their ability to force such discussions is likely to induce management to preemptively take such potential discussion and critique into
account.[21] There is no single standard for the appropriate ratio of worker-directors to total board members, either in current US proposals or
in European codetermination models. In Germany, workers represent
one-third to one-half of the directors for companies that fall under the
codetermination mandate. In the French model, the proportion of
worker representatives depends on the size of the company, ranging
from two directors to half of the board.[22] In the US context, the Accountable Capitalism Act proposed that workers elect two-fifths of the board,
while the Corporate Accountability and Democracy Act proposed that
workers elect 45 percent. This article proposes that policymakers
consider parity, or at the minimum one-third, as long as decision-
making is properly structured, as described below.

The impact of worker representation depends on whether certain
decisions require a supermajority. Corporate bylaws should require over
two-thirds of board directors to vote in favor of significant corporate
decisions, such as dissolution or merger.[23] Sufficient numbers are also
important so that workers have the opportunity to choose directors who
represent different worker constituencies, for example, from different
occupations, departments, or middle management.

Should the worker-director be required to be a worker or simply
elected by the workforce? On the one hand, limiting directors to current
workers means that individuals will themselves be able to bring their
perspective as a worker to the board. On the other hand, it may be best
to leave the choice up to the workforce; the key issue is to ensure that
management is not actually behind the choice of who serves on the
board. One way to limit management's ability to influence the choice of
worker-directors is to require a nomination process in which a worker
must pass a certain threshold of support from other workers before they
are able to stand for election, much as a political candidate must demonstrate a certain level of support through signature-gathering before they
can be added to an election ballot. Another approach is to ensure that

workers have an annual meeting in which no management is present (although the complex position of middle management could complicate the picture). Workers should hold elections by secret ballot, and a neutral arbiter should count the ballots and certify the election. In a unionized firm, if the units for collective bargaining and worker representation on the board are the same, there may be synergies between the election for worker-directors and union positions such as shop steward. However, it is not necessarily the case that the units will be the same, nor should it be assumed that the same individuals who are elected for union leadership are automatically best suited for the board. The role of the union in collective bargaining over terms and conditions of employment and resolution of grievances is distinct from workers engaging in the entrepreneurial and financial decisions that take place at the board level.

Who "Counts" as a Worker?

Two types of questions arise when considering who "counts" as a worker and thus may participate in worker-director elections and serve as one of the worker representatives on the corporate board. The first considers the reality of the "fissured" workplace, and whether nonformal employees who have a relationship with the employer of substantial control should be counted as workers.[24] The second question is how far up the hierarchy to go, given that the US economy has substantially moved away from a twentieth-century industrial model, where the distinction between the shop floor and management was clean. Who counts as a worker and who counts as management in the twenty-first century's largest corporations?

The US workplace has become increasingly fissured; under these circumstances, the creation of new policies that require *employees* to choose board representatives could inadvertently lead to even greater fissuring of the workplace, as management chooses to avoid the requirement by taking further measures to outsource and use contractors. In some sectors, occupations that used to be housed within a company are now spun off to other companies, who themselves would be subject to policies that require worker representation on boards. In other cases, where workers are wrongly misclassified as independent contractors instead of as employees, they should be appropriately reclassified as employees and participate in worker representation. In these cases, there may be a need to consider how findings of "joint employer status" under the Fair Labor Standards Act should require employees to participate in board elections for both employers. With the rise of the service economy, large workplaces no longer neatly divide into "shop floor" and "management": even workers who are low-paid and generally devoid of workplace power can be designated as "management" in order to avoid unionization.

The second question is how far up the hierarchy to go when considering who within the workforce should vote for the worker-directors. One option is to simply include all workers except for the executive suite. This is based on the assumption that officers of the corporation and the top tier of management already participate in the board and do not require additional board representation. All other "workers"— whether they would traditionally be considered management or not—should participate in the process of securing representation on corporate boards.

Should worker-director slots be assigned to different occupational groups or different pay bands? Or, more generally, should the worker-director slots simply be open to anyone the workers elect, or should there be a means of ensuring more proportional workforce representation? The risk of simply leaving elections open to the entire workforce is that individuals who are high-level managers could use implicit or explicit means to win the election, thus purporting to represent the workforce while continuing to further the interests of management. On the other hand, given the lack of uniformity in how large workplaces are currently structured, drawing boundaries to ensure some kind of proportional representation of different portions of the workplace may be complex. One important issue is that, where a workforce has both unionized and nonunion workers (excepting senior management), election districts should distinguish between the unionized and the nonunion workforce, so that the union can be involved in electing worker-directors for the bargaining unit. Another complication is the reality of multinational corporations whose employees span the globe. The creation of a requirement that only the US workers elect worker-directors for a multinational corporation may incentivize further offshoring, but inclusion of an international workforce may be logistically difficult (though recent policy work on international corporate taxation may shed light on such complex questions).

The policy recommended here is for the National Labor Relations Board (NLRB) to be tasked with drawing up election districts such that worker-directors are proportionally representative of the major occupational groups within a firm, along the same lines that a unit would be drawn up for collective bargaining purposes.[25] Though this leaves determination of the units up to an entity whose leadership is politically appointed, it is the only federal agency with the experience required to determine where the workforce ends and management begins on a case-by-case basis. The term "manager" is used by many corporations as a job title for employees whose work is clearly not managerial. Legislation can seek to create units by excluding "exempt" employees, that is, the type of employees who are exempt from overtime and generally considered to be middle management or above but who are not executives of the firm; however, it will be impossible statutorily to fine-tune the dividing line for each firm. There should be flexibility and delegation to an administrative agency to determine the structure of election districts, following the general principle of representation being proportionally assigned to different strata among the workforce. This will ensure that the basic goal of voice for the workforce through board representation is met, rather than board "worker-directors" simply reflecting the interests of executive management.

What Should the Fiduciary Duties of Worker-Directors Be?
Another critical piece of reform is to clearly broaden the fiduciary duties of all corporate directors to make them accountable to the corporation itself and its multiple stakeholders, rather than shareholders. Benefit corporations, now an option in the majority of states, allow corporations to choose to bind directors to a fiduciary duty that requires consideration of the effects of their decisions on multiple stakeholders, definitively moving away from shareholder primacy. Such a redefinition of fiduciary duty has been proposed as a complementary reform in the Accountable Capitalism Act. A more detailed description of the Model Benefit Corporation Act and how to institute such a reform for all corporations can be found in the work of Frederick Alexander, Andrew Kassoy et al.[26]

Critics will still argue that worker-directors will be partisan toward the workforce and unable to uphold the same (revised and clarified) fiduciary duties as other directors. However, all directors come to the board with some set of interests. Currently, many corporate directors are former corporate executives or individuals with deep managerial or financial experience. Yet by virtue of joining the board, they are committing to uphold the fiduciary duties of care and loyalty, requiring due diligence and barring self-dealing. As with other directors, there may be individual instances when fulfilling board fiduciary duty creates conflicts (due to personal relationships or other idiosyncratic issues), and in these instances worker-directors should recuse themselves from those specific decisions. However, any shareholder-director could be thought of as having a conflict between their duty of care and loyalty to the corporation and their own personal interest as a shareholder in making as much money as quickly as possible; but that is why fiduciary duties and clear processes for conflicts of interest are established in the first place.

The Importance of Worker Organizations

For worker-directors to represent workers, there must be some sort of organizational structure in place. Works councils in Europe operate as part of an institutional structure that makes clear what the councils' role is: they do not bargain over the terms and conditions of employment, which happens at the sectoral, regional, or national level, and they do not bargain over the social wage (health care, retirement, leave policies). Their role is therefore to provide a forum for collective discussion over the production and innovation process between workers and management.[27] Richard Freeman and Edward Lazear further delineate works councils in Europe as having different emphases: paternalistic (where management dominates), consultative (which function mainly to inform and consult workers), and representative (where the works council has actual power in decision-making).[28]

In the United States, only 6.2 percent of private sector workers were members of unions in 2019 (4.1 percent in retail, 2.9 percent in leisure and hospitality, 8 percent in private education and health care, and 8.6 percent in manufacturing).[29] Unions that are chosen to be the exclusive representative of the workforce have the responsibility to bargain with management over the terms and conditions of employment and do not bargain over decisions that fall within the "zone of entrepreneurial control."

Joel Rogers and Wolfgang Streeck describe a number of conditions that should be met.[30] First, workers' councils should be prohibited from any discussion (and certainly bargaining) over the terms and conditions of employment: this is not their function, although this would leave nonunionized workers with no way to collectively bargain. Second, the councils should serve to provide a forum for worker-directors to hear directly from the workforce, so they need to have some permanent form, procedures, and boundaries.

The third critical question concerns their engagement with management. In the European case, the main function of the works council is to engage with management over enterprise-specific issues. In the US, under current labor law, councils could run afoul of NLRA section 8(a) (2), passed as part of the 1935 Wagner Act to end the practice of company unionism (even though the public largely supported works councils as they existed at the time).[31] Rogers and Streeck suggest that this prohibition was too broadly drawn by its drafters and that two issues must be disentangled: councils where employees freely choose to engage with management over production and entrepreneurial decisions, and councils that function in the spirit of a "company union," where management controls who sits on the council and uses it as a way to preempt employee free choice.[32] In other words, the Wagner Act sought to disallow the paternalistic type of works council but did not distinguish the consultative and representative roles of workers' organizations sufficiently.

One solution for works councils that Rogers and Streeck propose (along with Clyde Summers) is that councils be established only when a majority of employees freely chooses to establish them through a secret ballot, since it is clear that councils violate section 8(a)(2) when they are unilaterally established by management.[33] However, this directly contradicts the idea that worker-directors need a permanent forum within which to engage with the workforce to ensure faithful representation. Another way to potentially establish them with the current NLRA in place could be to structure councils so that they only have an "information and consultation" function vis-à-vis management along with electing worker-directors. The NLRB's ruling in *Electromation* found that worker organizations formed to solely focus on increasing company productivity, efficiency, and quality control would be allowed.[34] This would potentially require amending section 8(a)(2) to distinguish between the role of councils while preserving employees' right to determine exclusive representation in collective bargaining. It is also complex to distinguish between the terms and conditions of employment that can be bargained over and consultation over business decisions, which often directly involve the workforce—for example, on which side of the line does outsourcing fall?[35]

A final option is to construe workers' organizations in the United States as being solely a channel between the nonmanagement workforce and their duly elected board representatives, with no management consultation or engagement. Though this would mean that such organizations do not improve productivity and the flow of information and consultation between workers and management, they would likely not run afoul of section 8(a)(2) because there would be no engagement with management. They would provide a forum for workers to bring issues to their representative, although the worker-directors would be bound through their own fiduciary duties to confidentiality for much of what boards typically discuss.[36] This largely one-way channel may be necessary for the workforce to elect representatives, but they would not fulfill many of the functions that make the combination of codetermination and works councils effective in Germany and throughout much of Europe. A final issue is, if these organizations must be chosen by the workforce, then if the workforce chooses not to establish them, it is unclear how worker-directors would then be chosen. Ultimately the best structure for workers' organizations needs to be thoughtfully considered in the context of other available options for industrial relations reform.

Conclusion

Workers are crucial stakeholders for the success of large corporations, the drivers of the US economy. The corporate-governance model of shareholder primacy, in which directors are supposed to maximize shareholder wealth, does not reflect the institutional factors that contribute to innovative enterprises.[37] This essay proposes that workers should elect a substantial proportion of the corporate board of directors, sufficient to provide them with the ability to collectively veto major corporate decisions, as in Ferreras's conception of bicameralism. How this policy would fit into the institutional context in the United States is the main question this essay attempts to answer. American labor law focuses on collective bargaining at the enterprise level; the impacts of worker representation on corporate boards are distinct from the collective bargaining focus on the terms and conditions of employment. Many procedural and substantive questions are likely to arise if a policy of codetermination or economic bicamerialism is adopted in the US, and this essay has laid out some of the major questions that will need to be addressed, as well as a range of potential policy solutions. The challenges of actually implementing such a policy should not stand in the way of such a commonsense and fundamental reform that is necessary for rebalancing power within the corporation and ensuring long-term economic and social prosperity.

IV.

Nuts and Bolts of Economic Bicameralism

7

Islands and the Sea:
Making Firm-Level Democracy Durable

Max Krahé

Firms are islands of planning embedded in a sea of markets. In her anchor chapter, as in her book, Isabelle Ferreras zooms in on firms' inner structures, highlighting both the importance of democratizing firms, and the promise of economic bicameralism as a first step for doing so.[1] In this chapter, I offer a complementary take. Rather than zooming in on firms themselves, I focus on the seas in which they are embedded. My main claim is that a durable democratization of our division of labor requires *combining* firm-level democratization with the democratization of market structures. The swift, turbulent waters of financial markets in particular must be tamed, else they threaten to erode the internal democratization that can be achieved within firms.

I illustrate the mechanism behind this possible erosion by, first, giving a stylized example of a structurally similar islands-within-a-sea constellation: that of Western states embedded within international markets for goods and capital. After World War II, these increased democratic control over their respective divisions of labor and capped this arrangement with tight financial regulation, particularly of international finance. As time went by, however, states gradually reliberalized finance, allowing a global (private sector–driven) financial system to reemerge. Through the pressures this created on individual states, a significant amount of control over the division of labor was returned to private financial actors. In the first section I briefly sketch this general story before zooming in on one particularly striking example in section two: the decision of the French socialists to liberalize finance during the 1980s.

From this example, the next section extracts a causal mechanism— "bribing capital"—via which the inner democratization of islands is threatened by interactions across the sea. This mechanism constitutes a specifically financial version of the "degeneration thesis": the thesis that democratized firms, when embedded in a capitalist society, will degenerate over time to resemble capitalist firms. However, the mechanism highlighted here differs from two other prominent versions of the degeneration thesis: unlike the conception advanced by Sidney and Beatrice Webb, it does not locate the drivers of degeneration in alleged internal faults of democratized firms, such as indiscipline or excessive conservativism.[2] And unlike the traditional Marxist conception, the focus here is on financial markets, which differ from product markets in the incentives and pressures that they create for firms.[3]

The final section and the conclusion then turn toward constructive proposals for responding to this mechanism. Since detailed proposals for democratizing financial markets have already been advanced, I consider how these would fit together with Ferreras's proposal for democratizing the firm.[4] The preliminary conclusion is that these proposals mesh well, mutually reinforcing each other, but that at least three open questions remain.

Islands and the Sea: A Stylized Example

As is well known, during and after World War II, the extent of public control over the division of labor expanded dramatically in the capitalist core. "Democratic institutions challenged the basic operations of the capitalist economy," and income and wealth inequality declined significantly.[5] Full employment, strong trade unions, the nationalization of certain commanding heights of industry, and tightly regulated financial sectors replaced the discretionary control that owners of capital and senior managers had previously held.

Public control over the division of labor is not necessarily democratic.[6] In this case, however, the extension of public control took place in the context of democratizing societies. Women's suffrage was introduced in France in 1944, in Italy in 1945, and in Japan in 1946. In the

US, "between the late 1950s and the early 1970s . . . nearly all formal restrictions on the suffrage rights of adult citizens were swept away, and the federal government assumed responsibility for protecting and guaranteeing those rights."[7] These developments rendered public control over the division of labor more democratic than it would otherwise have been.

During the 1970s and 1980s, this Keynesian social democratic settlement started to give way to what may be called *neoliberal globalism*.[8] The defining feature of this new settlement was that markets, and the corporations embedded within them, were clad in depoliticizing armour, "to [re]inoculate capitalism against the threat of democracy."[9] Via independent central banks, deregulated but publicly backstopped financial systems, commercial federalism, and a range of other reforms, democratic control over the division of labor was hollowed out.[10]

Of importance to the argument developed here, this new settlement and the financial liberalization at its heart were not wrought onto states by an outside force; they were actively pursued or strategically tolerated by states and governments who could have acted otherwise.[11] Examples of choices in this vein include the Bank of England overseeing the reemergence of offshore currency markets (the so-called eurodollar markets) in London during the 1950s, in violation of the spirit of Bretton Woods regulations;[12] the decision by the US government strategically to tolerate the growth of these dollar-based markets in the 1960s,[13] in order to entice foreigners to hold on to their US dollars and reduce downward pressure on the currency; and the decision by the New York State government in the late 1970s to legislate "international banking facilities" (IBFs), which allowed New York–based banks to conduct offshore business from their New York offices.[14]

In each of these cases, national or subnational governments were able to achieve an outcome they desired—the revival of a local industry or the protection of their currency—through what looked like a marginal concession to the financial sector. This is not surprising: given its quantitative precision and intense focus on profits, financial capital moves quickly, so that resources are rapidly redeployed in response to changing incentives, leading—potentially—to additional growth, new jobs, or a stabilized currency. Further, given the competitive nature of many financial markets, a relatively small concession can attract relatively large resources—until a similar concession is made by another potential borrower. Over time, of course, the combined result of many small concessions is a large shift in the balance of power: whereas at the beginning of the period in question, capital was ruled, at period's end, capital rules.[15]

In this mechanism, the degeneration of democratic control is not triggered by internal processes like declining participation, indiscipline, or excessive conservativism, as in the Webb conception. Nor is it triggered by an all-out pursuit of profit, as in the orthodox Marxist conception: the state actors in question did not act as profit-maximizers, nor were they externally constrained to do so. While they certainly cared about economic growth, they also pursued financial liberalization to avoid social and political conflict, to protect or attract jobs (in the case of IBFs in 1970s New York), or to protect the national currency and economy (in the case of US strategic toleration of offshore dollar markets as well as in the French example covered below).[16]

More broadly, the mechanism described in this chapter is compatible with the existence of significant frictions and inefficiencies, which create significant degrees of freedom for the organization of economic activity and thus undermine the case for the orthodox-Marxist version of the degeneration hypothesis. Instead of negative pressures, what drives the mechanism at stake here is a *positive* temptation emerging out of deregulated capital markets. Where banks or other financial firms can easily issue new credit or redirect financial flows, those willing and able to make material concessions to capital providers can quickly attract purchasing power for whatever project the recipient deems worthy.[17] Out of many small concessions, however, emerges a social order in which capital providers gain more and more decision-making power, at least over those who depend on access to borrowing.

Zooming In: Financial Deregulation and the End of Social Democracy in One Country

The potency of this temptation to trigger fundamental departures from the Keynesian social democratic settlement was revealed most strikingly not in Reagan's US or Thatcher's UK but rather in François Mitterrand's France. As with UK and US strategic toleration of the emergence and growth of offshore dollar markets, French financial deregulation, too, was driven by the advantages it offered to state actors.[18] What rendered this case so striking was that it was implemented by a socialist government that had been elected on a strongly anti-capitalist platform, demonstrating how even in the absence of Webbian internal changes, concessions to capital can take place.

In 1981, after years of mixed economic results in France, Mitterrand was elected to the presidency of the Fifth Republic. He and his party promised to slow inflation and restore mass prosperity through a program of downward redistribution, nationalization, and economic stimulus.[19]

However, once Mitterrand's government started implementing this program, it became clear that downward redistribution, large-scale nationalization, and full-employment fiscal and monetary policies were not easily compatible with France's integration into global product and financial markets. While the early Mitterrand government pursued full employment, both the British and American governments had started to prioritize price stability over full employment.[20] France's openness to trade, combined with this divergence between how France and its trade partners regulated their respective domestic divisions of labor, created a persistent balance of payments deficit.

This deficit was driven both by trade and by financial flows: tradewise, aiming at full employment through boosting aggregate demand meant that French consumers had comparatively high purchasing power, part of which went on imports from France's trading partners.[21] Given that the trading partners in question did not run an equally expansive macroeconomic policy, the reciprocal demand for French exports was lower, tilting the balance of trade toward deficit.

Besides the trade effects of full employment, there was also a capital flow effect of the divergence between France and its trading partners' social orders. The share of national income going to capital in France was lower, indeed considerably lower, than in any other G7 economy in the early 1980s (see fig. 7.1), despite a capital stock of comparable size.[22]

Given that capital was reaping a smaller annual flow on the basis of a similar stock, capital outflows from France were not just a shock reaction to the new government but also a commercially rational response to more profitable opportunities elsewhere.

At the time, the franc was part of the European Monetary System (EMS), a fixed currency regime and precursor to the euro. In the context of currency outflows through both trade and capital movements, this meant that the Bank of France had to purchase francs in order to ensure that its exchange rate did not fall below the agreed floor. Given that it

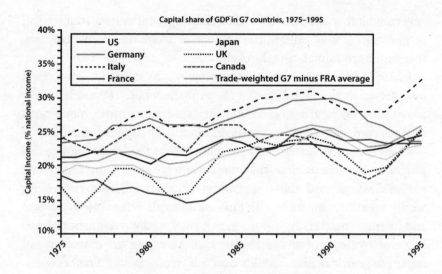

Figure 7.1 The capital share in France and other G7 countries, 1975–1995.
Source: author, based on Thomas Piketty, *Capital in the Twenty-First Century*
(Cambridge, MA: Belknap Press, 2014), figure 6.5.

had to use its foreign currency and gold reserves to do so, and given that those were finite, the French government was forced to choose between taking France out of the EMS—and hence the process of deeper European integration—or restructuring French society domestically to bring the balance of payments into a stable equilibrium again.

Between June 1982 and March 1983, the government chose domestic restructuring: although it required harsh austerity, the Elysée's economic staff projected that it would require *less* austerity than a decoupling from the international division of labor via tariffs and a move to floating exchange rates, which a rival faction of the government advocated. The reason that exit was considered to require more austerity was that the devaluation that would follow EMS-exit would drive up the costs of essential imports, especially oil. Unless domestic demand was drastically curbed, this sudden increase in the import bill would tilt the trade balance further into deficit, causing additional downward pressure on the currency, driving up oil import prices even further, and so on. At the limit, France would require an International Monetary Fund bailout similar to the UK's IMF bailout in 1976—an unacceptable outcome for the socialist government.

Resembling much of US and Swedish financial deregulation in this respect, it was above all to ease the pain of this domestic restructuring that Mitterrand opted to accompany austerity with the deregulation of finance.[23] In particular, deregulation allowed credit growth—that is, an increase in society-wide leverage. Both the newly created debt and its mirror image, the financial assets that represent claims to repayment, helped take the edge off austerity: credit, by allowing increased consumption in the face of stagnant incomes; assets, by giving capital a predictable source of profits in economically uncertain times.

Quantitatively, the most important effect of deregulation was to allow for the real interest rate to increase—drawing purchasing power away from spending and into savings, thereby reducing demand and so reducing inflation—without dampening credit growth, the usual consequence of an increase in interest rates. In particular, the real short-term interest rate increased from an average of around 0 percent during the 1970s to 4–5 percent in 1984–1987, its highest level since 1953. Despite this increase, real credit growth increased from 0 percent in 1981 and around 3 percent in 1982–1984 to around 5 percent in 1985–1990, with spikes of 9 percent and 8 percent respectively in 1988 and 1989.[24] At the same time, inflation fell from an annual rate of 13 percent in 1981 to a rate of 3 percent in 1986.[25]

In contrast, prior to deregulation, attacks on inflation meant that the *encadrement du crédit* "had to be tightened rather than loosened, exceptional tax levies had to be multiplied," and "interest rate policy [had to be] more deflationary than before."[26] Tackling inflation had meant curtailing credit, which had meant lower investment, lower consumption, and lower growth. Deregulation temporarily dissolved this binary choice between "high growth, high inflation" and "low inflation, low growth." It permitted credit growth even as interest rates increased, thereby allowing households to maintain consumption (and invest in assets, especially housing) despite lower-than-expected wage growth, and firms to invest despite initially low profits. This significantly softened the backlash against Mitterrand's turn toward austerity.

Yet deregulation was not costless. The consequences for the distribution of economic *decision-making power* were clear. Prior to reforms, most credit had been allocated by state or semipublic financial institutions.[27] Through the tool of credit allocation, choices about which sectors to prioritize, what kinds of firms to support, and which regions to foster had been in public hands. After the reforms, it was "large banks" that "assumed an active role in industrial investment decisions by virtue of their strategic position between the [newly created] financial market on the one hand and indebted industrial borrowers on the other."[28]

The Causal Mechanism: "Bribing Capital"

What causal mechanism can we extract from the stylized example just offered? And how does it apply to firms embedded in financial and product markets, as opposed to states embedded in an international financial and economic order?

Analytically speaking, the mechanism behind French and international financial liberalization was a particular kind of collective-action problem. At critical junctures, national governments could profit individually from what I call "bribing capital": since financial firms and investors are reliably profit-seeking, governments could indirectly command the resources that financial firms and investors controlled, by engineering changes in regulations or by tolerating questionable novelties that rendered profitable whatever activity or outcome the government in question desired.[29] Thus the Bank of England could contribute to a renaissance of the City of London by tolerating Midland Bank's arbitrage operations in the 1950s; 1970s New York could boost its financial sector, and hence its own finances, by creating IBFs; the American state could alleviate pressure on its gold reserves and on its domestic system of financial regulation by refusing to extend Regulation Q to offshore dollars; and the French state, as explored in greater detail below, could foster noninflationary borrowing through deregulation of its financial sector, thus reducing the need for austerity in difficult times.

This constitutes a classic collective-action problem for actors who are committed to the value of democracy: like the combustion of fossil fuels, each individual act of attracting financial resources through bribing capital channeled energy to what was perceived to be a worthwhile goal; but across many such acts, the collective consequences were devastating, for their sum was the evisceration of democratic control over the division of labor. Over time, they created an economy whose future structure and whose macroeconomic condition largely depended (and continues to depend) on the decision-making of private capital investors, banks, asset managers, and other financial firms.

Three points bear highlighting here. First, this transformation was not wrought onto national governments against their resistance by powerful banks and corporations. Instead, even though they were broadly speaking democratic, it was the national governments *themselves*— though no doubt with the encouragement of financial and other interests—who decided it was in their interest to take the individual steps that led from Bretton Woods to neoliberal globalism.[30]

Second, once a sizeable international financial market had been re-created (i.e., controls on outflowing capital had been lifted or their circumvention had become tolerated practice in key states, especially the US and the UK), states could access large amounts of noninflationary additional resources (which could then be used for whatever domestic project the government of the day deemed valuable) through capital-attracting reforms. This explains the temptation of financial deregulation even for social democratic states: in any particularly tough conflict, a bout of financial deregulation could be used to break the impasse, by channeling additional resources attracted through bribing capital to the relevant veto player, without having to tax another party to the negotiations at the same time. Zero-sum problems or, in the case of the unexpected growth slowdown of the 1970s, even negative-sum problems, could thus be transformed into positive-sum (or less harshly negative-sum) ones, rendering them more amenable to bargained resolution. Of course, the perceived positive sum relied on a temporal illusion: the additional resources that turned zero or negative sums into positive sums were checks written on the future. Eventually, these checks would be cashed, either out of future growth, necessitating that its fruits would fall to the financial sector, or, if future growth did not suffice, through austerity and upward redistribution.

Third, the effects of such acts on *other* governments did not depend on the motivation or the internal processes of the government in question. Regardless of the internal decision-making procedure that gave rise to acts of bribing capital, the consequences for other governments were that, if they wanted to attract or even just hold on to footloose capital, they had to match or exceed the terms of this bribe. A race to the bottom, or, more accurately, a beauty pageant in which investors and banks sat as the jury, resulted. This race to the bottom became visible, for example, in the spread of central bank independence, which did little to lower the cost of reducing inflation, while it *did* depoliticize and thereby de-democratize distributional conflict, assuring banks and investors of public support in emergencies and curtailing more radical political experimentation.[31] It can also be seen in the global decline of corporate income tax, whose worldwide average declined from 47 percent in 1980 to 26 percent in 2020; the decline in capital taxation more generally; and the gradual and global relaxation of banking regulation.[32]

This explains why democratizing firms is not enough to durably democratize the division of labor. Where bicameral firms are embedded in deregulated financial markets, even bicameral firms are likely, from time to time, to decide to bribe capital. In particular, because financial markets shift resources quickly—there is no need, unlike in product markets, to build them up through many profitable transactions over time—even a bicameral firm that does not prioritize profits will be tempted to offer attractive terms to financiers in order rapidly to attract resources to whatever project their two chambers deem most worthy of investment. The French example was a case of this: although the government was ideologically opposed to giving private investors control over the country's economic future, it implemented financial deregulation in order to weather an otherwise-difficult period.

The impact on other bicameral firms will be that, if these other firms want to undertake significant investments themselves, they either need to optimize their own operations for profit (to generate the required financing internally), or they themselves need to "bribe capital" to attract outside funds. In this manner, a process is initiated through which, across many iterations, the judgments of capital providers (in the case of external financing) or the criterion of profitability (in the case of internal financing) end up dominating the decision-making even of bicameral firms—even if none of the firms intended this outcome.

Suggestive empirical evidence for the operation of this mechanism comes out of Germany. A recent quasi-experimental study of codetermination found productivity, firm size, and fixed capital investment all unchanged or even slightly improved through codetermination: "Shared governance does not appear to induce firms to become smaller or less productive."[33] This suggests that neither Webbian nor Marxist processes of degeneration took place at scale. However, Thomas Piketty's analysis of German capital shows that codetermination leads to lower *market* valuations of German firms relative to otherwise-comparable British or

French firms: "This model of shared social ownership . . . can be at least as efficient economically as Anglo-Saxon market capitalism [but] the stakeholder model inevitably implies a lower market valuation."[34]

This creates precisely the temptation outlined above: positively, where firms reorganize themselves internally to give greater weight to the wishes of capital, they can in principle drive up their own market valuation, which would allow for more borrowing against the now-stronger collateral of their share price, or for the acquisition of new resources through sale of a small part of the now more valuable company. Negatively, where there is a market for corporate control, it creates the threat of private equity investors or corporate raiders taking over a firm, implementing the relevant restructuring, and then selling at a profit.

The presence of this implicit threat may explain why Simon Jäger et al. find that "worker representation on corporate boards does not appear to shift worker bargaining power."[35] The great danger of this mechanism, in other words, lies in the fact that it may operate *even where internal democratization leaves productivity and efficiency unchanged or improved.*

Synergies between Democracy in the Firm and Democracy in Finance

How can this process be arrested? How can democratic control over the division of labor as a whole, and in particular over its development over time, be assured in the face of this possible temptation?

Democratizing financial corporations themselves is unlikely to solve this problem. Two outcomes can be imagined: the sociology of finance suggests that a many financial service workers internalize the goal of profitability. If so, even bicameral banks and financial firms would remain receptive to bribes to capital, so that the collective action problem would remain in place.

Alternatively, if the introduction of bicameralism were to change the culture of financial firms, the collective action problem would be solved, but at the cost of introducing new inequities. Firm-level democracy in contemporary economies would then still leave the financial sector in charge of capital allocation. While this power would then be exercised in a discretionary fashion, as opposed to being exercised in pursuit of profit only, it is not clear why the workers of this sector, who constitute no more than 1 to 2 percent of the population, should wield this power over all other citizens. By rendering bribes to capital less predictably effective, this might slow down or arrest the mechanism at hand, but it would do so at the risk of creating a "bankers' democracy."

A more promising solution lies in legally mandating firm-level democracy across the entire economy, as Ferreras proposes: just as Germany mandates (certain forms of) codetermination for firms of a certain size and legal type, countries could require firms to be bicameral once they cross certain thresholds. By taking the option of surrendering corporate control to private capital off the table, this has the potential of resolving the collective action problem at the heart of the mechanism described here.

However, the mixed results from the German case summarized above, especially the absence of visible wage gains, improved working conditions, or other signs of improved labor bargaining power, suggest that here, too, there remain limits. While mandatory bicameralism prevents the permanent surrender of control, thus surely weakening the mechanism at stake, it does not prevent the "renting out" of control: firms in which both chambers credibly commit to meeting the wishes of financiers, whether in the form of higher dividends, via favoring some projects or processes over others, or via wage restraint, will likely still benefit from cheaper and/or more ample access to capital, giving them a leg up in competition with other bicameral firms.[36] Moreover, legal forms are malleable; even if an outright relinquishment of labor's control rights is made illegal, enterprising lawyers might find suitable proxy arrangements over time.[37] The temptation remains, albeit in weaker form.

If democratizing financial corporations does not solve the problem, and if making bicameralism mandatory attenuates but does not fully solve it, what could be done in addition? Supposing that the will for reform is strong—as it likely would be, in a scenario where the introduction of economic bicameralism is on the table—economic bicameralism could be accompanied by significant financial reform. In accordance with the "all affected" principle, the financial sector could be subjected to control by the demos as a whole. Proposals along these lines have been advanced by Tom Malleson, Robert Hockett, Fred Block, and others.[38]

Practically, democratizing finance consists in two steps: first, harnessing financial flows, so they can be required to follow a compass other than pure profitability; second, ensuring that the thus-created control is exercised democratically and sustainably. Block's proposals have certain shortcomings on the first dimension,[39] Malleson's on the second,[40] but Hockett's proposals appear, based on their current elaboration, to achieve both.

First, concerning the harnessing of financial flows, through offering citizens and firms direct access to checking accounts at the Federal Reserve, it ensures that financial flows can be guided effectively.[41] This is because Federal Reserve deposits, by virtue of their security, would attract large amounts of corporate and private money away from private deposit institutions; this would allow a spread to be created, if desired, between lending and borrowing with and without explicit public support, bringing financial flows under public control and allowing them to be harnessed toward publicly desired ends.

Second, concerning the democratic and sustainable exercise of the thus-created control, note that under Hockett's proposals, private banks could still pursue lending and investing that is not approved by the Fed, as long as this is sufficiently profitable to allow the bank to pay an interest rate that offsets the greater risk attached to depositing money there (presumably in time deposits, not demand deposits) as opposed to in a Fed account. This creates a safety vent that signals when public lending neglects projects that, according to the dollar votes cast by citizens in product markets, are widely desired. In this manner, it renders public control over the financial system more sustainable in the long run.[42]

How would this kind of financial system interact with bicameral firms? Although this is a complex question, a robust answer to which requires seeing their interaction play out in practice, it appears as though there would be strong synergies. If bicameral firms are less aggressive about pursuing profits—a reasonable assumption, it seems to me—then the pressure they would exert on profit-inhibiting regulations (whether financial regulation, on which this paper has focused, or social and environmental regulation, which are equally central in directing markets toward democratically desirable outcomes) would be reduced. While any individual bicameral firm may, through some contingent constellation, happen to go for aggressive profit maximization, insofar as *other* bicameral firms would be less likely to copy this than profit-maximizing firms would be (especially if they are backed by a financial sector that only gives mild preference to the profit-aggressive firm, as opposed to

flooding such a firm with capital, as a purely profit-maximizing financial sector likely would), this pressure would propagate less quickly. In
this manner, democratized firms would be less likely to undermine
democratic control over the economy as a whole and hence stabilize
democratization in finance.

Conversely, a democratized financial sector would stabilize firm-level
democracy. As the historical example demonstrated, democracy at the
level of individual islands can be hollowed out, even if all important
islands are democratized and if no individual island intends this, if
small surrenders of control are capable of attracting large amounts of
capital. Insofar as a democratized financial sector would be less responsive to attempted bribes of capital, since much of capital would no
longer be deployed in pursuit of maximum profit, this mechanism
would be rendered inoperative or at least greatly weakened and slowed
down.

Conclusion: Firms, Finance, and Democracy in the Division of Labor

Ferreras's work highlights the importance of firms in our division of
labor. Since markets are practically never perfectly competitive—due to
the existence of multiple equilibria, frictions, and transaction costs,
economies of scale, externalities, and other features—firms have considerable discretion in their decision-making.[43] Moreover, as Herbert
Simon points out, a hypothetical alien visiting earth, "equipped with a
telescope" through which "firms reveal themselves, say, as solid green
areas" and "market transactions show as red lines connecting firms,"
would see a world of "large green areas interconnected by red lines," not
"a network of red lines connecting green spots."[44] Firms, in other words,
dominate much of economic decision making. Of the problems and
inequities that we face today, many are rightfully attributed to firms and
their internal decision-making.

And yet, green blobs live in the shadow of red lines. Because firms,
despite their market power, are by and large subject to hard budget
constraints, their internal behavior is strongly shaped by the external
ecosystem they face. Where finance is deregulated and large pools of
footloose capital swirl around the world, or can quickly be summoned

into being through credit creation, firms (and countries) who (credibly) promise pliancy and high returns to finance can command immense resources, giving them a leg up in competition. Over time, finance-pleasing firms can use this to outcompete their rivals, who, due to the hard budget constraint they face, must eventually adapt or perish. As mentioned at the outset, this argument resembles the classic degeneration thesis put forward by the Webbs and a number of Marxist theoreticians. However, unlike in the Webb version, this mechanism does not presuppose any internal deterioration; and unlike in the Marxist version, it is not the immediate pressure to compete in product markets that starts the vicious cycle but, rather, the positive temptation to attract resources toward desirable projects. Democratizing the internal governance of firms may slow this process down, but on its own it will likely not arrest it. To render firm-level democracy sustainable, finance must be democratized, too.

The work of Hockett, Block, Malleson, and others provides convincing answers for doing so. As I show above, not only is democratizing finance compatible with democratizing firms, the two reforms mutually support each other. This makes a progressive version of "package reform," combining the introduction of bicameral firms with democratization of the financial sector, a more attractive proposition than either reform in isolation.[45]

Does this mean that these changes suffice, in combination, to durably democratize control over the division of labor?

The jury is out. At least three questions remain open: first, the problem of ossification or, from a market perspective, "inefficiency." Firm-level democracy under current conditions does not appear to inhibit productivity.[46] But it is unclear how robust this result is: hitherto, democratized firms have always operated in ecosystems dominated by profit-maximizing, nondemocratic firms and in the context of financial markets where capital is overwhelming allocated according to profitability. We do not know, therefore, if *the combination* of democratized firms and democratized finance would *also* be secure against ossification and inefficiency. The very purpose of democratizing finance, after all, is to render firms' access to capital less sensitive to pure profit maximization. This does not dispel budget constraints, but it does not exactly harden them either.[47] The question of dynamism and efficiency over time therefore remains open.

Second, the proposals so far have focused on democratizing a division of labor in one country. But recall the reason why President Mitterrand implemented the *tournant de la rigueur*: international imbalances. Where a democratized division of labor implies higher wages and a larger labor share, trade with capital-friendly countries is likely to be uneven. How to prevent the buildup of international imbalances remains a key open question for sustainably democratizing the division of labor, although arguably one that is more urgent for small, open economies such as individual European states than for large, significantly more closed ones like the United States or the EU as a whole.

Finally, there remains the question of mergers and acquisitions (M&A), of firms splitting and recombining, and of the market for corporate control. Industrial firms, for example, used to employ cleaning, catering, and other nonmanufacturing workers directly, at wages and conditions comparable to their core workforces. Under cost pressure, these have been outsourced, or, where firms did not aggressively profit-maximize in this way, private equity firms purchased such companies, "streamlined" them, and then sold them off again at a profit.[48] In this manner, M&A can be another mechanism that puts pressure on firms to be profit maximizing, again constraining the scope for firm-level democracy to permit real agency and substantial deviation from how a nondemocratic, profit-maximizing firm would behave. How to regulate M&A is thus a further question in the great task of democratizing the division of labor.

8

Are Bicameral Firms Preferable to Codetermination or Worker Cooperatives?

Thomas Ferretti and Axel Gosseries

Democratic ideals have led prominent scholars to propose the extension of democratic reforms to the economic sphere.[1] For John Stuart Mill,

> the form of association . . . which . . . must be expected in the end to predominate, is not that which can exist between a capitalist as chief, and workpeople without a voice in the management, but the association of the labourers themselves on terms of equality, collectively owning the capital with which they carry on their operations, and working under managers elected and removable by themselves.[2]

Workplace democracy would require the transformation of economic organizations, typically to involve elements of worker representation within firms through worker suffrage, election of executives, deliberative spaces, and accountability mechanisms.

A renewed interest in economic and workplace democracy has led to a flourishing of strategies to move firms toward this ideal.[3] While such strategies often rely on existing and tested forms of workplace democracy such as worker cooperatives or codetermination, a recent proposal by Isabelle Ferreras is economic bicameralism.[4] It is inspired by historical attempts at democratizing states through bicameral parliaments.

At the state level, a variety of institutional forms can generate the intrinsic and instrumental benefits of democratic rule. Historically, *bicameral legislatures* may have eased the access of emerging groups to representation and power while securing the previously hegemonic group (e.g., the aristocracy) some level of control.[5] Today, bicameralism is more often seen as a checks-and-balances strategy ensuring that no special interest group captures power in both chambers, or as a way of representing both a country's population in general and its territories' specific sensitivities. Ferreras argues that promotion of *economic bicameralism* within firms, this time with one chamber representing capital owners and another representing workers, can serve as a transitional step toward economic democracy.

Such a proposal should be evaluated on at least two grounds: its effectiveness at meeting normative targets, and whether it does better than alternatives. If we are to transform economic organizations to replace the dominant investor-owned model, we should choose the organizational form that best achieves our normative ideals. Is economic bicameralism better at achieving them than alternatives such as codetermination or worker cooperatives?

Section 1 introduces our normative framework. We stress that a mere parallel between states and firms cannot suffice to justify workplace democracy. Adequate justification requires that costs in terms of negative-freedom restrictions and eventual loss of economic productivity be outweighed by the benefits of democratization.

Section 2 compares the relative capacity of bicameralism and alternatives to deliver the expected benefits of firm-level economic democratization. Those benefits are assessed in terms of (a) reducing domination and bargaining power inequalities, (b) improving deliberation, and (c) unlocking epistemic benefits. We argue that bicameralism is weak on the first two fronts.

Section 3 investigates the economic costs of bicameral firms. Including two classes of patrons—investors and workers—in decision-making may lead to higher costs of contracting capital, higher costs of decision-making, and higher agency costs than alternatives.

1. Negative Freedom and the Necessity Test

The "parallel case" argument essentially claims, as Robert Dahl summarizes, that "if democracy is justified in governing the state, then it must also be justified in governing economic enterprises."[6] For Ferreras, the *critical intuition of democratic justice* denotes this expectation from workers to be treated with equal respect, whether in public life or in the workplace: "Democracies promise their citizens equality. But, even in political democracies, that promise has been shut out of the work-place."[7] Yet, the claim that democratic equality between citizens cannot be achieved unless a substantial part of the economy is composed of democratically ruled economic organizations requires an argument. For some may claim that citizens' equality is sufficiently protected even if their private organizations—such as their workplace or sports clubs— are not run democratically. Despite surveys showing that many workers want to participate in workplace decisions, not all of them do.[8] Some prefer working in authoritarian firms in exchange for other benefits such as fewer responsibilities or a lesser need to invest their own savings in their company.[9] Therefore, for the parallel case to success-fully justify workplace democracy, one should demonstrate that states and firms are relevantly similar such that democratic controls are *mandated* in both cases.[10]

One objection to the parallel case stresses that, while states and firms are in some way similar, namely because of the exercise of power within them, democratic institutions are *necessary* to protect us from state power but not to protect us from firm power. Contrary to states, the argument goes, "authoritarian" structures in economic organizations and employment relations result from free market contracts between consenting citizens. Therefore, workers can protect themselves from their firm's authority and power by simply ending their employment contract.[11] In response, one reason to restrict everyone's freedom of market contracting by mandating workplace democracy may be that workers often have little freedom to exit exploitative workplaces when they face high exit costs and few alternative job options, which means they cannot protect themselves from firm power so easily.[12]

Even so, a presumption against restrictions on *negative freedom* would recommend, if possible, remedying injustices without unneces-sarily restricting market freedoms. Indeed, one could distinguish *negative freedom* from legal constraints, *positive freedom* to pursue desired life projects, and *republican freedom* from domination.[13] While state restrictions on negative freedom are sometimes justified if neces-sary to improve people's freedom in other respects, negative freedom remains important. This has led some, like John Rawls, to propose a "general presumption against imposing legal and other restrictions on conduct without sufficient reason."[14] This simply stipulates that those legal restrictions of negative freedom that are unnecessary to achieve legitimate collective goals, such as securing positive and republican freedom to all, must be avoided. The reason for this presumption is *not* that negative freedom should prevail over other kinds of freedom. It is merely that once our legitimate collective goals are achieved, further restrictions on negative freedom are unnecessary. They would undermine parts of our freedom without reason.

This being said, a general presumption against restrictions on negative freedom is compatible with any state intervention deemed necessary to realize legitimate democratic or distributive goals.[15] Ferreras claims that "the liberal tradition and critical social theory have largely failed to expand the scope of the public sphere to include the firm."[16] But liberals do not need to assume that firms belong to the private sphere. Whether something belongs to the public or the private sphere is not what determines whether it should abide by public standards and be subjected to state regulations. Something as private as the family can be regulated if necessary to protect children's rights, and something as public as political speech may deserve protection from government interference if there is no sufficient reason to regulate it. The presumption against restrictions on negative freedom merely entails that regulation must be necessary to achieve legitimate democratic or distributive goals.

In this framework, in order to choose the regime best able to respect negative freedom while achieving our goals of securing everyone's positive and republican freedom, we must compare "ideal types" of social regimes without limiting ourselves to existing ones. Moreover, when choosing a social regime, we should not evaluate a part of the system without understanding how it fits into the overall system. Therefore, the regime best able to realize our goals could include institutions that seem prima facie unjust, such as undemocratic firms, but are not all-things-considered unjust because other parts of the social system compensate for apparent injustices.[17]

Consider two regimes. First, the ideal type of *welfare state capitalism*. This system would involve a strong, universal welfare state with market regulations securing a living wage, solid worker protections through strong unions, and investments in labor markets to facilitate job creation and social mobility. It would also include the universal provision of services such as health care and education, as well as ambitious universal asset holding or a basic income. But it would impose few restrictions on entrepreneurs' freedom to decide which firm structure to offer to labor suppliers, so that the most competitive firms (perhaps undemocratic ones) would come to dominate the economy. Contrast a different ideal type, which we will call *economic democracy*. It is identical except for heavier economic regulations mandating firms to adopt democratic structures or systematically subsidizing democratic firms, such as bicameralist workplaces or worker cooperatives, over alternatives. Because, evidently, all firms do not voluntarily evolve toward workplace democracy, the implementation of such a system will require some form of state coercion or financial incentive to democratize firms.

While current welfare states fail to secure everyone's dignity, republican freedom, and distributive fairness, a strong and universal welfare state capitalist system could perhaps achieve these goals.[18] If so, a presumption against restrictions on negative freedom would then mandate abstention from further restrictions mandating workplace democratization. Indeed, if such an ideal system could achieve our distributive goals, both freedom and social justice would be better protected: entrepreneurs and workers satisfied with working in undemocratic firms would remain free to do so, while workers unsatisfied with their situation or unfairly compensated in some firms would be compensated through universal social services. This hypothetical argument stresses an important point, which is that justification of the promotion of a specific form of firm governance—say, economic bicameralism—requires demonstrating that the associated restrictions on negative freedom are necessary to achieve desirable social goals, and that less restrictive alternative policies (such as an ambitious welfare state and universal social services of the kind described above) are insufficient for our purposes.

Applying this necessity test to the case of promoting workplace democratization, if alternative social regimes are sufficient to achieve our democratic and distributive goals, there might be good reasons for citizens in a democratic state to abstain from actively promoting workplace democracy, even if some workers would want more opportunity to join democratic firms. Even at the state level, while intrinsic or instrumental arguments for democracy may lead us to hold that every citizen should have a right to vote, there are good reasons to withhold decision-making power in some contexts. For example, while all citizens have a right to vote in national elections, they may not have a local right to vote against a national infrastructure project if the project's collective benefits far outweigh the interest of the local community. Similarly, state governments representing all citizens could legitimately judge that, all things considered, the benefits of tolerating undemocratic firms outweigh the interests of local workers wanting more power in their firm. As Gregory Dow underlines: "There might be good reasons for withholding control rights even when workers do want them. The interest of society as a whole may demand that other goals take priority, perhaps including efficiency goals."[19]

Suppose, for the sake of argument, that a universal welfare state capitalist system dominated by investor-owned firms is indeed more economically productive than economic democracy.[20] As a result, while respecting democratic equality, basic rights, and sufficient protection against domination, such a system would also help generate desirable distributive benefits overall—for example, through larger tax revenues increasing the state's capacity to fund important social services such as health care and education. In this case, there could be legitimate reasons to abstain from devoting resources toward workplace democratization (even if some want it)—for example, to maximize the situation of the least advantaged in society.

Hence, the "parallel case" argument is insufficient to justify any particular form of workplace democracy. One needs to demonstrate that the negative-freedom restrictions and eventual economic costs of such a proposal are necessary to realize the benefits of economic democratization, and that such benefits outweigh the claims of those who may gain from a system tolerating the existence of undemocratic, investor-owned firms.

2. Delivering Democratic Benefits

The framework above does not mean that workplace democracy cannot be justified. Indeed, restricting everyone's negative freedom of market contracting and regulating firms is often necessary to achieve democratic and distributive goals. Reviewing arguments in favor of democratic workplaces, Ferreras argues that "governments worthy of that name [should] meet the three basic conditions for just rule: being legitimate, reasonable, and intelligent."[21] Indeed, democratic firms could lead to more legitimate government by reducing domination, which would also favor distributive fairness.[22] They could foster more reasonable government by facilitating deliberation.[23] And they could lead to more intelligent government by unlocking the epistemic benefits of democratic decision-making, thus producing better-informed decisions.[24]

These arguments might succeed in justifying workplace democratization in general. Yet, they may not suffice to justify economic bicameralism in particular. While economic bicameralism proposes to balance the interests of capital owners and workers by recognizing "equality between capital and labor, providing both of them with equal power and equal political rights through their respective chambers," this may not be the most effective option to deliver democratic benefits compared to alternatives such as worker cooperatives or codetermination.[25]

(a) Legitimate Government by Reducing Power Inequalities

Democratic decision-making improves the legitimacy of decisions by representing all those affected and by forcing fairer bargaining between the interests at play. At the state level, constitutional democracies achieve this by combining constitutional rights, democratic representation, and other checks and balances to prevent both the tyranny of one and of the majority. This enables trust in public decisions by reducing power inequality and comforting everyone that no one has the power to unfairly impose their will on others.[26] In workplaces, forms of democracy can be justified along similar lines, to promote republican freedom from domination and to limit power inequalities between capital owners and workers.[27]

A quick look at existing firms might suggest that the organizational form best able to avoid power inequalities between capital owners and workers is one in which there are no external investors and the capital is owned by the workers themselves. Worker cooperatives fit this description. Worker-owners are entirely in control of the capital and decisions within their firm. Given adequate institutional design, this can significantly reduce domination at work. Moreover, giving workers full control over compensation decisions might create distributive benefits by reducing inequalities of income and wealth within firms.[28] Even in cases where significant inequalities in wages and capital ownership are allowed within worker cooperatives, a "one worker, one vote" rule can prevent such inequalities from translating into domination. In fact, worker cooperatives such as the ones belonging to the Mondragon Corporation (in Spain's Basque region), share similarities with bicameralism: the government council elected by the general assembly represents members' interest as investors, while social councils represent their interests as workers (although, consistent with today's political bicameralism, the same worker-members are represented by both types of "chambers").[29]

Instead of assigning both capital ownership and decision-making power entirely to workers, as in worker cooperatives, Ferreras's bicameralism takes as a starting point the dominant reality, in which nonworker ("external") investors own the capital. In keeping with early bicameral models at the state level, the goal is to improve the legitimacy of firm-level decisions by forcing a new and improved compromise between capital owners and workers. One problem is that, in most cases, investors have easier exit options than workers. While investors can almost costlessly invest elsewhere or sit on their capital, low-skilled workers must work and often have few alternative options. Thus, giving workers a formal voice over firm-level decisions may amount to an illusion, as it is insufficient to grant them any real bargaining power if capital owners can more credibly threaten to withdraw investments whenever they disagree with workers' preferences. This means that investors maintain stronger bargaining power. Thus, bicameralism appears to be worse than cooperatives at avoiding domination by capital owners.

Similarly, there is evidence that capital mobility creates power imbalances at the state level, too. Despite democratic governments giving a formal voice to all citizens, they cannot effectively tax the wealthy and have to reduce tax rates on mobile factors.[30] The problem is that capital owners, contrary to ordinary citizens, are free to move their wealth abroad and can do so relatively easily. Tom Malleson explains how the wealthy have frequently threatened states through powerful "capital strikes," forcing them to overturn democratic decisions.[31] This power imbalance partly explains the sharp decline of tax rates on corporate profits and capital gains in most countries in the past decades.[32] Interestingly, one condition for the historical success of early bicameral experiments in England may have been that lords enjoyed less mobility.

Firm-level codetermination models face similar problems as bicameralism. Investors remain in control of their investment decisions, and workers typically have only a minority of votes on the board, limiting workers' bargaining power. Recent empirical evidence suggests that

> from workers' perspectives, the introduction of codetermination in an individual firm results in either zero or very small positive effects on wage . . . typically, workers are either granted a minority share of the seats on their company's board, meaning they can always be overruled by unanimous shareholders, or they are given the right to form a shop-floor representative body with few substantive decision-making rights.[33]

In a nutshell, it seems that asymmetries in the credibility of threats between capital owners and workers rank both bicameralism and codetermination lower than worker cooperatives regarding their capacity to produce legitimate government and reduce domination.

(b) Reasonable Government by Fostering Deliberation

A second benefit of democratic decision-making consists in fostering reasonable solutions through deliberation between people (or groups) with different values and interests. This goes beyond considerations of bargaining power discussed above. The point is that institutions forcing deliberation also foster learning and mutual understanding, in some cases leading actors to change perspective. Instead of a compromise reached merely by mutual threats—including threats to leave—a consensus can be built on what is deemed fair and reasonable for all.[34] While some empirical literature suggests that deliberation could sometimes increase the polarization of opinions rather than bring people closer to a consensus, the hope is that adequate institutional design can foster some deliberative benefits.[35]

In the workplace, one organizational form fostering deliberation between representatives of capital owners and workers is the unicameral codetermination model, which usually brings together a majority of capital representatives and a minority of worker representatives on the same board of directors.[36] While codetermination faces the same problem as bicameralism regarding bargaining power imbalances, and while worker representatives are often a minority on the board, codetermination at least opens the opportunity for a true dialogue between representatives of capital owners and representatives of workers. They are all forced to take part in the same deliberative chamber, which makes it difficult to avoid listening to the other party. In the spirit of stakeholder capitalism, it would even be conceivable to add representatives of consumers and other stakeholders to the same board, institutionally guaranteeing the presence of a larger set of perspectives than the ones of capital owners and workers.[37]

Similarly, in state-level bicameral regimes, each chamber represents the whole population but in different configurations, and significantly different perspectives are expected to enter into dialogue in *each* chamber. A decision accepted in both chambers may seem more legitimate: a majority of representatives of the same population in two alternative configurations voted for it, reducing the risks of path dependency bias associated with a single configuration.

Instead, Ferreras's workplace bicameralism keeps capital owners and workers in *separate* chambers, which means that each chamber represents monolithic but divergent interests, with no institutional guarantee that deliberation will improve the legitimacy or quality of decisions. As she explains, the policy statement of newly appointed executives would need to obtain a majority vote in each chamber separately, giving a veto to each chamber.[38] Ferreras hopes that both chambers will meet together to deliberate and will be willing to hear each other out, since they both share an interest in the productivity of their firm.[39] Yet, her bicameral setting is not the one that renders such an essential dialogue most likely. Members of each chamber may stand firmly by their position and exercise their bargaining power to extract as much as they can for themselves. Both worker cooperatives and unicameral codetermination, which force representatives of capital owners to sit together with worker representatives, are in stronger positions to deliver the benefits generally associated with effective deliberation across the stakes.

(c) Intelligent Government by Unlocking Epistemic Benefits

A third benefit of democratic decision-making is that it can lead to more intelligent government by helping crucial information reach decision-makers more easily. This can lead to better-informed decisions and more effective policies.[40] In workplaces, any democratic reform can foster wiser and better-informed decisions by balancing the instrumental rationality of investors with the expressive rationality and knowledge of workers.[41] Indeed, democratic firms involving a variety of stakeholders would help to identify the concerns and interests of each group and to gather the information they have on the firm's operations. While capital owners or managers may have a better understanding of the market and competitive pressures on the firm, workers have a better understanding of shop-floor productive processes and organizational unfairness or inefficiencies. Bringing in everyone's knowledge and perspectives to the decision-making process is therefore valuable to improve workers' well-being as well as economic productivity.

To conclude, while all three models, including economic bicameralism, can deliver epistemic benefits to some degree, codetermination better fosters deliberation between capital and labor, and worker cooperatives better secure legitimate government and non-domination.

3. Three Economic Costs of Bicameralism

To arguments showing that alternative models of democratic firms can better deliver desired democratic benefits in ideal circumstances, one could object that bicameral firms are better in nonideal circumstances, where capital owners are already in a position of power in the economy. Based on historical developments in democratic representation, Ferreras argues that bicameralism would be a necessary transitional moment toward fully fledged democracy.

Indeed, state-level bicameralism arose in Europe in periods of transition from despotism to more democratic governments. The bicameral moment can be interpreted as a step toward this goal. In the English case, for example, the initial Upper House was partially reformed later so that some seats were no longer hereditary. Similarly, Ferreras underlines that the current power of capital owners is such that economic democratization cannot happen overnight. Hence, an initial compromise between capital owners and workers—each being given a chamber with equal power—might be seen as a more feasible step, acceptable to the current forces at play.[42] While underdelivering democratic benefits, economic bicameralism might be better at paving the way toward more comprehensive worker control in the future.

This transitional case assumes that economic bicameralism can sufficiently serve the interests of both capital and labor, to attract both investors and workers and to serve as a credible compromise. This not only depends on bicameral firms' capacity to deliver democratic benefits to workers, as discussed previously, but also on their capacity to avoid severe economic costs that could affect the economic productivity of the model. If bicameral firms face more severe economic costs than codetermination or worker cooperatives, this would undermine bicameral firms not only as an ultimate goal but also as a credible transitional option.

To be clear, the achievement of democratic and distributive goals such as improving positive and republican freedom for all may well take priority over economic productivity, which only has instrumental value. As long as democratic firms remain sufficiently productive to create decent jobs for their workers and to contribute to a productive economic system able to sustain a strong welfare state, some productivity can be traded off against other desirable goals.[43]

Moreover, democratic firms are not necessarily unproductive. While employee-owned firms usually face higher costs of raising capital and decision-making than investor-owned firms,[44] they can mitigate these costs through representative systems, higher employee motivation, and lower monitoring and agency costs.[45] Empirical evidence suggests that, in favorable circumstances, democratic models such as worker cooperatives and codetermination can be just as productive as conventional investor-owned firms, if not more so.[46]

Yet, some kinds of democratic firms are likely to be more productive than others. If economic-democratization proposals are to gather support and be considered credible, their relative productivity should be considered. Therefore, after comparing the relative capacity of worker cooperatives, codetermination, and bicameralism to generate democratic benefits, it is worth comparing the expected economic costs that these different models are likely to face. Arguably, if bicameral firms give workers substantial power over firm-level decisions, by giving both investors' and workers' chambers a veto, then they are likely to face higher costs than other democratic firms.[47] There are three reasons for this.

First, the cost of raising capital is likely to be lower in investor-owned firms than in employee-owned firms.[48] This is because investor-owned firms can attract external equity capital at a lower cost by giving control of the firm to investors—thus minimizing moral hazard—and without the need to pay any dividend until they show profits. By contrast, employee-owned firms often need to get their capital from debt financing. This leads to higher costs than equity financing because, as Henry Hansmann explains, "to avoid opportunism and moral hazard, debt financing is typically inflexible, requiring payment of interests and principal when due."[49]

While this is a challenge facing all democratic firms, worker cooperatives have an advantage over bicameralism. They do not rely on equity capital at all, only debt, which may be more costly but remains feasible in many contexts (especially when investing in non-firm-specific assets). Moreover, they can build up capital by relying on capital contributions from worker-members or even affiliated cooperative banks.[50] By contrast, the bicameral model still depends on attracting equity capital, which raises the problem of moral hazard. In a transition context in which various alternatives will coexist, investors may be reluctant to buy shares in a firm that gives significant power to workers. This could make it more costly, if not impossible, for bicameral firms to attract equity capital. Of course, this is only based on theories of transaction costs and some evidence about existing organizational models.[51] Since no bicameral firm has ever existed, future empirical evidence would be needed to confirm this argument.

Second, the cost of collective decision-making is likely to be lower in investor-controlled firms because of a higher homogeneity of investors' interests. By contrast, in employee-controlled firms, workers have more heterogeneous interests. For example, they may have different preferences for income or leisure, or have a stake in which plants to close or which processes to automate. Older employees closer to retirement, who may have more capital invested in the firm, may also prefer that more of the firm's earnings be invested in their pension funds while younger employees may prefer higher wages. Disagreement among decision-makers can result in conflicts, and mechanisms for resolving them can be costly because of time wasted, inefficient compromises, and opportunities for managerial malfeasance.[52]

While this is, again, a challenge facing all democratic firms, worker cooperatives can produce democratic benefits while reducing decision-making costs through democratic representation and promoting homogeneity of interest among members, compared to alternative forms of democratic firms.[53] By contrast, Ferreras's bicameral model involves the interests of both capital owners and workers, which are harder to reconcile. The decision mechanisms envisioned in this model—giving a veto to both chambers—seem likely to lead to costly gridlocks.

Third, agency costs derive from the need for principals (typically capital owners) to monitor agents (executives) to ensure that they act fully in accordance with the firm's interest and to avoid managerial opportunism. Agency costs are acute in investor-owned firms because investors are often widely dispersed. This requires mechanisms to exercise control over managers—for example, by tying their compensation to the firm's performance, which is costly. Interestingly, employees in worker cooperatives, being on site, are in a much stronger position to monitor managers and hold them accountable.[54] Yet, agency costs seem likely to be lower in both investor-owned and worker-owned firms, where managers are accountable to only one class of patrons, than in bicameral firms, where they are accountable to both at the same time.

Indeed, making executives accountable to more than one class of patrons makes it more difficult to monitor managers effectively and to align their interests with the ones of the patrons. Multi-fiduciary obligations allow for managerial opportunism and malfeasance. As Joseph Heath argues, when managers are given multiple objectives to fulfill, it can generate "multitask" agency problems, which makes it difficult to assess managerial performance:

> When managers are given two objectives that are not strictly complementary (such as making a profit *and* promoting domestic industry), they are essentially being freed from the obligation to do their best with respect to either. When asked to explain their failure to achieve one objective, they can point to the constraints imposed by the other, and it is essentially impossible for an observer to determine whether the manager has in fact made the best effort, or chosen the best policies.[55]

The problem is not that managers are unable to multitask but that self-serving managers in bicameral firms could intentionally play the interests of one chamber against the other in order to justify their decisions. This would render elusive the task of evaluating whether managers are actually doing their best to serve the interests of both investors and workers.[56] To prevent opportunism, bicameral firms would likely need to implement costly supervision mechanisms and incentive structures, raising agency costs. This would affect not only current investors but also would-be investors, who might factor in the risk of higher agency costs in their investment decisions, thus aggravating the cost of raising capital.[57]

To conclude, while all kinds of democratic firms face a variety of costs, some models can compensate for some of these costs in various ways, which can sustain our optimism about the productivity of some democratic firms. However, while all forms of democratic firms can produce desirable democratic benefits, worker cooperatives or codetermination involve fewer economic costs than bicameral firms. This is a reason to prefer worker cooperatives and codetermination over bicameralism. Indeed, in the case of bicameral firms, the conjunction of higher costs of raising capital, higher costs of decision-making, and higher agency costs appears likely to impair their productivity. This suggests that alternatives like codetermination and worker cooperatives are preferable, even as transitional options in nonideal circumstances.

Conclusion

While there may be a strong case for workplace democracy—in terms of its capacity to protect workers from domination in workplaces, improve deliberation, and generate epistemic benefits—bicameral firms may not be the best organizational form to deliver such benefits. Worker cooperatives are more suited to reduce domination and power inequalities at work. Codetermination is better suited to fostering deliberation and reasonable agreements between capital investors and workers. Moreover, both alternatives seem likely to be more productive compared to bicameral firms, which involve higher costs of contracting capital, higher costs of decision-making, and higher agency costs. Therefore, while the bicameral-firm model may provide us with still another interesting option, the balance of democratic benefits and economic costs seems to point toward alternative forms of workplace democracy.

9

Learning from Cooperatives to Strengthen Economic Bicameralism

Simon Pek

Isabelle Ferreras's excellent anchor chapter makes a compelling case for economic bicameralism. Bicameral firms give meaningful voice to labor investors and, in so doing, can help firms tackle a host of pressing social and environmental issues like climate change and inequality. Additionally, they can serve as a powerful intermediate step in the transition from capital investor–owned firms to worker cooperatives, which she views as a regulative ideal.

In light of these benefits, there is much to like about Ferreras's proposal. At the same time, I believe there are some specific ways in which bicameral firms could be strengthened to augment both of these benefits. In this article, inspired by Ferreras's identification of worker cooperatives as a regulative ideal, I seek to identify insights from research and practice on the governance of traditional worker cooperatives, multi-stakeholder cooperatives, and union cooperatives, with the ultimate aim of identifying potential improvements and refinements to the proposal of economic bicameralism. Ultimately, I identify three core refinements: (a) increasing the opportunities for labor investors to participate in firm governance and hold their representatives to account, (b) creating robust channels for other nonlabor stakeholders to influence firm decision-making, and (c) carefully delineating the role of labor unions vis-à-vis the chamber of representatives of the labor investors. All of these refinements are feasible and tailored to the unique features of the proposed bicameral firm, particularly its granting of formal decision-making authority to representatives of both labor and capital investors. As I elaborate below, these refinements strengthen economic bicameralism in different ways. Collectively, they will make bicameral firms more responsive to labor investors' and other stakeholders' needs, while also increasing the likelihood that those bicameral firms that are interested in transitioning into worker cooperatives are able to successfully do so by granting labor investors additional opportunities to develop their governance skills.

This chapter is structured in three main sections, each of which focuses on one of the abovementioned types of cooperatives, followed by a brief conclusion.

Learning from Worker Cooperatives: Strengthening Labor Investors' Participation and Control

I begin by discussing potential learnings from traditional worker cooperatives. In Ferreras's proposal, the primary way in which labor investors, as one of the firm's two core constituencies, participate in decision-making is through electing representatives to negotiate and deliberate on their behalf with representatives of capital investors. While no doubt a major improvement over investor-owned firms, this proposal could go further in terms of creating opportunities for labor investors to participate in firm decision-making more actively and hold their representatives to account more effectively. Research on worker cooperatives suggests that there is the risk that power may become centralized in an oligarchic manner, particularly when elections are used as the primary method to select representatives.[1] Worker representatives are not always descriptively representative of the broader workforce and may not be responsive to the diverse needs of the broader membership, including those of racial minorities (see Sanjay's Pinto's essay in this volume).[2] Furthermore, despite their synergies, representative and direct-voice structures are fundamentally distinct, and having access to the former does not mean that workers have access to the latter.[3] There is, therefore, the risk that labor investors who have access only to representative voice structures may lack the ability to influence decision-making in a more regular and unmediated way. What can we learn from worker cooperatives about fostering greater accountability and labor investor participation?

Member Participation in Worker Cooperatives

As the ultimate owners of their cooperatives, worker members are often afforded a wide range of opportunities to shape decision-making. Beyond their role in representative structures, whether as candidates or electors, members often have the opportunity to directly participate in cooperative decision-making in general assemblies. For instance, in individual worker cooperatives that comprise the Mondragon Corporation, the General Assembly is among the central governance organs—"the supreme authority expressing the social will of all the members."[4] It has responsibilities that include selecting workers' representatives on the governing council, approving major strategic plans, and, in some cases, considering a broader range of decisions.[5] Worker members have the power to call for an extraordinary general meeting to discuss decisions made by the governing council and, if necessary, to elect a new one.[6] Yet, as with their representative structures, direct structures for member participation face important challenges. The level of member participation in annual general meetings tends to be low.[7] Among those who attend, critical and informed engagement on the part of attendees is often lacking.[8]

Many worker cooperatives and researchers studying worker cooperatives have thus put a major emphasis on identifying practices and interventions to foster greater member participation and influence in the governance of their cooperatives. I highlight some salient examples here, though the literature is vast and practices vary widely across cooperatives. When it comes to increasing participation in general meetings, these include provision of token financial rewards and minimum attendance requirements to maintain membership.[9] When it comes to increasing members' ability to hold their representatives accountable, they can implement and promote recall mechanisms and carve out time in general assemblies for critical self-reflection.[10] More generally, they can pay careful attention to the cultivation and maintenance of a supportive organizational culture, disseminate information widely to members while ensuring members have the capacity to interpret it, reduce power and skill asymmetries through practices like job and task rotation, and create new opportunities for participation in decision-making like the mini-councils used in some of Mondragon's cooperatives and deliberative mini-publics, which are receiving increased attention in the context of cooperatives.[11]

Implications for Economic Bicameralism

We can draw important implications from these practices and experiences for the design of bicameral firms that will increase labor members' opportunities to meaningfully shape firm decision-making and develop their governance skills. In a general sense, they point to the importance of paying careful attention to how labor investors will be able to participate in decision-making and hold to account their representatives in the labor investors' chamber of representatives. When it comes to participation, bicameral firms should include extensive opportunities for labor investors to meet and deliberate together about their shared concerns and interests, to be able to provide more inclusive and refined input to their representatives and cultivate a sense of solidarity. While these interactions could take place in regular general assemblies for the entire workforce, they could also take place in various topic-specific working groups and committees or in department-wide subcommittees. Opportunities for labor investors to deliberate online through platforms like Loomio would be particularly helpful for larger and more geographically dispersed bicameral firms.[12] Bicameral firms should also consider granting labor investors the opportunity to ratify major decisions made by their representatives, such as major strategic reorientations and changes to labor policies. In terms of enabling labor investors to hold their representatives to account, bicameral firms should provide opportunities for labor investors to recall their representatives, receive comprehensive updates about their representatives' deliberations and decision-making processes, and engage in dialogue with their representatives in case labor investors wish to receive an account and explanation of certain decisions. Additionally, it will be crucial for bicameral firms to prioritize the development of an inclusive and democratic culture among labor investors, offer training and support for labor investors to better engage in firm-level decision-making, disseminate information widely and accessibly, and pay careful attention to inequalities and power asymmetries among labor investors.

Learning from Multi-stakeholder Cooperatives:
A More Prominent Role for Other Stakeholders

How should bicameral firms engage with nonlabor and non-capital-investor stakeholders like local communities, suppliers, and customers? To consider this, I now turn to identifying potential learnings from multi-stakeholder cooperatives. Ferreras's current proposal focuses on two crucial constituencies—labor and capital—which stakeholder theorists view as stakeholders of the firm.[13] While the debate over which stakeholders ought to be prioritized remains unsettled (see David Ellerman's and Marc Fleurbaey's contributions to this volume), there is no doubt that bicameral firms—like any other firms—will affect and be affected by a wide range of other stakeholders. Ferreras acknowledges this, arguing that they can channel their claims in three ways: shaping the context in which firms operate through the broader democratic process, shaping firm policy through having their concerns raised by labor investors (who are expected to have more regular and deeper connection with a variety of stakeholders), and shaping firm decisions through participation in consultation schemes. All three have important merits but also come with limitations.

First, in terms of stakeholder-interest protection through regulations, one conceptualization of the role of governments in stakeholder theory focuses on how they can use their regulatory and enforcement powers to create a "framework" that, ideally, fosters an environment for responsible conduct on the part of firms and stakeholders.[14] While this role has merits, including the ability to leverage governments' unique enforcement powers, Nicolas Dahan and colleagues highlight two important limitations.[15] The first is that governments' powers are jurisdictionally circumscribed, resulting in firms being able to shift their business activities to more favorable contexts. These jurisdictions may be less interested in or able to provide the same protections for stakeholders.[16] The second is that firms may also engage in lobbying or other forms of political influence to shape the nature of regulations and enforcement mechanisms for their own benefit. Beyond its more direct effects on regulations and, by extension, the extent to which stakeholders' interests can be protected, such actions can have major repercussions on the broader democratic system, including reducing citizens' voice in societal deliberations and their influence in policymaking.[17] To these two limitations we can add the risk that governments' increased adoption of this role may result in firms reducing their sense of responsibility for addressing stakeholders' interests over time.[18] Overall, while governments (particularly more responsive ones) will likely be able to help some other stakeholders advance their interests, this channel is unlikely to be sufficient and consistently effective.

Second, while labor investors may at times advocate for other stakeholders' interests or share those same interests, this should not be assumed. Research suggests that members of worker cooperatives do not always take into account broader social issues when making decisions. Camila Piñeiro Harnecker's study of Venezuelan worker cooperatives highlights that, despite expectations that workers in cooperatives would internalize the interests of the communities within which they are embedded, the workers are not necessarily aware of these broader interests, do not necessarily internalize those interests, and do not necessarily advocate for them even if they do internalize them.[19] This concern is echoed in other research on worker cooperatives, particularly on Mondragon, where scholars have documented how concerns about efficiency have threatened key social values.[20] In terms of labor advocacy through unions, in the context of the former Canadian Auto Workers union, their advocacy for the greater production and sale of personal transport vehicles was counter to the interests of other stakeholders, notably environmentalists and supporters of public transport.[21] Thus, we cannot expect that labor investors in a bicameral firm will be reliable and consistent advocates for other stakeholders' interests.

Finally, bicameral firms' establishment of consultative bodies to engage with stakeholders is a very important step, particularly when the previous two approaches fail to live up to their potential. At the same time, granting them merely a consultative role may leave their interests insufficiently protected while denying the firm access to important benefits. While labor investors undoubtedly have a strong claim for involvement in firm decision-making, in some circumstances other stakeholders may also. For instance, Jeffrey Moriarty points out that some of the core arguments used to advocate for employee participation in firm decision-making—for instance, that it is crucial for protecting employees' interests and promoting their autonomy—can often apply to other stakeholders, too.[22] He provides the example of a local community heavily dependent on a major local employer; the community may have more at stake than some employees, particularly those who have good job prospects elsewhere. While this debate is very much unresolved, even if we were to assume that labor investors' investments and claims are greater than those of other stakeholders, it is important to consider whether granting other stakeholders more formal participation in firm governance is attainable and worthwhile.

One approach to doing so that is rare in practice but has received attention from researchers for some time entails placing representatives from a broader array of stakeholder groups onto corporate boards. An overarching argument for such stakeholder representation is that it allows for greater consideration and balancing of stakeholders' interests.[23] It can also have important benefits for firms, including increasing stakeholders' commitment.[24] An argument gaining increasing attention draws on the notion of property rights. Stakeholders, including employees, often provide firms with valuable firm-specific investments (e.g., a supplier co-locating with one of its customers or purchasing highly customized production systems) that would be costly to reinvest elsewhere.[25] While these investments can be very valuable for firms, stakeholders may be less willing to provide them as they are difficult to fully protect through explicit contracts.[26] Granting these stakeholders formal involvement in firm governance can be a powerful way of reducing this concern.[27] At the same time, the presence of multiple stakeholder representatives on boards can impose important costs, including intra- and inter-stakeholder conflict, delayed decision-making, and reduced responsiveness.[28] Despite these arguments, empirical research on the benefits of stakeholder representation is very limited and inconclusive.[29] Research on the effects of outside directors—which may in some cases be stakeholder representatives—finds a positive relationship with corporate social responsibility performance.[30] More research is clearly needed on this this topic.

The Governance of Multi-Stakeholder Cooperatives

Let us now turn to research on multi-stakeholder cooperatives to identify potential refinements for economic bicameralism. Multi-stakeholder cooperatives are gaining increased research and practitioner interest, particularly in Québec and Italy.[31] Traditionally, cooperatives have been centered on a single category of members who own, control, and benefit from the cooperative.[32] Multi-stakeholder cooperatives, in contrast, involve multiple categories of members (typically between two and eight) who share the same mission but do not necessarily have the same interests.[33] While it is difficult to attribute this growing interest to a single cause, promising candidates include growing concerns about meeting the needs of a broader range of stakeholders, the ability to access more capital and resources, and a desire to overcome the limitations of pure forms of producer and worker cooperatives.[34]

In multi-stakeholder cooperatives, crucial decisions include which stakeholders should be a member, how the cooperative will be governed, and how surpluses are to be allocated.[35] In terms of who can be a member, the list of potential stakeholders is long, and choices vary across organizations and contexts. Margaret Lund grouped potential members into three categories: cooperative users (e.g., consumers, producers, institutional purchasers, distributors); producers (e.g., workers, professional employees); and support members (e.g., community members, investor members).[36] Different jurisdictions may emphasize different stakeholders. Québec, for instance, allows for up to a third of board seats to be granted to a category of stakeholder called "supporting members."[37] In terms of their governance, as with single-stakeholder cooperatives, a common approach is to follow a "one member, one vote" principle, with a twist, in that each member from each stakeholder group votes for a predefined number of seats.[38] In terms of allocating their surplus, approaches vary widely, and as with governance rights, these decisions are made democratically by the cooperative. Weaver Street Market, a retail multi-stakeholder cooperative in North Carolina, as an example, distributes the surplus to worker-members based on the number of hours worked.[39]

Multi-stakeholder cooperatives have many important benefits relevant to economic bicameralism. One broad category of benefits relates to how they can foster greater attention to relevant stakeholders' needs. They "offer potential for broadening democratic voice beyond the immediate member-users of cooperatives," enabling them to address a broader range of social and environmental issues.[40] They are premised on a longer-term horizon: "Multi-stakeholder cooperators are not interested in single transaction or even season of transactions, but rather in building a long term relationship based upon on a stable foundation of fair pricing, fair wages and fair treatment for all parties."[41] This focus on the development of longer-term networks of relationships can be a critical source of these cooperatives' resilience.[42] They can be particularly useful in helping address the interests of traditionally marginalized and excluded stakeholders in a manner that can "product a social surplus that goes beyond the simple sum of the parts."[43] At a minimum, including a broader array of stakeholders can serve as a signal that "embod[ies] and formalize[s] their desire to include the community in their collective project and to reaffirm their commitment toward their community."[44]

The second broad category pertains to more instrumental benefits. Bringing together a broad range of interests can help generate greater social capital and increase access to diverse information sources, while also reducing the costs associated with managing market transactions.[45] Formal inclusion in governance systems can encourage stakeholders to make a range of contributions to the broader cooperative. For instance, in Québec's multi-stakeholder cooperatives, those who support the cooperative and its social mission can provide a variety of resources, including volunteer work, materials, access to their networks, and financial investments (which, when totaled, can be significant) without receiving the same direct benefits that user-members would.[46] Multi-stakeholder cooperatives' governance structures also help proactively address the disagreements among stakeholders and foster closer ties to them.[47]

Despite these benefits, scholars and practitioners have emphasized that multi-stakeholder cooperatives come with important challenges that warrant attention. Perhaps the most oft-repeated concern relates to the increased complexities and transaction costs that accompany efforts to reconcile the diverse perspectives of multiple stakeholders.[48] Multi-stakeholder cooperatives create new areas for potential conflict, including how to distribute surpluses, who ought to be a member, how the cooperative ought to be governed, and what objectives should be prioritized.[49] This conflict, though, need not be a fair fight, as it is possible for a single class of members to dominate decision-making due to their greater power and access to information.[50] These challenges can become more salient as multi-stakeholder cooperatives grow and age.[51]

While these are important challenges, Catherine Leviten-Reid and Brett Fairbairn's review of the research finds that many multi-stakeholder cooperatives are able to avoid them and achieve effective and democratic governance.[52] Practices that can help mitigate these risks include the creation of spaces and processes for deliberation among different stakeholder representatives, development of clear decision-making processes, dissemination of information widely and in an accessible manner, maintenance of a focus on the overall objectives of the cooperative, and commitment to continuous learning and improvement.[53]

Implications for Economic Bicameralism

Our brief foray into the still relatively nascent literature on multistakeholder cooperatives suggests that such governance structures are becoming increasingly common, that they can have important benefits for both stakeholders and the cooperative, and that their costs and challenges can be surmounted. Collectively, these insights indicate that bicameral firms would benefit from going beyond consultative bodies to granting nonlabor and noncapital investor stakeholders more comprehensive opportunities to shape firm decision-making. There is a range of ways in which this could be accomplished as part of Ferreras's model, each with their pros and cons. First, either the labor or the capital chamber of representatives could be broadened to include representatives from other stakeholder groups. This approach would likely come with the greatest potential transaction costs and would inevitably grant the remaining chamber with only one stakeholder group (labor or capital investors) disproportionate influence over firm decision-making, which goes against economic bicameralism's emphasis on parity between these two constituencies. At the same time, it would grant other stakeholders an institutionalized means to influence firm decision-making within the existing bicameral model.

Second, bicameral firms could adopt a tricameral system of governance, whereby a third chamber representing nonlabor and noncapital stakeholders would be created to complement the two existing chambers (see Fleurbaey in this volume). Depending on the circumstances, it could have the same power as the two existing chambers, requiring a majority of representatives from all three chambers to approve major firm policies, or it could be given a consultative role. As in the case of Hossam Zeitoun and colleagues' proposal for a second board composed of randomly selected stakeholder representatives, such a tricameral approach would offer other stakeholders broader protections, though without the same decision-making costs as might occur with multiple stakeholder representatives on a single board.[54]

Third, building on Ferreras's proposal of consultative bodies, bicameral firms could institute more formalized stakeholder advisory panels in which stakeholder representatives offer their advice or recommendations on a particular topic that the firm has committed to consider and respond to in some way.[55] The stakeholder panels of the French industrial manufacturer Lafarge provide one such model, whereby a select group of stakeholder representatives meets biannually with the CEO and executive committee to critically review the company's sustainability performance and to jointly develop an action plan that the company commits to carry out.[56] While this approach would grant other stakeholders less overall influence, it is less likely to generate significant increases in transaction costs. It is also the most straightforward approach for subsequent transitions to worker cooperatives.

Regardless of which approach bicameral firms adopt, it will be important for each bicameral firm to carefully reflect on which stakeholders ought to be prioritized in different ways, given limited resources and transaction costs. Bicameral firms could draw on various tools when approaching this vexing challenge with their particular context, including the stakeholder salience model and stakeholder mapping techniques.[57] Ultimately, granting a broader range of stakeholders— including local communities, suppliers, and customers—a role in firm governance will help ensure that bicameral firms operate in a manner that genuinely takes into account their concerns and interests, and will enable firm management to leverage the unique resources these stakeholders can bring to firm governance.

Learning from Union Cooperatives: A Clear Delineation of Responsibilities

Finally, I turn to the role of labor unions in the bicameral firm. Ferreras grants them an important place in her proposal, describing how they can perform a range of functions, including training labor investors to run for elections, collectively representing the interests of labor investors, helping foster deliberation among groups with competing interests within bicameral firms, and advocating for labor investors in the political realm. This portion of her proposal connects to a rich body of research on the relationship between labor unions and worker ownership.

At first glance, it may appear that both the worker cooperative and labor union movements would be natural allies. Marina Monaco and Luca Pastrorelli argue that despite some important differences and tensions, "both movements share similar historical roots, common values and aims, and a methodology based on dialogue and workers' involvement."[58] Indeed, during the nineteenth century, some unions, including the Knights of Labor, were strong advocates of worker cooperatives.[59] Yet the relationship between these two movements is complex.[60] It has at times been characterized by divergent approaches and limited mutual support stemming from the unions' desire to protect their own interests and core competencies, plus broader concerns that firm-level interventions might come at the expense of the broader labor movement (see Mackin and Rothstein in this volume). The recent growth in interest in union cooperatives from both movements, which is well illustrated by the commitment in 2009 of both Mondragon and the United Steelworkers to pursue them, shows promise in increasing mutual synergies between them.[61] Drawing on the small but growing body of research on this phenomenon, along with other conceptual work on the role of unions in worker-owned firms (notably Ellerman's analysis of the unions' or union-like bodies' role as a "legitimate opposition" in democratic firms), I seek to distill implications for Ferreras's model of the bicameral firm.[62]

The Dynamics of Worker Representation in Union Cooperatives

At their core, union cooperatives are "worker co-op[s] where at least some of the employees are represented by a union."[63] Examples include Cooperative Home Care Associates, a Bronx-based home care agency whose workers are represented by the Service Employees International Union.[64] While they can take on a range of different forms, they tend to take on a structure similar to traditional worker cooperatives—with a general assembly, board of directors, and management—with the addition of a labor union committee that is granted the authority to represent workers qua workers in domains including collective bargaining and handling grievances.[65]

Union cooperatives have several benefits. At their core, they can help overcome the challenges facing both movements: overall declines

in unionization and union bargaining power for labor unions, difficulties accessing resources and investment, difficulties scaling up, and
frequent negative perceptions of their viability for worker cooperatives.[66] Both cooperatives and labor unions can learn a lot from each
other's dominant logic.[67] For workers, despite being represented as
owners on the board of directors, they may lack robust representation as
workers, particularly in large worker cooperatives. In this way, union
representation can overcome the limitations of bodies such as
Mondragon's Social Council, which had only an advisory role that was
seen as insufficient by many workers.[68] While the need for unionization
in worker cooperatives may not be apparent, Carmen Huertas-Noble
notes:

> Conflicts between worker-owners and their selected management
> can mirror conflicts in other workplaces and conflicts may also arise
> among worker-owners in non-management roles. In one rarely
> occurring but conceivable example, individual worker-owners can
> lose their membership by a vote of a majority of other worker-owners
> and thus lose their ownership interest.[69]

Representation through a labor union can help ensure that workers'
interests are captured in collective bargaining agreements, rules and
terms of employment are transparent and applied fairly, and grievances
can be filed and resolved in a professional manner.[70] Additionally, it can
result in more productive conflict management and a more integrative
approach to bargaining.[71] Furthermore, union cooperatives have the
potential to increase overall solidarity between worker-owners and
broader struggles over labor rights and economic justice.[72] Finally, affil-
iation with labor unions can increase worker cooperatives' ability to
organize and can grant them access to crucial resources, including
support networks, political connections, and financing.[73]

At the same time, union cooperatives come with important challenges. First, there is the possibility that unionization may threaten the
autonomy of worker cooperatives. In contrast with worker cooperatives,
labor unions tend to be more centralized in order to gain power and
may use industry-wide master agreements to ensure consistency across
organizations.[74] Ultimately, this may threaten worker cooperatives' ability to make autonomous decisions, such as changing pay and benefits

to match their specific circumstances like periods of economic hardship.[75] Second, there is a risk that labor unions may inadvertently, or in some cases deliberately, come to dominate workers' governance structures, such as the board of directors. Union leaders may perceive other institutions of worker representation as a threat to them and their legitimacy.[76] This may give rise to the risk of "competition over labor representativity" or, in some situations, union attempts to dominate other representation bodies.[77] Alison Barnes and Craig MacMillan document how a union was able to secure over 85 percent of the positions on a nonunion employee representation body.[78] One participant in their study who serves as an elected, nonunion representative reflected:

> I probably felt more frustrated than constrained because I did feel as though it was union dominated, and I have nothing against unions . . .
> I just felt it was a very biased representation because it was union heavy and discussion was quite union focused.[79]

Third, there is a risk that the presence of unions and their leadership in collective bargaining may lead to antagonism.[80] This was among the most significant sources of tension when the potential role of unions was discussed at Mondragon.[81] Finally, there is a risk that labor unions may not adequately represent the diverse interests of the union membership, which is important to the success of unionized employee stock ownership plans.[82]

These challenges highlight the importance of carefully delineating the role and responsibilities of labor unions in worker cooperatives to avoid unintended consequences. Ariana Levinson makes a compelling case for the separation of powers between labor unions and the worker cooperative and the implementation of policies to avoid potential conflicts of interest.[83] The bankruptcy of the appliance manufacturer Fagor Electrodomésticos points to the problems that can arise when the roles and responsibilities of the Social Council vis-à-vis the Governing Council become blurred, notably delayed and less effective decision-making.[84] Importantly, the delineation of roles ought to take into account the broader interests of both movements to increase the likelihood that each one will be willing to support and collaborate with the other.[85]

Implications for Economic Bicameralism

In sum, the research on union cooperatives suggests that labor unions can make important contributions to bicameral firms (and would likely benefit from them in turn). At the same time, we must be sensitive to the importance of carefully delineating their roles and responsibilities so that the partnership will be as fruitful as possible. While a full analysis of what this delineation ought to look like in practice is beyond the scope of this chapter, I outline my main suggestions for what the role of unions in bicameral firms ought to be, which are somewhat more muted than those put forward by Ellerman and by Ferreras in her proposal.[86] I begin by highlighting two roles for labor unions that I see as congruent with Ferreras's proposal. First, unions should be deployed to provide consistent and high-quality training and education to labor investors and their representatives across bicameral firms about the broader labor movement, contemporary labor issues and trends, and how to exercise their democratic rights and responsibilities. As an example, they could organize workshops and dialogues about trends in pay, benefits, and grievances across firms in similar industries. Second, they should continue their crucial advocacy for workers' rights and promising initiatives like the bicameral firm in the political realm.

At the same time, I propose two modifications to Ferreras's proposal. First, in terms of the role of labor unions in collective labor investor representation, labor unions should not play a direct role in representing labor investors in formal negotiations or collective bargaining with the executive committee or capital investors. In a bicameral firm, particularly one with the robust participatory and accountability practices I discussed earlier, the labor investors' chamber of representatives would already be able to collect and synthesize the interests of labor investors and advocate for them as part of their broader representative role. The addition of a labor union as another form of collective interest representation for labor investors in this context would likely lead to antagonism and fracturing among labor investors and their representatives as they undertake their delicate work. If, as I suggested above, labor unions were to use their expertise in bringing forward robust information about contemporary pay and benefits trends in the industry, labor investors would be well placed to consider these as they channel their broader interests to their representatives for negotiations. Such a clear division of labor would also mean there would be a single entity that labor investors could hold accountable if they felt their interests were not sufficiently advocated for. At the same time, labor unions should be deployed to represent labor investors in grievances in order to ensure that the benefits, working conditions, and voice mechanisms they negotiated are respected. They are well suited for this role given their extensive expertise in this domain and their independence from both management and labor investors' representatives. Second, given my earlier arguments about the importance of empowering labor investors as a constituency and the risk that labor unions may inadvertently co-opt elections for worker representatives, to avoid unduly influencing the process, I do not think they should play a role in advocating for or providing special assistance to specific labor investors running for election. Providing this type of support to preferred labor investors may lead to a dynamic in which the interests of labor unions dominate the chamber of representatives of the labor investors, which may not be the same interests as those of labor investors. As noted above, though, they should be available to provide general education and training to all interested labor investors. Collectively, these refinements will enable labor investors to influence firm decision-making in a more streamlined and effective manner, while also providing labor investors in a particular firm with more direct opportunities to develop their governance skills.

Concluding Reflections

In this chapter, I explored the possibility of strengthening economic bicameralism by learning from research and practice on traditional worker cooperatives, multi-stakeholder cooperatives, and union cooperatives. Through this exercise, I identified three core sets of refinements: strengthening labor investors' opportunities to participate in firm governance and more effectively hold their representatives accountable; creating robust channels for nonlabor stakeholders to influence firm decision-making; and carefully delineating the role of labor unions vis-à-vis the labor investors' chamber of representatives. When taken together, I argue that these refinements will help strengthen bicameral firms' contributions to tackling pressing social and environmental issues by making them more responsive to labor investors and other stakeholders.

Additionally, for those bicameral firms interested in subsequent transitions into worker cooperatives, these refinements will increase the likelihood of successful transition by enabling labor investors to develop their governance skills in more ways. My hope is that these ideas will help spur further research, reflection, and experimentation on how economic bicameralism and other promising alternatives to capital investor–owned firms can be continuously refined and improved over time.

V.

Economic Democracy:
The Big Picture

10

The Prospects for Economic Democracy: Learning from Sweden as Failed Case

Bo Rothstein

When analyzing the prospects for some form of economic democracy in the current political situation, it may be useful to look back on failed attempts. Obvious cases include, of course, the policies of nationalization of industries and central planning of the economy; but since there exists today (for good reason) little enthusiasm for these two models, not much needs to be added. It should suffice to mention that one of the major and decisive defeats of the union movement in Europe, the 1984–1985 miners' strike in the United Kingdom, came against a state-owned industry. The complete failure of Soviet-style central planning of the economy has made that model of "economic democracy" outdated. More promising is, for example, the proposal launched by Isabelle Ferreras, summarized in the lead essay of this volume, to democratize corporations through a bicameral system, where employees and owners/shareholders would each have a chamber for governing the corporation.[1] It should, however, be noted that there already exist many other institutional frameworks for employees to establish democratic forms of governing the enterprises in which they work.[2] Companies that are owned and/or governed by their employees (through a cooperative, a stock option plan, or an employee trust) have been a subject of empirical study for almost four decades. Overall, the results seem quite clear.

Economically, such companies perform on average better than firms governed by outside capitalists/owners/investors, and they pay somewhat higher wages.[3] Studies also indicate that the combination of ownership and control is an important factor in increased productivity.[4] In addition, they have far less turnover of personnel, who are more satisfied with their working conditions.[5] In many cases, such companies are contributing to decreasing economic inequality because, in addition to their salaries, employees also benefit from the capital in the company, usually in the form of substantially higher pensions.[6] To this one can add research showing that people working in employee-owned cooperative firms tend to be more pro-democratic and civic oriented.[7] Given these positive results, the starting point for this chapter is a straightforward counterfactual question: Why has economic democracy in the form of employee-owned and/or -governed companies not been on the political agenda in Sweden? The reason for focusing on Sweden is that this is a country with the highest degree of union membership among the countries of the Organisation for Economic Co-operation and Development (OECD), with a world record in having the longest tenure of a social democratic party in government, and with strong cooperative traditions in sectors such as agriculture and housing. Yet the country has comparatively very few such employee-owned or -governed companies, and the issue of economic democracy has been "stone dead" in the political debate since the early 1980s.[8] According to a report from the European Union, Sweden has the fewest and weakest institutional devices in place for supporting employee ownership.[9] Moreover, there is no large and well-known employee-owned company in the country— such as the Mondragon conglomerate in Spain, the John Lewis company in the United Kingdom, or Publix in the United States—that can work as a showcase or model. Paradoxically, the Western country that in many aspects is the antithesis of Sweden, the US, has a much-larger proportion of its workforce working in companies where the employees are the majority owner or own a significant part of the shares. The approximately 7,000 companies with employee stock ownership plans (ESOPs) now employ about 10 percent of the workforce, and in more than 4,000 of those firms, the employees are the majority owners.[10] Moreover, the establishment of such companies is not a politically controversial matter since both the Democratic and Republican Parties support the ESOP model. It is thus a real puzzle why economic democracy has failed in Sweden. Below, I will present three answers. The first is the huge failure of the wage-earner funds model that was presented by the Swedish confederation of blue-collar unions (Landsorganisationen, or LO) in the late 1970s. The second concerns two major theoretical mistakes by the Marxist and social democratic left. And the third is the resistance from the union movement, especially the blue-collar unions.

The Failure of the Wage-Earner Funds Model for Economic Democracy

The well-organized and strong labor movement in Sweden has not always been silent about economic democracy. In the 1970s, the LO launched the idea of "wage-earner funds" as a model for establishing economic democracy. The original proposal was very radical indeed, suggesting that all large companies should be required by law to put 20 percent of their profits into union-controlled funds. While the plan was presented as a Swedish model for establishing economic democracy on a large scale, the origin of the idea behind the funds was to handle the problem of "excess profits" caused by the Swedish blue-collar unions' solidaristic wage policy. This wage policy was intended to keep the union movement united by refusing the idea that wages should be set by the profit levels of different corporations. Instead, similar jobs should get similar pay regardless of what the specific firms (or branches) could pay. This led to a situation where wages were comparatively low in very profitable firms.[11] Thus, it was argued that workers subsidized profits in these companies, and such profits were termed "excess profits" in the Swedish debate.[12] The wage-earner funds were meant to make it possible for unions to acquire control over this capital. This background is important to show that the original goal was not democracy at the workplace; rather, it was to solve the problem of "excess profits" caused by the unions' wage policy. After a decade of very intense political strife about this policy, a much watered-down version was implemented by a Social Democratic government in 1983. The funds were then abolished by a conservative-led administration in 1992, and the issue has never since returned to the agenda.[13] Even the word "fund" has become almost a forbidden term within the Social Democratic Party.[14]

The wage-earner funds differ from the more successful Social Democratic reforms (pensions, health care, schooling, sick leave, paid parental leave, etc.) in that they were not connected to any specified social rights for the individual and did not cater to citizens in general but to a specific, class-based segment of the population. Nor, contrary to earlier successful reforms, were they based on the principle of universalism.[15]

The implications for individual employees working in the companies where these union-controlled funds owned shares were never clear. An empirical study of how the funds operated showed that employee influence through shareholding in companies was insignificant.[16] It was also not obvious how the situation for the employees in the companies where the funds would have a considerable influence through ownership of shares would differ from that in the companies where the funds did not invest. And, as argued by Jon Elster, "from the point of view of promoting social justice, it seems perverse to give employee voting rights only to workers in firms which for some reason happen to be chosen as investment objects for the funds."[17]

No plan was presented as to the types of company or branches of industry in which the funds would become owners. Nor was there any connection with the individual wage-earner's economic situation: in the government committee that prepared the policy, the unions and the Social Democratic Party said no to any form of individual profit-sharing. It was also unclear what the funds would imply for the individual employee's prospects for influencing their working conditions.

Seen from an ideological perspective, the wage-earner funds were thus a very "un–Social Democratic" type of social reform. The policy would give central union officials ownership power, but it was never made clear what this power was going to be used for or how this would benefit ordinary members. From the perspective of income inequality and economic democracy, as well as from the huge amount of research about which types of social reform are likely to secure broad-based political support, the wage-earner funds were a particularly bad idea.

The wage-earner funds experience led to one of the most crushing defeats for the Swedish labor movement. The proposal managed to mobilize and unite the often-divided center-right parties in Sweden and to radicalize the employers' federation, as well as many other business organizations that had been keen on collaborating in various neo-corporatist arrangements with the unions and the state under Social Democratic leadership.[18] Moreover, the labor movement lost the battle for public opinion on this issue. When the wage-earner fund idea was introduced, about half of LO members supported the policy, but when they were established it was only one in four.[19] The ideological defeat over the wage-earner funds can thus be seen as the starting point for the end of the dominance of the Social Democratic Party in Swedish politics. In sum, the negative experience with the funds has unfortunately made economic democracy a "no go" area—not only for the Swedish Social Democrats but also likely for most social democratic parties in Europe—ever since.

The Left's Misunderstanding of Capitalism and Markets

If we define the "political left" in Sweden as radical social democrats, union activists, the Left Party (Vänsterpartiet), and leftist public intellectuals (including radical feminists and people challenging various forms of ethnic discrimination), very few have been engaged with issues concerning economic democracy. Surprisingly, the enormous increase in economic inequality that has occurred since the early 1980s in most OECD countries—and Sweden is one of those countries where inequality has increased the most—has also not been of much concern to the political left.[20] Yet, according to a recent study by a leading Swedish political scientist, inequality has reached a level where there is a clear threat to social cohesion.[21] A recent report from the Nordic Council shows that Sweden is now the most unequal country in the region.[22] This has occurred despite very strong unions, which makes the lack of interest of the political left in policies, such as employee ownership/control, that could work against this development quite surprising.[23]

A major mistake in the discussion about economic democracy is that the political left has confused markets with capitalism.[24] As shown by, for example, Fernand Braudel, the leading figure in the French Annales school of historians, markets are much older than capitalism and will in all likelihood remain when capitalism has faded away.[25] In short, markets and capitalism are two very different things.[26] Capitalism should be defined as an economic system where those who are in possession of the capital invested in a corporation also have the management *power* over the corporation. But—and this is very important—the right of the capital owners to have this management power cannot come from their ownership of capital. Instead, as developed by David Ellerman, it comes from the construction of the "renting contract":

When labour (= the workers) and capital (= the capital owners) meet
in the market-place, it is not legally preordained which way the rental
contract will be made. Capital may hire labour, labour may hire
capital or some third party may hire both labour and capital. The
direct control rights over the use of the capital and the labour in
production are determined by the direction of that rental contract—
by who hires what or whom."[27]

This *contract theory of power over the corporation* fundamentally changes
the parameters for establishing economic democracy. Not realizing the
importance of this logic has probably been the second most important
mistake by the socialist and Marxist left over the last hundred years.[28]
People who invest their pension money in state bonds do not as a consequence have ownership rights over the state—indeed they do not have
even a minimal right to command what the state is going to do.[29]

The policy that would follow from the contract theory of power over
production is that shares traded on the stock market, which give ownership over corporations, would first be transformed into bonds. Then, in
a radical (revolutionary) one-shot transformation, or in a more gradual,
reformist manner, seats on the board would be transferred to representatives of the employees, as I suggested in my first article about this
issue.[30] The company bonds would be traded and give a dividend related
to the firm's profit, and their value would thus be based on how the
market valued the economic situation of the corporation. But these
corporate bonds would not give their owners the right to have any
influence over the running of the company. Since a very large part of
today's capital invested in large corporations comes from pension and
mutual funds, this would not make any difference in practice to the
large majority of shareholders.[31] This is especially the case for the very
large and growing index funds that are now the largest owners of shares
in the Swedish and many other stock markets. These index funds are
explicitly eschewing the responsibilities of exercising corporate governance, thereby creating a "power vacuum" that should be filled by the
democratic representation of the workforce in the firm.

The logic of Ellerman's contract theory is easy to understand. When
a number of persons decide to start a business together and get a loan
from the bank, the bank, which is the owner of the capital used in the
firm, does not decide how they will operate their company. Capitalism

can and should be defined as a society where those who own (or control in the name of the owners) the capital of a firm exercise managerial power in the relations of production. According to Marx, the central source of power in a society is located in the relations of production, that is, who has the right to command in the work process; and this in turn comes from the ownership of the capital. If so, democratic social-ism cannot become a reality just by changing who these owners are (the state, the central planners, the unions, the pension funds, etc.). Instead, democratic socialism must logically be defined as the situation where those who work in a company democratically wield the *power* over the relations of production. Thus, we can rephrase the initial question to, "Why has social democracy not been able to establish liberal democratic socialism in Sweden?"

The left's critique of the market has often been based on the idea that markets are built on and will increase selfish, "economic man" behav-ior. The neoliberal right has argued that markets must be built on self-interest. However, in a large research project where anthropologists collaborated with economists, it was found that both of these dominant notions can be completely wrong.[32] These scholars organized experi-ments aimed at measuring whether people were willing to share a sum of money they were given with another person whom they did not know and would not interact with again. Many such experiments have been performed over the years, showing that people are generally far less selfish than the *Homo economicus* model assumed. But this inter-disciplinary project indicated a caveat. The experiment was conducted in fifteen small communities, some with Indigenous peoples, who lived off various forms of farming, livestock, fishing and hunting. The results were similar to those in industrialized Western countries: the hypothe-sis about the dominance of self-interest was not supported. Yet there were also quite-large differences between the various groups in terms of how much the individuals were willing to share with "the other." The researchers also measured the degree to which these groups were inte-grated into market relationships, by measuring how much of their food intake came from goods they bought from other groups. The result, quite surprising for several of the researchers (some with a strong Marxist orientation), was that the more market-integrated these groups were, the *less* selfish and the more generously they behaved in the experiment. Conversely, the more hierarchically (read: as a planned economy) production was organized, the more selfish the individuals proved.[33]

These results indicate that both the "left" and the "right" may have been wrong (for more than 150 years!) about what type of human behavior markets enhance or engender. Well-functioning markets are probably not as inherently associated with egoistic behavior, as both neoclassical and Marxist economic thinking have taken for granted. Already in 1972, the Nobel laureate in economics Kenneth Arrow wrote:

> Virtually every commercial transaction has within itself an element of trust, certainly any transaction conducted over a period of time. It can be plausibly argued that much of the economic backwardness in the world can be explained by the lack of mutual confidence.[34]

For any productive organization, be it private, cooperative, or public, internal trust turns out to be utterly important for efficiency.[35]

Unions against Economic Democracy

After the historic defeat in the battle over the wage-earner funds, the powerful LO went silent about economic democracy. However, in 2014, the LO asked the renowned Harvard labor economist Richard B. Freeman to write a report within the framework of its project, "Full Employment and Solidaristic Wage Policy." In this report, *Workers Ownership and Profit-Sharing in a New Capitalist Model?*, Freeman argued that to do something about the huge increase in economic inequality in Sweden (and most similar countries), unions needed new policy instruments. One such instrument would have employees derive income additionally from the capital in their firms, through various forms of ownership.[36] Freeman presented a very convincing argument that the best strategy for unions, now also facing decline in membership, was to take a lead in promoting this development. His arguments were built on much the same empirical sources as presented here, showing that such firms performed on average very well. However, when he presented the report to the LO, the LO chair, Karl-Petter Thorwaldsson, told him, "We are never going to do this."[37] As I have shown elsewhere, the Swedish union movement has no interest or organizational support when members want to buy a company or otherwise take full control over their workplaces.[38]

For his superb documentary about employee cooperatives, *Can We Do It Ourselves?*, Patrik Witkowsky and his collaborators interviewed researchers, public intellectuals, and individuals working in or managing cooperatives.[39] One interviewee was the chief economist at the LO, Ola Pettersson. When asked why union members who were seeking help to take over their enterprises and turn them into cooperatives received no help, he replied: "We do not have an organization that can respond to these initiatives, so I am not at all surprised about the answers that they got." He also stated that this issue was not at all on the LO agenda. Similarly, according to Svante Nycander, one of the most knowledgeable analysts of industrial relations in Sweden, when different forms of profit-sharing have been discussed, Swedish blue-collar unions have been opposed—one reason being that they feared their members would adopt a "capitalist mentality."[40]

Take the well-known Swedish car company Volvo. In 2008, the company was owned by Ford, which, because of its own economic problems, wanted to sell Volvo. The civil engineers' union at Volvo took an initiative to transform the company into an employee-owned corporation, forming a special consortium to organize the takeover.[41] However, the plan could not be realized, for several reasons. One was that the large public pension funds in Sweden—in which the unions have a considerable influence—refused to provide any credit. Another was that the blue-collar union at Volvo refused to support the idea. In both cases, the reason seems to have been that none of them had confidence in the idea that employees could manage a large corporation like Volvo.[42] Today, Volvo is owned by a Chinese capitalist with strong ties to the Communist Party, an organization not known for its internal democracy.[43]

One of the few large-scale profit-sharing plans in Sweden was introduced in one of the largest banks in Sweden (Svenska Handelsbanken) in 1973. The employee-controlled foundation is now the largest shareholder, and an employee retiring after three decades of work receives about $2 million: the amount is strictly related to how long the person has worked in the bank, regardless of whether they were a cleaner or the chief executive. When this scheme was introduced, the Swedish

Employers' Confederation was firmly against it—but so was the Swedish Union of Bank Employees (Banktjänstemannaförbundet).[44]

There are probably many reasons for this lack of interest in any form of employee-owned or -managed firms on the part of the comparatively strong Swedish union movement. Primarily, I suspect that it has not so much to do with ideology per se but, rather, stems from two somewhat different perspectives: *organizational interest* and *organizational learning*. The main idea of the former is that when forced to choose between strengthening the organization and striving to realize ideological goals, most organizations will prioritize their strength.[45] Unions in Sweden have built their strength on being skilled in playing the "adversarial negotiation game"—not only in wage negotiations but perhaps even more so in operating the large and complicated Swedish system of industrial-relations laws, of which they are a well-integrated component.[46] These laws are about codetermination, how to handle layoffs, employment protection, safety regulations, board representation, and so on.

Much of this power works as a "selective incentive" for employees to become union members. For example, if there will be layoffs and one knows union officials will have a considerable say in who has to go, one would do well to become a member. Also, if one runs into a serious conflict with the employer—perhaps over working conditions, harassment, or discrimination—it can be very costly to take legal action against the company as an individual, making it much safer to have the union officials onside.[47] Almost all the industrial-relations laws in Sweden are based on the idea that employees have rights as union members, not as individuals: the whole system is constructed such that the union is one party and the management the other, engaged in almost day-to-day negotiations, at least in larger companies. If the employees would become the owners of the company and/or have the right to appoint the management, the very raison d'être of Swedish unions would simply evaporate.

The organizational learning perspective focuses on the huge amount of competence invested in how to operate this system of negotiations. It has been developed over many decades, with union officials undergoing massive amounts of training (formal and "on the job") to develop skills as negotiators. If their members would govern the companies by some form of representative democracy, this competence in negotiating with representatives of the owners would become almost worthless: there would be no one sitting on the other side of the table. Even if employees only received substantial compensation as dividends, wage negotiations would become less important. This is what in classical sociology is known as a "trained incapacity."[48]

While the Swedish blue-collar unions may favor economic democracy ideologically, as organizations they seem to perceive that they have much to lose and little to win by supporting firms governed by the people who work in them. This is probably the reason why we see many more such corporations in the US. History can be very ironic: a country with a very weak union movement, which only organizes 7 percent of the workforce, has a considerable number of employee cooperatives, while Sweden, where unionization is almost ten times as high, has very few such firms. In sum, the Swedish experience does not give much support to the positive role ascribed to strong unions for establishing economic democracy.[49] One way forward is that, given the many positive examples that now exist, Swedish unions could be convinced that this would be one way to counter the increased economic inequality. Since traditional wage negotiations have become an ineffective tool against this problem, unions must find a new agenda, and new tools, in their battle against inequality.

Conclusions

I think there are important lessons to learn from the failed Swedish case for economic democracy. First, we should not conflate markets with capitalism, since these are very different economic models. The many surprisingly good results from the studies of democratically governed firms mentioned above all come from firms that operate in (regulated) market economies. Second, we should not put much faith in established blue-collar unions for support for economic democracy. If employees run their firms through various forms of democratic representation, unions will lose much of their current "raison d'etre." Third, in line with the contract theory of power over the corporation presented above, the main mistake with the wage-earner funds was that they were built on the fundamental capitalist idea—that it is ownership of capital that gives power over the corporation. It was by owning capital, not by changing the rental agreement between capital and labor, that workers (read: central union officials) believed they would acquire control of their workplaces. As I have argued elsewhere, it is astonishing that over a century and a half of socialist thought have not confronted this basic capitalist idea: that owners of capital should have the right of command in the relations of production. The idea behind the wage-earner funds was in fact fundamentally the same idea as that on which capitalism is based: that ownership of capital should give owners the right to command in the production process. Indeed, this is a nice example of what Antonio Gramsci called bourgeois ideological hegemony.[50] The "voice strategy" that is the foundation of Isabelle Ferreras's bicameralist idea that focus on democratizing power inside firms (as presented in chapter 1 of this volume) is certainly a challenge against the traditional left's focus on the central role of ownership.

Lastly, I think it is important to recognize that democratically governed companies will be very different in size, production, social environment, and type of market in which they operate. We should therefore not expect them to have very similar institutional structures for democracy. This implies that the argument for democratic corporations should not be based on a "one size fits all" model. This is certainly also true for the established national political democracies that exists today. The Swiss democracy is very different from the Danish democracy, and both are very different from the British type of democracy. We should expect to see the same large variation in institutional arrangements for economic democracy that we encounter when we look at how nations around the world have established political democracy. Isabella Ferreras's bicameral model is very interesting and convincing, not least because of the historical parallel to political democracy, but there are likely many other models for establishing economic democracy.

11

Ferreras and the Economic Democracy Debate

Christopher Mackin

The valuable work of Isabelle Ferreras, summarized in her essay "Democratizing the Corporation," helps to fill in the contours of the worthy aspiration known as economic democracy. This response proposes three lines of inquiry that constructively challenge her efforts and hopefully add to a broader discussion within the economic democracy field.

The first line of inquiry regards the issue of context. How does the project Ferreras describes of promoting the democratic firm relate to contemporary political and economic conversations? The present political moment is dominated by the appearance of both right- and left-wing populisms that aspire to assert, and in some cases "take back," control. How does the theory of the democratic firm and the broader frame of economic democracy speak to questions of nationalism, sovereignty, and ownership?

The second line of inquiry is one of justification. How do Ferreras's arguments in favor of the democratic firm comport with a broad range of other arguments that have been asserted in support of these ideas? Is there a justificatory hierarchy of arguments in support of the democratic firm to be recognized while anticipating contests with status quo "neoliberal" arrangements? How can the case for the democratic firm in particular and economic democracy more generally move from a marginal arrangement that can be tolerated to one that can compete with mainstream models of the firm?

The third line of inquiry regards transition: the movement from prevailing undemocratic arrangements to democratic ones. This topic circles back to political context, but for our purposes I will focus on a limited set of perennial questions that challenge architects of social change. Should the transition to democratic arrangements be voluntary and "paid for" or externally imposed by legislative fiat? Any hoped-for transition to the democratic firm, as described by Ferreras and others, involves both perceived and legally very real changes in prevailing property rights. How should that challenge of transition be met?

Economic Democracy as Politics

Beginning with the issue of context, Andrew Cumbers of the University of Glasgow recently took stock of political themes that appear to have driven the success of populist uprisings in the UK, Europe, and the United States.[1] Citing Brexit and related movements, Cumbers claims that conservative movements have succeeded largely through slogans and emotional appeals to "take back control" that successfully draw the attention of voters skeptical of supranational bureaucratic projects such as the European Union. Bicameralism may well be motivated by the aspiration to reform workplaces in order to better represent the interests of working people. It will also be judged by how well it responds to concrete realities and controversies transforming national economies in the current moment.

Cumbers argues that, rather than reject the populist critique outright, progressive forces should connect populism with specific structures for what he calls "economic democracy" at the individual, enterprise, and national policymaking levels. Using democratically owned firms as an anchor for his arguments, Cumbers joins Ferreras, Bo Rothstein, and others in challenging a social democratic policy consensus that has been focused exclusively on supranational wage and labor market policy initiatives pursued through collective bargaining. His challenge exhorts progressive forces to expand their portfolio of approaches to workplace change and to be attentive to facts and circumstances emerging in national contexts.

The issue of context may be strengthened by reference to a concrete case. In January 1999, the legendary Swedish automaker Volvo was sold to American based manufacturer Ford Motor Company for $6.4 billion. Coming on the heels of a 1998 merger of Chrysler and Daimler-Benz, the sale to Ford assumed an air of inevitability that commentators in Sweden and abroad attributed to iron laws of globalization. With automobile manufacturing being a distinctly export-oriented sector, it was difficult to argue against measures that promised to increase global market share, even if those measures led to the loss of control of one of Sweden's leading national assets. The idea of Volvo passing over to foreign hands was unpopular, but resistance, particularly in the face of claims that a sale could protect wage and benefit standards, appeared to be futile. The desire to continue Swedish ownership of Volvo was derided by some as sentimental corporate patriotism. The $6.4 billion sale to Ford went through.[2]

Eleven years later, near the tail end of the dramatic American recession of 2007–2009, it was clear that the Ford strategy had failed, and once again Volvo was put up for sale. Volvo's labor unions debated the prospects. A surprise alternative proposal was put forward by the Swedish Association of Graduate Engineers Union (Sveriges Ingenjörer) to pursue a Swedish-controlled employee buyout.[3] That alternative was rejected in favor of the idea of union support for the sale of Volvo to another foreign-owned global partner. In August 2010, Zhejiang Geely Holding Group, a private company with close ties to the Chinese government, successfully secured ownership of Volvo for $1.8 billion, a 72 percent decline in value from the original sale to Ford in 1999. In recent years, the commercial fortunes of Volvo have revived, but serious concerns about Chinese ownership remain.[4]

How does this seemingly routine globalization-plus-economic-crisis narrative speak to the challenge Ferreras poses in her paper? In one respect, it does not at all. The arguments of "Democratizing the Corporation" take place largely outside of a discussion of political and economic trends. They aim instead to persuade readers that regardless of situational context, economic institutions can and should perform according to democratic structures and norms long accepted in the political sphere.

Still, we might retrospectively consider how a bicameral governance arrangement might have led to a different path for Volvo. Would a labor investors' chamber composed of representatives selected by Volvo workers have agreed to the initial sale to Ford in 1999 or to the subsequent sale to the Chinese in 2010? Might that labor investors' chamber have been able to come up with alternative production plans that could have retained Swedish control of Volvo?

Even more compelling might be a thought experiment about how the introduction of a bicameral arrangement might fare today with the benefit of over two decades of "foreign" ownership under Swedish belts. Does the social democratic consensus that rejected ownership paths still prevail in Sweden today? Or has the loss of local and national ownership and control of a company such as Volvo not only damaged the economic future of workers, engineers, and managers but also damaged the more general appeal of social democratic politics?

Defenders of the road taken at Volvo may suggest that campaigns to "take back control" of "sovereign" assets amount to sentimental corporate patriotism. Evidence regarding the weakened condition of social democratic parties in Scandinavia and in other parts of Europe suggests otherwise. The response to these questions speaks to the relevance of what Cumbers and others describe as populist dimensions of economic life. Reform agendas that neglect these questions—that take place "above" specific facts of ownership, control, and sovereignty—do so at considerable political risk.

Justificatory Schemes—Ranking Arguments for Economic Democracy

A second line of inquiry provoked by Ferreras's essay pertains to justificatory schemes. Arguments in support of the idea of economic democracy may not be prevalent, but neither are they new. Whatever their vintage, the central question is whether they can be persuasive. Our question is whether there exists a justificatory hierarchy among the broad array of arguments in support of these ideas that is equal to the task of overcoming those prevailing mainstream ideologies. If there is, we should privilege it and use it accordingly.

Looking first from history, most every industrialized country in the world has some kind of economic democracy footprint with intellectual pioneers associated with the idea—Robert Owen and the Rochdale Pioneers in Britain, Ernst Wigforss in Sweden, and José María Arizmendiarrieta in the Basque Country of Spain, to name three such leaders.

Each of these leaders appealed to moral intuition regarding community and justice to justify their preference for economic democracy.

In the United States, a nineteenth-century labor movement consisting of two labor organizations, the Knights of Labor and the National Labor Union, framed these ideas as an alternative to wage employment. Since then, a modest collection of approximately 400 cooperative firms inspired by countercultural norms and a much larger mainstream cohort of over 6,500 firms organized as employee stock ownership plans (ESOPs), motivated by its original political champion in the US Congress as a form of inclusive "worker capitalism," have created a recognized footprint on American soil.[5]

Ferreras's essay proposes a specific alternative road to economic democracy: bicameralism. Ferreras's justifications are well articulated and compelling. Following John Dewey and Mary Parker Follett, she makes the case that democratic arrangements lead to more meaningful and expressive work that contributes to human flourishing.[6] Before Ferreras, Carole Pateman, C. B. MacPherson, and Ronald Mason focused similarly on the cultivation of civic virtue made possible through greater autonomy and voice regarding workplace arrangements.[7] This is a seemingly full basket of affirmative arguments. Unfortunately, while these arguments can help build popular support, they leave in place the dominant justificatory frameworks that lend support to the status quo.

In the United States and most Western economies, the dominant justificatory frameworks for evaluating economic models taught in universities and enforced through public policy have not been historical, moral, or psychological. Those prevailing frameworks have a dual character. They are firstly consequentialist, insisting, through empirical research evidence, that economic arrangements must produce maximum performance, what is commonly referred to as "Pareto optimal" efficiency.[8] Secondly, they are liberal if not libertarian, stressing the centrality of consent and choice exercised by workers in the labor market toward employment in the conventionally structured employer–employee workplace.[9] Taken together, these two frameworks are the intellectual pillars, the foundational defenses of modern economic life. Efforts to break free of these defenses and pose alternatives must eventually reckon with, if not overcome, their persuasive power.

To a significant degree, the scholarly home of most reform efforts featuring more democratic, inclusive ownership models have chosen to

work within the consequentialist framework. Research in support of
more participatory models has sought to demonstrate that the primary
consequentialist goals of competitive, allocative efficiency both within
the firm and in competitive economic terrain in the marketplace is
not sacrificed in order to achieve what mainstream critics regard as
ambiguous moral ends. Participatory democratic arrangements remain
"Pareto optimal."

While their evidence is not beyond dispute, the empirical, consequentialist research project has produced a considerable body of data
that more democratic arrangements do unlock latent performance
potential.[10] Any costs or, more precisely, any lost opportunity costs
sacrificed to investments in time devoted to different forms of participatory deliberation or any short-term sacrifice in financial resources
dedicated to sharing the reward of ownership are, according to the
thrust of this research, eventually overcome by a newly motivated and
more productive workforce. A growing archive of evidence to defend
their claims has been established.[11]

Despite their accomplishments, two large problems haunt both the
moral/psychological and the empirical/consequentialist schools of
thought that embrace workplace or economic democracy. The first is
performative. The second is philosophical.

It has been argued by Richard Marens and others that within the
massive curricular scope of schools of management across the globe,
scholars have made it their business for more than a century to advise
business owners how to maximize motivation and efficiency by introducing incentives, forms of work organization and ideology that *simulate*
the idea of democracy and shared ownership without having to sacrifice
the legal fact of either democracy or ownership.[12] The choice between
real or simulated ownership is sometimes made explicit, with mainstream advisors counseling the prudence of dispensing a "sense of
ownership" without needing to dilute the finite holdings of the real
shareholders.

It is tempting to regard those efforts as a conscious ruse, a knowing
wink enjoyed between the class consisting of owners of property—
specifically corporations—in need of an obedient and productive
workforce and a dutiful international brigade of academic servants ready
and willing to meet that need in exchange for economic and institutional
support. In some cases, that is a valid interpretation. It is also the case,

however, that there are scholars and professionals working in these disciplines who sincerely apply insights about participation outside the for-profit private sector in schools, nonprofits, and government, where their contributions have proven to have objective merit.

Insofar as they have served within the for-profit sectors as agents of corporations with conventional ownership structures, those same management thinkers and practitioners credibly believe that they serve employees as well as owners. Far better, they reason, to train for and structure open, participatory work environments than the traditional autocratic alternative. Cracking the nut of how to actually restructure underlying property-sharing arrangements of the for-profit corporate sectors that might support the overlay of participatory management practices is a challenge most believe is either beyond their ken or something of a fool's errand. Better to *simulate* shared ownership, they reason, than to do nothing at all.

The problem facing economic democracy advocates is that simulated democracy and simulated ownership, while falling short of the full-throated promise of truly democratic arrangements that retain the rights to govern management and enforce more equitable compensation arrangements, still appear to work. Choose whatever missing virtue or quality conventional capitalist arrangements impose upon workers (e.g., too few incentives, too little recognition, too little participation), and scholars and professional management-consulting entities stand ready to fill the identified gap with structures, practices, and ideas that respond to the challenge at hand.[13]

Simulated democracy may fall short of the real thing, but it appears that it can serve to mollify those frustrated by traditional arrangements. Persuasive scholarly and activist work on behalf of genuine democracy can and will continue to make inroads with open and perhaps particularly young minds. The contest ahead, however, is not solely intellectual. For a relatively small investment, at least in comparison to giving up actual ownership, substitutes for democracy are available for purchase off the shelf.

The second philosophical challenge is more subtle. It builds from a bedrock ideological stance that defends status quo arrangements and that characterizes the modern liberal order. That stance maintains that, however unjust the critics of the status quo might paint the contemporary workplace to be, workers (and engineers and managers) "consent" to these arrangements. Until or unless critics can defeat the cardinal principle of consent either with law or with norms, it will carry on. Law can and does circumscribe the absolute freedom of employers (e.g., minimum wages, workplace safety), but the essential facts of property remain.

Regardless of the power of revealing critiques that unmask the truth of how firms (not corporations) operate, financial rewards and governance power reside in corporate law. That law sanctions arrangements that treat workers (and most managers and engineers) as a variable cost, a rented factor of production. Those taken-for-granted rental relationships confirm the legitimacy of those arrangements on a day-to-day basis.

In November 2019, a revealing public debate was staged in New York City by a group called Intelligence Squared between multimillionaire libertarian icon John Mackey, founder of Whole Foods Groceries (now sold to Amazon) and author (with Raj Sisodia) of *Conscious Capitalism: Liberating the Heroic Spirit of Business* and University of Massachusetts economist and avowed socialist Richard Wolff, a recent convert to the cause of workplace democracy. The proposition that structured the debate—pro (Mackey) versus con (Wolff)—was "Capitalism is a blessing."[14]

At a key juncture, when Mackey challenged Professor Wolff to describe his alternative, Professor Wolff was ready. He triumphantly recounted the (to him) compelling performance statistics of the Mondragon Cooperative Group in the Basque region of Spain. There was evidence in this data, according to Wolff, of a true workable and scaled alternative to status quo arrangements. The debate, however, was not done. Knowing ahead of time that the Mondragon case was likely to cited, Mackey next pulled out a file that summarized the latest Mondragon statistics. He read them aloud and pronounced himself unimpressed. The EBITDA (earnings before interest, taxes, depreciation, and amortization) of these companies was moderate at best, and the growth of the system was stalled. If this was the alternative, it barely qualified on consequentialist economic-performance grounds.

It was, however, Mackey's final riposte that revealed the depth and complexity of our second challenge. He and his right-wing sidekick Katherine Mangu-Ward, editor in chief of *Reason* magazine, struck a plaintive note. Why, they complained to Professor Wolff and his left-wing companion, *Jacobin* magazine founder Bhaskar Sunkara, do you criticize us, defenders of status quo arrangements? We are not particularly impressed with your so-called Mondragon alternative, but we in the status quo are not attempting to shut you down. If people wish to work for Mondragon-like companies, they should, according to liberal and libertarian principles, be allowed to. Consent is the bedrock foundation of this position, a position that is not disturbed by the existence of alternatives.

This somewhat surprising complaint reveals both the strength and the weakness of prevailing workplace arrangements. As long as defenders can revert to the seemingly unassailable ground of consent, they and their accumulated law, wealth, and control over the means of education will exercise what appears to be hegemonic control over the future design of the workplace. Protests that the scope of choice that workers perceive as possible is artificially narrow and coercive are valid. And campaigns to expand the imagined scope should be supported. But that critique does not cancel or, in any real way, inhibit the real-world functioning of enterprise and labor markets that power economic life. Choice may be limited, but it does exist. Workers consent to participate under existing arrangements. So perhaps a deeper critique of choice and consent is required.

The task of overcoming the cardinal principle of consent and rendering a convincing judgment that existing employment and ownership arrangements are morally indefensible—fraudulent or worse—may seem large. It has, however, been taken up in the past in other settings with lasting results. Two institutions, that of chattel slavery and the coverture marriage contract, both ubiquitous and in their time seemingly permanent institutions of society, eventually dissolved when effectively confronted by moral arguments from abolitionists and feminists.[15] The tradition of inalienable rights—rights that cannot be denied "even with consent"—is the tradition that did much of the intellectual work of achieving those ends. It is very likely that this tradition will have a prominent role to play in the debates ahead about the future of economic democracy.

In particular, the field of economic democracy should consider whether there is a justificatory hierarchy of arguments to deploy against the status quo. Traditions of deontological philosophy, associated with Kant and others, arguably offered the most hospitable setting for the deployment of inalienable-rights arguments that helped to defeat slavery and the coverture marriage contract. David Ellerman has substantively applied those same arguments against the institution of the modern employment contract. His revival and critique of Locke's eighteenth-century labor theory of property carries that critique into economic and political theory.[16]

The ambition of normative theory in the field of economic democracy should be large. It should rise to be able to put forward arguments that approach or equal the standards of legitimacy and truth to be found in our institutions of law. In the law there is relatively little ambiguity about the existence of a justificatory hierarchy. Legal claims rendered against individuals, associations, and corporations are not opinions or preferences. They are put forward and argued subject to procedural demands for fairness, evidence, and due process. Verdicts of guilt and innocence are rendered. Responsibility is assigned to responsible agents.

Of course, judgments of legitimacy and truth remain "intersubjective" even in the law. They are not flawless. They do not exist outside of history. They enjoy their legitimacy because judges and juries, and the governments and the publics that establish them, are persuaded based on rules of evidence and moral arguments that individuals are responsible for their actions and therefore judged guilty or innocent of crimes. But law cannot be reduced to the status of a subjective opinion. Nor can law be reduced to a complaint, however worthy, about contingent and potentially coercive arrangements where, for example, workers or management find themselves with limited bargaining power.

It is an ambitious claim to assert that moral critiques of prevailing ownership, control, and employment arrangements in our workplaces can approach the certainty enjoyed by courts of law. But, at the very least, political theory needs to confront this challenge. No single line of reasoning will be equal to the task ahead. Contributions can and should come from whichever corner we can discover. Resistance to these ideas is real and formidable and requires theoretical and analytical tools that are equal to the task. If it is agreed that there is a justificatory hierarchy of arguments in support of these ideas, we should privilege that hierarchy and use it accordingly.

Thoughts about the Transition

Near the end of "Democratizing the Corporation," Ferreras addresses the task of "From Here to There," sketching preliminary thoughts about how the move from status quo to democratic arrangements might take place. When considering that topic, attention turns to comparable examples to be found in different corners of the world. While the reach of bicameralism is more extensive, including jurisdiction over income rights such as profit sharing, the closest analogue to Ferreras's design is codetermination, or *Mitbestimmung* in Germany.

Like bicameralism, codetermination focuses on governance and voice concerns. It is largely silent on the topic of ownership and property rights. Other European countries, including Sweden, make use of similar designs. What these approaches share is an assumption that the workplace-democratization agenda should be conceived and administered at a federal level. Their focus is on corporate governance measures mandated by national and, where possible, international law.

Ferreras's approach can be contrasted to Anglo-American approaches to these questions. That tradition favors voluntary, property-based ownership-sharing designs, often encouraged by tax incentives. Ownership sharing is not an income-based approach. It involves the use of securities or stock, instruments that carry corporate governance power and that store the gradual appreciation of wealth. While there are Anglo-American (and European) designs that presume that workers acquire stock, usually at a discount, the most prominent ownership-sharing structure in the United States makes use of ESOPs. This form of employee ownership does not rely upon at-risk capital investments by workers and managers. Out of a total of 6,500 ESOP companies, 4,000 such firms (or 62 percent) are majority owned by their employees.[17]

Ferreras does introduce the idea of ownership as an option that might be pursued by labor investors, but securing ownership is not framed as a priority or an explicit goal of the bicameralism project. She cites the tax-favored status enjoyed by ESOP firms in the United States and argues that bicameral (and eventually democratic, unicameral) firms should likewise secure privileged tax and legal status, including the restriction of limited legal liability protections (presently enjoyed by all corporations) to democratic firms.

There are notable differences between Ferreras's approach and that pursued by three ownership-based models familiar to the contemporary conversation: the Meidner Plan of Sweden in the 1970s, the UK Labour Party leader Jeremy Corbyn's "Inclusive Ownership Plan/Fund" of 2019, and the US senator Bernie Sanders's "Corporate Accountability and Democracy Plan" of 2019–2020.[18] Of these three, the Meidner and Corbyn plans failed to launch. The Sanders plan, conceived as part of a 2020 campaign for president, was also frustrated.

Rothstein and others describe the only partially implemented Meidner Plan of 1970s Sweden as a complex transfer of corporate stock ownership to labor interests.[19] According to the original Meidner design, earnings from that stock were designed to be shared through a formula governed not by workers and managers within individual firms but by Swedish unions. Funds were to accumulate in a centralized structure, to be later distributed according to a "solidaristic" economic-sharing design.

More relevant to this discussion, however, are the mechanisms these various plans imagine for the actual transfer of shares. Shares of stock that represent existing property interests in the Meidner, Corbyn, and Sanders plans are not purchased or earned.[20] They are, rather, transferred through legislative fiat. It has been fairly argued that this mechanism is simply a variant on common taxation privileges of the state or, more precisely, an extension of familiar compensation practices, usually restricted to top executives, that involve the granting of shares. To business owners, public shareholders, and the public at large, however, these plans would divert very large amounts of stock that would substantially dilute existing shareholders. To critics, these designs would amount to an overt "taking," a legally sanctioned transfer of ownership rhetorically branded by certain displeased opponents as "expropriation."

In the summer of 2019, when the Corbyn Inclusive Ownership Fund proposal came under attack in the *Financial Times* and elsewhere, a list of sympathetic economists signed a letter stating that it was a "category error" to suggest that the fund would "cost" companies or that the state would "seize" shares. As they wrote,

> The proposal neither reduces the book value of corporate entities, nor
> does it require them to pay cash out. By requiring companies to issue

new shares and give them to a mutual fund, mirroring the existing practice of issuing shares for executive compensation, it ensures instead that workers share in the wealth they create.[21]

This rebuttal effectively highlights the precedent of shares being deployed as a compensation benefit by management, typically for management alone, without any kind of balancing compensation to existing shareholders. When that (routinely) takes place, no cries of expropriation fill the air. That qualification does not deny, however, that the Corbyn plan did involve significant dilution of existing shareholder stakes and relies upon an externally imposed "requirement" to transfer shares.

Because Ferreras focuses primarily on structures for voice that would flow from adoption of bicameralism, it is not clear what role ownership plays in her framework. The choice to elide the shareholding question under bicameralism is a large one, however, and is not merely political. It has implications for the economic deal which these ideas offer for workers. The implied economic benefit bicameralism offers appears to proceed from the assumption that worker representatives in new bicameral roles can apply leverage to discussions about compensation and benefits. Even if successful, such a "wage-led," "income-based" approach to overcoming economic inequality is problematic on several grounds.

One of the primary public policy rationales in support of employee ownership in the United States focuses on the wealth-sharing potential of broadly shared ownership.[22] The American framework generally achieves those ends without workers risking their own capital. While the economic participation opportunities of the dominant American ESOP model are strong, it should also be emphasized that this same model is relatively weak on the issue of voice. There are no requirements for worker representation on corporate boards. Nor are there prohibitions against such participation. However, economic democracy strategies that focus exclusively on voice cede the wealth-accumulation opportunities of ownership to established narrow interests. Concentrated share ownership is one of the largest drivers of economic inequality.[23]

Perhaps the most remarkable feature of the American experience with employee ownership of firms, primarily through ESOPs, has been the bipartisan political support this idea has long enjoyed. Arguably, the two biggest supporters in the US Congress for a number of years have also been two of the most ideologically different. Representative Dana Rohrabacher, a Republican (since retired) from Orange County, California, and Senator Bernie Sanders, an independent (allied with the Democratic Party) of Vermont provide the outer edges of right-wing to left-wing political support.[24] In the ideological middle, they are joined by a substantial mix of Republicans and Democrats.

Four reasons that this highly unusual cross-ideological consensus appears to hold up over time include the following:

- Ideological affinity: Conservative thinkers are drawn to the self-reliant features of shared ownership. They believe that solving problems of economic inequality should happen primarily in the economy, through work and not through the hand of government. They are drawn to a simple and triumphant-sounding meme that "the problem with capitalism is that there are too few capitalists."[25] Liberal and left thinkers are drawn to shared ownership both because of how it acknowledges the contribution of workers and because it confers legitimacy to the general idea of economic democracy. Leaving to the side the complexities of introducing democratic practices at the firm level, their endorsement also focuses on the distinction between income and wealth and stresses the importance of how employee ownership opens up the possibility of wealth sharing among workers.

- Transactions for market value and tax breaks: In the United States, employee ownership happens on a voluntary basis, primarily when companies are "sold" to legal trusts representing those employees. Sales to those trusts are tax advantaged for the seller, involving deferral of capital gains tax. Sellers receive market value for their holdings. On a going-forward basis, the taxable income of companies is reduced by direct proportion to the percentage of broad-based employee ownership held by employee stock ownership trusts. The "arm's length" market-value transactional character of these arrangements involving the actual payment by buyers and the "receipt of financial consideration" to sellers of these firms helps confer legitimacy to the process. This approach contrasts with designs promoted by Corbyn in 2019, and by Sanders in 2019 and 2020, that propose to transfer economic value without financial consideration to existing property owners through legislative fiat.[26]

- Minimal risk for workers: The sale of companies to legal trusts representing workers does not involve financial risk for workers. Sales are made possible by the aforementioned legal trusts that represent workers and managers taking out loans repaid through the cash flow of the ongoing enterprise. These loans are secured by the assets of the firm.

- Earned wealth: The fact that shared ownership comes about through arm's-length market-value transactions, and that future wealth sharing is contingent upon the competitive performance of the firm, introduces an "earned" (rather than "granted") psychology to the transition from conventional to more democratic ownership.

It is far easier to gain consensus on the value of shared ownership than it is on means to achieve it. A default assumption for many on the left is that the only way such transfers will ever happen is by a kind of Meidner Plan national legislative mandate or, more dramatically, as was the case in the case of the Argentinian *empresas recuperadas* (recovered businesses) of 2002, by literal expropriation.[27] As worthy as those efforts have been, they overlook a much more practical and immediate approach that recognizes that businesses routinely change hands, particularly when founders reach retirement age. There is, in other words, a substantial supply of scaled and successful businesses with willing sellers. The opportunity, well short of the imagined drama of expropriation, is that they can be acquired.

If resources and incentives can be mustered to support employees, they can become the buyers of these firms without mandates and without expropriation. The architects of American ESOP legislation executed the first step in how to take advantage of this opportunity by marrying tax incentives for sellers to legal structures representing employees as buyers while minimizing risk. ESOP designs are not ideal, particularly in the realm of voice, but they can be improved. They have achieved sufficient scale in the American context—6,500 companies representing 12 million workers—that they cannot be easily dismissed.[28]

A reasonable rebuttal to these arguments focuses on the difference between very large publicly traded Wall Street or City of London companies that, strangely, seem to have become the primary imagined model of economic life and the millions of "Main Street," nontraded, small- to medium-sized firms owned by families, management, and investment groups. On this point, scholars and journalists would be well served to familiarize themselves with the facts on the ground in their respective countries. Knowing who owns the companies in a given geography, how that ownership is structured, and when it might change hands should serve as a prelude to the advancement of an economic democracy agenda.

Using US statistics, in a first category of approximately 4,000 publicly traded firms (which comprise less than 1 percent of the combined count of private and public companies), stocks are actively traded on public markets. Considering large numbers of individual investors, mutual funds, and institutional shareholders, the achievement of controlling interest in those firms would appear to be a formidable challenge for economic democracy advocates.

In the second general category of private or closely held firms, also referred to as small to medium enterprises (SMEs), the companies may not dominate headlines, but they are plentiful. In the United States, approximately 350,000 out of a total of 17 million mostly small firms employ more than fifty employees. Reverting to a primary narrative of this paper, that considerable "lower-middle market" sector of privately held firms presents a promising target for economic democracy. Those firms, largely owned by the "silver tsunami" of business founders late in their careers, will eventually be put up for sale, potentially to employees.[29]

Even with the more crowded and formidable universe of publicly traded companies, there may be paths forward. In a provocative 2021 essay entitled "When Capital Relinquishes Ownership," Rothstein describes the workings of index funds, a newly ascendent and prominent investment product that explicitly eschews the responsibilities for exercising corporate governance voice.[30] The abandonment of voice by the formal legal owners of publicly traded firms has created a vacuum into which, he believes, the workers of those firms—and not their unions or the state—should be escorted to assume their proper role as the true governors of the firms where they work.

Rothstein's arguments deserve broad consideration. He has uncovered what can be described as nothing less than a legitimation crisis that undermines claims that we are living in democratic societies. The low level of shareholder voting even in actively managed funds of publicly traded companies, combined with a complete and unabashed voting vacuum among index funds, reveals a fundamental flaw plaguing the publicly traded sector. Outside investors, it can be argued, were never the proper governors of enterprise life. They invest for economic returns. Voice needs to reside somewhere. Rothstein and others assert that voice should reside with those who are governed in these firms, the community of blue- and white-collar workers.

How might it be practically possible for transformations to employee ownership to happen? We have alluded to the crucial role that public policy initiatives in the United States play in attracting the interest of incumbent owners of privately held companies. In addition, recent developments underway outside of public policy directives with scaled capital sources, including large family offices, foundation endowments, and union and public pension funds looking to engage in "social impact" investing, bode well for the employee-ownership field. Investments from these sectors should enable the field to move progressively "upmarket" to larger opportunities in both the publicly traded and closely held business worlds. Operating under the rubric of "ESG" (environmental, social, and governance), the participation of these investors should strengthen the potential and visibility of this sector.

Some of the largest sources of capital in the world exist in sovereign wealth funds (SWFs), such as Norway's $1.4 trillion Government Pension Fund. By choosing to deploy capital with investment groups that know the employee-ownership market, SWFs can help launch a new category of "sovereignty respecting" investment. SWFs can and should invest not primarily within their own borders but instead across borders, ideally on a reciprocal basis. These investments can provide competitive returns to investors while simultaneously privileging or ceding affirmative "local" ownership and control to the managers and workers in the countries where funds are placed. Using this investment thesis, the sovereignty of important assets within nation states, including "marquee" and scaled examples such as Volvo, can be made without sacrificing returns. [31]

If economic democracy becomes recognized as a promising new frontier, it should be possible to direct some percentage of its reformist energy, in both public policy and private initiative realms, toward the project of persuading scaled capital sources to provide alternatives to conventional investment structures that routinely concentrate wealth. What the economic democracy field needs are new and expert intermediary institutions and financing mechanisms that can join forces with workers and managers to deploy these funds toward more democratic and distributed ends.[32]

Conclusion

There are indications that the project of "Democratizing the Corporation," as portrayed by Ferreras, has achieved a level of interest to be able to contend with traditional social democratic measures for policy space. Gross inequalities in wealth and irresponsible stewardship, particularly of our largest corporations, facilitated by the structure and design of our capital markets, understandably strain the patience of thinkers and activists who wish to act to address that inequality immediately and at scale.

There is, however, more than one path forward for the economic democracy idea. Peremptory decisions that would assign or even restrict economic democracy to legislative mandates would be shortsighted and unwise. That approach would needlessly sacrifice evident cross-ideological appeal that is politically necessary to first organize and then maintain economic democracy as a new category of structural reform.[33]

A core challenge of the so-called transition from the status quo to more democratic arrangements will be sorting out the extent to which these reforms should be imposed or induced, mandated or voluntarily encouraged. These topics should be debated candidly and at length, taking into account a more complete appreciation of facts on the ground that describe our local economies and what might be done to change them.

12

Five Principles of Economic Democracy

Ewan McGaughey

If we were to "place the economy under a democratic microscope," it is universally seen that absolutism is rampant, power is unaccountable, and the principle of "one person, one vote" is as rare as it is precious.[1] As an old labor lawyer once told the US Congress, "The contrast between our political liberty and our industrial absolutism [is the prime source of social conflict]."[2] Today's economy has concentrated income and wealth to dangerous extremes of inequality, and will go further without positive change. The concentration of the votes in the economy, whatever the "variety of capitalism," is even more extreme.[3] Shareholders monopolize most votes in the corporations that make decisions over our wages, firm investment, our environment, and our public lives. Power begets wealth, and (under our laws today) wealth begets power. Shareholders are mainly asset managers like BlackRock, State Street, and Vanguard, or banks like Deutsche, Unicredit, or Société Générale. In the US a group of roughly twelve people control the policies on vast number of votes in our economy, and in Germany, the UK, or France matters are hardly better.[4] There they do not invest their own labor, capital, or custom in companies. In standard form contracts for financial services, they take over other people's voting rights, from other people's money, and other people's labor.

Against this absolutism, the early twentieth-century movement for an "industrial democracy" achieved three main changes.[5] First, there developed a system of *minimum rights at work*, enforceable through adjudication and in the courts, and coordinated globally through

International Labour Organization Conventions. Second, there are rights to collective bargaining, which are most successful where organized across sectors, so that people have voice with *negotiating power to get fair terms* beyond the minimum. Third, *rights to vote in enterprise* spread, to elect work councils with binding rights in management, to elect directors on boards, to appoint pension trustees that oversaw workers' capital, and for members of the public to codetermine enterprises that were state owned or specifically regulated. More complex than "one person, one vote" for a parliament or a president, the multi-stakeholder interests in the economy have meant that experiment has lasted. There is no single best model, but with the experience, evidence, and data accumulated in the twenty-first century, we can identify five main principles: universality of voice, votes at work, votes in capital, votes in public services, and enabling experiment. This chapter will set out these principles and assess how the pathbreaking proposals for a "bicameral firm" from Professor Isabelle Ferreras compare at each point, before returning to a general summary, and concluding.

Five Principles

1. Universality
The first principle of economic democracy is the universal right to play a deliberative part in government. This includes political as well as economic institutions. Democracy means that power and "administration is in the hands of the many, not the few."[6] At the core, this is "one person, one vote," but our democracy is also "based on the view that each person has equal value," and everyone "stands upon an equal foot."[7] As the old enemies of political democracy in the nineteenth century knew, the "principle of equality . . . is a very jealous power." In his campaign against extending voting rights in the UK, Robert Lowe, the "father of modern company law," warned other members of Parliament that once we have a democratic basis for politics, "you must remember that you cannot look at that alone, but you must look at it in reference to all your other institutions."[8] Lowe also opposed the so-called "grinding tyranny" of trade unions and lost this campaign, as well. Political and economic democracy advanced together: the Second Reform Act, 1867,

extended the franchise, and the Trade Union Act, 1871, upheld the freedom to organize and bargain.

Thus, the vote in politics was just one part of a greater bill of rights that includes economic voice. From the 1920s, the German trade unions sought extension of democratic norms to all economic entities and for people's votes to count directly in enterprise "without a detour through the state."[9] Equally it was seen by the New Deal architects, in the words of President Franklin D. Roosevelt, that we needed the "development of an economic declaration of rights, an economic constitutional order."[10] In short, the future of democracy is the extension of the vote and equal participation in every social institution.[11] Everyone who contributes to an enterprise, just like a polity, has a symmetrical right to participate in its government.[12] "Everyone," says the 1948 Universal Declaration of Human Rights, "has the right to take part in the government of his country, directly or through freely chosen representatives."[13]

There is an inherent tension in any system that attempts to maintain economic absolutism but also sustain political democracy. In Nazi Germany, the abolition of political parties went hand in hand with the abolition of free trade unions, and "reprivatization," after Hitler's promise to his "Circle of Business Friends" to make politics safe for capitalism.[14] The destruction of workers' rights to vote for company boards was soon followed by the elimination of investor rights, by cementing control of shares in the hands of bank cartels. As Johannes Zahn, a crazed Nazi banking lawyer and drafter of the 1937 Public Companies Act, said, "Democracy of capital will vanish, just as it did in politics."[15]

The opponents of economic democracy are also, at best, ambivalent about political democracy. For example, Ludwig von Mises was a member of the Austrian fascist party and wrote that Mussolini's fascists were justified as an "emergency makeshift" to ward off communism. Indeed they were "full of the best intentions" and had "saved European civilization."[16] In 1931 he wrote that the "capitalistic social order" was "an economic democracy in the strictest sense of the word," on the view that consumer spending is sovereign and each penny is like a vote.[17] As this seemed ever more absurd, the opponents of democracy turned to attack the basis of a vote as a whole. "The expressions of preferences in voting will be less precise," wrote George Stigler, "than the expressions of preferences in the marketplace because many uninformed people will

be voting and affecting the decision."[18] By 1983, Michael Jensen and
William Meckling argued that calls for economic democracy were
simply an "attack on freedom" and that no analogy could be drawn
between "free enterprise" and the "political state."[19] This view maintained that codetermination, such as that in Germany, would inevitably
devolve into economic squalor, like Marshal Tito's Yugoslavia.[20] Principle free and evidence free, this line of argument hijacked words to
protect its goal of unrestricted corporate power, run by a cartel of asset
managers and banks. As business interests in the US consistently back
extremist Republicans who legitimize the January 2021 attack on the US
Capitol, drive gerrymandering, limit the franchise, or lie that the
November 2020 presidential election was stolen, it is doubtful that
politics can remain stable and democratic while the economy is not. The
principle of democracy is for every social institution, and the principle
is universal. This fact is well acknowledged by Professor Ferreras and is
essential to the view that firms are political entities, just as governments
are economic ones.[21]

2. Votes at Work

The second main principle is that everyone should have the right to vote
at work, regardless of the legal form of enterprise in which they invest
their labor. "Labor is the superior of capital," said President Abraham
Lincoln in his first annual message, "and deserves much the higher
consideration."[22] Since most enterprise is cooperative, or carried out in
networks, labor law has long looked past the classical forms of contract,
property, and corporate personhood to ensure that everyone has the
right to participate in enterprise on an equal foot. The right to vote at
work is a human right, enshrined, among other places, in the European
Social Charter (article 22) and the Indian Constitution (article 43A) and
embedded in the national legal systems of a majority of member countries of the Organisation for Economic Co-operation and Development
(OECD), as well as Brazil and China.[23] While English-speaking countries are behind, the governing bodies in the best universities, such as
Cambridge, Oxford, University of Toronto, or Harvard, are majority-
elected by staff and alumni, and there is a rich history and cross-party
political support for labor's right to vote.[24]

There are many models for votes at work. Many countries, such as
Sweden, require that at least one-third of company boards be elected.

Germany transformed its two-tier board system to give between one-third and parity worker representation on the supervisory board in companies with over 500 staff. Cambridge University, like many others, creates majority representation for staff who have the status of fellows or higher, counts staff as "members" of the corporation, and grants the right to pass "graces" that bind management.[25] Democratic proposals in the United States range from advocating election of one-third of directors to be worker elected in listed companies, to 40 percent in $1 billion federal companies, to 45 percent in $100 million companies.[26] This follows the view that "every employee should be guaranteed the right to vote at work, and have a voice in setting their pay, regardless of the kind or size of company or firm they work for."[27] In the Clean Slate project, it has also been proposed that a supermajority of company boards, with 40 percent worker representation, should be needed for decisions involving redundancy, restructure, insolvency, or wage changes.[28] In Belgium, as well as new Flemish Green Party proposals for worker representation, the Socialist Party has put forth a radical plan for a "bicameral" model of governance, with a chamber of investors and a chamber of workers together electing another executive board (this could even be called "tricameral").[29] Similar to trade union governance, the differing models of proposal often match models of governance inherited from politics.[30] There is not yet an International Labour Organization convention, much less one that includes workers' capital (below), but there are drafts, and a debate about this is starting.[31]

The empirical research on votes at work is now extensive, and it suggests strong behavioral, qualitative, and quantitative support for representation in enterprise. The behavioral evidence shows that people are happier and more productive at work when they have voice.[32] Qualitative studies demonstrate that higher degrees of trust, confidence, and cooperation result when staff elect management. Codetermination reduces strikes.[33] Codetermination, along with all other labor laws, is closely correlated with raising employment, reducing unemployment, and decreasing inequality.[34] Codetermination, particularly where works councils have voice over dismissal and redundancy decisions, is strongly correlated with higher innovation, measured by the number of patent filings.[35] Other empirical research, with varying methods, has also sometimes concluded that the empirical effects are small, but this depends on how the studies are done, and to the extent that economic evidence is uncertain (if at all), we return to the principle that everyone has the moral, political, and human right to vote at work.[36] As below, the public and investors may often legitimately have the right to vote in an enterprise, but workers always do and in principle should hold at least half of the governance power, if not more.

The principle of votes at work encompasses the proposal for a bicameral firm but acknowledges that a bicameral firm is one among many models that could operate to achieve the goal of ensuring that workers have meaningful autonomy in their lives at work.

3. Votes in Capital

The third principle is that every investor has a right to vote on their capital, especially to control the policies for use of voting rights on shares that their money buys: it does not accept that "shareholders" should monopolize voting rights in firms. Indeed, workers' capital— people saving for retirement—makes up the majority of money in the share markets. Yet just as the worker who invests labor in a company is often separated from real influence over their enterprise, without positive legal rights, the true investors behind pensions, life insurance, and mutual funds, or even retail shareholders, are routinely separated from control over the votes that their money buys. Pension fund trustees are often dominated by employers, and they typically delegate investment services to asset managers, such as BlackRock, State Street, Vanguard, Schroders, or Legal & General. All too often, asset managers use standard form contracts to take over shareholder votes. Asset managers and banks sell pension and financial products to companies, where (using other people's money) they exercise shareholder voting rights. In mass self-dealing, fund managers can influence an employer to shift all workers' pensions from collective schemes to individual accounts, and then charge more fees. In the US, BlackRock, State Street, and Vanguard combined would be the largest shareholder in 438 of S&P 500 companies. They have fewer than fifty people in their corporate governance departments, meaning that less than fifty people dominate the vast majority of votes in the US economy. These outcomes are significant and deliberate. If pension fund growth had continued as it was doing, before Reagan and Thatcher drove closure of collective pensions and more individualized savings, workers' capital would have already become a majority of the stock market.[37]

Despite better workplace codetermination, the position on votes in capital is probably worse in continental Europe than in the UK or US. In Germany, three banks—Deutsche Bank, Commerzbank, and UniCredit—control around 60 percent of all voting rights in public company shares: we do not know the exact numbers because public data collection was canceled in 2005.[38] This illegitimate bank power (*Bankenmacht*) dates from a 1930 bank cartel deal and its codification in the 1937 Nazi Stock Corporation Act. It required that share certificates be deposited in a bank for safekeeping and that banks would take over the votes.[39] This practice probably violates EU competition law on state support for agreements that restrict competition, but it is not gone yet.[40]

The movement for votes in capital has two main features: first, to ensure that all pension or other capital funds are controlled by elected representatives; and second, to ensure that all financial intermediaries vote solely according to policies determined by elected representatives, not by themselves. For example, one of the earliest pension plans to guarantee beneficiary representation was the Teachers Insurance and Annuity Association. Today, most major Canadian pension funds are governed according to collective agreements that give equal power to employee and employer representatives.[41] The UK's standards are lower, foreseeing a minimum of merely one-third representation, and some, such as the Universities Superannuation Scheme, failing to even meet this. There is a power for the government minister to raise the required threshold of "member-nominated trustees" to one-half at any time.[42]

Democratic standards within funds are necessary but not sufficient: there also need to be systems to control the behavior of all intermediary agents, such as banks and asset managers, where they perform investment services for funds. A key example of reform was passed in Switzerland after 2013, placing a duty on pensions to determine a shareholder voting policy and for banks (who are functionally equivalent to asset managers) to follow that voting policy on shares.[43] Similarly, in the US, the Bernie Sanders Corporate Democracy and Accountability plan calls to "ban asset managers voting on other people's money, unless they are following instructions, just like we banned broker-dealer voting in the Dodd-Frank Act."[44] This will mean more, not fewer, votes are cast because replacing asset managers and banks with elected representatives of the real investors will ensure more engagement and a greater degree of corporate accountability. It will solve the systematic underinvestment in voting activity when asset managers or banks remain as so-called stewards.[45]

How does the principle of votes in capital fit with the proposal for a bicameral firm? This is one of the more muted points of discussion in Professor Ferreras's proposals: while it is said that capital should have its own chamber, this leaves unanswered the problems of accountability in capital-holding institutions. This is problematic because there is little or no moral case for any voice, of any stakeholder, to exercise power with other people's money, or other people's labor, if they are not accountable through the vote. It is also not clear why unrepresentative capital should have the privilege of its own chamber within enterprises as a mandatory norm: many enterprises may be entirely governed by workers. Yet the bigger picture is that, in most modern economic systems today, most capital ultimately is workers' capital, and so every worker who has savings should be entitled to participate in its use, as much as they do at work.

4. Votes in Public Services

The fourth main principle is that everyone needs the right to vote in public services, where consumers can no longer effectively "vote with their feet" and competitive markets fail to uphold the public interest. Democratic, competitive enterprise is likely to advance the public interest much of the time, but education, health, banking, energy, water, agriculture, housing, transport, communications, the media, the military, and sport have always been publicly financed, publicly owned in whole or part, subject to sector-specific regulation, or all three. When markets fail, when there is no broadly equal distribution of assets and finance for production, democratic societies alter the general rules of private enterprise. The student, patient, passenger, ratepayer, or viewer becomes more than just a "consumer"; they are rightly treated as a member with a legitimate voice in economic governance.

In the mid-twentieth-century system of nationalization developed in the UK, the leading theory advanced by former minister for transport Herbert Morrison was that only experts should be appointed to public company boards, and that labor or consumer voting rights would (ostensibly) distract from that.[46] These "experts" would therefore be appointed by the (apparently) biggest expert of all, the government minister, who just happened to be someone like Morrison. The distance between nationalized company boards and the people they were meant to serve was probably a leading cause for dissatisfaction with public ownership. Indeed, some of the most successful public enterprises, particularly in education, did give voting rights to the otherwise-consumer. For instance, the University of Toronto Act, 1971, gives both students and alumni roughly a third of the votes for the governing body, alongside staff and the lieutenant governor. The Spanish health service and the UK National Health Service give patients and residents' groups, alongside doctors and nurses, the right to vote for hospital boards.[47] In France, Germany, and Switzerland, ratepayers, local residents, or passengers have the right to codetermine the management of public services from water to electricity to transport.[48] Wikimedia, which runs some of the world's largest websites, gives the vote to registered account holders (particularly editors) for half of its board.[49] When consumers can no longer truly "vote with their feet," a democratic economy should give those service-users votes for real.

Like the principle of votes in capital, the principle of votes in public services goes a step beyond the discussion of a bicameral firm. In essence, this acknowledges that a third stakeholder comes into play when competitive private enterprise fails to protect the consumer or public interest. If it is accepted that there cannot always be plural centers of economic power through workable competitive enterprise, it is necessary to admit a third interest group into enterprise governance: the service-user. However, this principle does not require a third chamber, nor is it wedded to any single institutional arrangement. It simply claims that the consumer and public voice should be heard through the right to vote.

5. Experiment

The fifth main principle is that basic standards of economic democracy must leave room for experiment. Like all labor, investor, consumer, or public rights, in international or EU law the principle of subsidiarity requires that, rather than imposing rigid models, political entities and enterprises should be allowed to act as "laboratories of democracy."[50] There are two reasons for this. First, experimentation with new forms of institutional governance is more likely to improve governance systems than fixing maximum norms in law would do. For example, in US labor law, the National Labor Relations Act of 1935 was interpreted (despite silence in the act) to "preempt" states from passing their own stronger protections for workers to collectively bargain.[51] This led to an "ossification" of labor law, and no state could build beyond the supposed, pitifully weak federal maximum.[52] Second, social consensus on minimum principles is more likely to be achieved than consensus on a detailed plan and therefore better capable of building political coalitions to effect change. This is the approach that is adopted in EU law and international law and the most effective model to advance economic democracy in every country.

Firms as Political Entities

Given these five principles of economic democracy—of universality, votes at work, votes in capital, votes in public services, and experiment—what further comparisons can be made with Professor Isabelle Ferreras's proposals for "economic bicameralism"? Ferreras's basic thesis is that "firms are political entities," and she therefore rejects the distinction between political and economic democracy.[53] She says that corporate governance must, at least, be legitimate, reasonable, and intelligent and proposes that (similar to the Belgian Socialist proposals that her work has inspired) firms should be required to have two elected "chambers," one from investors, the other from workers. Each should have veto rights against the other, on all issues, and any other system would "create an incomplete form of bicameralism."[54] This has provoked broad discussion, and a related campaign for "democratizing work" galvanized widespread online support.[55]

A first main criticism of the "bicameral" proposal is that if capital and labor each have two chambers with vetoes against one another, there is a risk of "deadlock."[56] This critique has an element of truth, since the very process is designed to ensure that the status quo is maintained in absence of agreement. Ferreras contends that "deadlock is unlikely because both parties would suffer so greatly from the diminished productivity that would ensue," and this may be true.[57] It should be noted that most systems of corporate law do have mechanisms—such as general meeting decisions, buyouts, or liquidation—to overcome deadlocks on a board.[58] But also, in collective bargaining and strike action, like in most contract dealings, deadlock without agreement is the default. What is likely or unlikely to happen is simply an empirical question, which requires evidence to answer, but it would seem that the risk of deadlock is not one that should speak against the proposal as a whole. However, it could also be desirable to avoid any problem of deadlock by allocating supermajority rights to workers or other stakeholders on issues where they have the greatest legitimate interests.

Second, a deeper question is, why should investors be given their own chamber and, indeed, have veto rights over issues that the workforce is legitimately interested in deciding alone? Given that all companies need labor, and that most but not all need capital, it seems arguable that labor is ultimately the superior "factor of production," if one chooses to frame it this way. More substantively, there are vastly more people who invest their labor in companies, and relatively fewer people (yet more diversified through shareholding portfolios) who invest capital. Capital is also owned very unequally. If firms are political entities, the principle of equality—that all must stand upon an equal foot—would appear to speak against fixing a minimum participation rate for capital investors at "one-half," and for labor to be given the other half, and therefore a maximum participation rate. The true intention of Ferreras's proposals appears to be to increase worker voice, not limit it, unlike the example of the Taft-Hartley Act of 1947, which imposed a maximum threshold for unions to appoint one-half of multi-employer pension funds. That was, and remains, wrong in principle.[59] On the contrary, many enterprises do and should involve institutions with majority worker voice.

Third, whatever the rights of capital, it is vital to emphasize that shareholders are often not the real investors: they are investing other people's money. Parallel proposals to democratize capital funds are as necessary as proposals to democratize firms. However, in the case of a capital fund, there is no credible argument for giving fund managers— or their subordinate workers—a voice equal to the real investor because the fund belongs to the beneficiaries. This has implications both for the extent of a bicameral proposal (which probably did not envisage extension to pension funds, although they are also "firms") and the operation of an "investor chamber" within a bicameral firm. Does an investor chamber represent the real investors, or unaccountable financial intermediaries? If the latter, there seems to be little legitimacy in maintaining a full investor chamber, packed with asset managers or banker appointees.

Fourth, in public enterprise, it would appear that a general model for capital and labor may need to change. Another key stakeholder comes into play: the member of the public. If one sought to use a bicameral model in public enterprise, it could be argued that members of the public should elect the "investor" chamber, rather than the state that provides finance. But it is still not entirely clear that a "bicameral" model can represent the multiplicity of interests at stake, nor that it should replace the vast variety of experiments in public stakeholder voice.

Fifth, the model of bicameralism appeals to the UK Parliament's experience with the House of Commons and the House of Lords, and other bicameral legislatures. However, these political models are themselves deeply contested. As Ferreras notes, the House of Lords was temporarily abolished in the English Civil War, but also its power was virtually eliminated by the landmark Parliament Acts of 1911 and 1949, together ensuring that the Lords could only delay legislation by one year, and money bills not at all.[60] This is what enabled the creation of the welfare state, taxed the aristocracy, reformed land, and enabled modern democracy to develop. The UK Labour Party has proposed abolishing the upper house, and Sweden in fact did abolish its upper chamber from 1970. It is clear that in many countries two chambers of parliament work, but they are not always equal. For example, the UK's House of Commons can override the House of Lords. Bicameralism is not the only way of dividing power. Similarly, it would appear better that a flexible view is adopted and experiment allowed. What matters most is not so much the form of the model but achievement of the principles of economic democracy in substance.

Conclusion

Today ever fewer people view it as legitimate to say that the corporation (and even less the firm or enterprise) is "merely a vehicle for organizing capital [investors]." The better, and dominant, view that has guided the great New Dealers, the Universal Declaration, and corporate governance since the Great Depression is that a corporation is a "social institution" designed to advance the public interest.[61] Shareholder interests must represent the real investors, not unaccountable asset managers on Wall Street, Bay Street, in the City, Frankfurt, La

Défense, or Milan. Shareholders must in any case be "subordinated to a number of claims by labor, by customers and patrons, by the community."[62] It follows that the bicameral firm is an important model in thinking about the next steps in economic and social democracy and is ripe for realization in law. A firm and an enterprise are at once political, social, economic, and above all human entities, real organisms embedded in our environment and ecosystem as a whole.[63] The theory of the firm, and the law of enterprise, looks past legal form and focuses on function and effect. If the five principles of universality, votes at work, votes in capital, votes in public services, and experiment are upheld, then economic democracy can become social reality very soon.

13

Economic Democracy against Racial Capitalism: Seeding Freedom

Sanjay Pinto

In the mid-1990s, as neoliberalism was consolidating its global reach, Ellen Meiksins Wood's *Democracy against Capitalism* offered a trenchant account of liberal democracy's failure to extend democratic voice and representation into the economic realm.[1] Picking up the mantle today, Isabelle Ferreras's proposal for economic bicameralism offers a powerful vision for advancing economic democracy.[2] Right at the time of the COVID-19 pandemic, the economic impact of which reverberated widely but unevenly across the globe, her plea to expand the rights and claims of labor could not have been more timely. Countless workers have lost their livelihoods, others have been compelled by economic necessity to work in harrowing and unsafe circumstances, and many have been plunged into further economic insecurity. In the United States and elsewhere, these conditions have spurred demands for protection, voice, and dignity in the world of work—grassroots energy that might coalesce around the kind of vision that Ferreras puts forward.

Alongside and intertwined with struggles for workers' rights and economic justice, recent times have seen a cascade of uprisings contesting structural racism across different arenas. In the US, the killings of George Floyd, Breonna Taylor, and many other Black Americans by law enforcement agents prompted a new wave of movement activity asserting the intrinsic value of Black lives and demanding police accountability, set against a pandemic that disproportionately impacted the well-being and economic security of Black communities.[3] The Movement for Black

Lives has been interlinked with "Fight for 15" organizing to raise the minimum wage and other struggles for economic fairness, building on years of movement building at the intersection of economic and racial justice, and recent organizing has highlighted how race shapes the undervaluation of many jobs deemed "essential" during the pandemic.[4] Helping to frame these efforts is a growing body of work on "racial capitalism": the functioning of racial differentiation to subordinate Black and Brown people in processes of capital accumulation while bolstering the dominion of capital over labor, historically and in the present.[5]

In conversation with Ferreras's conception of economic bicameralism, this chapter makes the case for a more direct confrontation between the aspirations of economic democracy and the realities of racial capitalism. Focusing particular attention on the American context, the argument draws inspiration from the work and vision of two iconic figures in the unfinished struggle for Black liberation, W. E. B Du Bois and Fannie Lou Hamer. It considers how efforts to expand power and voice for workers must contend with the racial hierarchy that marks the socioeconomic division of labor and the related use of racial distinctions to thwart labor solidarity. The chapter begins by briefly examining the historical roots of American racial capitalism in slavery and conquest. It then considers how movements agitating for greater workplace democracy have intervened at the intersection of racial and class inequality. Against this backdrop, it draws lessons for how economic bicameralism might help to challenge racial capitalism as it exists today.

Racial Capitalism in America: A Short Sketch

"Progressive actors in history have fought to emancipate colonies, slaves, ethnic groups, or women," Ferreras writes. "Now it is time to emancipate workers" (this volume, p. 28). The racial capitalism framework provides a set of resources for understanding liberation from legacies of slavery and colonialism as a work in progress and a central concern for any project to emancipate workers. As such, it can help to fill a set of gaps and misapprehensions in existing theory. In *Democracy against Capitalism*, for example, Wood minimized the relevance of "identity" to the core project of democratizing the economy.[6] The argument advanced here shows why grappling with the role of race in capitalism's core dynamics must be central to this endeavor.

In a foundational text, Cedric Robinson asserts that "the tendency of European civilization through capitalism was . . . not to homogenize but to differentiate—to exaggerate regional, subcultural, and dialectical differences into racial ones."[7] According to Robinson, the propensity of political and economic elites to *racialize* group differences, and subordinate based on these differences, first hinged on ethnic and national distinctions within Europe. It then took hold globally through trans-atlantic slavery and settler colonialism, with Black and Brown people exploited in ways that benefited specific economic and political actors while helping to underwrite nation-building and capitalist development in the global North.[8] As Walter Johnson put it in a piece reflecting on Robinson's legacy, "There was no such thing as capitalism without slavery: the history of Manchester never happened without the history of Mississippi."[9]

Charting the origins of racial capitalism in the United States, Cheryl Harris unpacks how whiteness itself has functioned as a form of property, serving as a basis for exclusion from fundamental citizenship and ownership rights. "The racialization of identity and the racial subordination of Blacks and Native Americans provided the ideological basis for slavery and conquest," Harris notes.[10]

> Although the systems of oppression of Blacks and Native Americans differed in form—the former involving the seizure and appropriation of labor, the latter entailing the seizure and appropriation of land—undergirding both was a racialized conception of property implemented by force and ratified by law.[11]

Harris's account captures key mechanisms of racial capitalism.[12] One is the exploitation of labor by capital, a core concern and point of departure in Ferreras's discussion of economic bicameralism. Robinson, Harris, and others have shown how racial distinctions have structured the terms of exploitation, which is most starkly evident in the case of slavery but continues through the racially differentiated valuation of work in contemporary labor markets. A second is the expropriation of personhood and land that has laid the ground for capital accumulation. Long after the original sins of slavery and colonialism, expropriation continues through multiple forms of racialized dehumanization and practices that extract profit from communities of color while denying them the means for accumulating wealth, often saddling them with debt.[13] Building on recent contributions to the literature on racial capitalism, I would add to these another mechanism, marginalization, by which some are deemed surplus to the requirements of capital accumulation.[14] Racial differentiation looms large in who is rendered expendable in this manner, as evident in the racially inflected application and impact of austerity politics and the ways in which recent economic restructuring, though widely felt, often impacts employment and economic security in communities of color most acutely.[15]

Facing the confluence of labor-market segmentation with residential segregation and other forms of racial inequality, many people of color experience the oppressive force of these dynamics in ways that are closely intertwined. Long after the end of slavery and Jim Crow, for example, many Black women continue to experience exploitation in direct-care jobs, providing underpaid childcare and long-term care services that serve as the foundation for others to reap much-larger rewards in the labor market.[16] Despite helping to support core processes of capital accumulation that enrich others, many have zero or negative wealth, deprived of major assets such as homes or cars. And, as Gabriel Winant aptly put it in a discussion focusing on the health care sector, frontline direct-care workers are "indispensable" in a collective sense but "disposable" as individuals, considered easily replaceable.[17] The insecurity and marginality they experience, often living in zones without other good employment options, feeds into the conditions for their continued exploitation.

Long predating contemporary discussions around racial capitalism, W. E. B. Du Bois captured another aspect of whiteness as property that helps to explain the persistence of these mechanisms in our time. In *Black Reconstruction*, Du Bois told the story of why and how the project of achieving racial equality had foundered. A key factor, in his estimation, was a "public or psychological wage" of whiteness that served to compensate for the hardship many white workers face themselves, preventing them from seeing the humanity of workers of color and the broad interests they shared in creating a more equitable society.[18] The psychosocial gratification of racial domination served as a smoke screen for exploitation.

David Roediger builds from Du Bois's formulation to trace how the "wages of whiteness" developed historically in relation to slavery and evolving conceptions of freedom. Indenture and other "gradations of unfreedom" experienced by white workers as late as the eighteenth century led many not to distinguish their own circumstances all that sharply from those of enslaved Black people, Roediger argues.[19] By the first half of the nineteenth century, however, most white workers had exited indenture and occupational positions such as domestic service that placed them in closer structural proximity to the enslaved. Although there were currents of labor republicanism that challenged "wage slavery," large segments of the white working class came to jointly embrace "free" labor and whiteness as markers of their superiority.[20] Du Bois noted the mass refusal of many Black people to continue laboring under plantation slavery during the Civil War as a historic labor action—a general strike that also brought in some exploited white workers.[21] However, when emancipation was declared in 1865, large-scale damage to multiracial solidarity had already been done. The wages of whiteness reinforced Black subordination and hampered the formation of broad working-class coalitions that could resist wage slavery, working toward the uplift of people of all colors.[22]

These fissures have continued to shape the contours of American politics, social relations, and social policy. In the late nineteenth century, the Populist Party advanced an agenda favoring redistribution and robust social citizenship rights. However, in the South, where the party had its strongest base, white elites leveraged the wages of whiteness to cleave its farm-labor coalition along racial lines, halting its progress.[23] During the New Deal era, with this political dynamic entrenched, southern Democrats intent on preserving conditions of racialized subjection within their spheres of influence blocked the coverage of farmworkers and domestic workers under landmark labor and employment protections.[24] And, in the mid-1940s, spooked by the growing success of Black and white industrial workers seeking to unionize, a coalition including southern Democrats and northern Republicans passed legislation that substantially narrowed the range of tactics organized labor had at its disposal.[25] It is in this environment that movements pressing for greater democracy in the world of work have evolved and intervened.

Movements for Workplace Democracy and the Struggle for Racial Equality

In the 1880s, two decades after the end of the Civil War and just before the Populist Party reached the height of its influence, the Knights of Labor, a national labor federation, had a membership that was 700,000 strong and included large numbers of Black and Chicano workers.[26] Embodying labor republican values, significant elements within the federation sought to challenge wage slavery by advancing worker ownership and control over the means of production, and the Knights organized hundreds of producer and worker cooperatives around the country.[27] Many of these unionized cooperatives had significant numbers of members of color, including a cotton gin run by Black worker-owners in Alabama.[28] Yet, the Knights were not immune from the racially charged xenophobia of their day. Mirroring the 1882 Chinese Exclusion Act, the federation barred exploited Chinese immigrant workers from joining its ranks.[29]

The storyline of the Knights calls attention to a complicated history. Movements pressing for workplace democracy have challenged racial capitalism. However, they have also reflected, and, through action and inaction, reinforced it. Like the evolution of social policy in America, the development of the labor movement has been stymied by the wages of the whiteness. Indeed, these histories are closely interlinked. Without a strong and encompassing labor movement helping to anchor left coalitions, conservative economic and political elites have been better able to turn back progressive change; weak and fragmented labor and social rights have constrained the power and reach of organized labor.

During the early postwar period and the years leading up to it, workers of color demanded inclusion within a rapidly expanding labor movement, and a number of industrial unions affiliated with the Congress of Industrial Organizations (CIO) successfully organized multiracial worker populations.[30] Also during the postwar decades, some unions were able to make headway in areas where personal services and other work performed disproportionately by people of color and women had been systematically devalued—a trend that has continued in some areas of the economy in recent decades, even as overall union density has ebbed.[31] Postwar unionization helped to

advance better wages and benefits for millions of working people, bringing particular gains for Black workers.[32]

Despite this powerful impact, it is also true that many unions
bolstered or shied away from addressing patterns of racial hierarchy and
racist exclusion. Across the US, unions in different sectors have been
complicit in excluding people of color, women, and immigrants from
accessing entire segments of the labor market.[33] Even when members of
marginalized groups have made their way into union jobs, union representatives and members have too often subjected them to mistreatment,
constrained their job mobility, and kept them at the edges of union
decision-making processes.[34] Bruce Nelson documents how many of the
CIO unions noted for their multiracial organizing nonetheless reinforced patterns of occupational closure along racial lines, keeping
workers of color out of the most highly paid jobs.[35] And Operation
Dixie, launched in 1946 to organize industrial workers in the South,
ultimately stalled due not only to external factors (including the passage
of the Taft-Hartley Act) but also to decisions by CIO leaders to limit the
role of Black organizers and those judged too radical.[36]

Cooperatives of the sort organized by the Knights of Labor in the late
nineteenth century have had a much smaller footprint and structural
role than that of unions, which flows in part from the more direct challenge they pose to capitalism's foundational distinction: the dominion
of capital over labor. They are of special relevance to discussions
around democratizing the corporation since they function on a "one
member, one vote" basis—indeed, Ferreras sees economic bicameralism
as a potential transition point toward full worker ownership and control
of the sort embodied in worker cooperatives. Unfortunately, worker
co-ops have often reinforced racial exclusion in ways not unlike unions.
During the Depression, for example, Italian immigrant workers in
the San Francisco Bay Area created several garbage-collection worker
cooperatives, permitting Black workers to become associated only as
nonmembers.[37] But there are also notable examples of racially diverse
worker co-ops whose members have taken special pains to promote
radical inclusion along multiple dimensions.[38] And there is a long
history of worker co-ops and other forms of mutualism created within
communities facing acute social marginalization, including, in recent
years, numerous domestic worker co-ops formed by immigrant women
of color.[39]

Jessica Gordon Nembhard documents a rich tradition of Black co-operation and mutualism forged under conditions of racial subjugation and terror. This includes Black networks of mutual aid and resistance that emerged on slave plantations and in maroon settlements created by fugitives from bondage. It also encompasses an underappreciated history of Black cooperative development in the US.[40] As part of documenting this history, Gordon Nembhard highlights a lesser-known work published by Du Bois in 1907, *Economic Co-operation among Negro Americans*, in which he cataloged 154 existing Black-owned co-operatives (including consumer, credit, producer, and transportation co-ops) and hundreds of Black-run mutual aid societies.[41] Though he was not very optimistic about prospects for further growth at the time of this study, Du Bois continued to refer to cooperatives quite frequently when imagining what a more just economy and society might look like.[42]

Du Bois's bona fides as a radical democrat were not clear-cut, showing significant evolution over the course of his career. In *The Souls of Black Folk*, published in 1903, he put forward an elite-driven conception of Black progress spearheaded by a "talented tenth" within the race.[43] By the time he published *Black Reconstruction* in 1935, he had become more preoccupied with diagnosing the challenges confronting workers of color in both the global North and South and how those within the "dark sea of human labor" could mobilize collectively to improve their conditions.[44] Du Bois's views on the role on cooperatives evolved as part of this shift. All along, he saw cooperatives as a means of advancing Black self-determination and independence in the face of persistent racism. But, as his class analysis sharpened, he also came to envision a role for both cooperatives and unions as part of a broader push for "industrial democracy." "The disfranchisement . . . of the mass of workers . . . is the most vital disfranchisement in the world," he wrote in an article in *The Crisis* magazine in 1930.[45]

Fannie Lou Hamer's Freedom Farm Cooperative is a historically significant example within the tradition of Black cooperation and mutualism mapped by Gordon Nembhard and Du Bois. Priscilla McCutcheon notes that the Freedom Farms project was inextricably bound up both with Hamer's experience of exploitation as a sharecropper two generations removed from slavery and the skill she developed as an expert agriculture producer.[46] Best known for her trailblazing advocacy for the extension of voting rights, Hamer also consistently intervened in struggles for basic subsistence. Indeed, she was highly skeptical of political formations that failed to directly connect to and concern themselves with these struggles. In the 1960s, Hamer was closely involved with the work of the Mississippi Freedom Democratic Union (MFDU), a movement of poor, mostly Black workers closely tied to the Mississippi Freedom Democratic Party. Many, like Hamer, were sharecroppers employed by white landowners. The MFDU organized strikes and other actions and mobilized mutual aid, including relief for workers who faced employer retaliation due to their activities.[47]

Freedom Farm Cooperative, which Hamer founded in 1969, aimed to create an independent base of employment in Mississippi's Sunflower County while also attending to other basic challenges such as low rates of land and home ownership. The organizational complex employed dozens of people in co-op enterprises and clerical roles, administered a cooperative pig bank that helped to provide food and financial support to many families in the area, and anchored the development of hundreds of affordable housing units, among other initiatives.[48] Hamer knew that housing and food insecurity were literally forcing Black communities around her into submission, compelling them to accept the extractive terms of employment they were handed. In addressing basic consumption needs, the Freedom Farm project sought to safeguard basic well-being, enable a degree of autonomy from exploitative economic relationships, and establish a refuge permitting people to contest racial exclusion in the political arena while still having access to the basic means of life—in short, to start seeding a local foundation for liberation from the twin evils of racial oppression and economic compulsion.[49] Though beset by practical challenges and relatively short-lived, the project's scope and capacious vision of freedom stands as an important example of responding to racial capitalism holistically, in ways that reached well beyond the realm of paid work.[50] Today, an initiative in Jackson, Mississippi, bearing the Freedom Farm name and inspired by a similarly expansive vision carries forward this legacy.[51]

Bicameral Firms, Economic Democracy, and the Cause of Freedom

The background outlined above provides some grounding for thinking through how Ferreras's conception of economic bicameralism might be leveraged to help confront and overturn some of the core dynamics of racial capitalism, advancing greater freedom and inclusion in the economy and society more broadly. The discussion that follows addresses two broad questions that flow from this prospect. First, how could the internal structure and workings of bicameral firms be configured in ways that challenge invidious forms of racial differentiation? Second, how might bicameral enterprises fit within a larger set of struggles that advance the kind of broad, liberatory agendas that Du Bois and Hamer envisaged?

Economic bicameralism brings labor into parity with capital, offering a blueprint for recalibrating capitalism's foundational inequality at a firm level. In turn, it raises a set of questions around how to ensure equality, including racial equality, among labor investors. One important issue is how to prevent racism from infecting the associational life and representational structures of the labor chamber of the bicameral firm. This might be addressed by creating caucus structures such as those that have been established within union bodies and ensuring that structurally disadvantaged groups receive formal representation within the chamber of the labor investors.[52] However, even in worker cooperatives that are highly inclusive in their formal structures, the convergence of race, gender, and occupational position have been shown to bear heavily on who exerts authority in practice.[53] Challenging the ways in which racial capitalism penetrates the inner workings of the bicameral firm would thus require a further set of commitments.

Ronald Takaki observed that "racial inequality and occupational stratification have come to coexist in a mutually reinforcing and dynamic structural relationship."[54] One of the Gordian knots of racial capitalism, this entanglement raises two important issues for economic bicameralism. One has to do with the cultivation of solidarity. In firms with an elaborate division of labor and high degrees of job and occupational differentiation, divergent economic interests can often undermine cohesion in the ranks of labor.[55] The presence of racialized hierarchy and the continuing potency of the wages of whiteness only adds to the challenge, demanding strategies for countering white supremacy and bridging racial divides. For bicameral firms with more radically egalitarian designs, a second issue has to do with the transformation of underlying hierarchies. Of course, patterns of occupational stratification and racial segmentation have a complex set of sources that originate well beyond the boundaries of any individual firm. However, within firms, the transformation of hierarchy could include opening pathways for job and occupational mobility, contesting norms that undervalue certain work, recasting underlying divisions of labor in ways that more evenly distribute tasks of conception and execution (an issue Ferreras raises in discussing the potential benefits of economic bicameralism)—and directly accounting for race in effectuating all of these shifts.

Another set of issues related to the structure and workings of bicameral firms has to do with pathways to entry as labor investors. If the very organs meant to channel workplace democracy have been known to block racial inclusion, this raises questions around who would be included in the demos of the bicameral firm in the first place. The problem is particularly vexing since racially exclusionary patterns often materialize in ways that are subtle and largely unconscious, as in the case of many worker cooperatives that emerged from the social networks of white progressives amid the counterculture of the 1970s.[56] Hiring and recruitment policies at the firm level matter in addressing such patterns. Government policy also has an important role to play in combating discrimination at an individual firm level and in addressing broader forms of structural marginalization with racially disparate effects. For example, misclassification of workers as independent contractors is a form of workplace "fissuring" that has grown rapidly in recent years, relegating people undertaking essential functions of firms to peripheral, nonemployee status and depriving them of associated rights.[57] Checking misclassification through policy could expand the terrain for workplace democracy, and, since workers of color are overrepresented among the misclassified in many parts of the economy, it could also help to promote greater racial inclusion.[58]

The promise of economic bicameralism as a force for racial equality would also depend on addressing how racial wealth gaps shape the makeup of the investor class. Du Bois noted that poverty and a lack of accumulated wealth were factors inhibiting the growth of cooperatives in Black communities—patterns that were linked to his later analysis in *Black Reconstruction* showing how most freed slaves were denied land-ownership and forced into extractive forms of wage labor, including sharecropping arrangements that frequently left them indebted.[59] Over time, a range of racist practices, including redlining and predatory lending, have perpetuated and worsened racial wealth gaps, particularly for Black and Latinx communities in the US.[60] The persistence of racial wealth gaps contributes to these communities being less likely to serve as capital investors in the contemporary economy, which would undoubtedly affect the racial demographics of the chamber of capital within bicameral firms.[61] In turn, these demographics could be expected to shape decisions about where bicameral firms get formed, and for whose benefit. Du Bois and Hamer were ultimately concerned with how cooperative approaches could address the marginalization Black communities experienced both as workers seeking fair employment and as consumers seeking access to basic goods and services. Ensuring that bicameral firms could answer this call on a large scale would require thinking through a set of strategies to enable communities of color to build wealth and meaningfully participate in investment decisions related to enterprise formation.

Economic bicameralism holds promise for creating more democratic workplaces and, under the right conditions, better serving community needs for a variety of goods and services. It can be distinguished from forms of mutual aid and cooperation that enable people to meet basic needs outside the domain of the market—what George Caffentzis and Silvia Federici have in mind in their discussion of the "reproductive commons."[62] Core elements of Hamer's Freedom Farm project can be seen as embodying this sort of commoning approach. Under conditions in which a variety of racially oppressive dynamics pervaded market relations, the ways it addressed needs for food and housing were part of an effort to alleviate market dependency and provide an alternate means of subsistence. Such efforts should be seen as complementary to those seeking greater voice and fairness within markets. Both are part of a larger set of struggles to challenge racial capitalism, build economic democracy, and advance the cause of freedom.[63]

Economic bicameralism, on my reading, is best seen as a pragmatist formulation in the Deweyan sense: it seeks to deepen democracy in ways that are responsive to the evident limitations and possibilities of contemporary conditions.[64] In that spirit, I want to bracket the general question of what role the market and private corporations should play in our economic life in an ideal sense, focusing on how bicameral firms could connect to existing social and institutional ecologies to advance systemic change in desirable directions from where we are now. The links to state power are pivotal. Ferreras stresses the important role of the state in establishing the preconditions for economic bicameralism, and the foregoing discussion hinted at some specific areas where applications of state power could help to leverage bicameral firms as a force for greater racial equality and inclusion. We would need to add to these a host of other mechanisms ensuring democratic accountability to the communities and polities in which democratic firms (and indeed all firms) are embedded, and measures providing stronger supports allowing people to exit the market when needed.[65] This point deserves emphasis in a neoliberal environment where far too much power is ceded to corporations, with many damaging consequences that often fall disproportionately on communities considered expendable (environmental racism being just one example).[66]

State power might align with economic bicameralism in particular ways in parts of the economy where "essential" goods and services are being delivered (e.g., care provision and food production and distribution). The pandemic environment witnessed the emergence of a discourse of valuing frontline essential workers (e.g., home care workers and grocery store clerks). But the shift was largely rhetorical, as rates of pay and other concrete indications of value remained mostly unchanged, leaving many essential workers struggling to meet basic needs for themselves and their families. In many parts of the US, policymakers have actively promoted racialized exploitation within direct-care systems by setting reimbursement rates at low levels, assuming that the women of color who remain concentrated in these jobs can provide these services cheaply.[67] Thus, a strategy to improve conditions for direct-care workers might pair economic bicameralism with lobbying around raising these reimbursement rates—something that new infrastructure investments could help enable.[68] Over the medium to long term, perhaps economic bicameralism could be a transition point for bringing specific kinds of services back into the public sector, where they arguably belong, while retaining the kind of worker voice afforded by the chamber of labor investors.

Ferreras notes a potential role for unions in shaping the ecology for economic bicameralism, serving as a vehicle for the mobilization of labor investors. As the remaining vestiges of the postwar settlement continue to erode, several unions in the US have recently been exploring approaches that hark back to the efforts of the Knights of Labor in the late nineteenth century.[69] In a context where capital is growing ever more hostile, unions are looking at worker co-ops and other alternative enterprise models that could deepen worker voice and help to create more aligned bargaining partners over the long term. For example, the nation's largest health care union—an organization with a rich set of historical connections to the civil rights movement—already has a contract with the nation's largest worker cooperative, a home care agency.[70] Inspired in part by this example, the union has explored the creation of worker cooperatives as a strategy to retain good jobs for its mostly Black and Brown members while keeping needed services in underserved communities.[71] Although the aim is to create fully cooperative structures, arrangements akin to economic bicameralism have also been explored as a more pragmatic alternative in the near term.

The picture sketched here is distinctively American in important respects, but the confrontation between economic democracy and racial capitalism holds broader relevance, including in the metropoles of Europe. Here, immigration flows continue to follow old colonial routes and the intracontinental core–periphery circuits traced by Cedric Robinson. With racial, ethnic, and national differences often forming a basis for labor-market segmentation in ways not unlike those seen in the US, and amid trends of rising immigration, far-right parties have been gaining ground with anti-immigrant rhetoric and appeals to national purity.[72] In many cases, these parties have made significant inroads among segments of the working class that have previously been core constituencies of left political coalitions.[73] At a time when capital is challenging long-standing labor and social settlements even in the heartlands of coordinated capitalism, these kinds of fractures could be hugely consequential.[74] Perhaps it is time to experiment with ideas such as economic bicameralism that could advance equality, counter alienation, and help inspire new forms of solidarity.

As Du Bois came to emphasize in the latter stages of his career, the intersection of capitalism with racial oppression is ultimately global in character. Du Bois recognized capitalist exploitation as a problem that traversed boundaries of race and nation—indeed, his analysis of the wages of whiteness sought to draw attention precisely to the factors obscuring this reality. Yet, it was also evident to him that the "dark sea of human labor"—Black and Brown workers in both the global North and global South—remained concentrated in the bottom rungs of the global economic division of labor, working under the most coercive conditions.[75] Nearly one hundred years later, even with substantial shifts in class structures and the rising wealth and power of many countries in the global South, this basic pattern remains. And the wages of whiteness continue to cloud the humanity of Black and Brown people, dampening prospects for collective action across multiple arenas, from local worksites to global networks of production and distribution. As the historical record makes clear, movements to build economic democracy must directly confront the "color line" that Du Bois posited as the central problem of his time or risk buttressing the very forces standing in the way of human freedom.[76]

VI.
Conclusion

14

A Response to My Readers

Isabelle Ferreras

Let me begin by offering my profound thanks to the interlocutors in this volume. I am grateful for their comments and insights. In this brief response, I do not directly respond to each of them but rather make some general comments by way of reply to the most pressing themes.

The COVID-19 pandemic threw into sharp relief many aspects of social life, in particular the indisputable fact that workers are "essential." Indeed, the least-recognized, worst-paid, most ill-considered, and "low-skilled" workers among us were declared exactly that by governments around the globe. Our economic system, however, continues to resolutely ignore their importance. Indeed, it remains organized according to the very opposite principle: that workers are secondary and disposable. This is evident not only in the way the market economy operates but also in the way that power is structured inside the firm, which is governed as if workers were anything but essential. The immense and surprising popularity of the op-ed written by Julie Battilana, Dominique Méda, and myself at the onset of the COVID crisis to highlight this fact shows an immense appetite around the world to move beyond the current economic regime by democratizing firms, decommodifying labor, and decarbonizing the planet.[1] The resonance of that discussion means that the real utopia put forward in this volume is now being more seriously discussed across the world than at the time the anchor essay was written. Indeed, the basic principle underpinning the democratization of firms affirmed in the "Democratizing Work" op-ed is the philosophical principle that I identified throughout my study of democratic transitions of political entities under conditions of despotism, which I called "bicameral moments." The principle is that the disenfranchized constituency (i.e., workers in the case of the firm) "should get the right to collectively validate or veto the [firm's] decisions." Applying this principle to corporations gives us economic bicameralism.[2]

The excellent contributions of my coauthors in this volume will no doubt propel forward the dissemination of these ideas even faster. Nevertheless, it is true that since we wrote that call to repair ourselves and our earth, we have not seen the massive democratic renewal that is required. Instead, we've seen more democratic regress, more inequality, more mass death from a viral pandmic, more corporate looting in the public health disaster, more environmental destruction, as well as Russia's 2022 invasion of Ukraine. Yet, without a doubt, much of the public is disgusted with all of this, sick to death of their everyday bullying by those who imagine themselves the "masters of mankind."[3] The present seems like a hinge, ready to swing open to new possibilities. Perhaps, just perhaps, a simple proposal, like granting workers the collective veto right to validate the decisions of the firm, that is, making firms bicameral—thereby giving regular people more control over at least parts of their lives—will strike a chord and become popular enough to inspire a politician or two to run ahead of the crowd that calls for it.[4]

What Is Economic Bicameralism?

"Economic bicameralism," once again, refers to a specific principle in political philosophy and philosophy of law—guaranteeing veto power to a once-ignored constituency (in this case, the workers of the firm)—in order to democratize the institution in question (in this case, the corporation). In the context of capitalist firms, it recognizes in firm governance two types of investors needed for firm success—capital investors and labor investors—and accords them equal rights and thus mutual veto power. The basic idea is simple, straightforward, and because of that immensely powerful.

In recognizing these two constituencies, as discussed in the lead essay to this volume, economic bicameralism is situated in the tradition of German codetermination. However, since it grants veto power to each constituency on its own, it differs quite profoundly from most of the German experience where workers have merely remained the "junior partner" of capital (it differs even further from the non-German European experience, where workers' rights are weaker still). There is one exceptional case in the history of the German codetermination that may be said to converge with economic bicameralism: coal, steel, and mining firms with more than 1,000 employees, where workers are, unusually, granted true parity and the nomination of a firm's director of human resources must be approved by a majority in the firm's works council. Such firms are the only known example of economic bicameralism in action.[5]

Economic bicameralism, it bears repeating, grants workers (via their representatives) the right to validate or veto *all* major decisions in the firm; in practical terms, this means granting the same rights to workers as those currently enjoyed by capital investors in the governance of the firm. To enact this philosophical principle, organizational arrangements could take many forms. My anchor essay focused on one clear-cut and concrete example to make the proposal understandable, but in retrospect it seems that my vocabulary choices have led to some confusion. For example, I wrote of a "two-chamber parliament" as a way to highlight the idea that workers would enjoy this collective veto right at the legislative level. Yet, what I meant by this was not at all that the two chambers must be physically separated or distanced from one another. The point is, rather, that the governing authority of the firm must be shared between two bodies of equal power—a majority in each chamber being necessary to validate its decisions. It is not a matter of great importance whether the two chambers meet in physically distinct rooms or separate buildings, or whether they sit together. It goes without saying that regardless of whether they primarily meet in one physical space or two, there will need to be all kinds of regular inter-chamber (as well as intra-chamber) deliberation, through regular formal meetings, joint subcommittees, ad hoc gatherings of various representatives, and so on. This will drive the epistemic value of such a firm government, powering the third justification for bicameral government: its intelligence.

If the two chambers *do* meet together, this would constitute a single board or parliament. While technically a single board could be described as "monocameral," the crucial principle remains the same: worker representatives must be empowered to validate or veto all decisions via their own majority vote; thus a majority vote from *both* constituent bodies would be required to validate decisions. Clearly the practical arrangements for the implementation of this principle will vary depending on specific country traditions. In the case of a country with no tradition of works councils, such as the United States, for example, Sharon Block and Ben Sachs have proposed that economic bicameralism be implemented through a supermajority board vote by the workers' representatives, whatever their actual number on a given board might be. Whether they constitute 30, 40, or 50 percent of a board's members, their collective veto right remains clear.[6] Julie Battilana and I have suggested that the term "dual-majority board" might be used to describe the application of the principle of economic bicameralism in "monocameral" contexts such as the US.[7]

It is important to reiterate that although I believe economic bicameralism would be immensely beneficial here and now, it is not the ultimate ideal. I see it, rather, as a transitional demand to help shift ownership and control away from the capital investors to what I take to be the long-term goal: worker ownership and control. In other words, the deepest purpose of economic bicameralism is to help build a realistic bridge from here to a future society based (among other things) on cooperative firms where labor investors, the only people actually governed by the firm, are able to truly self-govern. Providing such a bridge is, as I see it, the specific task of a real utopia, as illuminated by the work of Erik Olin Wright.

Economic Bicameralism's Theory of Change

I take it for granted that many people are fed up with being bullied at work. My hypothesis is that if straightforward and compelling principles—such as the right to be respected at work and the importance of sharing power through a mutual veto—could be brought to bear, and if such a proposal were stated in terms that anyone could understand, and without threatening the viability of the firm, it might have a chance of attracting a critical mass of supporters within social movements and mainstream left political parties.

Assuming, as all evidence suggests, that firms set up this way would operate reasonably well, their functioning would naturally expand the opportunities, as well as the skills and capacities, of those interested in taking a more decisive role in running the firms themselves. Hence the bicameral firm is a first step on the journey toward worker cooperatives. It will surely sometimes stumble and have reversals. It will certainly require a different sort of financial system to fully prosper and grow (more on this below). But if we think of the firm as a political entity, this should not daunt but inspire.[8] Because one thing economic bicameralism gives workers immediately is more control over their lives. It gives them the agency that they neither now possess nor have the incentive to develop. I believe that once they have tasted substantial authority in the workplace, they will be unlikely to give it up without a fight.

The Likely Outcomes of Economic Bicameralism

If a country were to mandate that all sizable firms enact economic bicameralism, what should we reasonably expect to be the costs and benefits?

In economic terms, the most important point to reiterate is that the evidence is now robust and compelling that enhanced worker voice does not overly damage the productivity of the firm: this has been seen with respect to employee stock ownership plans (ESOPs), worker co-ops, and codetermined firms.[9] It is true that firms that institute bicameralism may face some additional costs. For instance, the aim of the firm will no longer be profit above all else; rather, profit maximization will be balanced with other goals such as employment stability and rising wages, and hopefully to some degree other nonpecuniary goals such as protecting the environment, as Battilana, Michael Fuerstein, and Matthew Lee showed in the case of "hybrid organizations."[10] Bicameral firms may also face more costs than conventional ones in that they may be more willing to pay their taxes and be less inclined to hide their profits in tax havens;[11] such firms will also be far less likely to consider offshoring their production to cheaper labor sources in the Global South.[12] Nevertheless, the evidence suggests that such costs are likely to be more or less offset by the benefits that increased voice can bring: increased motivation, less conflict, less absenteeism, reduced costs of monitoring, and so on.

Max Krahé (chapter 7) is right to point out that firms are islands in the market sea. How well bicameral firms operate will depend to a significant degree on the surrounding market system, in particular the financial system. Will bicameral firms be able to acquire the loans and other types of financial support that they require on good terms and without surrendering democratic control? Clearly, bicameral firms will struggle in the international competition if the only way that they can finance their operations is by relying on the conventional capitalistic infrastructure of private banks and stock markets (which will always prefer to finance corporations that offer control in return for invest- ment). It is important to remember that the financial infrastructure that exists today has been developed over the centuries in order to facilitate conventional business enterprises; it is not designed to foster demo- cratic firms. So for bicameral firms to flourish over the long term, they will clearly require some kind of complementary financial system. In the short term, the bicameral firm will acquire finance from private capital markets, banks, and perhaps the state (either via preferential loans or public banks set up specifically to help finance bicameral firms). Bicam- eral firms will still be able to receive finance from traditional private markets; they just may not receive as favorable terms as conventional firms. Clearly, the goal must be to remake the financial system to recog- nize that the provision of credit (like the provision of electricity or water) is at root an essential public service and so should be organized like a public utility with democratic oversight. Of course, how best to do this is a complicated issue, but some excellent suggestions are offered in Fred Block and Bob Hockett's *Democratizing Finance*—another volume in the Real Utopias series that Erik Olin Wright envisioned as a compan- ion to this one.[13]

What can we realistically expect from the bicameral firm in terms of its social benefits? Simon Jäger and coauthors' recent review of codeter- mination makes for sobering reading in this regard.[14] The authors find that codetermination brings little social benefits in terms of wages, the labor share, income inequality, or the quality of industrial relations as proxied by strikes, and gives workers basically no influence over corporate strategy. It does, however, mildly improve subjective job quality, enhance control over decisions related to working conditions, and perhaps provide small influence over layoffs and wages. They attribute these weak outcomes (correctly, in my view) to the fact that in the vast major- ity of codetermined firms, workers remain very much junior partners, lacking anything like equal power or authority (for instance, in most cases workers control only a minority of seats, around 20 to 40 percent, and their role is widely seen as facilitating communication, not at all as running the firm).[15]

It should nevertheless be pointed out that Jäger and colleagues are on the pessimistic side of the spectrum in terms of interpreting the social benefits of codetermination in the literature. Other studies have found that codetermination, even with the limited power granted to workers, does provide enhanced economic security, more employment, more shop floor decision-making power, as well as reduced inequality across society.[16] For instance, Felix Hörisch finds that looking at society as a whole, and controlling for union strength, "codetermination has a strong equalizing effect on the distribution of income."[17] Nevertheless, Jäger and colleagues are surely right that the basic reason why the social benefits are not larger is that workers in codetermined firms simply lack the power to demand them. Hence there is every reason to expect those outcomes to be significantly different in a bicameral firm where workers would no longer be junior partners but instead equal ones and would thus enjoy adequate power to demand those benefits.

Indeed, when we look at different kinds of organizations where workers do have substantially more governing power than minority board-level representation, such as worker co-ops, we do in fact see more robust social benefits: there is less inequality, more job security, sometimes more meaningful avenues for democratic participation, and clear increases in well-being in the sense that co-op workers are typically highly resistant to returning to work at conventional undemocratic firms. Of course, not everything is roses; co-ops can be stressful places to work because even though increased power and responsibility are generally positive things, they can also be heavy things.[18]

Given that bicameral firms would provide workers with an amount of power and authority somewhere between minority board-level representation and worker co-ops, we should expect the benefits to fall somewhere in that range, as well. Beyond these well-documented benefits, bicameral firms may also provide other kinds of benefits in terms of various social issues and positive externalities that impact the places where they live (such as protecting the local environment, ensuring their firm pays its taxes to sustain the community's public services, and so on) over and above conventional firms, which are governed by shareholders who either don't live in the impacted community or who do but are rich enough to not care about the public provision of basic goods.[19] It stands to reason that bicameral firms, with workers at the helm, would have different (and better) incentives in this regard. Indeed, improving the relationship between firms and public authorities would be a major positive outcome, and one of ever-increasing relevance, as we race to restrain firms from trespassing beyond ecological boundaries, which can only be set in place through strong public decisions applied to the whole economy.

One further cautionary note: even though we have good reason to expect bicameral firms to improve the quality of regular people's working lives, they will remain very much works in progress. As Sanjay Pinto (chapter 13) usefully reminds us, even firms that are formally democratic can fail to live up to their promise of genuine equality; this is obviously true in terms of race, but it is also true in terms of gender and ability. Ongoing experimentation, rooted in the commitment to the ideal of equality of all labor investors, will be necessary to build a democratic and egalitarian culture into the mortar between the bricks of a formally democratic structure.

At the industry and economy-wide level, an economic fabric made of bicameral firms would be a game changer in terms of labor's bargaining power. It is reasonable to expect that the conditions would then be set to move beyond capitalism if this is desired by the majority. As for the planet, it is certainly clear that moving beyond capitalist extractivism is urgently needed. In sum, we should not expect economic bicameralism to be a magic bullet that solves all of society's problems. Should society adopt economic bicameralism, there will not likely be any significant economic costs in terms of general productivity, but there will be sizable benefits. In short, it is a necessary but not a sufficient condition for moving toward a future that is democratic and sustainable.

A Voice, Not Ownership, Approach

Economic bicameralism takes an explicitly political "voice" approach to building power, rather than an economic "ownership" approach. Here I learn, with Bo Rothstein (chapter 10), from the Swedish failure in the ownership approach and agree with David Ellerman (chapter 4) that workplace democracy is about avoiding domination and exercising freedom, not declaring property rights. Acquiring "ownership of the means of production," the historic goal of the Marx-inspired left, is neither necessary nor sufficient for that. Control of how those means of production are used, and gaining a residual claim on the surplus that follows from their use, is of course one way to express part of the social-ist ideal. But given the immense obstacles in the way of an ownership path to democratic control—in particular the fact that it would require relatively poor workers coming up with the money to buy the relatively expensive firms in which they work from the current shareholders, a truly immense undertaking—such a path is not at all a short-term possibility.[20] To be clear, I do think the ownership path is an important part of the long-term strategy. The ESOP model in general, and in particular the ESOP-co-op proposal articulated by Ellerman, galvanized by having government offer tax breaks for worker-owned firms, strike me as effective strategies for slowly transitioning ownership of the economy over to workers. Nevertheless, a voice approach is still needed.

Currently, capital investors assume the central rights of governing. But this has much less to do with efficient production than a simple usurpation of power. With extraordinary obfuscation of this basic fact, capital organizes this usurpation through corporate or company law (which organizes the rights of capital investors among themselves); by labor law (which organizes the renting out of labor investors to capital investors' representatives); and by commercial law (which organizes the flow of input and output generated by the activity of the firm). All of these subject labor to capital investors' domination. But there really is no good economic, much less moral, reason why they should have such one-sided power. There is no reason why labor investors should not govern their own life at the workplace, which is what economic bicam-eralism makes possible.

Who Should Have a Say in Firm Governance?

Economic bicameralism is based on an investor model, according to which those who directly invest in the activity of the firm, those who generate its service or product, and who, in return, are governed by its rules should have a voice in its government. In particular, this means that the workers—that is, the *labor investors, the only ones governed by the rules of the firm*—must be included in the firm's government.

Contrary to Marc Fleurbaey (chapter 3), Ewan McGaughey (chapter 12), and Lenore Palladino (chapter 6), I do not believe that the owners of capital should be privileged in the governance of its everyday operations. Why? Because they are simply a source of rented capital. And that capital, while enabling value-producing activity, is by itself simply a store of value. The owners' welfare is obviously affected by firm success, but they are not governed by its decisions in anything like the same way, or to the same degree, as are those actually involved in laboring.

Although I accept that for the time being—as a matter of transition— firm governance must include labor *and* capital investors, it might well be asked whether capital investors are truly "governed" by the firm and so deserving (above and beyond the rental payments they receive for the use of their capital) a say in the governance of the firm. Ultimately, I do not think the inclusion of capital investors in governance can be justified; for the time being I simply accept it as part of the political reality. However, the truth is that capital investors are not truly *governed* by the firm but only *affected* by it, as are other stakeholders. In fact, only one specific category of capital investors is truly governed by the firm: those who invest their labor, putting mind and body in action at once. This is the case of the entrepreneur, and indeed those investors should be represented through the labor investors' chamber of representatives, not that of capital. In contrast, the role of the typical capital investor should be gradually phased out of a firm's government structure, to be replaced, if at all, by a simple rental agreement, as Ellerman and others have long proposed.

The term "labor investors" is unpleasant to some critical ears and has been objected to as a concession to the vernacular of capitalism. In the spirit of Gramsci, however, I think we must make incursions against the cultural hegemony of neoliberalism by fighting to reclaim this term. I see the term as a statement against the disempowerment of workers who are treated in word and deed as merely another type of stakeholder. But they are not simply one stakeholder among many. While providers of capital do mobilize assets, such assets are always external to themselves. So, while they are impacted by the success or failure of their investment, they are not governed in an intimate, everyday way by the decisions of the firm; moreover, they benefit from the protections of *limited liability* in exchange for their investment (in other words, their greatest risk is seeing the value of their assets drop). By contrast, a worker *invests* not just their skill, time, and effort, but their entire person—their physical self, their intelligence, and their self-respect. And as the COVID pandemic has shown all too clearly, they risk their health and sometimes even their lives. It is high time we reclaimed the term "investment" to assert workers' central importance and their rights. Without workers, a corporation would be nothing but a pile of assets, static and useless. In addition, I see the term "labor investor" as a useful tool to help us overcome, or at least mitigate, the fissuring strategies of corporations. It helps us argue that regardless of whether one is formally classified as "employee" or "subcontractor," everyone who invests their labor in bringing a firm's product or service into existence while being governed by its decisions should properly (and legally) be considered "workers" and given the right to representation and a vote in the government structure of the firm. This is crucial to reconstituting the contemporary corporation—with its amorphous, tentacled, transnational, and diffuse reach—into a distinct political entity tractable to democratic oversight.

Why not include other stakeholders in firm governance? I disagree that stakeholders have an equally legitimate place in the legislative branch of firm governments. Stakeholders, in my view, are *affected* but not *governed* by the decisions of the firm.[21] The basic contrast is clear enough: while workers, being governed by the rules of the firm, are subjected to the rules and decisions of the firm in ways that are temporally extensive (often forty hours per week for years on end) and morally profound (workers can face real coercion, domination, and the severe sanction of being fired), stakeholders like consumers are typically impacted in ways that are occasional, fleeting, and morally less significant. That does not mean that stakeholders should be abandoned, just that their needs and rights are better protected by a democratic state (via regulations) and information and consultative rights (via institutions such as works councils that should be improved to include environmental stakeholders at the firm level) rather than by inclusion into the legislative branch of the firm government and the operations and minutiae of an organization that is largely separate from them.[22] After all, the firm, while vast in the extent of its effects, remains a relatively distinct entity, with a distinct purpose of producing tradable value.[23] It is not a school or church or political party but rather an economic actor. Here is what I suggest: limiting firm government to those intimately governed by its rules, and including the affected stakeholders in its governance via consultation and information mechanisms.

The Central Role of Unions

A number of interlocutors in this volume, in particular Simon Pek (chapter 9) and Bo Rothstein (chapter 10), have rightly asked about the role of unions in the project of economic bicameralism. I cannot emphasize strongly enough the critical role of unions in the project of democratizing the corporation. Collective bargaining, particularly at the industry level, remains of critical importance to ensuring decent wages and conditions across the industry. Safeguarding their key role in the economy will bring broad benefits, chief among them more equal societies.[24] Unions are necessary if we are to win the fight for the decommodification of labor throughout society and if we wish to keep the promise of equality, not as a mere philosophical ideal but as a practice that includes concrete social provisions (health, education, etc.) as Carly Knight (chapter 2) rightly argues. But the unions that do this, of course, must be more oriented toward social justice, community, and the environment than the typical "business unions," which see themselves as basically insurance companies, selling slightly higher paychecks and slightly more security. We require unions that are more universal, inclusive, and democratic in their vision of the political community they help create.

In his insightful chapter, Rothstein argues that unions will inevitably resist economic bicameralism on the grounds that it will undermine their traditional role and raison d'être. It is true that many unions, in Sweden and elsewhere, have developed extensive knowledge, practice, and expertise in bargaining with management in a conventional across-the-table kind of way, which economic bicameralism would challenge. This is true in the same way that codetermination—which also allows worker representatives to join the managerial side of the table—does indeed add a new function to the role of unions.

However, it is wrong to suspect that most unions will or should reject this. For one thing, many unions *already are* doing this kind of work. For instance, the European Trade Union Confederation (ETUC), the umbrella organization including the vast majority of trade union members in Europe, has been supporting board-level employee representation for years and has an active "Democracy at Work" campaign.[25] Indeed, the 2015 Paris Manifesto elevated the demand for "Democracy at Work" to one of the three key "Priorities for a Better Europe." Specifically, and explicitly, the manifesto demands, "We want greater workplace and industrial democracy, freedom of association and the right to strike."[26] And this is no marginal organization: the ETUC represents 45 million members from eighty-nine trade union organizations in twenty-nine European countries. In December 2021, the confederation succeeded in having the European Parliament pass a resolution calling for "More Democracy at Work."

Second, unions would be making a severe mistake in resisting economic bicameralism. After all, workers and their union representatives gain nothing from distancing themselves from managerial power (except for the tranquilizing comfort that comes from continuing the current, precarious status quo). Joining a board does not mean that workers are "selling out" or "becoming capitalists"; it simply means they acquire power, are able to achieve better material and social outcomes, and, in the bigger picture, are one step closer to abolishing the need for a separate capitalist class that dominates workers from above.[27] Historically, the role of unions has always been twofold: to fight for better material and social outcomes for workers here and now, and, more broadly, to help to transform the oppressive economic system into a better, more just society. Economic bicameralism is a key advantage on both fronts. Some unions, of course, will prefer to simply continue with what they know and not ruffle any feathers. But for those unions who remain true to their basic goal and essential mission, to be the collective vehicle for enabling the flourishing of workers' citizenship in the economy, they will see economic bicameralism as not only one of their best strategies but also one of their strongest weapons.

Final Words

The capitalist firm is one of the most extractive institutions human beings have ever created; it extracts value from people and from the planet, to the point of extinction.[28] The advance of artificial intelligence makes the extractive potential of the undemocratic firm even more worrisome. Surviving the Capitalocene means leaving behind extractive capitalist governance.[29] Economic bicameralism remains a real utopia—a tool to help us find the exit; it does not pretend to be the necessary and sufficient condition to produce all the diverse changes that we need. It is necessary *and* insufficient—one crucial piece in the puzzle of defining a different future, grounded in the project of democracy rather than the despotism of capital. One critical outcome of economic bicameralism's implementation will be a change in the relationship between private and public power, between states and firms. Indeed, that is one of its most ambitious goals: to foster a far more mutualistic relationship between the different elements of our democratic society, one functional and beneficial enough to tackle the many crises we face.

As I was completing this conclusion, Vladimir Putin began his war against Ukraine. As bombs fall in Europe, I conclude by noting that despotism in the firm and despotism in the polis must be fought together; otherwise, in one way or another, they will succeed in destroying our democratic project altogether—not to mention habitable conditions on this planet. The political question is how the fight, which we know must be fought on both fronts, is best engaged at this particular moment in our history. What I'm suggesting is that focusing on despotism at work is a good place to start.

Notes

1 Introduction

1. Elizabeth Anderson, *Private Government* (Princeton, NJ: Princeton University Press, 2017).
2. For overviews of the evidence pertaining to employee stock ownership plans (ESOPs), codetermination, works councils, and worker cooperatives, see, respectively, Douglas Kruse, Richard Freeman, and Joseph Blasi, eds., *Shared Capitalism at Work: Employee Ownership, Profit and Gain Sharing, and Broad-Based Stock Options* (Chicago: University of Chicago Press, 2010); Simon Jäger, Shakked Noy, and Benjamin Schoefer, "What Does Codetermination Do?," National Bureau of Economic Research Working Paper (2021); John Addison, *The Economics of Codetermination: Lessons from the German Experience* (London: Palgrave Macmillan, 2009); Joel Rogers and Wolfgang Streeck, eds., *Works Councils: Consultation, Representation, and Cooperation in Industrial Relations* (Chicago: University of Chicago Press, 1995); Gregory Dow, *Governing the Firm: Workers' Control in Theory and Practice* (Cambridge, UK: Cambridge University Press, 2003); Tom Malleson, *After Occupy: Economic Democracy for the 21st Century* (New York: Oxford University Press, 2014); Chris Cornforth et al., *Developing Successful Worker Co-operatives* (London: SAGE Publications, 1988).
3. "List of Electoral Democracies," World Forum on Democracy, available at https://web.archive.org/web/20131016184935/http://www.fordemocracy.net/electoral.shtml.
4. Milan Babic, Eelke Heemskerk, and Jan Fichtner, "Who Is More Powerful—States or Corporations?," *The Conversation*, July 10, 2018, theconversation.com.
5. In 2021, for the sixteenth year in a row, Freedom House's index of democratic vitality showed more nations declining than maintaining or improving, as well as a clear counter-rise in authoritarian public practice. Freedom House, *Freedom in the World 2022: The Global Expansion of Authoritarian Rule* (Washington, DC: Freedom House, 2022).
6. On lobbying, for instance, in 2020 fifty-five large US corporations paid zero in federal corporate income taxes, yet those same companies spent $450 million on lobbying and political contributions in recent years: Josephine Fonger, "Corporations Are Spending Millions on Lobbying to Avoid Taxes," Public Citizen, August 11, 2021, citizen.org. As for media and PR, the *Citizens United* decision of the Supreme Court in 2010 prevents any restrictions on corporate expenditures for political campaigns; today, 90 percent of US media is controlled by only six large companies: Ashley Lutz, "These 6 Corporations Control 90% of the Media in America," *Business Insider*, June 14, 2012, businessinsider.com. See also Fred

Block, "The Ruling Class Does Not Rule: Notes on the Marxist Theory of the State," *Socialist Revolution* 3, no. 6 (1977); Thomas Christiano, "Money in Politics," in *The Oxford Handbook of Political Philosophy*, ed. David Estlund (Oxford: Oxford University Press, 2012); Joshua Cohen and Joel Rogers, *On Democracy* (Harmondsworth, UK: Penguin, 1983); Edward S. Herman and Noam Chomsky, *Manufacturing Consent: The Political Economy of the Mass Media* (New York: Pantheon, 1988); Charles Lindblom, "The Market as Prison," *Journal of Politics* 44, no. 2 (1982).

7. Joel Bakan, *The Corporation* (Toronto: Penguin Canada, 2004).

8. R. S. Foa et al., *The Global Satisfaction with Democracy Report 2020* (Cambridge, UK: University Centre for the Future of Democracy, 2020).

9. Across Europe, the average share of the vote for populist parties in national and European parliamentary elections has more than doubled since the 1960s, growing from 5.1 percent to 13.2 percent. Ronald Inglehart and Pippa Norris, "Trump, Brexit, and the Rise of Populism: Economic Have-Nots and Cultural Backlash," HSK Faculty Research Working Paper Series (2016).

10. For instance, contemporary Canadian employment law frequently cites the decision of Lord Evershed from 1959 that "wilful disobedience of an order will justify summary dismissal, since wilful disobedience of a lawful and reasonable order shows a disregard—a complete disregard—of a condition essential to the contract of service, namely, the condition that *the servant must obey the proper orders of the master and that, unless he does so, the relationship is, so to speak, struck at fundamentally.*" Philip R. White, "Grounds for Being Fired for Just Cause," *Employment Law 101*, employmentlaw101.ca, emphasis added.

11. This is, of course, not to say that there is no difference between a typical worker from the mid-1800s compared to now. Today, most workers in the rich countries have much more robust rights than earlier times, which somewhat limits what the employer can force the employee to do (e.g., employers can no longer force workers to handle dangerous materials like asbestos or fire a woman who becomes pregnant); they also have various labor-market protections (such as welfare and unemployment systems), and some have unions to protect them. Nevertheless, the basic facts—that the essential job an employee is to do what they are told, to be a subordinate and of lower status, to be subject to punishment through firing if they refuse their obedience, and have no power of accountability over their bosses—remain as true today as at the birth of capitalism.

12. See, for example, Rebecca J. Bentley et al., "A Longitudinal Analysis of Changes in Job Control and Mental Health," *American Journal of Epidemiology* 182, no. 4 (2015); H. Bosma et al., "Low Job Control and Risk of Coronary Heart Disease in Whitehall II (Prospective Cohort) Study," *British Medical Journal* 314, no. 7080 (1997); Michael G. Marmot, Martin J. Shipley, and Geoffrey Rose, "Inequalities in Death—Specific Explanations of a General Pattern?," *Lancet* 323, no. 8384 (1984).

13. Jim Clifton, "The World's Broken Workplace," *Gallup*, June 13, 2017, news.gallup.com.

14. Gallup, *State of the American Manager* (Washington, DC: Gallup, 2015), 8; "DoYou? 1 in 5 Employees Admit They Hate Their Boss," *StudyFinds*, April 21, 2018, studyfinds.org. In their study of daily life experience, Kahneman et al. found that the single most negative part of the day for most people was interacting with their boss. Daniel Kahneman et al., "A Survey Method for Characterizing Daily Life Experience: The Day Reconstruction Method," *Science* 306, no. 5702 (2004).

15. Josh Bivens and Lawrence Mishel, "The Pay of Corporate Executives and Financial Professionals as Evidence of Rents in Top 1 Percent Incomes," *Journal of Economic Perspectives* 27, no. 3 (2013): 57–78. Lawrence Mishel and Jori Kandra, "CEO Pay

NOTES FROM PAGES 4 TO 6

Has Skyrocketed 1,322% since 1978," *Economic Policy Institute*, August 10, 2021, epi.org.

16. Thomas Piketty, *Capital in the Twenty-First Century*, trans. Arthur Goldhammer (Cambridge, UK: Belknap Press, 2014); Robert Reich, *Saving Capitalism* (New York: Alfred A. Knopf, 2015); Joseph Stiglitz, *The Price of Inequality* (New York: W. W. Norton & Company, 2012).

17. Kimberly A. Clausing, "Does Tax Drive the Headquarters Locations of the World's Biggest Companies?," *Transnational Corporations* 25, no. 2 (2018). See also Nicholas Shaxson, *Treasure Islands: Tax Havens and the Men Who Stole the World* (London: The Bodley Head, 2011); Emanuel Saez and Gabriel Zucman, *The Triumph of Injustice* (New York: W. W. Norton & Company, 2019); Gabriel Zucman, *The Hidden Wealth of Nations: The Scourge of Tax Havens* (Chicago: University of Chicago Press, 2015).

18. Lucas Chancel et al., *World Inequality Report 2022* (Cambridge, MA: Harvard University Press, 2022), 168, 10.

19. Legally, corporations are structured according to the idea of "shareholder primacy," which means that shareholders are legally recognized as the only group that makes a risky investment into the firm, and so is the group who retains primary ownership and decision-making rights (to safeguard that ownership). Yet, as Ferreras and other contributors to this volume point out, the notion that shareholders are the only stakeholders who take any "risks" or make any kind of "investment" into the firm is quite absurd.

20. Mikhail Bakunin, *Bakunin on Anarchism*, ed. Sam Dolgoff (Montreal: Black Rose Books, 1980); Peter Kropotkin, *The Conquest of Bread* (Oakland: AK Press, 2007 [1892]).

21. See Anton Pannekoek, *Workers' Councils* (Cambridge, MA: Root & Branch, 1970 [1936]); G. D. H. Cole, *Guild Socialism Re-stated* (London: Leonard Parsons, 1920); Bertrand Russell, *Proposed Roads to Freedom* (Cornwall, NY: Cornwall Press, 1918); Jessica Gordon Nembhard, *Collective Courage: A History of African American Cooperative Economic Thought and Practice* (University Park: Penn State University Press, 2021). In recent years, prominent works on workplace democracy include Carole Pateman, *Participation and Democratic Theory* (Cambridge, UK: Cambridge University Press, 1970); Michael Walzer, "Town Meetings and Workers' Control: A Story for Socialists," *Dissent* 25 (Summer 1978); Robert Dahl, *A Preface to Economic Democracy* (Berkeley: University of California Press, 1985); David Ellerman, *Property and Contract in Economics: The Case for Economic Democracy* (Cambridge, MA: Blackwell, 1992); Dow, *Governing the Firm*; Malleson, *After Occupy*; Richard D. Wolff, *Democracy at Work: A Cure for Capitalism* (Chicago: Haymarket Books, 2012); Isabelle Ferreras, *Firms as Political Entities* (Cambridge, UK: Cambridge University Press, 2017); Anderson, *Private Government*.

22. John Stuart Mill, *Principles of Political Economy* (Toronto: University of Toronto Press, 1965 [1848]), book 4, chapter 7.

23. Probably the most ambitious attempts to institute workplace democracy across society as a whole occurred in anarchist-controlled Catalonia during the Spanish Civil War and, to a certain degree, in Yugoslavia in 1950–1990. Alan Whitehorn, "Yugoslav Workers' Self-Management: A Blueprint for Industrial Democracy?," *Canadian Slavonic Papers* 20, no. 3 (1978); Sam Dolgoff, ed., *The Anarchist Collectives* (Montreal: Black Rose Books, 1990).

24. Huber Eveleyne and Stephens John, *Development and Crisis of the Welfare State* (Chicago: University of Chicago Press, 2001); Walter Korpi, "Power Resources and Employer-Centered Approaches in Explanations of Welfare States and Varieties of

Capitalism: Protagonists, Consenters, and Antagonists," *World Politics* 58, no.2 (2006); Jonas Pontusson, *Inequality and Prosperity: Social Europe vs. Liberal America* (Ithaca, NY: Cornell University Press, 2005).

25. In US law, for instance, unions are legally barred from making decisions that fall within the so-called entrepreneurial zone.

26. Cole, *Guild Socialism Re-stated*, 20.

27. Kruse, Freeman, and Blasi, *Shared Capitalism at Work*.

28. Joseph R. Blasi, Richard B. Freeman, and Douglas L. Kruse, *The Citizen's Share* (New Haven, CT: Yale University Press, 2013), 164.

29. John T. Addison, *The Economics of Codetermination: Lessons from the German Experience*; Jäger, Noy, and Schoefer, "What Does Codetermination Do?"; Ewan McGaughey, "The Codetermination Bargains: The History of German Corporate and Labor Law," *Columbia Journal of European Law* 23 (2016).

30. Jeremy Corbyn proposed giving workers one-third of board seats. Elizabeth Warren's Accountable Capitalism Act proposed that workers elect 40 percent of the board, while Bernie Sanders's Corporate Accountability and Democracy Act proposed that workers elect 45 percent.

31. There is now extensive empirical evidence showing that ESOPs and codetermined firms are just as productive as conventional firms, with no serious efficiency problems, and somewhat higher levels of worker satisfaction: Jäger, Noy, and Schoefer, "What Does Codetermination Do?"; Kruse, Freeman, and Blasi, *Shared Capitalism at Work*. Unions can be expanded by legislation that makes them easier to form (such as simple "card check" rules for membership) and harder to intimidate; ESOPs can be expanded by providing favorable tax treatment (as already happens to a degree); and codetermination is typically imposed by legal fiat. See, for instance, Chris Riddell, "Union Certification Success under Voting versus Card-Check Procedures: Evidence from British Columbia, 1978–1998," *Industrial and Labor Relations Review* 57, no. 4 (2004).

32. Dow, *Governing the Firm*; Joyce Rothschild and J. Allen Whitt, *The Cooperative Workplace* (Cambridge, UK: Cambridge University Press, 1986); Stefano Zamagni and Vera Zamagni, *Cooperative Enterprise: Facing the Challenges of Globalization* (Cheltenham, UK: Edward Elgar, 2010).

33. Although an inspiring model in many ways, Mondragon has struggled in the last couple of decades to retain its democratic character due to challenges with globalization and the acquisition of large competitors, which have led to a majority of its total workforce being conventional employees, not cooperative members. Tom Malleson, "What Does Mondragon Teach Us about Workplace Democracy?," *Advances in the Economic Analysis of Participatory and Labor-Managed Firms* 13 (2013); William Foote Whyte and Kathleen King Whyte, *Making Mondragon: The Growth and Dynamics of the Worker Cooperative Complex* (Ithaca, NY: ILR Press, 1988).

34. Malleson, *After Occupy*; David Schweickart, *After Capitalism*, 2nd ed. (Lanham, MD: Rowman & Littlefield, 2011); Wolff, *Democracy at Work*; Erik Olin Wright, *Envisioning Real Utopias* (London: Verso, 2010).

35. The number of worker co-ops comes from Prushinskaya, and the number of total employing businesses from the Small Business and Entrepreneurship Council. Olga Prushinskaya, "Worker Co-ops Show Significant Growth in Latest Survey Data," Fifty by Fifty, February 18, 2020, fiftybyfifty.org; "Facts & Data on Small Business and Entrepreneurship," Small Business and Entrepreneurship Council, sbecouncil.org.

36. The one exception to this is German firms in the mining, coal, and steel industries with more than 1,000 employees. These have genuine parity, and shareholders do

not have a tiebreaking vote. Jäger, Noy, and Schoefer, "What Does Codetermination Do?," 9.

37. The evidence backs this up: Vitols finds that companies with board-level employee representation do indeed have a higher effective tax rate than companies without workers on the board. Sigurt Vitols, "Board Level Employee Representation and Tax Avoidance in Europe," *Accounting, Economics, and Law: A Convivium* (2021).

38. Robert Scholz and Sigurt Vitols, "Board-Level Codetermination: A Driving Force for Corporate Social Responsibility in German Companies?," *European Journal of Industrial Relations* 25, no. 3 (2019).

1. Democratizing the Corporation

1. This chapter was the anchor essay for the Real Utopias Conference scheduled to take place in March 2020, in Stockholm at the Institute for Future Studies. It was completed in 2019. The conference had to be postponed to January 2021 due to the COVID-19 pandemic. Since the other chapters in this volume comment on this original essay, its content could not be substantially revised after the conference. This explains why the references have not been updated.

2. Joshua Cohen and Joel Rogers, *On Democracy: Toward a Transformation of American Society* (New York: Penguin, 1983).

3. To mention a few: in the United States, Elizabeth Anderson's *Private Government: How Employers Rule Our Lives (and Why We Don't Talk about It)* (Princeton, NJ: Princeton University Press, 2017) has received wide attention, while Elizabeth Warren's proposed Accountable Capitalism Act, introduced in August 2018, would require that at least 40 percent of the boards of all major US corporations be elected by their employees. In 2018, in the United Kingdom, the Labour Party's new platform has included worker ownership funds and board members chosen by workers. In Belgium, the Socialist Party has included the proposal of the bicameral firm in its new federal platform. In France, the new PACTE law includes two or three employee representatives on the boards of large firms, and in the summer of 2017 the CFDT, one of the country's main unions, named codetermination as one of its major demands. Since the writing of this essay, many relevant developments have taken place. In particular, the COVID-19 crisis brought attention to the fate of "essential" workers. Another notable development is the fact that the philosophical principle of bicameralism to reform corporate governance was affirmed at the start of the pandemic (May 2020) in the Democratizing Work Manifesto, written by myself, Julie Battilana, and Dominique Méda, and signed by more than 6,000 scholars across the five continents. The manifesto argued that "workers should get the right to collectively validate or veto the [firm's] decisions." See democratizingwork.org; Isabelle Ferreras, Julie Battilana, and Dominique Méda, eds., *Le Manifeste Travail: Démocratiser, démarchandiser, dépolluer* (Paris: Le Seuil, 2020); Isabelle Ferreras, Julie Battilana, and Dominique Méda, eds., *Democratize Work: The Case for Reorganizing the Economy* (Chicago: University of Chicago Press, 2022).

4. Erik Olin Wright and Joel Rogers, *American Society: How It Really Works* (New York: W. W. Norton, 2015).

5. The following analysis draws from more substantial developments to be found in Isabelle Ferreras, *Critique politique du travail: Travailler à l'heure de la société des services* (Paris: Presses de Sciences Po, 2007); Isabelle Ferreras, *Gouverner le capitalisme? Pour le bicamérisme* économique (Paris: Presses Universitaires de France, 2012); and Isabelle Ferreras, *Firms as Political Entities: Saving Democracy through Economic Bicameralism* (Cambridge, UK: Cambridge University Press, 2017).

6. Aristotle characterizes this relationship as despotic. Ferreras, *Firms as Political Entities*. Ellerman is the contemporary author who has highlighted most powerfully this dimension of the employment contract. See David Ellerman, "On the Renting of Persons: The Neo-Abolitionist Case against Today's Peculiar Institution," *Economic Thought* 4, no. 1 (2015): 1–20.

7. Indeed, the first known employment contracts in antiquity were for the hiring of slaves from one master to another within the context of the despotic master-slave relationship. See Paulin Ismard, *La cité et ses esclaves: Institutions, fictions, experiences* (Paris: Le Seuil, 2019). And the quest for emancipation has always been an issue central to economic relations. For the modern era in the United States, see Caitlin Rosenthal, *Accounting for Slavery: Masters and Management* (Cambridge, MA: Harvard University Press, 2018). For a retrospective looking back from modern era, see Alex Gourevitch, *From Slavery to the Cooperative Commonwealth: Labor and Republican Liberty in the Nineteenth Century* (Cambridge, UK: Cambridge University Press, 2014).

8. Anderson, *Private Government*.

9. Paddy Ireland, "Property, Private Government and the Myth of Deregulation," in *Commercial Law and Commercial Practice*, ed. Sarah Worthington (Oxford: Hart, 2003), 85–123. Quoting Robert Hale, "Force and the State: A Comparison of 'Political' and 'Economic' Compulsion," *Columbia Law Review* 35 (1935): 149.

10. David Weil, *The Fissured Workplace: Why Work Became So Bad for So Many and What Can Be Done to Improve It* (Cambridge, MA: Harvard University Press, 2014).

11. The available literature in sociology and political science cannot illustrate more clearly the fact that markets are products of the state, and that sets of rights enforced by the state are needed to empower corporations and make these so-called free markets operate.

12. Danilo Martuccelli, *Grammaires de l'individu* (Paris: Gallimard 2002).

13. As will be made clear, and contrary to what the economic theory of the firm asserts, corporations enjoy legal personality, meaning that people own shares in corporations. No one, however, owns corporations themselves, let alone firms. Legally speaking, they are both entities owned by no one.

14. For a clear-cut example, see the Nobel Prize in Economics acceptance lecture by Oliver Hart, "Incomplete Contracts and Control," December 8, 2016, available at nobelprize.org.

15. Charles F. Sabel, "Learning by Monitoring: The Institutions of Economic Development," in *The Handbook of Economic Sociology*, ed., N. J. Smelser and R. Swedberg (Princeton, NJ: Princeton University Press, 1994), 138–65.

16. About practices of worker involvement developed by innovative business in the past decade, see the practices inspired by self-defining "liberated" firms. Brian Carney and Isaac Getz, *Freedom Inc.: Free Your Employees and Let Them Lead Your Business to Higher Productivity, Profits, and Growth* (New York: Crown Business, 2009), and "reinvented" organizations pushing toward more horizontal decision-making processes, as well as "sociocracy" and "hollacracy" as modes of self-management. Frédéric Laloux, *Reinventing Organizations: A Guide to Creating Organizations Inspired by the Next Stage of Human Consciousness* (Brussels: Nelson Parker, 2014). For empirical and growing evidence of this reality, see the How Report, 2016, howmetrics.lrn.com. Based on comprehensive data collected from 16,000 employees in seventeen countries, the data shows that self-governing organizations based on some of the practices just mentioned outperform their peers and generate increased worker satisfaction.

17. The most popular has been Graeber's critique of "bullshit jobs." David Graeber, *Bullshit Jobs: A Theory* (New York: Simon & Schuster, 2018). Informed by Habermas's conception of emancipation as a knowledge-constitutive interest for the critical sciences, the perspective of our own work, inspired by Erik Olin Wright's *Real Utopias* anti-cynical approach, sees social scientists as responsible for identifying the potential contained in reality, however dark it may be, and helping it to flourish. Jürgen Habermas, *Knowledge and Human Interests*, trans. J. J. Shapiro (Boston: Beacon Press, 1971).

18. Some renewed attention has been given to the issue. For the critical social theory, see Christophe Dejours et al., *The Return of Work in Critical Theory: Self, Society, Politics* (New York: Columbia University Press, 2018); Lisa Herzog, *Reclaiming the System: Moral Responsibility, Divided Labour, and the Role of Organizations in Society* (Oxford: Oxford University Press, 2018). For the liberal tradition see, in particular, Martin O'Neill, "Three Rawlsian Routes towards Economic Democracy," *Revue de Philosophie* économique 9, no. 1 (2008): 29–55; Jeffrey Moriarty, "Rawls, Self-Respect, and the Opportunity for Meaningful Work," *Social Theory and Practice* 35, no. 3 (2009): 441–59; Sandrine Blanc and Ismael Al-Amoudi, "Corporate Institutions in a Weakening Welfare State: A Rawlsian Perspective," *Business Ethics Quarterly* 23, no. 4 (2013): 497–525.

19. Indeed, research has proven that above a certain threshold, the nominal value of compensation, even increasing compensation, has no impact on worker performance. See Daniel Pink, *Drive: The Surprising Truth about What Motivates Us* (New York: Riverhead, 2009).

20. See Ferreras, *Gouverner le capitalisme?* and *Firms as Political Entities*; Pink, *Drive*; Dominique Méda and Patricia Vendramin, *Reinventing Work in Europe: Value, Generations and Labour* (London: Palgrave MacMillan, 2017); Anca Gheaus and Lisa Herzog, "The Goods of Work (Other Than Money!)," *Journal of Social Philosophy* 47, no. 1 (2016): 70–89.

21. Particularly salient is the example of Google, which set up an internal group to learn more about teamwork and the best way to build productive teams. "The project, known as *Project Aristotle*, took several years and included interviews with hundreds of employees and analysis of data about the people on more than one hundred active teams at the company. The Googlers looked hard to find a magic formula—the perfect mix of individuals necessary to form a stellar team—but it wasn't that simple. 'We were dead wrong,' the company said," and ultimately concluded, against their own expectations, that "the best teams *respect* one another's emotions and are mindful that all members should *contribute* to the conversation *equally*. It has less to do with who is in a team, and more with how a team's members interact with one another." These findings are clear-cut: the expectation of equality as a fundamental principle for organizing the "conversation" and "contributions" speaks for how work is fundamentally an experience that mobilizes people's conceptions of democratic (in)justice. Aamna Mohdin, "After Years of Intensive Analysis, Google Found the Key to Good Teamwork Is Being Nice," *Quartz*, February 26, 2016, qz.com.

22. See, for instance, the first transnational general assembly of bikers, delivering for Uber Eats, Deliveroo, etc., from eight European countries, which convened on October 25–26, 2018, in Brussels to "fight platform abuse." "Transnational Couriers' Assembly #riders4rights," *Alter Summit*, altersummit.eu.

23. "We believe that Google should not be in the business of war," its employees stated in a letter publicized by the *New York Times*. Scott Shane and Daisuke Wakabayashi, "'The Business of War': Google Employees Protest Work for the Pentagon," *New York Times*, April 4, 2018, nytimes.com.

24. "As the people who build the technologies that Microsoft profits from, we refuse to be complicit," the employees said in the letter, obtained by the *Seattle Times*. "We are part of a growing movement, [comprising] many across the industry who recognize the grave responsibility that those creating powerful technology have to ensure what they build is used for good, and not for harm." Rachel Lerman, "Microsoft Employees Call on Company to Cancel Contract with ICE," *Seattle Times*, June 19, 2018, seattletimes.com.

25. Georgia Wells and Kirsten Grind, "Inside Twitter's Long, Slow Struggle to Police Bad Actors," *Wall Street Journal*, September 3, 2018, wsj.com.

26. Matthew Weaver et al., "Google Walkout: Global Protests after Sexual Misconduct Allegations," *Guardian*, November 1, 2018, theguardian.com.

27. Based on extensive research of more than 35,000 leaders and interviews with 250 C-level executives led by Rasmus Haugaard and Jacqueline Carter, *The Mind of the Leader* (Cambridge, MA: Harvard Business Review Press, 2018) concludes that "organizations and leaders aren't meeting employees' basic human needs of finding meaning, purpose, connection, and genuine happiness in their work. 77% of leaders think they do a good job of engaging their people while 88% of employees say their leaders do a bad job with engagement, and 65% of employees would forego a pay raise to see their leaders fired." This speaks volumes about the extent to which employees put their own conceptions of justice before economic gain. Unsurprisingly, the solutions put forth in the business literature are individual-centered and not structural: "To solve the leadership crisis, organizations need to put people at the center of their strategy. They need to develop managers and executives who lead with three core mental qualities: Mindfulness, Selflessness, and Compassion." Another figure highlighted in the book is worth mentioning, as well: "And this is despite the fact that $46 billion is spent each year on leadership development." That is a substantial amount of money, which could be put to better use reforming and nurturing structures of firm government capable of seriously taking employee voice into consideration.

28. Ferreras, *Gouverner le capitalisme?* and *Firms as Political Entities*.

29. See the most complete study carried out in the United States on American workers' expectations regarding representation and participation in work, Richard B. Freeman and Joel Rogers, *What Workers Want* (Ithaca, NY: ILR Press / Russell Sage Foundation, 2006). A figure stands out: in the United States, which is traditionally considered to be rather hostile to unions, unionization has now dipped below 7 percent in the private sector—but, at the time of the survey it was around 10. Yet, 90 percent of American workers stated that they were in favor of a form of independent organization for employees in their companies, whose purpose would be to represent workers and communicate their viewpoints to management.

30. Cohen and Rogers, *On Democracy*.

31. I do agree with Marxists about the potentially destructive nature of capitalism's internal contradictions. I differ from Marx and the Frankfurt school, however, in that I do not see democracy as an ideological layer superimposed on the capitalist structure of society. Rather, I see it as a full alternative, as a potential underpinned by a lively critical intuition that challenges the current ordering of social forces within the capitalist system.

32. By "political rights" I refer to the rights associated with participation in governing the joint endeavor of the firm—specifically, the right to a say in choices related to present and future goals and outcomes. This takes place in a democratic context, where participants recognize each other as enjoying equal political rights. In other types of political contexts (monarchic, plutocratic, etc.), political rights are

distributed unequally; capitalism is one such power system, since it accords political rights to capital investors only.

33. On workers' suffering in Western economies, see Dejours et al., *The Return of Work in Critical Theory.*

34. Ferreras, *Firms as Political Entities.*

35. Jean-Philippe Robé, "The Legal Structure of the Firm," *Accounting, Economics, and Law* 1, no. 5 (2011).

36. For more on the political history and theory of the corporation, see the groundbreaking David Ciepley, "Beyond Public and Private: Toward a Political Theory of the Corporation," *American Political Science Review* 107, no. 1 (2013): 139–58. The perspective proposed here rests on a political theory of the *firm*, which offers a somewhat different perspective from Ciepley's focus on a political theory of the *corporation.* Ferreras, *Gouverner le capitalisme?* and *Firms as Political Entities.* Our own perspective takes the *reductio ad corporationem* seriously and, instead of suggesting we salvage the corporation from its capital investors, suggests we complete the process of organizing its power structure according to standards that live up to our democratic commitment as a society. If we take the difference between the corporation and the firm seriously, we must spend more time envisioning how to seriously organize the representation of labor investors, rather than falling for the siren song of corporate social responsibility, which never contests shareholder primacy but is built on the assumption that capital investors are the legitimate constituency of the firm, as it remains conflated with the corporation.

37. Paddy Ireland, "Corporate Schizophrenia: The Institutional Origins of Corporate Social Irresponsibility," in *Shaping the Corporate Landscape,* ed. Nina Boeger and Charlotte Villiers (Oxford: Hart, 2018). For a list of recent cases across the five continents, see European Network of Corporate Observatories, "The EU and the Corporate Impunity Nexus," The Transnational Institute, October 2018, tni.org.

38. See Adam Winkler, *We the Corporations. How American Businesses Won Their Civil Rights* (New York: W. W. Norton, 2018).

39. Jean-Philippe Robé, *L'entreprise et le droit* (Paris: Presses Universitaires de France, 1999), and "The Legal Structure of the Firm." Note that it is therefore inappropriate to discuss the question of firms in terms of property rights: although economic theory refers to a firm's owners, firms, like corporations, fall outside the scope of the concept of property. As Robé has shown, it is empirically wrong and legally unfounded to describe firms as having owners: whereas the shares of a corporation, at least, are owned by its shareholders, there is no exact correlate for the firm. And yet, this legal reality has gone completely unnoticed by even the world's most distinguished economists, who continue to base their economic theories of the firm on the fallacy that it has owners. In his 2016 Nobel acceptance speech, for example, Oliver Hart, a professor at Harvard, discussed the "control rights" of the "owner of firm." Returning to Habermas's distinction between the two knowledge-constitutive interests served by science, it is reasonable to ask what interests are served by maintaining this fallacy. Habermas, *Knowledge and Human Interests.*

40. On the similarities between firms and states, to justify using the tools and concepts of political science and political theory to study firms, see Hélène Landemore and Isabelle Ferreras, "In Defense of Workplace Democracy: Towards a Justification of the Firm-State Analogy," *Political Theory* 44, no. 1 (2016): 53–81. For a thoughtful critique justifying the specifics of the disanalogy, see Abraham Singer, *The Form of the Firm: A Normative Political Theory of the Corporation* (New York: Oxford University Press, 2018).

41. Virgile Chassagnon, "The Network Firm as a Single Real Entity: Beyond the Aggregate of Legal Distinct Entities," *Journal of Economic Issues* 45, no. 1 (2011): 113–36.

42. Robé, "The Legal Structure of the Firm," 36.
43. Echoing a campaign promise by then-presidential-candidate Donald Trump, his son-in-law Jared Kushner declared to the *Washington Post* on March 26, 2017: "The government should be run like a great American company. Our hope is that we can achieve successes and efficiencies for our customers, who are the citizens."
44. Trump's despotic disposition has carried over to his public office. This was abundantly evident in James Comey's testimony to the Senate Intelligence Committee in June 2017 after he was fired by the Trump administration. Comey reported that the new president was trying to establish "some sort of patronage relationship with [Comey]" and had no respect for or understanding of the idea that a public servant might choose to act with independence in pursuit of the common good, rather than engaging in the kind of subordinate relationship that Trump expects of anyone employed by "his" organization.
45. Wright and Rogers, *American Society*; Archon Fung and Erik Olin Wright, "Deepening Democracy: Innovations in Empowered Participatory Governance," *Politics and Society* 29, no. 1 (2001): 5–41.
46. Braudel describes the economic system as comprising three layers: one of exchange among people who know each other personally (which is not necessarily monetized, as in gift exchange); market exchange among individuals and groups (via markets, where competition is intense and trade is mediated by money); and, finally, capitalism (where important producers attempt to influence policymakers in order to define favorable rules of the game; at this upper level, the free market is actively restrained in order to favor consolidation and monopolies, capture the regulatory state, and foster accumulation of wealth). Fernand Braudel, *La dynamique du capitalisme* (Paris: Flammarion, 1985). For a necessary companion refection to this one on the corporation, see Malleson on how to democratize the market system: Tom Malleson, *After Occupy. Economic Democracy for the 21st Century* (New York: Oxford University Press, 2014). On the specific crux of how to democratize finance, see in particular Fred Block and Robert Hockett, eds., *Democratizing Finance* (London: Verso, 2022).
47. The birth of the Yellow Vest movement in France in November 2018 illustrates this vague feeling of being subject to the powerful forces of the transnational corporations, which have become more powerful than our states; it is an angry social movement with no clear claims or demands, only a general outrage at the notion that they should pay higher fuel taxes while the wealthiest capital owners accrue still more money and influence. See French economist Thomas Coutrot's analysis of voting behavior in France's 2017 presidential elections. Coutrot found that voters whose work was closely monitored and controlled (that is, who had little to no autonomy in the way their work was organized) were significantly more likely to either vote for the extreme-right candidate or abstain from voting. Thomas Coutrot, "Travail et bien-être psychologique," *DARES*, March 2018, dares. travail-emploi.gouv.fr. See also Mounk's powerful analysis of the rise of populist/anti-democratic resentment in Western nations: Yascha Mounk, *The People vs. Democracy: Why Our Freedom Is in Danger and How to Save It* (Cambridge, MA: Harvard University Press, 2018). Mounk's work shows a growing loss of faith in representative democratic politics as it is currently structured—not a lessened desire for voice. This has the perverse effect of causing voter behavior that eventually draws power away from voters who see demagogic or authoritarian strongmen as the solution to their problems. This, of course, directly echoes Polanyi's analysis of fascism as the "last resort solution" of a people desperate for a government that was responsive to their needs rather than to the prevailing economic interests of

the time. Karl Polanyi, *The Great Transformation* (New York: Rinehart & Co, 1944). For more on this, see Ferreras, *Firms as Political Entities*.

48. In the case of contemporary US workplaces, Anderson even speaks of "communist dictatorship" ruling the lives of employees. Anderson, *Private Government*.

49. German *Mitbestimmung* (codetermination) was put in place after the Second World War and is unique and remarkable as a system of industrial relations at the firm level: corporations with more than 2,000 employees are supervised by a board composed of an equal number of employee and employer representatives. But while formal parity exists, in most firms it is the case that all tie votes are broken by the president of the board, who is elected by the employer representatives, giving them a de facto majority. German legal scholars thus refer to it as "false parity," a point to which we will return later on.

50. See the tremendous success of Mondragon and Ellerman's radical defense of workers as the sole legitimate investor-owners. Malleson, *After Occupy*; Amanda Latinne, *The Mondragon Cooperatives: Workplace Democracy and Globalization* (Cambridge, UK: Intersentia, 2014); Ellerman, "On the Renting of Persons."

51. Ellerman, *Property and Contract in Economics* and "On the Renting of Persons"; Malleson, *After Occupy*; Sanjay Pinto, "Worker Co-operatives and Other Alternative Forms of Business Organization," in *Handbook of the International Political Economy of the Corporation*, ed. Christian May and Andreas Noelke (Cheltenham, UK: Edward Elgar, 2018).

52. David Weil, *The Fissured Workplace: Why Work Became So Bad for So Many and What Can Be Done to Improve It* (Cambridge, MA: Harvard University Press, 2014).

53. In the United States, this is already a legal possibility thanks to federal ESOP legislation, which allows workers to set up a trust that can contract loans with which they then buy back the firm's shares from its previous owners.

54. For more on possible connections between corporate governance and environmental sustainability, see Florence Jany-Catrice and Dominique Méda, *Faut-il attendre la croissance?* (Paris: La Documentation française, 2016); Tim Jackson and Peter Victor, "Does Slow Growth Increase Inequality? Some Reflections on Piketty's 'Fundamental' Laws of Capitalism," Passage Working Paper (2014); and Tim Jackson, *Prosperity without Growth? Foundations for the Economy of Tomorrow* (London: Routledge, 2016).

55. For a more comprehensive perspective on the different dimensions and levels involved in the project of economic democracy, see Malleson, *After Occupy*.

56. Ferreras, *Firms as Political Entities*.

57. As this battle continues, this stance is being taken more and more frequently in courts; see, for example, in May 2018, the major decision by the California Supreme Court to limit the right of platforms to classify their workers as independent contractors. The same decision was handed down by France's highest court in November 2018.

58. For a discussion that fits this line of reasoning, of a failed attempt by the freelancer cooperative SMart, based in Brussels, to organize Deliveroo bike drivers, see Julien Charles, Isabelle Ferreras, and Auriane Lamine, "Economie de plateforme et entreprise fissurée: Quelle perspective d'émancipation pour les travailleur-se-s?," *Politique*, December 7, 2018, revuepolitique.be.

59. This is typically the case of family-owned firms or firms with a strong family tradition. But these cases have become the exception. See Colin Mayer, *Prosperity: Better Business Makes the Greater Good* (Oxford: Oxford University Press, 2018).

60. The bias of the current system, in which the corporation holds despotic power over the firm, is very perceptible in the way risk is assessed for capital and labor

investors. Noncompetition, confidentiality, and intellectual-property-ownership clauses have become commonplace in US labor contracts, extending over months or even years, during which labor investors cannot seek a similar job or position; at the same time, their employer can fire them at will. How would the law view a similar agreement between corporate entities? How could a worker impose a parallel obligation on an employer through the employment contract (i.e., if I quit, you cannot hire any new person to perform the services I perform for the corporation for a period of two years)? The seeming outrageousness of these hypotheticals highlights how risibly little assessment of labor-investment risk there really is.

61. Again, this holds true until the day corporations are able to forego labor investors entirely and use robots instead, but for many firms this remains firmly in the realm of science fiction. And in any case, for the moment, if their investments are to have any value, capital investors in firms continue to depend on labor investors.

62. This is an especially daunting project, as the economy has become global and the state a local player. Taking this challenge seriously, see in particular Joshua Cohen and Charles Sabel, "Extra Rempublicam Nulla," *Justitia Philosophy and Public Affairs* 34, no. 2 (2006): 147–75. And, from the perspective of the operation of global firms, see Jean-Philippe Robé, Antoine Lyon-Caen, and Stéphane Vernac, eds., *Multinationals and the Constitutionalization of the World Power System* (London: Routledge, 2016).

63. The functioning of the US Congress should not be taken as concrete evidence for the (in)efficiency of the institutional invention of bicameralism. Indeed, the reader should bear in mind that this case is an extreme one: the oppositional forces of the American system of checks and balances are strong enough to block one another entirely. This seems counterproductive in the case of the firm, where aligning the powers of the two chambers to appoint the executive branch would appear to be necessary to produce the kind of environment that respects each chamber's interests and acknowledges their shared goals.

64. According to Norton, parliamentary models all fall somewhere along a spectrum, which ranges from "policy-influencing" on one end to "policy-making" on the other. Philippe Norton, "Parliament and Policy in Britain: The House of Commons as a Policy Influencer," *Teaching Politics* 13, no. 2 (1984): 198–221. Here, Norton is elaborating on Polsby's classic analysis, which contrasted parliaments that functioned as "arenas" with those functioning as "policy transformers." Nelson Polsby, "Legislatures," in *Handbook of Political Science: Governmental Institutions and Processes*, ed. Nelson Polsby and Fred Greenstein (Boston: Addison-Wesley, 1975), 257–319. According to Norton the weak legislature of British Parliament falls on one end of this spectrum—parliament as arena. At the other end of the spectrum, the US Congress, with a broad parliamentary mandate that allows it to draft and propose laws, is an example of parliament as policy transformer. Most countries, including most in continental Europe, lie somewhere between these two extremes. Norton, "Parliament and Policy in Britain," 20. Norton further nuanced his idea with reference to Blondel's concept of "legislative viscosity," which measures a legislature's influence on the legislation process. Philippe Norton, "La nature du contrôle parlementaire," *Pouvoirs* 3 (2010): 134–94. "Legislative viscosity" describes the extent to which a legislature is able to resist the advance of a law drafted by the executive branch of government by slowing it or even blocking it (through veto power), and to force the executive branch to negotiate, change the text of the draft law, and accept proposed amendments. This viscosity may go so far as to allow the legislature to propose its own laws. If a legislature holds all these powers, it is considered to be highly "viscous."

65. Erik Olin Wright, *Envisioning Real Utopias* (London: Verso, 2010).
66. Francis Delpérée, "Les Secondes Chambres parlementaires," *XIXè Session de l'Académie internationale de Droit constitutionnel portant sur les Secondes Chambres parlementaires* XIII (2004): 1–13.
67. For more in-depth discussions of the history of bicameralism, see Ferreras, *Gouverner le capitalisme?* and *Firms as Political Entities.*
68. Donald Shell, "The History of Bicameralism," *Journal of Legislative Studies* 7, no. 1 (2001): 9.
69. The United Kingdom and the United States use different terms to describe the same idea: in general, the English refer to the theory of mixed government and Americans to checks and balances.
70. See Federalist Paper 39 by James Madison: "The House of Representatives will derive its powers from the people of America; and the people will be represented in the same proportion and on the same principle as they are in the legislature of a particular State. So far, the government is national, not federal. The Senate, on the other hand, will derive its powers from the States as political and coequal societies; and these will be represented on the principle of equality in the Senate, as they are now in the existing Congress. So far, the government is federal, not national." Giancarlo Doria, "The Paradox of Federal Bicameralism," *European Diversity and Autonomy Papers* 5, no. 41 (2006): 13.
71. Gordon Wood, *The Creation of the American Republic* (Chapel Hill: University of North Carolina Press, 1969), 552.
72. Elaine Swift, *The Making of an American Senate: Reconstitutive Change in Congress, 1787–1841* (Ann Arbor: University of Michigan, 1996), 47.
73. Doria, "The Paradox of Federal Bicameralism," 24. Doria also points out that bicameralism was a ready solution for the American founding fathers, since the federated states were already organized into bicameral parliaments. According to Doria, this is further proof that America's founders were motivated not by the goal of a federal union but by their desire to achieve a balance of power; indeed, at the state level this was the principle used to justify bicameralism.
74. Shell, "The History of Bicameralism," 9.
75. Obviously, these arguments ignored the fact that they were taking place on stolen land, in a system that did not recognize the rights of women and included the practices of slavery and indentured servitude, which of course throws the legitimacy of their claims into question in a much deeper and more fundamental way. We do not wish to minimize the tragic injustice of colonialism as a whole. Rather we hope to draw attention to the way in which these seeds of democratic equality developed in the United States, with the goal of continuing to extend and deepen the project of democratic equality. Though it cannot repair the damages done in the past, it might bring some greater measure of justice to the present and the future.
76. John Stuart Mill, *Considerations on Representative Government*, in *Liberty and Other Essays* (Oxford: Oxford University Press, 1998 [1861]), 385.
77. Shell, "The History of Bicameralism," 10.
78. Hélène Landemore, *Democratic Reason: Politics, Collective Intelligence, and the Rule of the Many* (Princeton, NJ: Princeton University Press, 2012); Hélène Landemore, "Deliberation, Cognitive Diversity, and Democratic Inclusiveness: An Epistemic Argument for the Random Selection of Representatives," *Synthese* 190, no. 7 (2013): 1209–31; Hélène Landemore and Jon Elster, eds., *Collective Wisdom: Principles and Mechanisms* (Cambridge, UK: Cambridge University Press, 2012).
79. Franz Gamillscheg, "La Cogestion des travailleurs en droit allemand: Bilan à la lumière du jugement du Tribunal constitutionnel fédéral du 1er mars 1979," *Revue internationale de droit comparé* 32, no. 1 (1979): 57–74.

80. On the distinction between management and government, see Ferreras, *Firms as Political Entities*. In sum, management looks to means, and government to ends. Both are important, and means are always meaningful to the establishment of ends, but, contrary to inclusive participatory management techniques, the goal of economic bicameralism is to guarantee labor investors a deciding voice in the *government* of their firms, and thus of their (work) lives, rather than keep them in the position of a dominated serfs serving the ends established by a more or less benevolent despot. It should function as a critique of the naivete of the movements for "liberated firms" and "reinvented organizations." Carney and Getz, *Freedom Inc.*; Laloux, *Reinventing Organizations*. These movements are leading to more intelligent forms of capitalism, but it still leaves the government of firms (and thus the determination of the ends of capitalism) squarely in the hands of capital investors. If these movements become willing to address this structural issue, their impact on the course of human development will be significantly different.

81. For a careful discussion of the differences between the "logics of collective action" of capital and labor, see Claus Offe and Helmuth Wiesenthal, "Two Logics of Collective Action: Theoretical Notes on Social Class and Organizational Form," in *Political Power and Social Theory: A Research Annual*, vol. 1, ed. Maurice Zeitlin (Greenwich, CT: JAI, 1980), 67–116.

82. Florence Jaumotte and Carolina Osorio Buitron, "Inequality and Labor Market Institutions," IMF Staff Discussion Note 31 (2015).

83. Richard B. Freeman and James L. Medoff, *What Do Unions Do?* (New York: Basic Books, 1984).

84. Elections should be considered as just one possible way to appoint representatives. Sortition is at least as relevant a way. See Landemore, "Deliberation, Cognitive Diversity, and Democratic Inclusiveness"; John Gastil and Erik Olin Wright, eds., *Legislature by Lot* (London: Verso, 2019). Contemporary reflections on the ills of elections are very relevant in the context of firms. Firms should be conceived as useful laboratories of deliberation and, as such, help pave the way to enhance the selection practices that can best nurture a vibrant democracy at the macro-level.

85. Offe and Wiesenthal, "Two Logics of Collective Action."

86. My understanding of economic bicameralism rests on the idea of a fundamental conflict between capital and labor. I see them, in the Marxian tradition, as incommensurable. The proposal does not rest on a naive view of a shared community of interests; rather, it seeks to organize this fundamental conflict in order to make the most productive use of it, rather than subject society in general, and labor investors in particular, to its most deleterious ills. The conception of the political that lies behind it is Arendtian and agonistic.

87. In a world made of cities ruled by plutocrats, we would welcome it as a positive development if some cities entered a bicameral moment and began their internal democratization by establishing a bicameral legislature representing the plutocrats and the people, and giving this second chamber the same veto power as enjoyed by the first chamber. Of course, the construction and democratization of a global structure encompassing these cities, governing their common fate (especially if they were located on the same threatened planet) and mutual externalities, should be considered a fitting and urgent endeavor. But both goals are and should be considered complementary, not mutually exclusive.

88. Joel Rogers and Wolfgang Streeck, *Works Councils: Consultation, Representation, and Cooperation in Industrial Relations* (Chicago: University of Chicago Press, 1995).

89. Ewan McGaughey, "Democracy in America at Work: The History of Labor's Vote in Corporate Governance," *Seattle University Law Review* 42 (2019): 697–753.

90. Julie Battilana and Isabelle Ferreras, "From Shareholder Primacy to a Dual Major-ity Board," Aspen Institute Business and Society Program Report Series, August 2021.

91. At the site and country level, some corresponding committees should provide for useful representation, as is the case in Germany with codetermination, which is organized at the level of the corporate structure (*Unternehmen*) and at the level of the worksite (*Betriebsrat*). The present essay cannot elaborate on the complexity of this internal architecture, but it is clearly a major dimension of economic bicam-eralism that proper internal channels of representation will have to be established and relevant devolution of power carefully thought out, especially in the case of a transnational firm.

92. See the very informative database about EWCs maintained by the European Trade Union Institute, ewcdb.eu.

93. Stefan Rüb, *World Works Councils and Other Forms of Global Employee Representa-tion in Transnational Undertakings: A Survey*, Arbeitspapier 55 (Düsseldorf: Hans Böckler Stiftung, 2002).

94. Ernest Mandel, *Autogestion, occupations d'usines et contrôle ouvrier* (Paris: Maspero, 1973), 9. This idea fits with Gorz's idea of "achievable intermediate goals" capable of opening up a "practical way forward" to democratic socialism. André Gorz, *Stratégie ouvrière et néo-capitalisme* (Paris: Seuil, 1964).

95. Ralf Dahrendorf, *Class and Class Conflict in Industrial Society* (Stanford, CA: Stanford University Press, 1957).

96. Morris R. Cohen, "Property and Sovereignty," *Cornell Law Quarterly* 13 (1927): 26.

97. See Thomas Piketty, *Capital in the Twenty-First Century*, trans. Arthur Goldham-mer (Cambridge, UK: Belknap Press, 2014).

98. Ireland, "Corporate Schizophrenia."

99. Mill, *Considerations on Representative Government*, 385.

100. Jany-Catrice and Méda, *Faut-il attendre la croissance?*; Jackson, *Prosperity without Growth?*

101. Polanyi, *The Great Transformation*.

102. Wright and Rogers, *American Society*.

103. According to the figures published by the US Center for Disease Control and Prevention, processing BLS data: "Productivity losses linked to absenteeism cost employers $225.8 billion annually in the United States, or $1,685 per employee." "Worker Illness and Injury Costs U.S. Employers $225.8 Billion Annually," CDC Foundation, January 28, 2015, cdcfoundation.org.

104. Douglas Kruse, Richard Freeman, and Joseph Blasi, *Shared Capitalism at Work: Employee Ownership, Profit and Gain Sharing, and Broad-Based Stock Options* (Chicago: University of Chicago Press, 2010); Joseph R. Blasi, Richard B. Freeman, and Douglas L. Kruse, *The Citizen's Share: Putting Ownership Back into Democracy* (New Haven, CT: Yale University Press, 2014).

105. See Block and Hockett, *Democratizing Finance*.

106. In short: in the tradition of the Frankfurt school, and in particular the work of Habermas, my research seeks to support emancipation, being the core "knowledge-constitutive interest" of the critical sciences, through identifying the emancipatory "critical intuitions" of actors as a means to reinforce them using a reconstructive approach, in the sense of the "reconstructive ethics" proposed by Jean-Marc Ferry. Habermas, *Knowledge and Human Interests*; Ferreras, *Gouverner le capitalisme?*; Jean-Marc Ferry, *L'Éthique reconstructive* (Paris: Le Cerf, 1996).

107. Ferreras, *Critique politique du travail*. From the seminal work of Weber to the contem-porary studies of the spirit of capitalism led by Boltanski and Chiapello, we know that

capitalism, in the efforts it requires, needs an ethos to generate true anthropological commitment. Luc Boltanski and Eve Chiapello, *The New Spirit of Capitalism*, trans. Gregory Elliott (London: Verso, 2006). In the past ten years, propositions to "free" or liberate the firm, to flatten the hierarchy, to "reinvent organizations," or to give more autonomy to workers have been taught in business schools. Carney and Getz, *Freedom Inc.*; Laloux, *Reinventing Organizations*. They reflect the current practices of innovative businesses that seek to return some degree of power and autonomy to workers. These "agile" practices speak for the sheer force of capitalism as it instrumentalizes and recycles its critiques to draw strength from them.

108. Herbert Marcuse, *One-Dimensional Man: Studies in the Ideology of Advanced Industrial Society* (Boston: Beacon Press, 1964).
109. Piketty, *Capital in the Twenty-First Century*.
110. Alain Supiot, ed., *Face à l'irresponsabilité: La dynamique de la solidarité* (Paris: Collège de France, 2018); Robé et al., *Multinationals and the Constitutionalization of the World Power System*; Virgile Chassagnon, *Économie de la firme-monde: Pouvoir, régime de gouvernement et regulation* (Bruxelles: De Boeck, 2018).
111. Sabel, "Learning by Monitoring."
112. Isabelle Ferreras and Julien Charles, "La citoyenneté au travail: Enjeu pour les organisations et la sociologie," in *Travail et care comme expériences politiques*, ed. Matthieu de Nanteuil and Laura Merla (Louvain-la-Neuve: Presses universitaires de Louvain, 2017), 165–78; Coutrot, "Travail et bien-être psychologique"; Mounk, *The People vs. Democracy*; Lawrence Lessig, *America, Compromised* (Chicago: University of Chicago Press, 2018).
113. Richard Heede, *Carbon Producers' Tar Pit: Dinosaurs Beware: The Path to Accountability of Fossil Fuel Producers for Climate Change and Climate Damages*, Plenary Conference Address (Edinburgh: Institute for New Economic Thinking, Climate Accountability Institute, 2017); Peter C. Frumhoff, Richard Heede, and Naomi Oreskes, "The Climate Responsibilities of Industrial Carbon Producers," *Climatic Change* 132 (2015): 157–71.
114. See the *Carbon Majors Report*, last updated 13 November 2021, available at climateaccountability.org.
115. Jackson, *Prosperity without Growth*; Jany-Catrice and Méda, *Faut-il attendre la croissance?*; Isabelle Cassiers, ed., *Redefining Prosperity* (London: Routledge, 2015).
116. Jackson, *Prosperity without Growth*; Olivier De Schutter, "The Political Economy of Food Systems Reform," *European Review of Agricultural Economics* 44, no. 4 (2017): 705–31.

2. The Progressive Era's Public Firm

1. "Watered stock" refers to stock that was issued at a higher value than its actual value, which, prior to new legal protections in the early twentieth century, exposed stockholders to greater liability.
2. During this period, the word "trust" was used in public discourse to refer to any large corporation that operated nationally. James Dill, *National Incorporation Laws for Trusts* (Cambridge, MA: Harvard University, 1902).
3. Chicago Conference on Trusts, *Chicago Conference on Trusts Speeches, Debates, Resolutions, Lists of the Delegates, Committees, etc., Held September 13th, 14th, 15th, 16th, 1899*, ed. Civic Federation of Chicago (Chicago: Civic Federation of Chicago, 1899), 500.
4. Ibid., 43.
5. Ibid., 68.

6. The first antitrust state law was enacted by Kansas in 1889. By 1890, the date of the Sherman Antitrust Act, fourteen states had antimonopoly provisions in their state constitutions. Henry R. Seager and Charles A. Gulick, *Trust and Corporation Problems* (New York: Harper, 1929).

7. Lincoln Steffens, "New Jersey: A Traitor State," *McClure's Magazine* 24 (1905): 41.

8. Chicago Conference on Trusts, *Chicago Conference on Trusts Speeches*, 569.

9. Camden Hutchinson, "Progressive Era Conceptions of the Corporation and the Failure of the Federal Chartering Movement," *Columbia Business Legal Review* 2017, no. 3 (2018): 1017–99.

10. Elizabeth Warren, "Companies Shouldn't Be Accountable Only to Shareholders," *Wall Street Journal*, August 14, 2018.

11. David Ciepley, "Beyond Public and Private: Toward a Political Theory of the Corporation," *American Political Science Review* 107, no. 1 (2013): 139–58; Hélène Landemore and Isabelle Ferreras, "In Defense of Workplace Democracy: Towards a Justification of the Firm–State Analogy," *Political Theory* 44, no. 1 (2016): 53–81; Elizabeth Anderson, *Private Government* (Princeton, NJ: Princeton University Press, 2017); Isabelle Ferreras, *Firms as Political Entities: Saving Democracy through Economic Bicameralism* (Cambridge, UK: Cambridge University Press, 2017); Abraham A. Singer, "The Corporation as a Relational Entity," *Polity* 49, no. 3 (2017): 328–51; Abraham A. Singer, "The Political Nature of the Firm and the Cost of Norms," *Journal of Politics* 80, no. 3 (2018): 831–44.

12. Singer, "The Political Nature of the Firm," 831.

13. In his dissent on *Citizens United*, Justice Stevens argued that the framers had very different views of the purpose of corporations than we have today—"purposes that had to be made consistent with public welfare."

14. Jason Kaufman, "Endogenous Explanation in the Sociology of Culture," *Annual Review of Sociology* 30, no. 1 (2004): 335–57; Oscar Handlin and Mary F. Handlin, *Commonwealth: A Study of the Role of Government in the American Economy: Massachusetts, 1774–1861* (Cambridge, MA: Belknap Press, 1969); Ronald Seavoy, *The Origins of the American Business Corporation, 1784–1855: Broadening the Concept of Public Service during Industrialization* (Westport, CT: Greenwood Press, 1982); Herbert Hovenkamp, *Enterprise and American Law, 1836–1937* (Cambridge, MA: Harvard University Press, 1991).

15. Handlin and Handlin, *Commonwealth*, 97.

16. James S. Coleman, *The Asymmetric Society* (Syracuse, NY: Syracuse University Press, 1982), 37.

17. Henry Hansmann and Reinier Kraakman, "The Essential Role of Organizational Law," *Yale Law Journal* 110, no. 3 (2000): 387–440; Henry Hansmann, Reinier Kraakman, and Richard Squire, "Law and the Rise of the Firm," *Harvard Law Review* 119 (2005): 1335–403; Ciepley, "Beyond Public and Private."

18. Ciepley, "Beyond Public and Private," 156.

19. Ibid., 145.

20. Gregory A. Mark, "The Personification of the Business Corporation in American Law," *University of Chicago Law Review* 54, no. 4 (1987): 1441–83.

21. Robert Ludlow Fowler, "The State and Private Corporations," *American Law Review* 25 (1891): 581.

22. Martin J. Sklar, *The Corporate Reconstruction of American Capitalism, 1890–1916* (Cambridge, MA: Cambridge University Press, 1988); Morton J. Horwitz, "Santa Clara Revisited: The Development of Corporate Theory," *West Virginia Law Review* 88 (1985): 173–224; Mark Hager, "Bodies Politic: The Progressive History of Organizational 'Real Entity' Theory," *University of Pittsburgh Law Review* 50 (1989): 575–654; Mark, "Personification of the Business Corporation."

23. Carly Knight, "Classifying the Corporation: The Role of Naturalizing Analogies in American Corporate Development, 1870–1930," Working Paper (2022).
24. Max Radin, "The Endless Problem of Corporate Personality," *Columbia Law Review* 32 (1932): 643–67.
25. John Dewey, "The Historic Background of Corporate Legal Personality," *Yale Law Journal* 35, no. 6 (1926): 661.
26. Gerald F. Davis, *The Vanishing American Corporation: Navigating the Hazards of a New Economy* (Oakland: Berrett-Koehler, 2016).
27. The definition of "public" that Ferreras employs is "the sociological notion of a specific 'interaction regime'" wherein members of a democratic public sphere treat one another with equality and respect (this volume, 19).
28. Robert A. Dahl, *A Preface to Economic Democracy* (Berkeley: University of California Press, 1985); Carole Pateman, *Participation and Democratic Theory* (Cambridge, UK: Cambridge University Press, 1970); David Schweickart, *After Capitalism* (London: Rowman & Littlefield, 2011), 47; Richard Wolff, *Democracy at Work: A Cure for Capitalism* (Chicago: Haymarket Books, 2012).
29. Dahl, *A Preface to Economic Democracy*, 57.
30. Ibid., 111.
31. Anderson, *Private Government*, 42.
32. William J. Novak, "The Public Utility Idea and the Origins of Modern Business Regulation," in *Corporations and American Democracy*, ed. Naomi Lamoreaux and William J. Novak (Cambridge, MA: Harvard University Press, 2017), 139–54.
33. Ibid., 160.
34. Dewey, "Corporate Legal Personality."
35. Rexford G. Tugwell, "The Economic Basis for Business Regulation," *American Economic Review* 11, no. 4 (1921): 643–58.
36. Felicia Wong, "The Emerging Worldview: How New Progressivism Is Moving Beyond Neoliberalism," Roosevelt Institute, January 15, 2020, rooseveltinstitute.org.
37. Paul Adler, "Democratizing Control," *Boston Review*, October 1, 2019, bostonreview.net.
38. Jared Bernstein, "Wages in the United States: Trends, Explanations, and Solutions" in *The Dynamics of Opportunity in America*, ed. Irwin Kirsch and Henry Braun (New York: Springer, 2016), 167–95.
39. Mark Mizruchi, "Berle and Means Revisited: The Governance and Power of Large US Corporations," *Theory and Society* 33, no. 5 (2004): 579–617; Frank Dobbin and Dirk Zorn, "Corporate Malfeasance and the Myth of Shareholder Value," *Political Power and Social Theory* 17 (2005): 179–98; Thomas A. DiPrete, Gregory M. Eirich, and Matthew Pittinsky, "Compensation Benchmarking, Leapfrogs, and the Surge in Executive Pay," *American Journal of Sociology* 115, no. 6 (2010): 1671–712; Barry Eidlin, "Why Is There No Labor Party in the United States? Political Articulation and the Canadian Comparison, 1932 to 1948," *American Sociological Review* 81, no. 3 (2016): 488–516; Nathan Wilmers, "Labor Unions as Activist Organizations: A Union Power Approach to Estimating Union Wage Effects," *Social Forces* 95, no. 4 (2017): 1451–78.
40. Erling Barth et al., "It's Where You Work: Increases in the Dispersion of Earnings across Establishments and Individuals in the United States," *Journal of Labor Economics* 34 (2016): S67–S97; David Autor et al., "Concentrating on the Fall of the Labor Share," NBER Working Paper Series (2017); David Autor et al., "The Fall of the Labor Share and the Rise of Superstar Firms," NBER Working Paper Series (2017); Nathan Wilmers and Clem Aeppl, "Consolidated Advantage: New Organizational Dynamics of Wage Inequality," *American Sociological Review* 86, no. 6 (2021): 1100–30.
41. Wilmers, "Labor Unions as Activist Organizations," 215.

42. Autor et al., "Concentrating on the Fall of the Labor Share."

43. Autor et al., "The Fall of the Labor Share and the Rise of Superstar Firms."

44. Suresh Naidu, Eric A. Posner, and Glen Weyl, "Antitrust Remedies for Labor Market Power," *Harvard Law Review* 132 (2018): 536; Efraim Benmelech, Nittai Bergman, and Hyunseob Kim, "Strong Employers and Weak Employees: How Does Employer Concentration Affect Wages?," National Bureau of Economic Research (2018).

45. Wilmers, "Wage Stagnation and Buyer Power."

46. Ryan A. Decker et al., "Where Has All the Skewness Gone? The Decline in High-Growth (Young) Firms in the US," *European Economic Review* 86 (2016): 4–23; Raven Molloy et al., "Understanding Declining Fluidity in the US Labor Market," Brookings Papers on Economic Activity (2016): 183–259.

47. Jacob S. Hacker, *Universal Insurance: Enhancing Economic Security to Promote Opportunity* (Washington, DC: Brookings Institution, 2006); Jacob S. Hacker, *The Great Risk Shift: The New Economic Insecurity and the Decline of the American Dream* (Oxford: Oxford University Press, 2006); Arne L. Kalleberg, "Precarious Work, Insecure Workers: Employment Relations in Transition," *American Sociological Review* 74, no. 1 (2009): 1–22; Arne L. Kalleberg and Steven P. Vallas, "Probing Precarious Work: Theory, Research, and Politics," *Research in the Sociology of Work* 31, no. 1 (2018): 1–30.

48. Peter Cappelli, *The New Deal at Work* (Cambridge, MA: Harvard Business School Press, 1998); Kalleberg, "Precarious Work, Insecure Workers."

49. Bureau of Labor Statistics, "National Compensation Survey: Employee Benefits in the United States," Bulletin 2715, 2008, bls.gov.

50. Based on tabulation from US Federal Reserve Board's Survey of Consumer Finances.

51. Jacob S. Hacker, Philipp Rehm, and Mark Schlesinger, "The Insecure American: Economic Experiences, Financial Worries, and Policy Attitudes," *Perspectives on Politics* 11, no. 1 (2013): 23–49.

52. Matissa N. Hollister and Kristin E. Smith, "Unmasking the Conflicting Trends in Job Tenure by Gender in the United States, 1983–2008," *American Sociological Review* 79, no. 1 (2014): 159–81; Davis, "The Vanishing American Corporation."

53. Kate Andrias and Brishen Rogers, *Rebuilding Worker Voice in Today's Economy* (New York: Roosevelt Institute, 2018).

54. Hacker, *Universal Insurance*.

55. Bruce G. Carruthers, "Financial Decommodification," in *Policy Shock*, ed. E. J. Balleisen et al. (Cambridge, UK: Cambridge University Press, 2017), 371–94.

56. Mike Konczal, *Freedom from the Market* (New Press, 2021).

57. Erik Olin Wright, "Basic Income, Stakeholder Grants, and Class Analysis," *Politics and Society* 32, no. 1 (2004): 79–87.

58. Karl Polanyi, *The Great Transformation* (Boston, MA: Beacon Press, 1944), 73.

59. Isabelle Ferreras, "Democratizing the Corporation, this volume, 15–60.

60. Chicago Conference on Trusts, *Chicago Conference on Trusts Speeches*, 511.

3. Workplace Democracy, the Bicameral Firm, and Stakeholder Theory

1. See Ferretti and Gosseries, "Are Bicameral Firms Preferable to Codetermination or Worker Cooperatives?," this volume, 165–79.

2. J. Heath, *Morality, Competition, and the Firm: The Market Failures Approach to Business Ethics* (Oxford: Oxford University Press, 2014); J. S. Harrison, J. B.

Barney, R. E. Freeman, and R. A. Phillips, eds., *The Cambridge Handbook of Stakeholder Theory* (Cambridge, UK: Cambridge University Press, 2019).

3. Marc Fleurbaey and G. Ponthière, "The Stakeholder Corporation and Social Welfare," *SSRN*, August 9, 2021, ssrn.com.

4. See, for example, Harrison et al., *The Cambridge Handbook of Stakeholder Theory*; Michael Magill, Martine Quinzii, and Jean-Charles Rochet, "A Theory of the Stakeholder Corporation," *Econometrica* 83 (2015): 1685–725.

5. Heath, *Morality, Competition, and the Firm*; J. Tirole, *The Theory of Corporate Finance* (Princeton, NJ: Princeton University Press, 2006).

6. Fleurbaey and Ponthière, "The Stakeholder Corporation and Social Welfare."

7. Ibid.

8. Ibid.

9. Heath, *Morality, Competition, and the Firm.*

10. Isabelle Fererras, "Democratizing the Corporation: The Proposal of the Bicameral Firm," this volume, 15–60.

11. Oliver Hart and Luigi Zingales, "Companies Should Maximize Shareholder Welfare Not Market Value," ECGI—Finance Working Paper 521 (2017).

12. Fererras, "Democratizing the Corporation."

13. Fleurbaey and Ponthière, "The Stakeholder Corporation and Social Welfare."

14. Ibid.

4. Fallacies about Corporations

1. Isabelle Ferreras, *Firms as Political Entities* (Cambridge, UK: Cambridge University Press, 2017); "Democratizing the Corporation: The Proposal of the Bicameral Firm," this volume, 15–60.

2. Frederic W. Maitland, *Frederic William Maitland: Historian*, ed. Robert L. Schuyler (Berkeley: University of California Press, 1960), 174.

3. Otto von Gierke, *Political Theories of the Middle Age*, trans. F. W. Maitland (Boston: Beacon Press, 1958), 88.

4. Karl Marx, *Capital*, vol. 1, trans. Ben Fowkes (New York: Vintage, 1977), 450–1.

5. Bo Rothstein, "Social Justice and State Capacity" *Politics and Society* 20, no. 1 (1992): 118; see also his chapter in this volume.

6. Ernest Barker, *Reflections on Government* (London: Oxford University Press, 1967), 105–6, emphasis added.

7. John Maynard Keynes, *The General Theory of Employment, Interest, and Money* (New York: Harcourt Brace Jovanovich, 1953), 135.

8. See the later distinction between the "corporation" and the "firm."

9. Christopher McMahon, *Authority and Democracy: A General Theory of Government and Management* (Princeton, NJ: Princeton University Press, 1994), 16, emphasis added.

10. Mark Theobald, "Briggs Mfg. Co.," *Coachbuilt* (blog), 2004, coachbuilt.com.

11. John Rawls, *Justice as Fairness: A Restatement* (Cambridge, MA: Belknap Press, 2001), 138–9.

12. Frank Knight, *On the History and Method of Economics* (Chicago: Phoenix Books, 1956), 68n40.

13. Paul A. Samuelson, *Economics*, 10th ed. (New York: McGraw-Hill, 1976), 52.

14. Stanley Fischer, Rudiger Dornbusch, and Richard Schmalensee, *Economics* (New York: McGraw-Hill, 1988), 323.

15. Frank Knight, "The Quantity of Capital and the Rate of Interest: I," *Journal of Political Economy* 44, no. 4 (1936): 438.

16. See Lynn Stout, *The Shareholder Value Myth: How Putting Shareholders First Harms Investors, Corporations, and the Public* (San Francisco: Berrett-Koehler, 2012); David Ciepley, "Beyond Public and Private: Toward a Political Theory of the Corporation," *American Political Science Review* 107, no. 1 (2013): 139–58; David Ciepley, "Wayward Leviathans: How America's Corporations Lost Their Public Purpose," *Hedgehog Review* (blog), 2019, hedgehogreview.com; and Jean-Philippe Robé, "The Legal Structure of the Firm," *Accounting, Economics, and Law* 1, no. 5 (2011).

17. Ciepley, "Beyond Public and Private" and "Wayward Leviathans."

18. For more on the corporate-governance debate, see David Ellerman, "Fallacies of Corporate Analysis," *Challenge* (February 2020): 1–23; David Ellerman, *Neo-Abolitionism: Abolishing Human Rentals in Favor of Workplace Democracy* (Cham, Switzerland: SpringerNature, 2021); and David Ellerman, *Putting Jurisprudence Back into Economics: On What Is Really Wrong with Today's Neoclassical Theory* (Cham, Switzerland: SpringerNature, 2021).

19. Ferreras, "Democratizing the Corporation," this volume, 15–60.

20. "In general, the shareholders are the members of the company and the terms 'shareholders' and 'members' may be used interchangeably." Brenda Hannigan, *Company Law*, 3rd ed. (Oxford: Oxford University Press, 2012), 304.

21. David Ellerman, "The 'Ownership of the Firm' Is a Myth," *Administration and Society* 7 (1975): 27–42.

22. Robé, "Legal Structure of the Firm," 4.

23. Brian Tierney, *Religion, Law, and the Growth of Constitutional Thought 1150–1650* (Cambridge, UK: Cambridge University Press, 1982), 19.

24. See John P. Davis, *Corporations* (New York: Capricorn Books, 1961); Robert L. Raymond, "The Genesis of the Corporation," in *Corporations: Selected Essays Reprinted from the* Harvard Law Review (Cambridge, MA: Harvard Law Review, 1966), 1–16.

25. Abram Chayes, "The Modern Corporation and the Rule of Law," in *The Corporation in Modern Society*, ed. E. S. Mason (New York: Atheneum, 1966), xix.

26. Merton H. Miller and Franco Modigliani, "Dividend Policy, Growth, and the Valuation of Shares," *Journal of Business* 34 (1961): 415.

27. Chayes, "The Modern Corporation and the Rule of Law," xix.

28. John Dewey, *Reconstruction in Philosophy*, rev. ed. (Boston: Beacon Press, 1948), 209.

29. Chayes, "The Modern Corporation and the Rule of Law," 39–40.

30. John J. Flynn, "Corporate Democracy: Nice Work If You Can Get It," in *Corporate Power in America*, ed. Ralph Nader and Mark J. Green (New York: Grossman Publishers, 1973), 106.

31. Robert Dahl, *After the Revolution? Authority in a Good Society* (New Haven, CT: Yale University Press, 1970).

32. Robert Dahl, *Preface to Economic Democracy* (Berkeley: University of California Press, 1985), 91. The footnote reads: "In clarifying my ideas on this question I have profited greatly from a number of unpublished papers by David Ellerman, cited in the bibliography, as well as numerous discussions with and papers by students in my graduate seminar on The Government of Economic Enterprises and my undergraduate seminar on Democracy at Work."

33. See Carole Pateman, *Participation and Democratic Theory* (Cambridge, UK: Cambridge University Press, 1970).

34. See Anton Menger, *The Right to the Whole Produce of Labour: The Origin and Development of the Theory of Labour's Claim to the Whole Product of Industry*, trans. M. E. Tanner (London: Macmillan & Co., 1899); Richard Schlatter, *Private Property: The History of an Idea* (New Brunswick, NJ: Rutgers University Press, 1951); David Ellerman, *Property and Contract in Economics: The Case for Economic*

Democracy (Cambridge, MA: Blackwell, 1992); Ellerman, *Neo-Abolitionism*; Ellerman, *Putting Jurisprudence Back into Economics.*

35. Eustace Percy, *The Unknown State: 16th Riddell Memorial Lectures* (London: Oxford University Press, 1944), 38.

36. For further development of the property-theoretic case for the democratic firm, see Ellerman, *Property and Contract in Economics*; Ellerman *Neo-Abolitionism*; Ellerman, *Putting Jurisprudence Back into Economics.*

37. Louis D. Brandeis, *The Curse of Bigness* (New York: Viking, 1934), 35.

38. Ferreras, "Democratizing the Corporation," this volume, 15–60.

39. David Ellerman and Tej Gonza, *Employee Stock Ownership Plans: A Generic Model* (Ljubljana: Institute for Economic Democracy, 2019).

5. Prospects for Democratizing the Corporation in US Law

1. I thank Isabelle Ferreras, Tom Malleson, David Ellerman, Ewan McGaughey, and anonymous reviewers for comments on earlier drafts. Thanks to Isabelle and Tom for inviting me to participate in this project.

2. Henry Hansmann and Reinier Kraakman, "The End of History for Corporate Law," Harvard Law School Discussion Paper 280 (2000): 1.

3. US corporate law operates at the state level. I focus on Delaware law, which is widely regarded as the most influential body of corporate law in the US.

4. Erik Olin Wright, *Envisioning Real Utopias* (London: Verso, 2010), 20.

5. Isabelle Ferreras, *Firms as Political Entities: Saving Democracy through Economic Bicameralism* (New York: Cambridge, 2017).

6. John C. Coffee Jr. "The Mandatory/Enabling Balance in Corporate Law: An Essay on the Judicial Role," *Columbia Law Review* 89 (1989).

7. Robert C. Clark. "Agency Costs versus Fiduciary Duties," in *Principals and Agents: The Structure of Business*, ed. John W. Pratt and Richard J. Zeckhauser (Boston: Harvard Business School Press, 1985), 55–61. Ellerman (this volume) offers a theory of incorporated associations that treats the board as an agent of association members. In this context he contends that corporate boards are "in theory" agents of shareholders, though he acknowledges that in practice this agency relation "is little more than a fiction." His approach constructs a powerful theoretical and normative rationale for treating boards as agents of a broader association membership. But, whatever its virtues as a normative model of how we might reconstruct corporate law, his theory is inconsistent with US law's current self-understanding of the shareholder–board relationship.

8. Deborah A. DeMott, "Shareholders as Principals," 2002, available at ssrn.com.

9. Clark, "Agency Costs versus Fiduciary Duties," 57.

10. Ferreras, *Firms as Political Entities.*

11. Margaret Blair, *Ownership and Control: Rethinking Corporate Governance for the Twenty-First Century* (New York: Brookings, 1995); Margaret Blair and Lynn Stout, "A Team Production Theory of Corporate Law," *Virginia Law Review* 85 (1999): 247–328; Bernard Black, "Corporate Law and Residual Claimants," UC Berkeley Program in Law and Economics, Working Paper Series (partial draft) 1999, available at scholarship.org.

12. Franklin A. Gevurtz, "The Historical and Political Origins of the Corporate Board of Directors," *Hofstra Law Review* 33, no. 1 (2004), citing Delaware Corporation Code 2007, §141a.

13. Clyde W. Summers, "Codetermination in the United States: A Projection of Problems and Potentials," *Journal of Comparative Corporate Law and Securities Regulation* 4 (1982): 157.

14. Elizabeth Warren, "Accountable Capitalism Act S.3348," 2018, section 6b, congress.gov.
15. See, for example, Lenore M. Palladino, "Ending Shareholder Primacy in Corporate Governance," Roosevelt Institute Working Paper (2019).
16. The law in some states, including Delaware, does allow "closely held" corporations to depart from the board requirement by allowing shareholders to run the corporation directly if bylaws are so modified.
17. This is speculative, of course. In principle, statutory law should allow for the creation of bicameral boards, and such laws would probably be upheld by the courts. But statutory law can come into conflict with common law tradition. LLC statutes in many US states, for example, allow board members to waive fiduciary duties. But courts have sometimes effectively reimposed fiduciary standards on board members, despite their claims that they were exempt. See, for example, *Skye Mineral Investors, LLC et al. v. DXS Capital (US) Limited et al.*, C.A. No. 2018–0059 -JRS (Delaware Chancery), 2020. The issues are complex, but the point is that tension between statute and common law can create uncertainties that take years or even decades to work out.
18. D. Gordon Smith, "The Dystopian Potential of Corporate Law," *Emory Law Journal* 57, no. 4 (2008), 989.
19. E. Norman Veasey and Christine T. Di Guglielmo, "How Many Masters Can a Director Serve? A Look at the Tensions Facing Constituency Directors," *Business Lawyer* 63 (2008): 6.
20. American Bar Foundation, Model Business Corporation Act, 3rd ed., 2002, §8.30a.
21. Robert C. Clark, *Corporate Law* (Blue Springs, MO: Aspen Law and Business Publishers, 1986), 123.
22. Jean-Phillipe Robé, "The Legal Structure of the Firm," *Accounting, Economics, and Law* 1, no. 5 (2011), 34.
23. D. Gordon Smith, "The Shareholder Primacy Norm," *Journal of Corporation Law* 23, no. 2 (1998): 285.
24. Ibid., 285–6.
25. *Aronson v. Lewis*, 473 A.2d 805 (Delaware Supreme Court), 1984.
26. Clark, *Corporate Law*, 123.
27. Blair and Stout, "A Team Production Theory of Corporate Law," 303.
28. *Unocal Corp. v. Mesa Petroleum Co.*, 493 A.2d 946 (Delaware Supreme Court), 1985.
29. *Revlon v. MacAndrews & Forbes Holdings, Inc.*, 506 A.2d 173 (Delaware Supreme Court), 1986, emphasis added. The following quote is from the same source.
30. Clark, *Corporate Law*, 141.
31. *Guth v. Loft, Inc.*, 5 A.2d 503 (Delaware Supreme Court), 1939.
32. *Re Walt Disney Co Derivative Litigation*, 906 A.2d 27 (Delaware Supreme Court), 2006.
33. D. Gordon Smith and Jordan C. Lee, "Fiduciary Discretion," *Ohio State Law Journal* 75, no. 3 (2014): 635.
34. Gibson Dunn, "A Corporate Paradigm Shift: Public Benefit Corporations," *Gibson Dunn*, August 9, 2016, gibsondunn.com.
35. Some scholars have argued that this "contract-based approach does not merit the same consideration in a company with widely dispersed ownership because the public stockholders do not have the same opportunity [as members of a closely held organization] to bargain" regarding the modification of fiduciary duties. If Delaware courts affirmed this reasoning, they would presumably be hostile to extending new organizational forms to the corporate context. Veasey and Di Guglielmo, "How Many Masters Can a Director Serve?," 11.
36. Lynn Stout, *The Shareholder Value Myth: How Putting Shareholders First Harms Investors, Corporations, and the Public* (San Francisco: Berrett-Koehler, 2012).

37. *Burwell, Secretary of Health and Human Services et al. v. Hobby Lobby Stores, Inc., et al.*, 573 US 682 (United States Supreme Court), 2014, 23. In Burwell, the alternative to profit maximization pursued by the corporation was the "religious freedom" to deny birth control coverage to employees due to its "immorality."
38. Smith, "Dystopian Potential of Corporate Law," 1005.
39. Dylan Riley, "An Anticapitalism that Can Win," *Jacobin*, January 7, 2016, jacobin. com.
40. Cf. Ezra W. Zuckerman, "The Categorical Imperative: Securities Analysts and the Illegitimacy Discount," *American Journal of Sociology* 104, no. 5 (1999): 1398–438.
41. Oliver Hart and Luigi Zingales, "Companies Should Maximize Shareholder Welfare Not Market Value," European Corporate Governance Institute Working Paper Series in Finance, 521 (2017), 21. The remainder of the paragraph draws heavily on this source.
42. As quoted in Hart and Zingales, "Companies Should Maximize Shareholder Welfare," 22.
43. Cf. John W. Meyer and Brian Rowan, "Institutionalized Organizations: Formal Structure as Myth and Ceremony" *American Journal of Sociology* 83 (1977): 340–63.
44. Lucian A. Bebchuk and Yaniv Grinstein, "The Growth of Executive Pay," Harvard Law and Economics Discussion Paper 510 (2009); Gerald F. Davis, *Managed by the Markets: How Finance Re-shaped America* (New York: Oxford, 2009); Matteo Tonello, "CEO and Executive Compensation Practices: 2017 Edition," Harvard Law School Forum on Corporate Governance, October 4, 2017, corpgov.law. harvard.edu.
45. Adam Goldstein, "Revenge of the Managers: Labor Cost-Cutting and the Paradoxical Resurgence of Managerialism in the Shareholder Value Era, 1984 to 2001," *American Sociological Review* 77, no. 2 (2012): 268–94.
46. Cf. Philip Selznick, *The Moral Commonwealth: Social Theory and the Promise of Community* (Berkeley: University of California Press, 1994); Meyer and Rowan, "Institutionalized Organizations."
47. See Ferreras, *Firms as Political Entities*.

6. Economic Democracy at Work

1. William Lazonick and Mary O'Sullivan, "Maximizing Shareholder Value: A New Ideology for Corporate Governance," *Economy and Society* 29, no. 1 (2000): 13–35.
2. Michael Jensen and William Meckling, "Theory of the Firm: Managerial Behavior, Agency Costs and Ownership Structure," *Journal of Financial Economics* 3, no. 4 (1976): 305–60.
3. Isabelle Ferreras, *Firms as Political Entities* (Cambridge, UK: Cambridge University Press, 2017); and "Democratizing the Corporation," this volume, 15–60.
4. Wilma Liebman, "Does Federal Labor Law Preemption Doctrine Allow Experiments with Social Dialogue?," *Harvard Law and Policy Review Online* (2017); Joel Rogers, and Wolfgang Streeck, "The Study of Works Councils: Concepts and Problems," in *Works Councils: Consultation, Representation, and Cooperation in Industrial Relations*, ed. Joel Rogers and Wolfgang Streeck (Chicago: University of Chicago Press, 1995); Stephen Silvia, *Holding the Shop Together: German Industrial Relations in the Postwar Era* (Ithaca, NY: Cornell University Press, 2013); Clyde Summers, "Industrial Democracy: America's Unfulfilled Promise," *Cleveland State Law Review* 28, no. 29 (1979); Clyde Summers, "Codetermination in the

United States: A Projection of Problems and Potentials," *University of Pennsylvania Journal of International Law* 4, no. 155 (1982).

5. Rogers and Streeck, "The Study of Works Councils."

6. Ewan McGaughey, "Democracy in America at Work: The History of Labor's Vote in Corporate Governance," *Seattle University Law Review* 42, no. 697 (2019); Bo Rothstein, "The Prospects for Economic Democracy: Learning from Sweden as Failed Case," this volume, 199–210.

7. William Lazonick, "Is the Most Unproductive Firm the Foundation of the Most Efficient Economy? How Penrosian Learning Confronts the Neoclassical Absurdity," Institute for New Economic Thinking Working Paper 111 (2020).

8. Ibid., 6. Lazonick and O'Sullivan, "Maximizing Shareholder Value"; Edith Penrose, *Theory of the Growth of the Firm* (Oxford: Oxford University Press, 1959).

9. Peter Drucker, *Concept of the Corporation* (Abingdon-on-Thames, UK: Routledge, 1946).

10. Lazonick, "Most Unproductive Firm."

11. Ibid.

12. Margaret Blair and Lynn Stout, "A Team Production Theory of Corporate Law," *Virginia Law Review* 85 (1999): 247–328.

13. John Parkinson, Gavin Kelly, and Andrew Gamble, *The Political Economy of the Company* (Oxford, UK: Bloomsbury Publishing, 2001).

14. Summers, "Codetermination in the United States," 170.

15. For a detailed history of the history of labor's voice in corporate governance in the 1800s and early part of the 1900s, see McGaughey, "Democracy in America at Work." For a detailed history of the movement for industrial democracy in the early twentieth century, see Joseph McCartin, *Labor's Great War: The Struggle for Industrial Democracy and the Origins of Modern American Labor Relations, 1912–1921* (Chapel Hill: University of North Carolina Press, 1998).

16. Liebman, "Federal Labor Law Preemption Doctrine"; Rogers and Streeck, "The Study of Works Councils."

17. This redefinition of fiduciary duty can be seen in the benefit corporation duties of directors: see Model Benefit Corporation Statute § 301(a).

18. Robert Scholz and Sigurt Vitols, "Board-Level Codetermination: A Driving Force for Corporate Social Responsibility in German Companies?," *European Journal of Industrial Relations* 25, no. 233 (2019).

19. Sanford Jacoby, "Employee Representation and Corporate Governance: A Missing Link," *University of Pennsylvania Journal of Business Law* 3, no. 449 (2001); Liebman, "Federal Labor Law Preemption Doctrine"; Rogers and Streeck, "The Study of Works Councils"; Summers, "Codetermination in the United States."

20. Kent Greenfield, *The Failure of Corporate Law* (Chicago: University of Chicago Press, 2007).

21. Summers, "Codetermination in the United States."

22. Edith Ginglinger, William Megginson, and Timothee Waxin, "Employee Ownership, Board Representation, and Corporate Financial Policies," *Journal of Corporate Finance* 17, no. 868 (2011).

23. Summers, "Codetermination in the United States."

24. David Weil, *The Fissured Workplace: Why Work Became So Bad for So Many and What Can Be Done to Improve It* (Cambridge, MA: Harvard University Press, 2014).

25. Summers, "Codetermination in the United States."

26. Frederick Alexander, "The Benefit Stance: Responsible Ownership in the 21st Century," *Oxford Review of Economic Policy* 36, no. 341 (2020); Andrew Kassoy et al., "From Shareholder Primacy to Stakeholder Capitalism: A Policy Agenda for Systems Change," *B Lab*, 2020, bcorporation.net.

27. Liebman, "Federal Labor Law Preemption Doctrine"; Rogers and Streeck, "The Study of Works Councils."

28. Richard Freeman and Edward Lazear, "An Economic Analysis of Works Councils," in *Works Councils: Consultation, Representation, and Cooperation in Industrial Relations*, ed. Joel Rogers and Wolfgang Streeck (Chicago: University of Chicago Press, 1995).

29. Bureau of Labor Statistics, "Union Members—2020," news release no. USDL-21–0081, January 22, 2021, bls.gov.

30. Rogers and Streeck, "The Study of Works Councils."

31. Liebman, "Federal Labor Law Preemption Doctrine."

32. Ibid.; Rogers and Streeck, "The Study of Works Councils."

33. Rogers and Streeck, "The Study of Works Councils"; Summers, "Codetermination."

34. Liebman, "Federal Labor Law Preemption Doctrine."

35. Liebman also considers whether or not establishment of works councils, or health and safety committees, at the state level could increase "social dialogue." Ibid. However, as worker representation on boards would need to be established at the federal level in order to ensure it in fact takes hold—otherwise companies could simply change their state of incorporation—the question of state-level establishment of works councils, though important for future policy design, is outside of the scope of this chapter.

36. Douglas Fraser, "Worker Participation in Corporate Governance: The U.A.W.-Chrysler Experience," *Chicago-Kent Law Review* 58, no. 949 (1982).

37. William Lazonick and Jang-Sup Shin, *Predatory Value Extraction: How the Looting of the Business Enterprise Became the US Norm and How Sustainable Prosperity Can be Restored* (Oxford: Oxford University Press, 2020).

7. Islands and the Sea

1. Isabelle Ferreras, *Firms as Political Entities: Saving Democracy through Economic Bicameralism* (Cambridge, UK: Cambridge University Press, 2017).

2. Sidney Webb and Beatrice Webb, *The Consumers' Cooperative Movement* (London: Longmans, Green & Co., 1921), 463–68; see also Robert Michels, *Political Parties: A Sociological Study of the Oligarchical Tendencies of Modern Democracy*, trans. Eden Paul and Cedar Paul (New York: Free Press, 1962).

3. See, for instance, Ernest Mandel, "Self-Management: Dangers and Possibilities," *International* 2, no. 4 (1975).

4. See, in particular, Tom Malleson, *After Occupy: Economic Democracy for the 21st Century* (Oxford: Oxford University Press, 2014); Fred Block, "Financial Democratization and the Transition to Socialism," *Politics and Society* 47, no. 4 (2019): 529–56; Robert Hockett, "Finance without Financiers," *Politics and Society* 47, no. 4 (2019): 491–527; Fred Block and Robert Hockett, eds., *Democratizing Finance: Restructuring Credit to Transform Society* (London: Verso, 2022).

5. Samuel Bowles and Herbert Gintis, *Democracy and Capitalism* (New York: Basic Books, 1986), 5; Thomas Piketty, *Capital in the Twenty-First Century* (Cambridge, MA: Belknap Press, 2014).

6. Besides the command economies of the Cold War, a striking example of how public control over the division of labor can clash with democratic principles is the historical practice of redlining in the United States.

7. Alexander Keyssar, *The Right to Vote: The Contested History of Democracy in the United States* (New York: Basic Books, 2009), 205.

8. Quinn Slobodian, *Globalists: The End of Empire and the Birth of Neoliberalism* (Cambridge, MA: Harvard University Press, 2018).

9. Ibid., 2.

10. By "commercial federalism" I refer to the deliberate construction of market orders that exceed the scope of existing democratic states. On the political consequences of this, see Friedrich Hayek, "The Economic Conditions of Interstate Federalism," in *Individualism and Economic Order* (Chicago: University of Chicago Press, 1948), 255–72.

11. Eric Helleiner, *States and the Reemergence of Global Finance: From Bretton Woods to the 1990s* (Ithaca, NY: Cornell University Press, 1994); Rawi Abdelal, *Capital Rules: The Construction of Global Finance* (Cambridge, MA: Harvard University Press, 2007).

12. Catherine R. Schenk, "The Origins of the Eurodollar Market in London: 1955–1963," *Explorations in Economic History* 35, no. 2 (April 1998): 221–38; Gary Burn, *The Re-emergence of Global Finance* (Basingstoke: Palgrave Macmillan, 2006).

13. Helleiner, *States and the Reemergence of Global Finance*, 81–100.

14. Vanessa Ogle, "Archipelago Capitalism: Tax Havens, Offshore Money, and the State, 1950s–1970s," *American Historical Review* 122, no. 5 (December 2017): 1452–54.

15. Abdelal, *Capital Rules*.

16. See, especially, Greta R. Krippner, *Capitalizing on Crisis: The Political Origins of the Rise of Finance* (Cambridge, MA: Harvard University Press, 2011).

17. See Hockett, "Finance without Financiers"; Mary Mellor, "Democratizing Finance or Democratizing Money?," in Block and Hockett, *Democratizing Finance*.

18. Abdelal, *Capital Rules*.

19. Peter A. Hall, "Socialism in One Country: Mitterrand and the Struggle to Define a New Economic Policy for France," in *Socialism, the State and Public Policy in France*, ed. Philip Cerny and Martin Schain (London: Frances Pinter, 1985).

20. In the American case with the Volcker shock starting in 1979, in the British case with Margaret Thatcher's austerity budgets of 1980 and especially 1981.

21. Peter A. Hall, *Governing the Economy: The Politics of State Intervention in Britain and France* (Cambridge, UK: Polity, 1986), 198.

22. Piketty, *Capital in the Twenty-First Century*, table S4.5.

23. See, respectively, Krippner, *Capitalizing on Crisis*; Mark Blyth, "Domestic Institutions and the Possibility of Social Democracy," *Comparative European Politics* 3, no. 4 (2005): 379–407. A comprehensive account of the history of financial deregulation in France is given by Benjamin Lemoine, *L'Ordre de la dette: Enquête sur ies infortunes de l'État et la prospérité du marché* (Paris: La Découverte, 2016); and Michael Loriaux, *France after Hegemony: International Change and Financial Reform* (Ithaca, NY: Cornell University Press, 1991), in English, with an emphasis on international linkages, in particular to US policy.

24. All figures author's calculations, based on Jordà Schularick and Alan Taylor, "Macrofinancial History and the New Business Cycle Facts," in *NBER Macroeconomics Annual 2016*, eds. Martin Eichenbaum and Jonathan A. Parker, vol. 31 (Chicago: University of Chicago Press, 2017).

25. Organisation for Economic Co-operation and Development, "National Accounts at a Glance," OECD National Accounts Statistics (2017), CPI Inflation.

26. Loriaux, *France after Hegemony*, 235.

27. Ibid., 226.

28. Ibid., 227.

29. Besides being reliably profit seeking, banks in particular are usually also keen to take on additional risk, since the downside costs of this risk are usually socialized, while the higher returns associated with it are privatized. See William H. Simon, "The Politics of Financial Reform," in Block and Hockett, *Democratizing Finance*.

30. See especially Helleiner, *States and the Reemergence of Global Finance*.
31. Adam Posen, "Why Central Bank Independence Does Not Cause Low Inflation: There Is No Institutional Fix for Politics," in *Finance and the International Economy*, vol. 7, *The Amex Bank Review Prize Essays*, ed. Richard O'Brien (Oxford: Oxford University Press, 1993); Sheri Berman and Kathleen McNamara, "Bank on Democracy," *Foreign Affairs*, March 1999; David M. Woodruff, "To Democratize Finance, Democratize Central Banking," in Block and Hockett, *Democratizing Finance*.
32. Elke Asen, "Corporate Tax Rates around the World," *Tax Foundation* 735 (2020): 8; Emmanuel Saez and Gabriel Zucman, *The Triumph of Injustice: How the Rich Dodge Taxes and How to Make Them Pay* (New York: Norton, 2019), 93, figure 5.1; Bruce G. Carruthers and Naomi R. Lamoreaux, "Regulatory Races: The Effects of Jurisdictional Competition on Regulatory Standards," *Journal of Economic Literature* 54, no. 1 (2016): 82, 85.
33. Simon Jäger, Benjamin Schoefer, and Jörg Heining, "Labor in the Boardroom," *Quarterly Journal of Economics* 136, no. 2 (2021): 713; this meshes with the assessment given in Malleson, *After Occupy*, 54–90.
34. Piketty, *Capital in the Twenty-First Century*, 144–6.
35. Jäger, Schoefer, and Heining, "Labor in the Boardroom," 720.
36. Having said this, the German evidence comes from firms with only one-third worker representation on boards (i.e., significantly less de jure power than what is envisaged in Ferreras's proposal, and so cannot be considered conclusive).
37. William L. Silber, "The Process of Financial Innovation," *American Economic Review* 73, no. 2 (1983): 89–95; Katharina Pistor, *The Code of Capital* (Princeton: Princeton University Press, 2019).
38. Malleson, *After Occupy;* Hockett, "Finance without Financiers"; Block, "'Financial Democratization"; Block and Hockett, *Democratizing Finance*.
39. The heart of Block's proposal is nonprofit credit unions and public investment banks. However, there were and are plenty of nonprofit financial institutions in existence already. Insofar as they offer lower rates of return than profit-oriented banks, they have remained marginal. In addition, in the case of US credit unions and German Sparkassen, it is not obvious that, when embedded in a market together with for-profit institutions, they will behave as desired. As Malleson shows, US "credit unions actually make a higher proportion of their home mortgages to richer people than comparable private banks," presumably to generate a margin that allows them to go into higher-risk lending to poorer households, showing the structural constraint that they are under. Malleson, *After Occupy*, 182. As a result, middle-class borrowers are not always well served by them. Germany's Sparkassen banks, in turn, were heavily invested in mortgage-backed securities prior to 2008, since these appeared to offer better returns than lending to local firms or households.
40. Because Malleson's proposal, drawing on Schweickart, abolishes private banking, it runs the risk of leaving even very high-return projects unrealized, if they are politically unfavored. Malleson, *After Occupy*, 153; David Schweickart, *After Capitalism*, 2nd ed. (Lanham, MD: Rowman & Littlefield, 2011). There is no safety vent, so to speak, which would allow citizens' votes in product markets to correct decisions made in the financial system. Were the financial system to become corrupt—a possibility of which Malleson is aware, and to which he proposes various countermeasures—pressure would likely emerge to "depoliticize it."
41. Hockett, "Finance without Financiers," 518–19.
42. As with any proposal that moves toward full reserve banking, there are questions about macroeconomic stabilization—with endogenous money creation ruled out,

the mechanisms behind aggregate demand fluctuations change significantly—and about who then makes lending decisions and how. But these problems do not seem prima facie insurmountable. There are questions, too, about how to counter the sociological power of existing financial interests, a question taken up by McCarthy: Michael McCarthy, "Three Modes of Democratic Participation in Finance," in Block and Hockett, *Democratizing Finance*. Here, too, solutions could be found, certainly in a context in which the introduction of bicameralism is already politically viable (e.g., through the use of mini-publics, sortition, and other forms of open democracy). See Hélène Landemore, *Open Democracy: Reinventing Popular Rule for the Twenty-First Century* (Princeton, NJ: Princeton University Press, 2020).

43. See John Cassidy, *How Markets Fail* (New York: Picador, 2009) for a compact overview.

44. Herbert A. Simon, "Organizations and Markets," *Journal of Economic Perspectives* 5, no. 2 (1991): 28.

45. Isabella Weber, *How China Escaped Shock Therapy: The Market Reform Debate* (London: Routledge, 2021).

46. Malleson, *After Occupy*, 54–90; Jäger, Schoefer, and Heining, "Labor in the Boardroom."

47. On the dangers of soft budget constraints, see Janos Kornai, *The Socialist System: The Political Economy of Communism* (Oxford: Oxford University Press, 1992). For ideas on how to tackle it without relying on the disciplining effect of a profit-oriented financial sector, see, for example, Pranab Bardhan and John Roemer, *Market Socialism: The Current Debate* (Oxford: Oxford University Press, 1993), esp. chapter 7.

48. Indeed, as Knight's contribution to this volume highlights, a large part of the increase in inequality has been driven by rising *between-firm* inequality (e.g., all lawyers in a law firm now earning much more than the food workers in the catering company that serves the law firm) rather than *within-firm* inequality (e.g., the CEO of a firm earning 300 times the median or average salary of the same firm). Jae Song et al., "Firming Up Inequality," *Quarterly Journal of Economics* 134, no. 1 (2019): 1–50.

8. Are Bicameral Firms Preferable?

1. The authors thank the editors of this volume, Tom Malleson and Joel Rogers, as well as Verso's anonymous referee for their helpful suggestions. John Stuart Mill, *Principles of Political Economy* [1848] *with Chapters on Socialism* [1879] (Oxford: Oxford University Press, 2008); Robert Dahl, *A Preface to Economic Democracy* (Berkeley: University of California Press, 1985).

2. Mill, *Principles of Political Economy*, IV.7.21

3. Axel Gosseries and G. Ponthière, "La démocratie d'entreprise," *Revue de philosophie économique / Review of Economic Philosophy* 9, no. 1 (2008): 3–9; Tom Malleson, *After Occupy: Economic Democracy for the 21st Century* (Oxford: Oxford University Press, 2014); Elizabeth Anderson, *Private Government: How Employers Rule Our Lives (and Why We Don't Talk about It)* (Princeton, NJ: Princeton University Press, 2017); Lisa Herzog, *Reclaiming the System: Moral Responsibility, Divided Labour, and the Role of Organizations in Society* (Oxford: Oxford University Press, 2018).

4. Henry Hansmann, *The Ownership of Enterprises* (Cambridge, MA: Harvard University Press, 1996); Gregory K. Dow, *Governing the Firm: Workers' Control in*

Theory and Practice (Cambridge, UK: Cambridge University Press, 2003); Isabelle Ferreras, *Firms as Political Entities: Saving Democracy through Economic Bicameralism* (Cambridge, UK: Cambridge University Press, 2017); Isabelle Ferreras, "Democratizing the Corporation," this volume, 15–60.

5. Ferreras, "Democratizing the Corporation."
6. Dahl, *A Preface to Economic Democracy*, 111.
7. Ferreras, "Democratizing the Corporation," 23.
8. Malleson, *After Occupy*, 47–9.
9. Tyler Cowen, in Anderson, *Private Government*, 108–16.
10. Iñigo González-Ricoy, "Firms, States, and Democracy: A Qualified Defense of the Parallel Case Argument," *LEAP* 2 (2014): 32–57, 39–42.
11. Robert Nozick, *Anarchy, State, and Utopia* (New York: Basic Books, 1974), 250–62; Abraham Singer, *The Forms of the Firm: A Normative Political Theory of the Corporation* (Oxford: Oxford University Press, 2019), 139–40.
12. Iñigo González-Ricoy, "The Republican Case for Workplace Democracy," *Social Theory and Practice* 40, no. 2 (2014): 232–54, 239–41; Anderson, *Private Government*, 33–44; Ferreras, "Democratizing the Corporation."
13. Anderson, *Private Government*, 45–8.
14. John Rawls, *Political Liberalism* (New York: Columbia University Press, 1993), 292.
15. Ibid., 292–3.
16. Ferreras, "Democratizing the Corporation," 23. For Ferreras, "to consider the work experience as nonpublic (private, in other words) means suspending the norms of equality in dignity and rights that underpin the democratic public sphere." Ferreras, "Democratizing the Corporation," 19.
17. John Rawls, *A Theory of Justice* (Cambridge, MA: Harvard University Press, 1971), 57; Christian Schemmel, "How (Not) to Criticize the Welfare State," *Journal of Applied Philosophy* 32, no. 4 (2015): 396.
18. Schemmel, "How (Not) to Criticize the Welfare State," 397–405.
19. Dow, *Governing the Firm*, 42.
20. This is not necessarily true. In fact, both theoretical arguments and empirical evidence suggest that some kinds of democratic firms, such as worker cooperatives, can be as productive as nondemocratic ones, at least in favorable contexts. Malleson, *After Occupy*, 72–6; Virginie Pérotin, "Worker Co-operatives: Good, Sustainable Jobs in the Community," *Journal of Entrepreneurial and Organizational Diversity* 2, no. 2 (2014): 34–47; Virginie Pérotin, "What Do We Really Know about Worker Co-operatives?," *Co-operative UK*, November 19, 2018, uk.coop; Singer, *The Forms of the Firm*, 157; Simon Jäger, Shakked Noy, and Benjamin Schoefer, "What Does Codetermination Do?," NBER Working Paper 28921 (2021), 2.
21. Ferreras, "Democratizing the Corporation," 31; see also Ferreras, *Firms as Political Entities*, 123–5.
22. Gosseries and Ponthière, "La démocratie d'entreprise"; González-Ricoy, "The Republican Case," 237–48; Malleson, *After Occupy*, 76–83.
23. Joshua Cohen, "Deliberation and Democratic Legitimacy," in *The Good Polity*, ed. Alan Hamlin and Philip Petit (Cambridge, MA: Blackwell, 1989).
24. *Hélène Landemore, Democratic Reason: Politics, Collective Intelligence, and the Rule of the Many* (Princeton, NJ: Princeton University Press, 2012).
25. Ferreras, *Firms as Political Entities*, 173, 174; Ferreras, "Democratizing the Corporation."
26. John Rawls, *Justice as Fairness: A Restatement* (Cambridge, MA: Belknap Press, 2001), 26; Frank Lovett, *A General Theory of Domination and Justice* (Oxford: Oxford University Press, 2010).

27. González-Ricoy, "The Republican Case," 237–48; Anderson, *Private Government*, 45–8.

28. Malleson, *After Occupy*, 76–83.

29. William F. White and Kathleen K. White, *Making Mondragon: The Growth and Dynamics of the Worker Cooperative Complex* (Ithaca: NY, ILR Press, 1991), 38, 291.

30. Michael Bennett, "The Capital Flight Quadrilemma: Democratic Trade-offs and International Investment," *Ethics amd Global Politics* 14, no. 4 (2021).

31. Malleson, *After Occupy*, 137–52.

32. Richard Murphy, John Christensen, and Jenny Kimmis, "Tax Us If You Can, 2nd Edition," *Tax Justice Network*, 2012, taxjustice.net, 5, 11. Shapiro explores other explanations for "why the poor don't soak the rich": Ian Shapiro, "Why the Poor Don't Soak the Rich," *Daedalus* 131, no. 1 (2002): 118–28.

33. Jäger et al., "What Does Codetermination Do?," 3.

34. Cohen, "Deliberation and Democratic Legitimacy."

35. Cass R. Sunstein, "The Law of Group Polarization," Law and Economics Working Paper 91 (1999).

36. Hansmann, *The Ownership of Enterprises*; Jäger et al., "What Does Codetermination Do?"

37. Jean-Philippe Deranty, "Book Review: *Firms as Political Entities*," *Critical Horizons* 20, no. 1 (2019): 95–8; Marc Fleurbaey, "Workplace Democracy, the Bicameral Firm, and Stakeholder Theory," in this volume.

38. Ferreras, *Firms as Political Entities*, 132; Ferreras, "Democratizing the Corporation."

39. Ferreras, "Democratizing the Corporation."

40. *Landemore, Democratic Reason.*

41. Ferreras, *Firms as Political Entities.*

42. Ibid., 174; Ferreras, "Democratizing the Corporation."

43. Dow, *Governing the Firm*, 41.

44. Hansmann, *The Ownership of Enterprises*, 57–65, 76–8; Singer, *The Forms of the Firm*, 149–51.

45. Hansmann, *The Ownership of Enterprises*, 77–8, 98–103; Malleson, *After Occupy*, 72–6.

46. Malleson, *After Occupy*, 57, 72–6; Jäger et al., "What Does Codetermination Do?," 2; Pérotin, "Worker Co-operatives"; Pérotin, "What Do We Really Know about Worker Co-operatives?"

47. Ferreras, *Firms as Political Entities*, 141; Ferreras, "Democratizing the Corporation."

48. Hansmann, *The Ownership of Enterprises*, 53–78.

49. Ibid., 56, 76. See also Dow, *Governing the Firm*, 185–6.

50. Whyte and Whyte 1991: 42–3; Hansmann, *The Ownership of Enterprises*, 76; Tom Malleson, "What Does Mondragon Teach Us about Workplace Democracy?," *Advances in the Economic Analysis of Participatory and Labor-Managed Firms* 14 (2013), 130–4; Malleson, *After Occupy*, 83–8.

51. Hansmann, *The Ownership of Enterprises.*

52. Ibid., 40–2, 89–90; Singer, *The Forms of the Firm*, 149–51.

53. Hansmann, *The Ownership of Enterprises*, 92–103.

54. Ibid., 36–8, 77; Singer, *The Forms of the Firm*, 93–6.

55. Joseph Heath, "Why Profit Is Not the Problem," Working Paper, 2017, available at academia.edu, 19–20.

56. Joseph Heath, "Business Ethics without Stakeholders," *Business Ethics Quarterly* 16, no. 4 (2006): 543. In fact, the multitask problem also applies to well-intentioned

managers who "may find themselves lacking the information that they need in order to determine how well they are doing, or whether they could be doing better." Joseph Heath and Wayne Norman, "Stakeholder Theory, Corporate Governance and Public Management: What Can the History of State-Run Enterprises Teach Us in the Post-Enron Era?," *Journal of Business Ethics* 53, no. 3 (2004): 258.

57. Singer, *The Forms of the Firm*, 95.

9. Learning from Cooperatives to Strengthen Economic Bicameralism

1. Chris Cornforth et al., *Developing Successful Worker Co-operatives* (London: SAGE, 1988); Tom Malleson, "Economic Democracy: The Left's Big Idea for the Twenty-First Century?," *New Political Science* 35, no. 1 (2013): 84–108; Simon Pek, "Drawing Out Democracy: The Role of Sortition in Preventing and Overcoming Organizational Degeneration in Worker-Owned Firms," *Journal of Management Inquiry* 30, no. 2 (2021): 193–206.

2. Mark Carley, "Board-Level Employee Representatives in Nine Countries: A Snapshot," *Transfer: European Review of Labour and Research* 11, no. 2 (2005): 231–43; Cornforth et al., *Developing Successful Worker Co-operatives*.

3. Mick Marchington and Adrian Wilkinson, "Direct Participation and Involvement," in *Managing Human Resources: Personnel Management in Transition*, ed. Stephen Bach (Malden, MA: Blackwell, 2005), 398–423.

4. Francisco Javier Forcadell, "Democracy, Cooperation and Business Success: The Case of Mondragón Corporación Cooperativa," *Journal of Business Ethics* 56, no. 3 (2005): 260.

5. Imanol Basterretxea, Chris Cornforth, and Iñaki Heras-Saizarbitoria, "Corporate Governance as a Key Aspect in the Failure of Worker Cooperatives," *Economic and Industrial Democracy* 4 (2020): 1–26; Forcadell, "Democracy, Cooperation and Business Success."

6. Fred Freundlich, Herv Grellier, and Rafael Altuna, "Mondragon: Notes on History, Scope and Structure," *International Journal of Technology Management and Sustainable Development* 8, no. 1 (2009): 3–12.

7. Bakaikoa Bakaikoa, Anjel Errasti, and Agurtzane Begiristain, "Governance of the Mondragon Corporación Cooperativa," *Annals of Public and Cooperative Economics* 75, no. 1 (2004): 61–87.

8. Sarah Hernandez, "Striving for Control: Democracy and Oligarchy at a Mexican Cooperative," *Economic and Industrial Democracy* 27, no. 1 (2006): 105–35; Moira Lees and Reimer Volkers, "General Trends, Findings and Recommendations," *Review of International Co-operation* 84, no. 4 (1996): 37–49.

9. Catherine W. Ng and Evelyn Ng, "Balancing the Democracy Dilemmas: Experiences of Three Women Workers' Cooperatives in Hong Kong," *Economic and Industrial Democracy* 30, no. 2 (2009): 182–206.

10. Hernandez, "Striving for Control"; Christopher Gunn, "Hoedads Co-op: Democracy and Cooperation at Work," in *Worker Cooperatives in America*, ed. Robert Jackall and Henry M. Levin (Berkeley: University of California Press, 1984), 141–70.

11. William I. Sauser, "Sustaining Employee Owned Companies: Seven Recommendations," *Journal of Business Ethics* 84, no. 2 (2009): 151–64; John Teta Luhman, "Theoretical Postulations on Organization Democracy," *Journal of Management Inquiry* 15, no. 2 (2006): 168–85; Ng and Ng, "Balancing the Democracy

Dilemmas"; Ignacio Bretos, Anjel Errasti, and Carmen Marcuello, "Is There Life after Degeneration? The Organizational Life Cycle of Cooperatives under a 'Grow-or-Die' Dichotomy," *Annals of Public and Cooperative Economics* 91, no. 3 (2020): 435–58; Simon Pek "Reconceptualizing and Improving Member Participation in Large Cooperatives: Insights from Deliberative Democracy and Deliberative Mini-Publics," *M@n@gement* (in press).

12. Gianluca Schiavo, Adolfo Villafiorita, and Massimo Zancanaro, "(Non-)Participation in Deliberation at Work: A Case Study of Online Participative Decision-Making," *New Technology, Work and Employment* 34, no. 1 (2019): 37–58.

13. R. Edward Freeman, *Strategic Management: A Stakeholder Approach*, 2nd ed. (Cambridge: Cambridge University Press, 2010).

14. Nicolas M. Dahan, Jonathan P. Doh, and Jonathan D. Raelin, "Pivoting the Role of Government in the Business and Society Interface: A Stakeholder Perspective," *Journal of Business Ethics* 131, no. 3 (2015): 665–80.

15. Ibid.

16. John Douglas Bishop, "The Limits of Corporate Human Rights Obligations and the Rights of For-Profit Corporations," *Business Ethics Quarterly* 22, no. 1 (2012): 119–44.

17. Daniel Nyberg, "Corporations, Politics, and Democracy: Corporate Political Activities as Political Corruption," *Organization Theory* 2, no. 1 (2021).

18. R. Edward Freeman et al., *Stakeholder Theory: The State of the Art* (Cambridge, UK: Cambridge University Press, 2010).

19. Camila Piñeiro Harnecker, "Workplace Democracy and Social Consciousness: A Study of Venezuelan Cooperatives," *Science and Society* 73, no. 3 (2009): 309–39.

20. George Cheney, *Values at Work: Employee Participation Meets Market Pressure at Mondragón* (Ithaca, NY: Cornell University Press, 1999).

21. Heath and Norman, "Stakeholder Theory, Corporate Governance and Public Management," 247–65.

22. Jeffrey Moriarty, "Participation in the Workplace: Are Employees Special?," *Journal of Business Ethics* 92, no. 3 (2010): 373–84.

23. Jeffrey Moriarty, "The Connection between Stakeholder Theory and Stakeholder Democracy: An Excavation and Defense," *Business and Society* 53, no. 6 (2014): 820–52.

24. Jeffrey S. Harrison and R. Edward Freeman, "Is Organizational Democracy Worth the Effort?," *Academy of Management Executive (1993–2005)* 18, no. 3 (2004): 49–53.

25. Heli Wang, Jay B. Barney, and Jeffrey J. Reuer, "Stimulating Firm-Specific Investment through Risk Management," *Long Range Planning* 36, no. 1 (2003): 49–59.

26. Cheryl Carleton Asher, James M. Mahoney, and Joseph T. Mahoney, "Towards a Property Rights Foundation for a Stakeholder Theory of the Firm," *Journal of Management and Governance* 9, no. 1 (2005): 5–32.

27. Hossam Zeitoun, Margit Osterloh, and Bruno S. Frey, "Learning from Ancient Athens: Demarchy and Corporate Governance," *Academy of Management Perspectives* 28, no. 1 (2014): 1–14.

28. Aimee E. Barbeau, "Deliberative Democracy and Corporate Governance," *Business Ethics Journal Review* 4, no. 6 (2016): 34–40; Saskia Crucke and Mirjam Knockaert, "When Stakeholder Representation Leads to Faultlines: A Study of Board Service Performance in Social Enterprises," *Journal of Management Studies* 53, no. 5 (2016): 768–93; see also Ferretti and Gosseries, "Are Bicameral Firms Preferable to Codetermination or Worker Cooperatives?," this volume, 168–79.

29. Silvia Ayuso and Antonio Argandoña, "Responsible Corporate Governance: Towards a Stakeholder Board of Directors?," University of Navarra: IESE Business School Working Paper, 2007.

30. Jason Q. Zhang, Hong Zhu, and Hung-bin Ding, "Board Composition and Corporate Social Responsibility: An Empirical Investigation in the Post Sarbanes-Oxley Era," *Journal of Business Ethics* 114, no. 3 (2013): 381–92.

31. See, respectively, Myriam Michaud and Luc K. Audebrand, "Inside Out, Outside In: 'Supporting Members' in Multi-stakeholder Cooperatives," *Management Decision* 57, no. 6 (2019): 1382–98; and Johnston Birchall and Silvia Sacchetti, "The Comparative Advantages of Single and Multi-stakeholder Cooperatives," European Research Institute on Cooperative and Social Enterprises Working Paper, 2017.

32. Margaret Lund, *Solidarity as a Business Model: A Multi-stakeholder Cooperatives Manual*, Cooperative Development Center, Kent State University, 2011.

33. Ibid.

34. Catherine Leviten-Reid and Brett Fairbairn, "Multi-stakeholder Governance in Cooperative Organizations: Toward a New Framework for Research?," *Canadian Journal of Nonprofit and Social Economy Research* 2, no. 2 (2011); Lund, "Solidarity as a Business Model"; Loren Rodgers, *Hybrid Cooperatives: Challenges and Advantages* (Oakland: National Center for Employee Ownership, 2008).

35. Lund, "Solidarity as a Business Model"; Rodgers, "Hybrid Cooperatives."

36. Lund, "Solidarity as a Business Model."

37. Michaud and Audebrand, "Inside Out, Outside In."

38. Lund, "Solidarity as a Business Model."

39. Ibid.

40. Thomas Gray, "Historical Tensions, Institutionalization, and the Need for Multi-stakeholder Cooperatives," *Journal of Agriculture, Food Systems, and Community Development* 4, no. 3 (2014): 27.

41. Lund, "Solidarity as a Business Model," 5.

42. Mario Pansera and Francesco Rizzi, "Furbish or Perish: Italian Social Cooperatives at a Crossroads," *Organization* 27, no. 1 (2020): 17–35.

43. Silvia Sacchetti and E. C. Tortia, "The Social Value of Multi-stakeholder Co-operatives: The Case of the CEFF System in Italy," in *Research Handbook on Sustainable Cooperative Enterprise: Case Studies of Organisational Resilience in the Co-operative Business Model*, ed. T. Mazzarol et al. (Cheltenham, UK: Edward Elgar, 2014), 291.

44. Michaud and Audebrand, "Inside Out, Outside In," 1388.

45. Roger Spear, Chris Cornforth, and Mike Aiken, "The Governance Challenges of Social Enterprises: Evidence from a UK Empirical Study," *Annals of Public and Cooperative Economics* 80, no. 2 (2009): 247–73; Birchall and Sacchetti, "Comparative Advantages."

46. Michaud and Audebrand, "Inside Out, Outside In."

47. Rodgers, "Hybrid Cooperatives."

48. Spear, Cornforth, and Aiken, "Governance Challenges of Social Enterprises."

49. Michaud and Audebrand, "Inside Out, Outside In"; Rodgers, "Hybrid Cooperatives."

50. Rodgers, "Hybrid Cooperatives."

51. Jean-Pascal Girard, "Governance in Solidarity," in *Co-operative Governance Fit to Build Resilience in the Face of Complexity* (International Co-operative Alliance, 2015), 127–33.

52. Leviten-Reid and Fairbairn, "Multi-stakeholder Governance in Cooperative Organizations."

53. Girard, "Governance in Solidarity"; Lund, "Solidarity as a Business Model"; Michaud and Audebrand, "Inside Out, Outside In."

54. Zeitoun, Osterloh, and Frey, "Learning from Ancient Athens."

55. AccountAbility and Utopies, "Critical Friends—The Emerging Role of Stake-holder Panels in Corporate Governance, Reporting and Assurance," March 2007.

56. Andreas Georg Scherer, Dorothée Baumann-Pauly, and Anselm Schneider, "Democratizing Corporate Governance: Compensating for the Democratic Deficit of Corporate Political Activity and Corporate Citizenship," *Business and Society* 52, no. 3 (2013): 473–514.

57. Ronald K. Mitchell, Bradley R. Agle, and Donna J. Wood, "Toward a Theory of Stakeholder Identification and Salience: Defining the Principle of Who and What Really Counts," *Academy of Management Review* 22, no. 4 (1997): 853–86; M. S. Reed and R. Curzon, "Stakeholder Mapping for the Governance of Biosecurity: A Literature Review," *Journal of Integrative Environmental Sciences* 12, no. 1 (2015): 15–38.

58. Marina Monaco and Luca Pastorelli, "Trade Unions and Worker Cooperatives in Europe: A Win–Win Relationship," *International Journal of Labour Research* 5, no. 2 (2013): 227–49.

59. Rob Witherell, Chris Cooper, and Michael Peck, "Sustainable Jobs, Sustainable Communities: The Union Co-Op Model," *Ohio Employee Ownership Center*, 2012.

60. Ibid.

61. Rob Witherell, "An Emerging Solidarity: Worker Cooperatives, Unions, and the New Union Cooperative Model in the United States," *International Journal of Labour Research* 5, no. 2 (2013): 251–68.

62. David Ellerman, "The Legitimate Opposition at Work: The Union's Role in Large Democratic Firms," *Economic and Industrial Democracy* 9, no. 4 (1988): 437–53.

63. Ariana R. Levinson, "Union Co-ops and the Revival of Labor Law," *Cardozo Journal of Conflict Resolution* 19, no. 3 (2018): 458.

64. Levinson, "Union Co-ops and the Revival of Labor Law."

65. Ibid.; Witherell, "Trade Unions and Worker Cooperatives in Europe"; Witherell, Cooper, and Peck, "Sustainable Jobs, Sustainable Communities."

66. Witherell, "Trade Unions and Worker Cooperatives in Europe."

67. Sanjay Pinto, "Practitioner Perspective: Economic Democracy, Embodied: A Union Co-Op Strategy for the Long-Term Care Sector," in *Organizational Imaginaries: Tempering Capitalism and Tending to Communities through Cooperatives and Collectivist Democracy*, vol. 72, Research in the Sociology of Organizations, eds. Katherine K. Chen and Victor Tan Chen (Leeds, UK: Emerald Publishing, 2021), 163–84.

68. Sharryn Kasmir, *The Myth of Mondragon: Cooperatives, Politics, and Working-Class Life in a Basque Town* (Albany: State University of New York Press, 1996).

69. Carmen Huertas-Noble, "Worker-Owned and Unionized Worker-Owned Cooperatives: Two Tools to Address Income Inequality," *Clinical Law Review* 22, no. 2 (2016): 341.

70. Huertas-Noble, "Worker-Owned and Unionized Worker-Owned Cooperatives"; Levinson, "Union Co-ops and the Revival of Labor Law."

71. Levinson, "Union Co-ops and the Revival of Labor Law"; Laura Hanson Schlachter, "Stronger Together? The USW-Mondragon Union Co-op Model," *Labor Studies Journal* 42, no. 2 (2017): 124–47.

72. Tom Clarke, "Alternative Modes of Co-operative Production," *Economic and Industrial Democracy* 5, no. 1 (1984): 97–129; Huertas-Noble, "Worker-Owned and Unionized Worker-Owned Cooperatives"; Schlachter, "Stronger Together?"

73. Pinto, "Practitioner Perspective"; Schlachter, "Stronger Together?"; Witherell, Cooper, and Peck, "Sustainable Jobs, Sustainable Communities."

74. Schlachter, "Stronger Together?"

75. G. L. Clark, "Challenges Facing Union-Led ESOPs: Commentary," *Environment and Planning D: Society and Space* 8, no. 2 (1990): 233–36.

76. Alison Barnes and Craig MacMillan, "The Difficult Challenge Faced by Hybrid Employee Voice in the Australian University Sector," in *Voice and Involvement at Work: Experience with Non-Union Representation*, ed. Paul J. Gollan (New York: Routledge, 2015), 101–24; Mark Hall et al., "Promoting Effective Consultation? Assessing the Impact of the ICE Regulations," *British Journal of Industrial Relations* 51, no. 2 (2013): 355–81.
77. Pierre Patry et al., "Trade Union Support for Labour Cooperatives: An Experiment in Cooperation between Brazil and Canada," *International Journal of Labour Research* 5, no. 2 (2013): 225; Hall et al., "Promoting Effective Consultation?"
78. Barnes and MacMillan, "The Difficult Challenge Faced by Hybrid Employee Voice in the Australian University Sector."
79. Ibid., 113.
80. Schlachter, "Stronger Together?"
81. Kasmir, *The Myth of Mondragon*.
82. Simon Pek, "Rekindling Union Democracy through the Use of Sortition," *Journal of Business Ethics* 155, no. 4 (2019), 1033–51; Clark, "Challenges Facing Union-Led ESOPs."
83. Levinson, "Union Co-ops and the Revival of Labor Law."
84. Basterretxea, Cornforth, and Heras-Saizarbitoria, "Corporate Governance."
85. Clarke, "Alternative Modes of Co-operative Production."
86. Ellerman, "The Legitimate Opposition at Work."

10. The Prospects for Economic Democracy

1. Isabelle Ferreras, *Firms as Political Entities: Saving Democracy through Economic Bicameralism* (New York: Cambridge University Press, 2017); Isabelle Ferreras, "Democratizing the Corporation," this volume, 15–60.
2. Jonathan Michie et al., eds. *The Oxford Handbook of Mutual, Co-operative, and Co-owned Business* (Oxford: Oxford University Press, 2017).
3. Joseph R. Blasi et al., "The Citizen's Share: Reducing Inequality in the 21st Century (New Haven, CT: Yale University Press, 2014); Joseph R. Blasi et al., "Evidence: What the US Research Shows about Worker Ownership," in Michie et al., *The Oxford Handbook of Mutual, Co-operative, and Co-owned Business*; R. C. May et al., "Encouraging Inclusive Growth: The Employee Equity Loan Act," *Challenge* 62, no. 6 (2019): 377–97; David Erdal, *Beyond the Corporation: Humanity Working* (London: The Bodley Head, 2011).
4. Corey Rosen, and Michael Quarrey, "How Well Is Employee Ownership Working?," *Harvard Business Review* 65, no. 5 (1987): 126–36; Lars Lindkvist, *Tänder tillsammans: Personalkooperativ inom vård och omsorg* (Stockholm: SNS förlag, 2007); Richard B. Freeman, *Workers Ownership and Profit-Sharing in a New Capitalist Model* (Stockholm: Swedish Trade Union Confederation, 2015).
5. Wolfgang G. Weber et al., "Psychological Research on Organisational Democracy: A Meta-analysis of Individual, Organisational, and Societal Outcomes," *Applied Pshychology: An International Review* 69, no. 3 (2020): 1009–71.
6. Patrik Witkowsky, *Personalägda företag och den amerikanska ESOP modellen* (Companion: Companion Stockholm, 2018); Janet Boguslaw and Lisa Schur, *Building the Assets of Low and Moderate Income Workers and their Families* (New Brunswick, NJ: Rutgers University Institute for the Study of Employee Ownership and Profit Sharing, 2019).
7. Weber et al., "Psychological Research on Organisational Democracy"; Andrew Timming and Juliette Summers, "Is Workplace Democracy Associated with Wider

Pro-democracy Affect? A Structural Equation Model," *Economic and Industrial Democracy* 41, no. 3 (2020): 709–26.

8. Sophie Nachemson-Ekwall, *Ett Sverige där anställda äger* (Stockholm: Global Utmaning, 2018).

9. Jens Lowitzsch and Iraj Haschi, *The Promotion of Employee Ownership and Participation* (Brussels: European Commission, 2014).

10. Witkowsky, *Personalägda företag*.

11. It also led to a very economically successful restructuring of the Swedish economy since less profitable (outdated) firms had to shut down, and resources and people power could be transferred to the more efficient parts of industry through a comprehensive "active labor-market policy." This combination of union wage policy, a strict financial policy to avoid inflation, and active labor-market policy to help the workforce to adjust was known as the Rehn model, named after the legendary union economist Gösta Rehn. See H. Milner, and E. Wadensjö, eds., *Gösta Rehn, the Swedish Model and Labour Market Policies: International and National Perspectives* (Aldershot, UK: Ashgate, 2001).

12. Bengt Furåker, "The Swedish Wage-Earner Funds and Economic Democracy: Is There Anything to Be Learned from Them?," *Transfer: European Review of Labour and Research* 22, no. 1 (2015): 121–32.

13. Ibid.

14. Bo Rothstein, "Det terminologiska misstaget," in *Kampen om Euron*, ed. Henrik Oscarsson and Sörren Holmberg (Gothenburg: Department of Political Science, University of Gothenburg, 2004), 121–32.

15. Bo Rothstein, "The Moral, Economic, and Political Logic of the Swedish Welfare State," in *The Oxford Handbook of Swedish Politics*, ed. Jon Pierre (Oxford: Oxford University Press, 2015): 69–86.

16. Philip Whyman, "An Analysis of Wage-Earner Funds in Sweden: Distinguishing Myth from Reality," *Economic and Industrial Democracy* 25, no. 3 (2004): 411–45.

17. Jon Elster, "The Possibility of Rational Politics," in *Political Theory Today*, ed. David Held (Cambridge, MA: Polity Press, 1991), 99; Jon Elster, "Rationality and Social Norms," *Archives Europennées de Sociologie* 31 (1991): 233–56.

18. Johannes Lindvall and Joakim Sebring, "Policy Reform and the Decline of Corporatism in Sweden," *West European Politics* 28, no. 5 (2005): 1057–74.

19. Mikael Gilljam, *Svenska folket och löntagarfonderna* (Lund: Studentlitteratur, 1988).

20. Jonus Pontusson and D. Weisstanner, "Macroeconomic Conditions, Inequality Shocks and the Politics of Redistribution, 1990–2013," *Journal of European Public Policy* 25, no. 1 (2017): 31–58.

21. Li Bennich-Björkman, "Krackelerar den sociala sammanhållningen," in *Demokratins framtid*, ed. Katarina Barrling and Sören Holmberg (Stockholm: Sveriges Riksdag, 2019), 191–210.

22. Nordic Council of Ministers, *State of the Nordic Region 2020* (Copenhagen: Nordiska Ministerrådet, 2020), pub.norden.org.

23. A search in the Swedish database Artikelsök, which registers most published op-ed articles, yields zero results for "ekonomisk demokrati" for the Swedish left-leaning magazine *Arena*.

24. Among the latest examples of this conflation of markets and capitalism is Martin Hägglund's much-acclaimed book *This Life: Why Mortality Makes Us Free* (London: Profile Books, 2019), esp. 278–81 and 304–8. In Hägglund's "democratic socialism," demand from individuals will have no effect on what is going to be produced. Instead, "we can decide through democratic processes how and what we produce, based on which abilities we seek to cultivate and which needs we have

to satisfy" (307). I suppose that when there are changes in tastes and fashion, for example from low- to high-heeled shoes, the majority will decide if production should follow—my guess is that in Hägglund's utopia, the majority would vote for very flat and truly "sensible" shoes.

25. Fernand Braudel, *Civilization and Capitalism: 15th–18th Century* (London: Fontana: 1985).

26. Erik Olin Wright, *How to Be an Anti-Capitalist in the Twenty-First Century* (London: Verso, 2019).

27. David P. Ellerman, "The Employment Relation, Property Rights and Organizational Democracy," in *Organizational Democracy and Political Process*, ed. Colin Crouch and Frank A. Heller (New York: Wiley, 1983), 269; see also David P. Ellerman, "On the Role of Capital in 'Capitalist' and in Labor-Managed Firms," *Review of Radical Political Economics* 5 (2007): 5–26.

28. The first main mistake was the idea that the industrial working class would be the engine behind a new (socialist) mode of production. Looking back at major economic transformations in history, this makes absolutely no sense: it was not the slaves who did away with slave society and created feudalism. Moreover, it was not the peasants that abolished feudalism and introduced capitalism. A subordinate social class can fight for more of "the pie" (slave rebellions, peasant upheavals, workers' striking), but they will not be able to bake the new pie. For this, a new social class is needed. Today, we see quite a lot of employee ownership in the high-tech sector, a process driven by the new "information and knowledge" class. For example, when six very successful young entrepreneurs in the "new economy" wrote an op-ed about what policies they requested from the government (published in the main Swedish daily newspaper, *Dagens Nyheter*, on March 13, 2015), their first demand was that government should make it easier for them to make their employees co-owners.

29. It should be added that the conflation of capitalism and the market economy is also standard among most neoclassical economists.

30. Bo Rothstein, "På spaning efter den socialism som flytt: Kapital och självstyre," *Zenit* 1 (1984): 50–62.

31. There is certainly a problem of how to handle entrepreneur-owners in this model, but I have presented a solution I think would work. Those who start a company using their own or borrowed capital should have the management rights, due to the company being their "intellectual property." However, when they leave the company, their shares would be transferred to bonds. Their heirs would inherit the capital as bonds—not shares that give them power over how to run the company. That power would be transferred to the employees. See Bo Rothstein, "Social Justice and State Capacity," *Politics and Society* 20 (1992): 101–26.

32. Joseph Henrich et al., *Foundations of Human Sociality: Economic Experiments and Ethnographic Evidence from Fifteen Small-Scale Societies* (New York: Oxford University Press, 2004).

33. Joseph Henrich et al., "In Search of *Homo economicus*: Behavioral Experiments in 15 Small-Scale Societies," *American Economic Review* 91, no. 2 (2001): 73–8; Henrich et al., *Foundations of Human Sociality*; Joseph Henrich et al., "Markets, Religion, Community Size, and the Evolution of Fairness and Punishment," *Science* 327, no. 5972 (2010): 1480–4.

34. Kenneth J. Arrow, "Gifts and Exchange," *Philosophy and Public Affairs* 1, no. 4 (1972): 357.

35. Don Cohen and Laurence Prusak, eds., *In Good Company: How Social Capital Makes Organisations Work* (Cambridge, MA: Harvard Business School, 2001); Gary J. Miller, *Managerial Dilemmas: The Political Economy of Hierachy*

(Cambridge, UK: Cambridge University Press, 1992); Gary J. Miller and Andrew B. Whitford, "Trust and Incentives in Principal-Agent Negotiations—The 'Insurance/Incentive Trade-off,'" *Journal of Theoretical Politics* 14, no. 2 (2002): 231–67.

36. Freeman, *Workers Ownership and Profit-Sharing.*
37. Email from Freeman to the author, December 15, 2020. Freeman says he has received similar negative comments about this idea from union leaders in Germany and Italy.
38. Bo Rothstein, ed., *Tillsammans: En fungerande ekonomisk demokrati* (Stockholm: SNS Förlag, 2012).
39. Patrik Witkowsky, *Can We Do It Ourselves?*, documentary film (Stockholm: Centrum för personalägande, 2015).
40. Svante Nycander, *Makten över arbetsmarknaden: Ett perspektiv på Sveriges 1900-tal* (Stockholm: SNS Förlag, 2002), 462.
41. The formal name of the union in English is the Association of Graduate Engineers.
42. Sophie Nachemson-Ekwall, *Ett Sverige där anställda äger* (Stockholm: Global Utmaning, 2018).
43. Stu Woo, "China Moves to Increase Oversight over Tech Companies," *Wall Street Journal*, September 23, 2019, wsj.com.
44. Jan Wallander, *Effektivitet, legitimitet och delägarskap* (Stockholm: SNS, 1989).
45. The statutes of the LO say that the organization will "promote societal development on the basis of political, social, and economic democracy."
46. Laura Carlson et al., *Swedish Labour and Employment Law: Cases and Materials* (Stockholm: Stockholm University, Faculty of Law, 2008).
47. Although almost 70 percent of the Swedish workforce is unionized, confidence in the unions is not high. The Society-Opinion-Media (SOM) institute at the University of Gothenburg has carried out surveys measuring confidence in various institutions since 1986, with the question about the unions asked almost every year. There are five possible answers—very low, low, intermediate, high and very high confidence—and the resultant measure can go from –100 (all respondents answer "very low") to +100 (all answer "very high"). The average for the unions over the years is about –15, and in no year is it a net positive. In comparison, the police and the courts score about +40, public radio/TV +45, and public health care +55. See J. Martinsson, et al., *Svenska Trender 1986–2017* (University of Gothenburg, SOM-Institute, 2018). This bears out that high union membership rate is to a considerable extent a result of the "selective incentives" stemming from the construction of industrial-relations laws. Cf. Bo Rothstein, "Marxism, Institutional Analysis and Working-Class Strength," *Politics and Society* 18, no. 3 (1990): 317–45.
48. Robert K. Merton, "Bureaucratic Structure and Personality," *Social Forces* 18, no. 4 (1940): 560–8.
49. This is not to say that unions could not have a positive role in democratically governed firms. For such arguments, see David P. Ellerman, "The Legitimate Opposition at Work: The Union's Role in Large Democratic Firms," *Economic and Industrial Democracy* 9 (1988): 433–57.
50. Rothstein, "Social Justice and State Capacity."

11. Ferreras and the Economic Democracy Debate

1. Andrew Cumbers, "Economic Democracy: Why Handing Power Back to the People Will Fix Our Broken System," *Portside*, December 30, 2019, portside.org.

2. See the account of this transaction at "Ford Buys Volvo Car Arm," *CNN Money*, January 27, 1999, money.cnn.com.

3. See Mattias Gothberg, "Så nära var Volvo att bli personalägt," *ETC*, Stockholm, Sweden, March 29, 2019. The Sverieges Ingenjorer employee buyout initiative was led by its then president, Magnus Sundemo. Lacking support from his union colleagues and without access to technical and financial resources, this plan dissolved, and Sudemo turned his support to the Chinese offer. Another union-led employee buyout effort of scale in the United States, initiated by union groups at United Airlines in 1994 and lasting until 2001, is described in Christopher Mackin, "United It Was Not," *Employee-Owned America*, September 2, 2020, employee-ownedamerica.com.

4. See Thomas Erdbrink and Christina Anderson, "Fears for Volvo Expose Sour Turn in Sweden's Ties with China," *New York Times*, June 14, 2020, nytimes.com.

5. ESOPs are made possible by federal tax law and the vision of a conservative Democratic politician, Senator Russell Long (deceased) of Louisiana. Long's early collaboration in the 1970s with attorney Louis Kelso made possible a nonconfrontational, voluntary road to employee ownership. Federal-level ESOP legislation creates enterprise level trust structures that represent workforces. Owners of closely held, non-publicly traded companies are encouraged by tax incentives to "sell" their companies to these trusts. This form of internal sale makes use of loans. As those loans are paid down, employees become owners of their firms without having to risk their own cash resources or personal property. Long and his successors in the US Congress designed tax incentives that have served to build up a significant niche of the American economy substantially owned by employees.

6. John Dewey, *Reconstruction in Philosophy*, rev. ed. (Boston: Beacon Press, 1948), 209; Mary Parker Follett, "The Giving of Orders," in *Classics of Public Administration*, eds. Jay M. Shafritz and Albert C. Hyde (Pacific Grove, CA: Brooks/Cole, 1992 [1926]), 66–74.

7. Carole Pateman, *Participation and Democratic Theory* (Cambridge University Press, 1970); C. B. Macpherson, *The Life and Times of Liberal Democracy* (Oxford: Oxford University Press, 1977); Ronald M. Mason, *Participatory and Workplace Democracy: A Theoretical Development in Critique of Liberalism* (Carbondale: Southern Illinois University Press, 1982).

8. "Pareto Optimality: Conditions and Composition," economicsdiscussion.net

9. Gregory N. Mankiw, *Principles of Economics*, 7th ed. (Stamford, CT: Cengage Learning); Michael C. Jensen and William H. Meckling, "Theory of the Firm: Managerial Behavior, Agency Costs and Ownership Structure," *Journal of Financial Economics* 3, no. 4 (1976): 305–60.

10. Douglas Kruse, Richard B. Freeman, and Joseph Blasi, *Shared Capitalism at Work: Employee Ownership, Profit and Gains Sharing and Broad-Based Stock Options* (Chicago: University of Chicago Press, 2010).

11. The largest collection of research evidence summarizing activity in this field is to be found at the Rutgers Institute for Employee Ownership and Profit Sharing (smlr.rutgers.edu).

12. Richard Marens, "Speaking Platitudes to Power: Observing American Business Ethics in an Age of Declining Hegemony," *Journal of Business Ethics* 94 (2010): 239–53.

13. Eric George, "Recruit and Retain Top Talent by Creating a Sense of Ownership," *Forbes*, March 1, 2022, forbes.com.

14. Intelligence Squared Debates, New York and online, November 12, 2019: see Open to Debate, "Does Capitalism Improve the Human Condition: Debate Clip," YouTube video, November 19, 2019.

15. Coverture marriage contracts were the accepted norm governing marriage until the late nineteenth century in the United States. According to that construct women were regarded as the property of their fathers, property that was passed over "in coverture" to their husbands on the occasion of marriage.

16. See David Ellerman, *Property and Contract in Economics: The Case for Economic Democracy* (Cambridge, MA: Blackwell, 1992); *Neo-Abolitionism: Abolishing Human Rentals in Favor of Workplace Democracy* (London: Springer, 2021).

17. NCEO, "Employee Stock Ownership Plan (ESOP) Facts," National Center for Employee Ownership, 2023, esop.org.

18. Rajeev Syal, "Employees to Be Handed Stake in Firms under Labour Plan," *Guardian*, September 24, 2018, theguardian.com; Bernie Sanders, "Corporate Accountability and Democracy," berniesanders.com.

19. See Bo Rothstein's essay in this volume, 199–210.

20. The Sanders approach to these issues operates on more than one level. Prior to the summer 2019 introduction of his Corporate Accountability and Democracy Plan featured in his presidential campaign, Sanders had been a regular sponsor of two more mainstream pieces of employee ownership legislation that focused on providing support to the kind of employee-ownership transactions that have been taking place in the United States for nearly forty years. Those transactions involve the voluntary sale of companies for market prices from their founder-owners to employees using bank credit and not risk capital from employees. The Worker Ownership, Readiness, and Knowledge (WORK) Act authorizes the US Department of Labor to provide education and outreach, training, grants, and other technical support for local and state programs dedicated to the promotion of employee ownership and participation. A second bill, The US Employee Ownership Bank Act, would provide loans and loan guarantees to employees to purchase businesses through employee stock ownership plans (ESOPs) or worker-owned cooperatives.

21. David Blanchflower et al., "The UK's Failing Economic Model Demands Such Bold Ideas," *Financial Times*, September 6, 2019, ft.com.

22. Jared Bernstein, "Employee Ownership, ESOPs, Wealth and Wages," *Employee-Owned S Corporations of America* (January 2016). Jared Bernstein joined the Biden administration's Council of Economic Advisors in December 2020.

23. Christopher Mackin, "Property Not Pay: Restoring the Middle through Ownership," in *The Many Futures of Work: Rethinking Expectations and Breaking Molds* (Philadelphia: Temple University Press, 2021); and "Defining Employee Ownership: Four Meanings and Two Models," *Journal of Participation and Employee Ownership*, 2023.

24. A more recent example of the bipartisan character of ESOP law appeared in May of 2023, a bill called the Employee Equity Investment Act (EEIA). This bill is co-sponsored by Democratic senator Chris Van Hollen of Maryland and Republican senator Marco Rubio of Florida. If passed, this bill will extend federal loan guarantees, familiar in the home mortgage market, to investment funds that supply worker and management groups with equity capital to acquire their firms.

25. An anecdotal illustration of how these ideas comport with Republican audiences can be found in Christopher Mackin, "Employee Ownership: The Road to Shared Prosperity," *Nation*, June 8, 2011, thenation.com.

26. See note 20 above. Senator Sanders has endorsed both "earned" and paid-for, as well as overt transfer approaches.

27. Matt Kennard and Ana Caistor-Arendar, "Occupy Buenos Aires: The Workers' Movement that Transformed a City, and Inspired the World," *Guardian*, March 10, 2016, theguardian.com.

28. See "Employee Ownership by the Numbers," National Center for Employee Owner-ship, February 2023, nceo.org.
29. See Mary Ellen Biery, "4 Things You Don't Know about Private Companies," *Forbes*, May 26, 2013, forbes.com; and North American Industry Classification System (NAICS) summary statistics for 2021, naics.com.
30. Bo Rothstein, "When Capital Relinquishes Ownership," *Social Europe*, June 25, 2021, socialeurope.eu.
31. Christopher Mackin, "Sovereign Wealth Funds Can Choose a Different Invest-ment Path," *Financial Times*, April 9, 2019, ft.com.
32. Richard C. May, Robert C. Hockett, and Christopher Mackin, "Encouraging Inclusive Growth: The Employee Equity Loan Act," *Challenge* 62, no. 6 (2019): 377–97.
33. John Case, "An Economy in Waiting," *New Republic*, July 8, 2018, newrepublic.com.

12. Five Principles of Economic Democracy

1. I am very grateful to Tom Malleson for comments. Tom Malleson, *After Occupy: Economic Democracy for the 21st Century* (New York: Oxford University Press, 2014), 1–24.
2. Louis Brandeis, "Testimony to Commission on Industrial Relations," *Industrial Relations Testimony* 8 (1916): 7659–60.
3. Ewan McGaughey, "From 'Capital and Ideology' to 'Democracy and Evidence': A Review of Thomas Piketty," *Economia, History, Methodology, Philosophy* 11, no. 1 (2020).
4. John C. Coates, "The Future of Corporate Governance Part 1: The Problem of Twelve," *Harvard Public Law* 19, no. 7 (2018).
5. Starting with Sidney Webb and Beatrice Webb, *Industrial Democracy* (London: Printed by the authors especially for the Amalgamated Society of Engineers, 1897).
6. Pericles in Thucydides, *History of the Peloponnesian War*, trans. Benjamin Jowett (1880).
7. *R (Animal Defenders Int) v SS for Culture, Media and Sport* (2008), UKHL 15, Baroness Hale; *Stoughton v. Reynolds* (1735), 93 ER 1023, a case on a church corporation's election: "We must therefore resort to the common right, which is in the whole assembly, where all are upon an equal foot."
8. Robert Lowe MP, Hansard HC Debs (July 15, 1867) column 1543.
9. Fritz Naphtali et al., *Wirtschaftsdemokratie. Ihr Wesen, Weg und Ziel* (Berlin: Verlagsges. des Allgem. Dt. Gewerkschaftsbundes, 1928); *Resolution des ADGB-Kongress 1928 in Hamburg über "Die Verwirklichung der Wirtschaftsdemokratie"* (1928).
10. Franklin. D. Roosevelt, "Campaign Address on Progressive Government at the Commonwealth Club in San Francisco, California" (1932).
11. Ewan McGaughey, "The Future of Democracy and Work: The Vote in our Economic Constitution," Sefton-Williams Memorial Lecture, *SSRN*, April 7, 2021, papers.ssrn.com.
12. Ewan McGaughey, "Participation in Corporate Governance," *SSRN*, November 4, 2014, papers.ssrn.com.
13. Universal Declaration of Human Rights (1948), article 21(1).
14. Sidney Merlin, "Trends in German Economic Control since 1933," *Quarterly Journal of Economics* 57, no. 2 (1943): 169; Ewan McGaughey, "The Codetermina-tion Bargains: The History of German Corporate and Labor Law," *Columbia*

Journal of European Law 23, no. 1 (Fall 2016): 135–76; Arthur Schweitzer, "Business Policy in a Dictatorship," *Business History Review* 38, no. 4 (1964): 413, 423–4; Arthur Schweitzer, *Big Business in the Third Reich* (London: Eyre & Spottiswoode, 1964), 104–5.

15. J. C. D. Zahn, *Wirtschaftsführertum und Vertragsethik im neuen Akitenrecht* (Berlin: De Gruyter, 1934), 105.

16. Ludwig von Mises, *Liberalismus* (Jena: Verlag von Gustav Fischer, 1927).

17. Ludwig von Mises, *Die Ursachen der Wirtschaftskrise: Ein Vortrag* (Tübingen: JCB Mohr, Paul Siebeck, 1931) republished in *The Causes of the Economic Crisis, and Other Essays before and after the Great Depression* (Auburn, AL: Ludwig von Mises Institute, 2006), chapter 3.

18. George Stigler, "The Theory of Economic Regulation," *Bell Journal of Economics and Management Science* 2, no. 1 (1971): 10–11.

19. Michael C. Jensen and William H. Meckling, "Corporate Government and 'Economic Democracy': An Attack on Freedom," in *Proceedings of Corporate Governance: A Definitive Exploration of the Issue,* ed. C. J. Huizenga (Berkeley: University of California Press, 1983). Cf. Isabelle Ferreras, *Firms as Political Entities: Saving Democracy through Economic Bicameralism* (Cambridge, UK: Cambridge University Press, 2017), 183, "firms are political entities."

20. Michael C. Jensen and William H. Meckling, "Rights and Production Functions: An Application to Labor-Managed Firms and Codetermination," *Journal of Business* 52, no. 4 (1979): 469, 503–4.

21. Ferreras, *Firms as Political Entities*, 183.

22. Abraham Lincoln, "December 3, 1861: First Annual Message," December 3, 1861, available at millercenter.org.

23. European Social Charter (1996), article 22; Constitution of India (1949), article 43A; BLER, "Board-Level Employee Representation across the EU," *Worker Participation*, 2016, worker-participation.eu; Constitution of Brazil (1988), article 11; Company Law of the People's Republic of China (1994), article 51.

24. Ewan McGaughey, "Votes at Work in Britain: Shareholder Monopolisation and the 'Single Chanel,' " *Industrial Law Journal* 47, no. 1 (2018): 76; Ewan McGaughey, "Democracy in America at Work: The History of Labor's Vote in Corporate Governance," *Seattle University Law Review* 42, no. 2 (2019): 697–8.

25. See University of Cambridge, Statute A.I.7. These rules plainly leave much to be desired, as many part-time, fixed-term, or nonacademic staff are unnecessarily excluded.

26. Reward Work Act of 2018, S.2605 and H.R. 6096; Accountable Capitalism Act of 2018, S. 3348.

27. Bernie Sanders, "Corporate Accountability and Democracy," 2019, berniesanders.com.

28. Benjamin Sachs and Sharon Block, "Clean Slate for Worker Power: Building a Just Economy and Democracy," *Centre for Labor and a Just Economy* (2019): 73.

29. European Trade Union Institute, "Belgian Political Parties Favour Co-determination of Employees in Company Boards," ETUI, 2020, etui.org.

30. Ewan McGaughey, "Democracy of Oligarchy? Models of Union Governance in the UK, Germany and US," KCL Law School Research Paper 2017–35 (2017).

31. See Ewan McGaughey, "The International Labour Organization, Economic Democracy and the Undemocratic Third," *King's Law Journal* 32, no. 2 (2021): 287, including a draft model ILO Economic Democracy Convention.

32. Paul Blumberg, *Industrial Democracy: The Sociology of Participation* (London: Constable, 1968), chapter 2.

33. See, for instance, Sigurt Vitols, "Prospects for Trade Unions in the Evolving European System of Corporate Governance," German Corporate Governance Network,

2005, gcgn.net; John T. Addison and Paulino Teixeira, "Strikes, Employee Workplace Representation, Unionism, and Trust: Evidence from Cross-Country Data," *SSRN* 10575 (2017).

34. Zoe Adams et al., "The Economic Significance of Laws Relating to Employment Protection and Different Forms of Employment: Analysis of a Panel of 117 Countries, 1990–2013," *International Labour Review* 158, no. 1 (2019): 1.

35. Viral V. Acharya, Ramin P. Baghai, and Krishnamurthy V. Subramanian, "Labor Laws and Innovation," *Journal of Law and Economics* 56, no. 4 (2013): 997.

36. See Simon Jäger, Shakked Noy, and Benjamin Schoefer, *What Does Codetermination Do?*, National Bureau of Economic Research, 2021.

37. McGaughey, "Participation in Corporate Governance," chapters 6(1) and (3), and note the charts on share ownership changes.

38. Deutsche Bundesbank, *Statistische Sonderveröffentlichung* 9 (2005) 32 and (1998) 32 give the last picture, to the author's knowledge.

39. Centralverband des deutschen Bank- und Bankiergewerbes (1930) BankA 1930–31, 116, Aktiengesetz 1937 §114; see also Aktiengesetz 1965 §135. This is history explained in McGaughey, "Participation in Corporate Governance," chapter 6.

40. Treaty on the Functioning of the European Union, articles 101 and 106(1).

41. See, for instance, the University Pension Plan Ontario, www.universitypension.ca.

42. Pensions Act 2004 §243.

43. *Verordnung gegen übermässige Vergütungen bei börsenkotierten Aktiengesellschaften 2013* (in German) or Regulation Against Excessive Compensation at Listed Companies 2013.

44. Sanders, "Corporate Accountability and Democracy."

45. See, for instance, Arad Reisberg, "The UK Stewardship Code: On the Road to Nowhere?," *Journal of Corporate Law Studies* 15, no. 2 (2015): 217.

46. Herbert Morrison, *Socialisation and Transport: Organisation of Socialised Industries with the Particular Reference to the London Passenger Transport Bill* (London: Constable, 1933).

47. National Health Service Act 2006, sch. 7, paras 3 and 9; John Carvel and Giles Tremlett, "Milburn Seeks Hospital Role Model in Spain," *Guardian*, November 6, 2001, theguardian.com.

48. See, for instance, We Own It, "Liberté, égalité, and a glass of fizzy water?," *We Own It* (blog), August 31, 2018, weownit.org.uk; Gemeindeordnung Nordrhein-Westfalen 1994 §§107–113; Hans-Liudger Dienel and Martin Schiefelbusch, *Public Transport and Its Users: The Passenger's Perspective in Planning and Customer Care* (2009).

49. Wikimedia Bylaws (2019), article 4, §§1–3.

50. Cf. *New State Ice Co v. Liebmann*, 285 U.S. 262 (1932).

51. See Archibald Cox and Marshall J. Seidman, "Federalism and Labor Relations," *Harvard Law Review* 64, no. 211 (1950); "Federalism and the Law of Labor Relations," *Harvard Law Review* 67, no. 1297 (1954); "Labor and Law Preemption Revisited," *Harvard Law Review* 85, no. 1337 (1972). This became a tragic part of Supreme Court jurisprudence in *Garner v. Teamsters Local 776*, 346 U.S. 485 (1953).

52. Cynthia L. Estlund, "The Ossification of American Labor Law," *Columbia Law Review* 102 (2002): 1527.

53. Ferreras, *Firms as Political Entities*, 183.

54. Ibid., 133

55. See democratizingwork.org; there are 6,722 signatories at the time of writing.

56. See the discussion in Thomas Piketty, *Capital and Ideology* (Cambridge, MA: Harvard University Press, 2020), 486–577.

57. Ferreras, *Firms as Political Entities*, 133–4.
58. For example, *Barron v. Potter* (1914) 1 Ch 895 and the Companies Act 2006 § 994ff.
59. Labor Management Relations Act 1947, codified at 29 U.S.C. §186(c)(5)(B).
60. Ferreras, *Firms as Political Entities*, 123.
61. Adolf A. Berle and Gardiner C. Means, *The Modern Corporation and Private Property* (1932), book 4, chapter 4, 355–6; the authors conclude that corporations should "serve . . . all society," not directors or shareholder interests.
62. Adolf A. Berle, "For Whom Corporate Managers Are Trustees: A Note," *Harvard Law Review* 45, no. 8 (1932): 1365, 1372.
63. O. Gierke, *The Social Role of Private Law* (1889), trans. Ewan McGaughey, *German Law Journal* 19, no. 4 (2018): 1017.

13. Economic Democracy against Racial Capitalism

1. Ellen Meiksins Wood, *Democracy against Capitalism: Renewing Historical Materialism* (Cambridge, UK: Cambridge University Press, 1995).
2. Wood, grounding her conception of economic democracy in a discussion of ancient Athens, does not clearly delineate what it would look like in the present day. However, given her theoretical priors, it would likely look quite different from the vision Ferreras advances.
3. See, for example, Phyllis Moen, Joseph Pedtke, and Sarah Flood, "Disparate Disruptions: Intersectional COVID-19 Employment Effects by Age, Gender, Education, and Race/Ethnicity," *Work, Aging, and Retirement* 6, no. 4 (2020): 207–28.
4. Maite Tapia, Tamara L. Lee, and Mikhail Filipovitch, "Supra-union and Intersectional Organizing: An Examination of Two Prominent Cases in the Low-Wage US Restaurant Industry," *Journal of Industrial Relations* 59, no. 4 (2017); Naomi Williams and Sheri Davis-Faulkner, "Worker Mobilization and Political Engagement: A Historical Perspective," in *Revaluing Work(ers): Toward a Democratic and Sustainable Future*, ed. Tobias Schulze-Cleven and Todd Vachon (Ithaca, NY: Cornell University Press, 2021), 121–40; Nicole Pangborn and Christopher Rea, "Race, Gender, and New Essential Workers during COVID-19," *Political Economy* 2 (2020).
5. Cedric J. Robinson, *Black Marxism: The Making of the Black Radical Tradition* (Harmondsworth, UK: Penguin, 2021). For a recent collection building from Robinson's formulation, see Justin Leroy and Destin Jenkins, *Histories of Racial Capitalism* (New York: Columbia University Press, 2021).
6. Wood was worried that a focus on factors such as race and gender would distract from and eclipse class politics. The line of analysis developed here is that this ship has already sailed but from a different point of origin: those in positions of power with an interest in turning back progressive change have played on racial distinctions to undermine working-class solidarity.
7. Robinson, *Black Marxism*, 26. Another narrower usage of the term focuses on how "white individuals and predominantly white institutions us[e] non-white people to acquire social and economic value." See Nancy Leong, "Racial Capitalism," *Harvard Law Review* 126, no. 12, as quoted in article abstract.
8. Robinson, *Black Marxism*. Robinson notes that English and Irish workers in the late eighteenth century did act in concert, including as part of the Chartist movement. However, by the mid-nineteenth century, English nationalism had largely overwhelmed this incipient class solidarity, and "the English people were at one with respect to the Irish Question," 41.

9. Walter Johnson, "To Remake the World: Slavery, Racial Capitalism, and Justice," *Boston Review* (2018). See also Eric Williams, *Capitalism and Slavery* (Chapel Hill: University of North Carolina Press, 2021 [1944]).

10. Cheryl Harris, "Whiteness as Property," *Harvard Law Review* 106, no. 8 (1993): 1707–91.

11. Ibid., 1715.

12. For a fuller accounting of these mechanisms, see Sanjay Pinto, "Racial Capitalism at Work: Evidence from a Covid-Era Survey," in *A Racial Reckoning in Industrial Relations: Storytelling as Revolution from Within*, ed. Tamara Lee et al. (Ithaca, NY: Cornell University Press, 2022).

13. See Keeanga-Yamahtta Taylor, *Race for Profit: How Banks and the Real Estate Industry Undermined Black Homeownership* (Chapel Hill: University of North Carolina Press, 2019); Michael C. Dawson and Megan Ming Francis, "Black Politics and the Neoliberal Racial Order," *Public Culture* 28, no. 1 (2016): 23–62.

14. For more on the sense in which I use the term "marginalization," see Iris Marion Young, *Justice and the Politics of Difference* (Princeton, NJ: Princeton University Press, 1990). Of course, there is also a long history of theorizing surplus populations in Marxist thought.

15. For more on how what I refer to as "marginalization" applies in the context of racial capitalism, see Gargi Bhattacharyya, *Rethinking Racial Capitalism: Questions of Reproduction and Survival* (London: Rowman & Littlefield, 2018); and Arun Kundnani, "The Racial Constitution of Neoliberalism," *Race and Class* 63, no. 1 (2021).

16. Evelyn Nakano Glenn, "From Servitude to Service Work: Historical Continuities in the Racial Division of Paid Reproductive Labor," *Signs: Journal of Women in Culture and Society* 18, no. 1 (1991): 1–43.

17. Gabriel Winant, "Deindustrialization, Working Class-Decline, and the Growth of Health Care," *New Labor Forum* 30, no. 2 (2021): 54–61.

18. W. E. B. Du Bois, *Black Reconstruction in America: Toward a History of the Part Which Black Folk Played in the Attempt to Reconstruct Democracy* (London: Routledge, 2017 [1935]).

19. David Roediger, *The Wages of Whiteness: Race and the Making of the American Working Class* (London: Verso, 1999), 25.

20. For more, see Alex Gourevitch, *From Slavery to the Cooperative Commonwealth, Labor and Republican Liberty in the Nineteenth Century* (Cambridge, UK: Cambridge University Press, 2014).

21. Du Bois, *Black Reconstruction*. I thank Mary Jirmanus for reminding me of this passage from Du Bois.

22. Roediger, *Wages of Whiteness*. See Williams and Davis-Faulkner, "Worker Mobilization and Political Engagement."

23. Alberto Alesina and Edward Glaeser, *Fighting Poverty in the US and Europe: A World of Difference* (Oxford: Oxford University Press, 2004).

24. Juan F. Perea, "The Echoes of Slavery: Recognizing the Racist Origins of the Agricultural and Domestic Worker Exclusion from the National Labor Relations Act, *Ohio State Law Journal* 72 (2011): 95–138.

25. Adam Dean and Jonathan Obert, "Rewarded by Friends and Punished by Enemies: The CIO and the Taft-Hartley Act," *Labor* 18, no. 3 (2021): 78–113.

26. Bill Fletcher and Fernando Gapasin, *Solidarity Divided: The Crisis in Organized Labor and a New Path Toward Social Justice* (Berkeley: University of California Press, 2008).

27. Gourevitch, *From Slavery to the Cooperative Commonwealth*.

28. Jessica Gordon Nembhard, *Collective Courage: A History of African American Cooperative Thought and Practice* (University Park: Penn State University Press,

2014). See also John Curl, *For All the People: Uncovering the Hidden History Cooperation, Cooperative Movements, and Communalism in America* (Oakland: PM Press, 2009).

29. Fletcher and Gapasin, *Solidarity Divided*.
30. Bruce Nelson, "Class, Race, and Democracy in the CIO: The 'New' Labor History Meets the 'Wages of Whiteness,' " *International Review of Social History* 41, no. 3 (1996): 351–74.
31. Alethia Jones, "Agents of Change: How Allied Healthcare Workers Transform Inequities in the Healthcare Industry," in *Structural Competency in Mental Health and Medicine*, ed. Helena Hansen and Jonathan Metzl (London: Springer, 2020); Roger Waldinger et al., "Helots No More: A Case Study of the Justice for Janitors Campaign in Los Angeles," UCLA Lewis Center for Regional Studies Working Paper, 1996.
32. Brantly Callaway and William Collins, "Unions, Workers, and Wages at the Peak of the American Labor Movement," *Explorations in Economic History* 68 (2018): 95–118.
33. Roger Waldinger and Thomas Bailey, "The Continuing Significance of Race: Racial Conflict and Racial Discrimination in Construction," *Politics and Society* 19, no. 3 (1991): 291–323.
34. Orley Ashenfelter and Albert Rees, *Discrimination and Trade Unions* (Princeton, NJ: Princeton University Press, 2015).
35. Nelson, "Class, Race, and Democracy in the CIO." See also Fletcher and Gapasin, *Solidarity Divided*.
36. Ibid.
37. Joyce Rothschild and J. Allen Whitt, *The Cooperative Workplace: Potentials and Dilemmas of Organizational Democracy and Participation* (Cambridge, UK: Cambridge University Press, 1989).
38. Joan Meyers and Steven Vallas, "Diversity Regimes in Worker Cooperatives: Workplace Inequality under Conditions of Worker Control," *Sociological Quarterly* 57, no. 1 (2016): 98–128.
39. See, for example, Ken Estey, "Domestic Workers and Cooperatives: Beyond Care Goes Beyond; A Case Study in Brooklyn, New York," *Working USA* 14, no. 3 (2011): 347–65.
40. Nembhard, *Collective Courage*, 33.
41. W. E. B. Du Bois, *Economic Cooperation among Negro Americans* (Atlanta: Atlanta University Press, 1907). See also Nembhard, *Collective Courage*, 73.
42. Nembhard, *Collective Courage*. See Nikhil Pal Singh, *Black Is a Country: Race and the Unfinished Struggle for Democracy* (Cambridge, MA: Harvard University Press, 2005).
43. W. E. B. Du Bois, *The Souls of Black Folk* (Minneola, NY: Dover Publications 1994 [1903]).
44. Du Bois, *Black Reconstruction*. See also Singh, *Black Is a Country*, for more on Du Bois's class analysis and the evolution of his economic thinking.
45. As quoted in Singh, *Black Is a Country*, 73.
46. Priscilla McCutcheon, "Fannie Lou Hamer's Freedom Farms and Black Agrarian Geographies," *Antipode* 51, no. 1 (2019); and Monica M. White, "'A Pig and a Garden': Fannie Lou Hamer's Freedom Farm's Cooperative," *Food and Foodways* 25, no. 1 (2017): 25–39.
47. Chana Kai Lee, *For Freedom's Sake: The Life of Fannie Lou Hamer* (Champaign: University of Illinois Press, 1999).
48. White, "'A Pig and a Garden'"; Lee, *For Freedom's Sake*.

49. McCutcheon, "Fannie Lou Hamer's Freedom Farms." Hamer herself experienced retaliation due to her civil rights activism—she and her husband were fired from numerous jobs by white employers due to her activism. See Lee, *For Freedom's Sake.*

50. For more on conceptions of freedom within the Black radical tradition, see Robin D. G. Kelley, *Freedom Dreams: The Black Radical Imagination* (Boston: Beacon Press, 2002).

51. Kali Akuno, "Building and Fight: The Program and Strategy of Cooperation Jackson," in *Jackson Rising: The Struggle for Black Self-Determination in Jackson, Mississippi,* ed. Kali Akuno and Ajamu Nangwaya (Wakefield: Daraja Press, 2017).

52. See, for example, Ruth Needleman, "Black Caucuses in Steel," *New Labor Forum* 3 (1998): 41–56.

53. Meyers and Vallas, "Diversity Regimes in Worker Cooperatives."

54. Ronald Takaki, "Reflections on Racial Patterns in America," *From Different Shores: Perspectives on Race and Ethnicity in America* (Oxford: Oxford University Press, 1994), 34.

55. As Erik Olin Wright observed, these interests can be so divergent that they place certain wage workers—those who are more professionalized, and who wield greater organizational control—in "contradictory class locations," rendering them conflicted over whether their loyalties reside with capital or labor. See Erik Olin Wright, *Classes* (London: Verso, 1990).

56. Rothschild and Whitt, "The Democratic Workplace."

57. For more on workplace fissuring, see David Weil, *The Fissured Workplace* (Cambridge, MA: Harvard University Press, 2014). For more on the implications of contemporary misclassification, see Jennifer Pinsof, "A New Take on an Old Problem: Employee Misclassification in the Modern Gig-Economy," *Michigan Telecommunications and Technology Law Review* 22 (2015): 341–73.

58. Charlotte Alexander, "Misclassification and Antidiscrimination: An Empirical Analysis," *Minnesota Law Review* 101 (2016): 907–62.

59. Nembhard, *Collective Courage*; Du Bois, *Black Reconstruction.* See also Dawson and Francis, "Black Politics and the Neoliberal Racial Order."

60. Taylor, *Race for Profit.*

61. Laura Sullivan et al., *The Racial Wealth Gap: Why Policy Matters* (New York: Demos, 2015).

62. George Caffentzis and Silvia Federici, "Commons against and beyond Capitalism," *Community Development Journal* 49, no. 1 (2014): 92–105.

63. See Sanjay Pinto and Mary Jirmanus, "Puntos en común: Vinculando las luchas del trabajo de reproducción social," in *Comunes reproductivos: Cercamientos y descercamientos contemporáneos en los cuidados y la agroecología* (Madrid: Los Libros de la Catarata, 2022).

64. See John Dewey, *Reconstruction in Philosophy* (Boston: Beacon Press, 1957).

65. Universal basic income, for example, could help to decommodify labor and increase the effective bargaining power of workers while ensuring a base level of economic security. See Phillipe Van Parijs, "Basic Income: A Simple and Powerful Idea for the Twenty-First Century," *Politics and Society* 32, no. 1 (2004): 7–39.

66. Dawson and Francis, "Black Politics and the Neoliberal Racial Order." Granted, the emergence and handling of water contamination in Flint, Michigan, shows how, absent strong accountability, public officials can show the same racially inflected callousness to the value of human life.

67. Eileen Boris and Jennifer Klein, *Caring for America: Home Health Workers in the Shadow of the Welfare State* (Oxford: Oxford University Press, 2015).

68. Sanjay Pinto et al., "Seizing the Moment to Make Our Care Systems More Equitable," Gender Policy Report, May 27, 2021, genderpolicyreport.umn.edu.

69. Sanjay Pinto, Camille Kerr, and Ra Criscitiello, "Shifting Power, Meeting the Moment: Worker Ownership as a Strategic Tool for the Labor Movement" (New Brunswick: Rutgers Institute for Employee Ownership and Profit Sharing, 2021).

70. Sanjay Pinto, "Economic Democracy, Embodied: A Union Co-op Strategy for the Long-Term Care Sector," in *Organizational Imaginaries: Tempering Capitalism and Tending to Community through Cooperatives and Collectivist Democracy*, ed. Katherine Chen and Victor Tan Chen (Bingley, UK: Emerald, 2021).

71. Leon Fink and Brian Greenberg, *Upheaval in the Quiet Zone: 1199SEIU and the Politics of Healthcare Unionism* (Champaign: University of Illinois Press, 2009).

72. For a discussion focused on guest workers in the German context, see Amelie Constant and Douglass Massey, "Labor Market Segmentation and the Earnings of German Guestworkers," *Population Research and Policy Review* 24, no. 5 (2005): 489–512. Lewis Davis and Sumit S. Deole, "Immigration and the Rise of Far-Right Parties in Europe," *IFO DICE Report* 15, no. 4 (2017): 10–15.

73. Philipp Adorf, "A New Blue-Collar Force: The Alternative for Germany and the Working Class," *German Politics and Society* 36, no. 4 (2018): 29–49.

74. Wolfgang Streeck, *Re-forming Capitalism: Institutional Change in the German Political Economy* (Oxford: Oxford University Press, 2009).

75. Du Bois, *Black Reconstruction*.

76. W. E. B Du Bois, *The Souls of Black Folk* (New Haven, CT: Yale University Press, 2015 [1903]).

14. A Response to My Readers

1. The op-ed turned manifesto "Democratizing Work" was published on May 16, 2020, in forty-six newspapers (including the *Wire-India*, *Meidaan-Iran*, *South China Morning Post*, *La Folha de Sao Paulo*, *Le Monde*, *Il Manifesto*, *Boston Globe*, *Le Soir*, *De Morgen*, and the *Guardian*) in twenty-seven languages, and signed by more than 6,000 scholars at the time, including Elizabeth Anderson, Nancy Fraser, Dani Rodrik, Thomas Piketty, Katharina Pistor, Marshall Ganz, Joshua Cohen, and Axel Honneth. It is available at democratizingwork.org. See also Isabelle Ferreras, Julie Battilana, and Dominique Méda, eds., *Democratize Work: The Case for Reorganizing the Economy* (Chicago: University of Chicago Press, 2022). In October 2022, we organized the first Global Forum on Democratizing Work, which gathered online more than 3,000 participants from eighty-five countries during three days for more than 120 panels, and launched national chapters in sixteen countries to discuss the three principles of the Democratizing Work manifesto.

2. Isabelle Ferreras, *Firms as Political Entities: Saving Democracy through Economic Bicameralism* (Cambridge, UK: Cambridge University Press, 2017).

3. Adam Smith, *An Inquiry into the Nature and Causes of the Wealth of Nations* (New York: Alfred Knopf, 1991 [1776]), 306.

4. For instance, as I write I see that the Spanish labor minister, Yolanda Díaz, has just announced that democratizing firms is the next frontier of the progressive agenda.

5. Sara Lafuente, "Dual Majorities for Firm Governments," in Ferreras, Battilana, and Méda, *Democratize Work*, 73–8.

6. Sharon Block and Benjamin Sachs, "Clean Slate for Worker Power: Building a Just Economy and Democracy," (Cambridge, MA: Labor and Worklife Program, Harvard Law School, 2020).

7. Julie Battilana and Isabelle Ferreras, "From Shareholder Primacy to a Dual Majority Board," in *A Seat at the Table: Worker Voice and the New Corporate Boardroom*

(Washington, DC: The Aspen Institute Business and Society Program Report Series, 2021).

8. Ferreras, *Firms as Political Entities.*
9. See, respectively, Douglas Kruse, Richard Freeman, and Joseph Blasi, eds., *Shared Capitalism at Work: Employee Ownership, Profit and Gain Sharing, and Broad-Based Stock Options* (Chicago: University of Chicago Press, 2010); Tom Malleson, *After Occupy: Economic Democracy for the 21st Century* (New York: Oxford University Press, 2014); Gregory Dow, *Governing the Firm: Workers' Control in Theory and Practice* (Cambridge, UK: Cambridge University Press, 2003); John Addison, *The Economics of Codetermination: Lessons from the German Experience* (London: Palgrave Macmillan, 2009); Simon Jäger, Shakked Noy, and Benjamin Schoefer, "What Does Codetermination Do?" (Cambridge, MA: National Bureau of Economic Research, 2021).
10. Julie Battilana, Michael Fuerstein and Matthew Lee, "New Prospects for Organizational Democracy? How the Joint Pursuit of Social and Financial Goals Challenges Traditional Organizational Designs," in *Capitalism beyond Mutuality? Perspectives Integrating Philosophy and Social Science*, ed. Subramanian Rangan (Oxford: Oxford University Press, 2018).
11. Sigurt Vitols, "Board Level Employee Representation and Tax Avoidance in Europe," *Accounting, Economics, and Law: A Convivium* (2021).
12. It is also likely that some firms will try to avoid the bicameral mandate by attempting to designate their workers as "independent subcontractors" or by bunching the number of employees to just below the threshold at which bicameralism becomes enforced. This is one more reason why we need a tractable concept of "labor investors" so as to accurately account for all those workers without whom the firm's production would not exist, *and* who are governed by the rules and decisions of the firm. All these labor investors, whatever their exact legal status, and wherever they live on the planet, must be included in the labor chamber.
13. Fred Block and Robert Hockett, eds., *Democratizing Finance: Restructuring Credit to Transform Society* (London: Verso, 2022).
14. Jäger et al., "What Does Codetermination Do?"
15. According to Harju et al., "Survey and in-depth interviews we conducted with worker representatives confirm that they view their role as about improving communication, information sharing, and cooperation, but do not believe their role comes with direct decision-making power." Jarkko Harju, Simon Jäger, and Benjamin Schoefer, "Voice at Work," *NBER Working Paper* 28522 (2021): 1–2.
16. Felix Hörisch, "The Macro-Economic Effect of Codetermination on Income Equality," Working Paper Mannheimer Zentrum für Europ ische Sozialforschung 147 (2012); Gary Gorton and Frank A. Schmid, "Capital, Labor, and the Firm: A Study of German Codetermination," *Journal of the European Economic Association* 2, no. 5 (2004): 863–905; E. Han Kim, Ernst Maug, and Christoph Schneider, "Labor Representation in Governance as an Insurance Mechanism," *Review of Finance* 22, no. 4 (2018): 1251–89; Harju et al., "Voice at Work."
17. Felix Hörisch, "The Macro-Economic Effect of Codetermination on Income Equality," 19–20. Moreover, the fact that quasi-parity codetermination is almost universally opposed by business is also indirect evidence that it likely does empower workers somewhat against the bosses. On this, compare Addison, *The Economics of Codetermination*, with Jäger et al., "What Does Codetermination Do?" For the role and evidence of codermination reducing equality, see also Thomas Piketty, *Capital and Ideology* (Cambridge, MA: Harvard University Press, 2020).
18. Malleson, *After Occupy*; Dow, *Governing the Firm*; Joyce Rothschild and J. Allen Whitt, *The Cooperative Workplace* (Cambridge, UK: Cambridge University Press, 1986).

19. Hélène Landemore, "Democratize Firms . . . Why, and How?," in Ferreras, Battilana, and Méda, *Democratize Work*, 47–54.
20. John Roemer points out that the US labor force contains approximately 150 million workers, and the market capitalization of the corporate sector is roughly $330,000 per worker. This means that, if workers were to own the firms in which they worked, each worker would have to invest this much on average in their firm. John E. Roemer, "Thoughts on Arrangements of Property Rights in Productive Assets," *Analyse und Kritik* 35, no. 1 (2013): 55–64.
21. There is of course an old and ongoing debate in democratic theory as to how to conceptualize the principle of affected interest. Interested readers should see Archon Fung, "The Principle of Affected Interests: An Interpretation," in *Representation: Elections and Beyond*, ed. Jack Nagel and Rogers Smith (Philadelphia: University of Pennsylvania Press, 2013); Robert E. Goodin, "Enfranchising All Affected Interests, and Its Alternatives," *Philosophy and Public Affairs* 35, no. 1 (2007): 40–68. I have proposed that the key criterion for taking part in governing the political entity should be whether one is *governed* by it.
22. Isabelle Ferreras, "From the Politically Impossible to the Politically Inevitable: Taking Action," in Ferreras, Battilana, and Méda, *Democratize Work*, 23–46.
23. Virgile Chassagnon, "The Network Firm as a Single Real Entity: Beyond the Aggregate of Distinct Legal Entities," *Journal of Economic Issues* 45, no. 1 (2011): 113–36.
24. Henry S. Farber et al., "Unions and Inequality over the Twentieth Century: New Evidence from Survey Data," NBER Working Paper 24587 (2018).
25. The key demands of which are a revision of the European Works Councils Directive; the inclusion of information, consultation, and participation rights for workers in specific pieces of European legislation (such as the Corporate Sustainability Reporting Directive); and a framework directive for information, consultation, and participation rights in European companies. Thanks to Sigurt Vitols (personal correspondence) for pointing this out to me.
26. European Trade Union Congress, "Paris Manifesto" (Brussels: ETUC, 2015), 4.
27. Julie Battilana and Tiziana Casciaro, *Power, for All: How It Really Works and Why It's Everyone's Business* (New York: Simon & Schuster, 2021). Even from a narrow perspective that sees the remit of unions as nothing more than bargaining over wages and working conditions, given the immense changes that technology and globalization are bringing to the twenty-first-century workplace, surely having a position in firm governance will mean that they have a much better vantage point to understand and deal with the workplace changes and so be much better situated to bargain effectively than if they remained locked out of the corporate boardroom.
28. See Ferreras, "From the Politically Impossible to the Politically Inevitable."
29. Isabelle Ferreras, "Democratizing Firms: A Cornerstone of Shared and Sustainable Prosperity" (Guildford: Center for the Understanding of Sustainable Prosperity Essay Series, University of Surrey, 2019).